Thanks
2013

From:
Mary Alice

Never Too Old

To Climb Walls

May God bless you,
Love Todd

Martha Sue Todd

Editor: Dorothea Stewart Gilbert

Note for Librarians: A cataloguing record for this book is available from Library and Archives Canada at www.collectionscanada.ca/amicus/index-e.html
ISBN 1-4251-0936-5

Printed in Victoria, BC, Canada. Printed on paper with minimum 30% recycled fibre. Trafford's print shop runs on "green energy" from solar, wind and other environmentally-friendly power sources.

TRAFFORD
PUBLISHING™
Offices in Canada, USA, Ireland and UK

Book sales for North America and international:
Trafford Publishing, 6E–2333 Government St.,
Victoria, BC V8T 4P4 CANADA
phone 250 383 6864 (toll-free 1 888 232 4444)
fax 250 383 6804; email to orders@trafford.com
Book sales in Europe:
Trafford Publishing (UK) Limited, 9 Park End Street, 2nd Floor
Oxford, UK OX1 1HH UNITED KINGDOM
phone +44 (0)1865 722 113 (local rate 0845 230 9601)
facsimile +44 (0)1865 722 868; info.uk@trafford.com
Order online at:
trafford.com/06-2694

10 9 8 7 6 5 4 3

DEDICATION

I dedicate this book in memory of my dear deceased husband, Carl G. Todd, who blessed me with his loving support for forty-one years, and in honor of my son, Glenn; his wife, Dee; and my grandchildren, Whitney Sue and Matthew, whose love, prayers, and encouragement surrounded me during my service in China. Equally, I dedicate this book in memory of my godly parents, the Reverend I. T. and Esther P. Stroud, who taught me at an early age, by example and by word, to love God and to serve Him with my life.

ACKNOWLEDGMENTS

These memoirs are being shared in my desire to inspire others to take the gospel to China, which has one-fifth of the world's population. The younger people are responding and sharing with their families and friends, but someone must first help them to understand Christianity. Many Chinese have never heard of Jesus Christ and the plan of salvation. They deserve to know our Jesus. Please be a volunteer and take the Good News to them.

Special thanks are due to these good friends who assisted me with my memoirs. I am greatly indebted to Chung Soo Kim, Vivre Abul, Joanna Worrell, Olivia Weeks, Darla Reed, and Maria Ahmadi, all of whom typed the manuscript straight from my handwritten copy. A young Chinese friend from Fujian Province in China, Zhi Cheng Lin, translated the menu of Guo Zin Lin's birthday dinner. Dorothea Stewart-Gilbert, retired English professor at Campbell University, Buies Creek, North Carolina, edited my manuscript and typed it twice, finally putting it on a disk and then a CD with assistance from Charles Lee Price and Joseph Price. Thanks also to the Dean of the College of Arts and Sciences at Campbell University, Dr. Mark Hammond, who performed miracles with Dorothea's computer.

Extraordinary thanks are due to my brother, Joe Stroud, and our good friend, Lib Roberts, for their concern and financial support of the four blind students now employed as masseurs in Fujian Province, China. Also, I want to express my undying gratitude and love to my other family members in addition to my son and his family, to friends, and to churches that supported me with their prayerful concern, love, and much-needed financial help.

Without the assistance of these fine friends, this book would never have been completed. I shall be forever grateful to each of them.

TABLE OF CONTENTS

INTRODUCTION

Amity Foundation, a Chinese organization founded in 1985, was the brainchild of Bishop K. H. Ting of Nanjing, China. Bishop Ting suggested, to the proper governmental and church officials, that foreign organizations be allowed to send English teachers into China since English is the universal language. They would teach in colleges and universities that requested their service. Sponsoring organizations are Christian; therefore, teachers volunteering for services would most likely be Christians. This was the beginning of Amity Foundation, a social organization and not a governmental or church organization.

Amity has dramatically expanded its services and is now classified as a developmental organization. Besides church-run projects, it emphasizes the importance of doing concrete projects that directly benefit people and of having people take responsibility for these projects.

Another important aspect of Amity is recognizing the importance of working in cooperation with the government. This attitude shows respect for authority and in turn merits respect from governmental authorities.

China is moving toward modernization; however, many of the inland rural areas still exist. No electricity, inadequate water supply, little or no medical service, poor housing for homes, schools, and churches – the needs go on. Amity leaders are looking for ways to focus on some of these areas and provide assistance for a better quality of life for remote village people and less fortunate urban citizens.

Besides the previously mentioned projects, Amity has been working to help provide educational opportunities for the blind and visually impaired, training for unemployed people whose jobs phased out, emergency shelters for earthquake victims as well as for those who lose their homes in yearly floods. Tents, blankets, food, and medicine are donated and distributed by the local officials. So this endeavor becomes a joint effort between the donors, distribution leaders, and recipients.

An integral part of my mission to China, Amity has expanded since its beginning in 1985, but its goal has remained the same: to help meet humanitarian needs by providing sustenance and by including the recipients in the equal distribution and rebuilding process. Its motto, which is closely related to that of the Chinese Protestant Church, is based on Matthew 22:36-39: "Glorify God and serve people." Obeying this scripture is easy when people love God with all their being and others as themselves. This was also the motto of the greatest teacher who ever lived, Christ Jesus. May that be the motto not only of Amity Foundation but for us as well.

CHAPTER 1

My Call and Preparation

"Train up a child in the way he should go: and when he is old, he will not depart from it."
(Proverbs 22:6 KJV)

How well I remember that night in early fall when my church was in a week-long revival! As I dressed, my nine-year-thoughts were on my need to accept Christ as Savior. Our family home was heated by open fireplaces in three of the six rooms in which we lived. I had gone into the bedroom to get my black patent leather slippers and just as I stepped into the short hallway to make my way to the fireplace to warm the shoes, I felt a sudden surge of inexpressible joy deep within my heart. With no second thoughts, I knew God had accepted my soul into His safe keeping. I was ecstatic!

Mother was busy as usual helping younger siblings get ready for bed because they were much too young for night meetings. I explained to her what had just happened but was greatly disappointed when she thought I was perhaps too young for such a major decision. In my heart, I knew beyond doubt that Jesus Christ had paid the penalty for my sins and I was a member of the family of God. It was only after I reached the age of eleven that Mother consented for me to make a public statement of my belief and finally experience baptism. How pleased her approval made me, but I knew the Holy Spirit of God had come into my life two years earlier. I'm sure Mother was advising what she felt was best for me.

Our church had no baptistery so on the appointed Sunday afternoon the church family gathered at a branch from Northeast River in rural Duplin County, N.C., for the baptism of only two candidates, one a young married lady and, of course, me. After this service, we went to the church for worship and Communion; even as a child I felt a sense of humility and pride as I partook of the bread and grape juice, a substitute for the wine. Communion was followed by the right hand of Christian fellowship, when all church members came by shaking the hands of us new members and making welcoming remarks such as, "God bless you," "Welcome into our church," etc. At last I was now a bona fide church member but more importantly a sinner saved by the blood of Jesus Christ.

Childhood moved quickly and Sunday School and Worship were the climax of each week. For several years my older sister, brothers, and I attended Sunday morning services at the nearby Pleasant View Presbyterian Church because the Missionary Baptist Church met on Sunday afternoon. That way we could attend both churches. As time went by, each church decided to have morning worship and since our father was a Baptist minister, we naturally went to the Jones' Chapel Missionary Baptist Church with him, Mother, and the younger children. There were nine children in our big, happy family, and in addition our paternal grandmother lived with us. Each Sunday we packed into the family car to ride the four miles to Jones' Chapel Missionary Baptist Church, and each Sunday, as well as the other six days, we twelve family members ate at a long table loaded with delicious food prepared by loving family hands. Those were pleasant, secure years for our large family.

When I was a junior in high school, our father gave a piece of land for a new church building nearer our home in a small settlement made up mostly of relatives. Dad was the major leader in both the older church and the new one now in Albertson, N.C. A plaque out in the front stands today in memory of both parents, the Reverend I. T. Stroud and Esther P. Stroud, two of the most committed and dedicated Christians I have ever known. Needless to say, all of us were proud of the new clapboard church located so near to our home that we could walk and no longer needed to pack into the family car to go to church.

The word "missionary" always fascinated me and shortly after the new church was open, Miss Katie Murray, a real live Baptist missionary, came to our church. She was the epitome of a missionary in my mind. She talked of her work on the mission fields in China! In my young heart, I knew God had a place for me to serve in China. Miss Murray planted that seed as she described the pressing needs of the poor, deserving Chinese, and I knew even then that one day, yes, one day with God's help I would go to China to share the love of Christ with Chinese. How could I have known that fifty-six years would elapse before that became a reality! I never gave up on that idea and fruition took place in 1988! A long time, but God was not idle, He had a plan, and it was finally realized.

Public schools were in session for only eight months during those years. The four months of summer vacations were spent babysitting younger siblings, helping around the house, and sweeping the big, sandy yard weekly, an unwelcome job. I was not permitted to help cook, and my older sister, mother, and grandmother took care of the family's culinary needs. With little experience in preparing and cooking food until after my marriage, I was lucky that my husband had acquired that skill by helping his mother in the kitchen as he grew up! Summers were long and sometimes very boring in my childhood until I could climb the large oak tree while grasping the book I was currently reading. Two limbs provided a perfect seat, and I could read until the baby woke up.

I graduated from B. F. Grady High School in Duplin County in 1938. Dad had decided that I would follow my elder sister and elder brother by attending Campbell College, a small junior institution in Buies Creek, Harnett County, North Carolina. On the first Sunday in June that year, after Sunday School in my church, a cousin, Cordelia Stroud, invited me to have lunch with her family. During the course of a typical country Sunday lunch, we discussed the new Presbyterian mission which was meeting for the second time that afternoon. When we decided to attend, I felt rather grown up, now being a high school graduate and participating in my first mission Sunday School.

Several people had already gathered as we arrived at the meeting point, an unfinished farm house which had been made available by the owner. A first cousin, whose daughter had just graduated with me, was the acting superintendent. She, the cousin with whom I had eaten lunch, and I were seated together about midway the large room with other adults. The other people assembled were unknown to me, but I felt a warm welcome and had settled down to participate in this the second Sunday School class of the new mission.

Shortly before we entered the building, low thunder rumbled in the southeast from a distant cloud. Hymns, scripture, announcements, and prayers made up the opening assembly. Soon afterwards the different age groups dispersed to their classes for the Sunday School lesson. My cousin was collecting donations on his Sunday School quarterly since offering envelopes were not yet available. Suddenly, my body began to shake uncontrollably, the cousin nearest me was on the floor, and the other cousin had to be carried out by her father. The coins actually melted on the Sunday School quarterly my cousin was holding to collect the donations. People were lying down, sitting, and crawling around looking dazed and shocked. Parents were racing about, frantically calling out for their children. I had to step over the bodies of several young men to get outside while clinging to the arm of my cousin. The smell of scorched clothes, singed hair, and burned paper was almost overwhelming. Pews and chairs were in disarray. Hymn books littered the floor as wails and loud weeping came from those unable to locate a family member. Two brothers, their sister, and an eight-year-old cousin were killed instantly by lightning. A third brother spent one week in the hospital. My only obvious injury was a perfect lightning streak which reached from my right shoulder to the elbow. It was not a deep burn, so after a few days it disappeared. Through the years, I have felt this was my mark from God to serve Him.

September rolled around and Dad loaded my one suitcase and trunk on the trailer he pulled behind his car. Off we went to Campbell College, now Campbell University, where I knew only the names of some faculty and staff my elder siblings had mentioned. I was determined to be a good student and make high grades. I was somewhat homesick when I saw that green Pontiac slowly disappear as Dad drove out of sight.

My first Sunday on campus I attended the Buies Creek Baptist Church and responded when the invitation was given by the pastor, Charles B. Howard, later Dr. Charles B. Howard. I came under the Watchcare of the church and dedicated my life to become a missionary. I never forgot that commitment.

World War II interrupted my plans to go to China as a missionary. After graduating from Campbell College, I went to East Carolina Teacher's College, now East Carolina University, in Greenville, North Carolina. There I majored in primary education with a minor in psychology. Upon graduation in 1942 I took my first job as a second grade teacher in the Pitt County School in Pactolus, North Carolina. Teaching was my field and I enjoyed working with students. My plans to become a foreign missionary to China were put on hold as China closed its doors to foreigners and deported missionaries. This change of regime merely stalled any dreams I had of going to the mission field in China.

During the following years, I met my handsome husband, Carl Glenn Todd, my first roommate's friend back at Campbell College. After a two-year courtship, we married in 1944 and enjoyed forty-one years together before God took Carl to be with Him. We were blessed with one son, Carl Glenn Todd, Jr., and now I am the proud grandmother of a beautiful granddaughter and a handsome grandson! A fairly small family but ones I deeply cherish and am extremely proud to call family. We still miss the patriarch of our small group, but I rest assured that God is taking good care of him.

Three weeks after my husband's funeral, my son's mother-in-law was diagnosed with inoperable cancer. The following fourteen months I spent most of the time helping with two grandchildren, cooking, housekeeping, etc., to free my daughter-in-law to be with her dying mother either in her home or in the hospital. After her mother's death, my son's wife was able to assume full duties of her home and children, and I found time to look for other ways to be useful.

Church has always been an important part of my life. From our childhood, our parents took us every Sunday to Sunday School and worship, with Dad a pastor during many of those years. Teaching Sunday School classes and helping in Daily Vacation Bible School, mission groups, choir, etc., were natural for me. Now in my retirement years, I realize God was training me for special services. I worked as a primary teacher, speech therapist, and elementary supervisor, and before going to China, as a teacher for six years in the education department of North Carolina Wesleyan College in Rocky Mount, North Carolina. God was teaching me unconditional patience, unconditional love, unconditional acceptance, and unconditional forgiveness, skills I desperately needed to acquire and use during all those years in preparation for my China mission and certainly during my years of the Lord's service in China.

God had not been idle during all those years of my preparation and family responsibilities. Shortly after the funeral of my daughter-in-law's mother, I learned of the plan through the Baptist Foreign Mission Board in Richmond, Virginia, whereby teachers could go to China as English teachers! Exuberant, excited, happy, and enthusiastic, I pursued the process, met the requirements, and in late August 1988 my son and two precious grandchildren took me to Raleigh-Durham International (RDU) Airport for my long awaited destination, Nanjing, China! God had finally opened the door for me to become a missionary teacher in the land of my childhood dreams!

CHAPTER 2

Heading to Nineveh

"And he said unto them, 'Verily I say unto you, there is no man that hath left house, or parents, or brethren, or wife, or children, for the kingdom of God's sake, who shall not receive manifold more in this present time, and in the world to come life everlasting."

(*Luke 18:29-30 KJV*)

The early morning flight from Raleigh-Durham International to Hong Kong began with a big surprise. I had been routed by Chicago for a connecting flight to Seattle and another connection to Hong Kong. My son, my ten-year-old granddaughter, and my five-year-old grandson were helping with luggage. Imagine the surprised faces when we were told that O'Hare airport in Chicago was closed because of fog! We did not panic, as the ticket clerk studied alternatives to get me to Seattle, where I was to meet other volunteers in the same organization, Cooperative Services International (CSI), a division of the Southern Baptist Foreign Mission Board.

After some minutes, which seemed like an hour to me, he finally produced a revised flight plan, not on United Airlines as my ticket had indicated but on American Airlines to Dallas-Fort Worth, Texas. This meant changing terminals as well as flight plans. My precious grandchildren struggled to help with the heavy luggage while we boarded the airport bus over to American Airlines. Looking back on this unexpected "hitch," I realize it kept us from getting too emotional at good-bye time. Silent sobs and unshed tears were in abundance as those precious three waved good-bye, and a paraphrase of Christ's words in Luke 18:29-30 came into my heart to comfort me. Indeed, anyone who gives up his home, siblings, parents, spouse, children, or property to follow Him shall have a hundred times as much in return and shall have eternal life. I know God will fulfill all of His promises.

After a tearful farewell, I walked away to enter the boarding corridor and heard my son say in very solemn tones, "Goodbye, Mama," and my grandson exclaim, "She's going to China!" My granddaughter was speechless and so was I. What began seemingly as a handicap for the flight was now resolved and I was on my way to China.

The flight to Seattle from RDU and Dallas-Fort Worth consumed much of the day; however, I arrived in good time for the next leg of the journey to Hong Kong. A peace settled over me as I chatted with other passengers and at times read or watched the movie being shown. Time slipped by quickly and on arrival in Seattle, one of the first people I saw was a lady in our group who would become my roommate for the next year during required conferences we attended. At last, I was on the West Coast and a "mere" fifteen hours flight away from Hong Kong.

We boarded the big United 747 at 4:00 p.m. and flew during the night hours. My seat was next to a Chinese gentleman who had apparently enjoyed a double dose of garlic with his last meal. This exposure encouraged me to walk up and down the aisles as much as possible! Some passengers slept but I was too excited to do much sleeping. The trip over was smooth, uneventful, and pleasant except for the garlic. The big plane performed well.

Hong Kong at last! Officials from our CSI organization were on hand to meet the volunteers. Another unexpected problem – my luggage did not come in on my flight! I would not leave the baggage claim department until checks could be made to find where the two bags were. I went to lost luggage and reported it. My "future roommate" waited just outside baggage claim for me. As I walked back by another carousel toward the exit, there sat my luggage which had evidently come in on a different plane at about the same time as my plane. What a surprise! What a relief!

My friend, who had waited so patiently for me, and I took a taxi to the YWCA, where reservations had been made for us. A hot meal and warm shower finalized the activities of that day except for a long, long thank you to a loving heavenly Father, who had kept me at peace in spite of the unexpected events of the past twenty-four hours. He promises to meet all of our needs and indeed He did and He does fulfill promises!

The YWCA was just down the hill from the Hong Kong Baptist Seminary. After a good night's rest and a hearty breakfast, the group went to the Seminary for orientation and Bible Study. The Book of Ephesians was the one studied. Later my notes came in handy as a Bible Study Group in Nanjing, where I was stationed, chose to focus on Ephesians! Coincidence – I don't think so! The YWCA became a little like home as we used it for several years during the annual Winter Conferences. It was conveniently located near the Seminary and major bus lines we needed for travel around the city.

The week ended with much prayer and good wishes. Then the group of around twelve volunteers headed into mainland China. The Chinese airplane was different from any other plane I had flown in before – seats too close together, fabric and padding worn, peanuts and watered-down Kool Aid drink for our lunch. After shaking and shuddering for an hour and a half, we landed in Nanjing, the city which I lived in, worked in, and loved for the next four years.

Amity Foundation, the Chinese organization through which we were assigned, sent personnel to help with luggage and take us to the hotel where we would be in conference for yet another week. Puzzled looks and an air of excitement and expectation filled the bus as we rode through one of the largest cities in China. People! People! Bicycles! Bicycles! Bicycles! After another week of orientation, expectations, warnings, etc., along with seventy other people from several countries in Europe, Canada, Japan, and Australia, we were finally dispersed to our assigned institutions.

Assignments were far flung from Nanjing, headquarters for Amity Foundation and Chinese Christian Council. New friends were leaving by buses and trains to their locations. Waving good-bye to them as they left for their various colleges or universities,

I had a sudden feeling of loneliness when they moved out of sight and a lump filled my throat. They had become like sisters and brothers in just a few short weeks. Now I knew no one around me very well.

Uncertainty lasted only a few minutes! A pleasant young lady came up to me and said, "Hello! I am Wang Li, your foreign affairs officer. I will take you to Southeast University and help you get settled." Another teacher from Germany was assigned to the same school. I had seen her during conference but knew nothing about her background. We were assigned connecting rooms in the guest house where we lived for the next four years. We are still good friends.

An old model car pulled up where we stood surrounded by baggage and accompanied by our foreign affairs officer, Wang Li. The back window and the back side windows were covered with a light green, slightly ruffled cloth. We could see out but could not be seen from outside! My German friend seemed less surprised as we were helped into the backseat along with bags that couldn't fit into the snug trunk. I didn't know whether I should feel like a corpse or a celebrity!

Despite its age, the car took us across the city to the guest house on the campus of Southeast University, a sixty-year-old school for engineers. My legs and body complained as we walked up four flights of stairs to #402, one bedroom with a bathroom and commode which functioned sometimes. A plunger and the housekeepers became good friends and frequent visitors! At last, at last, I am in my Nineveh. God had to intervene and assist, but I knew in my heart that He would not "leave me nor forsake me." The old car was faithful but God is more so! Nineveh, I'm here and ready to begin serving Chinese students in classrooms and in my new home.

CHAPTER 3

Settling In

"...Prepare ye the way of the Lord, make straight in the desert a highway for our God."

(Isaiah 40:3 KJV)

Room #402 faced an obsolete Olympic-sized swimming pool unused except as a receptacle for broken furniture parts, twisted bicycle wheels, and at least a trillion hungry mosquitoes. I soon learned that insect repellent was a must as those pesky rascals were very fond of my O positive blood! I soon found out just how long a container could last so it almost became a hoarded item in my closet.

Meals were served in a communal dining room. Each person was issued a washcloth which hung on a nail underneath that person's assigned number. My number was fifty-four. The same cloth was used for a week, and another clean one replaced the used one on Monday mornings. One sink with only cold water available accommodated all incoming diners! Needless to say, the six foreign teachers washed their hands in their living quarters before going over for a meal. Even so, each Monday morning, the cloth below number fifty-four was a different one.

A large glass cabinet against the wall displayed plates of foods available for lunch and dinner. We made our food choices by putting the number of a particular plate by the person's name on a long food list hanging near the cabinet. Each meal included one meat, rice, and one vegetable. Chicken, seafood, and pork were the usual meats served. Greens, potatoes, carrots, celery, cabbage, and cucumbers were the most commonly used vegetables. Fresh fruit was offered at times. The food was all right, but the lack of hot water and sanitation created major stomach disorders for most foreigners.

No health department officials checked periodically for "safety in dining." It was not uncommon to see a cook preparing vegetables on the dirty floor of the cooking area. Cats could be seen walking across the counters where plates were served. Chefs and other kitchen personnel seemed unmoved as an occasional rat raced across the kitchen and dining room. Eating in this environment became a hazard to my health, and constant stomach problems and hunger were always present. A remedy occurred when the five foreign teachers gave me a hot plate and one large pot for my birthday in October. At last! Now I could prepare and cook for myself. Problem solved.

My room was comfortable with a desk, two stuffed chairs, nightstand, coffee table, and a mirror over the desk, which caused the house manager to forget what he was saying as he observed himself in the mirror, turning his face from left to right. A narrow cot with a bamboo mat made a comfortable bed for my back, which requires a hard mattress. A closet provided small but ample space in which to hang clothes. I was pleased with my room and settled in for the school year.

The bathroom served as my kitchen for storing the big pot and hot plate. Of course, the rice bowls and the one large mixing bowl were usually washed in a large pan placed in the bathtub. Hot water was available from an electrical tank on the roof just above my room. It had no thermostat and often spewed out hot steam instead of water! The commode took frequent leaves and water had to be drawn from the other taps to do the work of the commode.

In spite of the inconveniences, I felt fortunate to be in a guest house with steam heat, electricity most of the time, and running water. Most of the students were not accustomed to such luxuries, and many areas of China were still without these services. As friendships developed, I allowed students to bathe in my tub or shower on the condition that it be kept secret. Our secret was never revealed. After each student's bath, I would find around the tub a black ring which I removed with available

Ajax cleanser and some fierce elbow "grease."

The first night on campus a young lady posed a question that was repeated many times during the next thirteen years. English Corner, a group of students that met once weekly for free conversation in English, was meeting with the six foreigners in attendance. After the introduction of the six, groups were formed with a different foreigner in each group. That young lady in my group asked, "Do you believe in God?" A little red flag went up in my mind as to why she would ask this question, but I could not and would not deny my heavenly Father. When I answered, "Yes, I do," she responded, "You can't see Him, so why would you believe in Him?" A large tree stood just outside the room and the wind was blowing. So I asked her, "Do you think the wind is blowing?" She answered, "Everyone knows the wind is blowing," and to this I replied, "But you cannot see it." "But I see the leaves moving in the wind," she said. My response was, "I see the effect God has in the lives of people who believe in Him." In early May this same student asked whether she could audit my class. After a few weeks, she asked whether she could attend church with me. I suggested she meet me at St. Paul's Church the next Sunday, and I was delighted to see her there. She became my interpreter and shortly before I left for summer in the U.S.A., she made a profession of faith! God did not give up on her. When I returned in late August, she was the first student I saw on campus. She flew into my arms and with tears streaming down her face exclaimed, "I told my best friend about Jesus and now she is a believer, too!" I explained to her that this is how Christianity can spread as each believer shares with non-believers. She was so radiant and happy that she is still telling others about God's love and salvation. If asked that one question today, "Do you believe in God?" she would answer with a resounding, "Yes, I do believe!"

A few days passed, allowing time for touring the campus and seeing our classrooms and Nanjing, my home for the next four wonderful years. Classrooms were rather bleak with scarred and cracked chalkboards probably from abuse by red guards when they were out to destroy "all the old." Communism, according to Mao Tse Tung, was going to provide a new society so the old schools and churches should be destroyed. The double desks were likewise scarred and damaged but eager students seemed not to notice, and only the foreigners commented on their condition. Those first few days were eye openers!

Finally, the dean, vice-dean, director, and several professors came to the guesthouse where foreign teachers were housed. The dean explained who would teach what and issued a schedule to each of us. He apparently thought we were all super people. This university had ten thousand students and he obviously wanted all of them to study English. I had been assigned way too many classes with too many students. Fifty students were not considered too many for one class, and I was to teach oral English! Having completed his mission, the dean left and the director of graduate school asked to speak to me. All of my classes were for graduate students.

As other teachers dispersed discussing assignments, the director and I remained seated. When he opened up his notebook, I naturally thought he had some special requests, plan, etc., for students who would soon graduate. He greatly surprised me by asking, "How much money do you have in the bank in America?" God came to my rescue and gave me the immediate response. "I did not have time to count it before I left," was my meek reply, but internally my thoughts were that it is none of your business! After that, we did have a short discussion relative to achievement levels of students, study materials – most of which had been destroyed by red guards earlier, and evaluations – a joke.

Three levels of graduate work were offered: Master's One, Master's Two, and the Doctoral program. The director explained, "Master's One will receive a grade between seventy and eighty, Master's Two will receive a grade between eighty and ninety, and Doctoral candidates will receive grades between ninety to one hundred." Doctoral students were the poorest achievers of all. Many were older men in their late thirties or forties sent back to school by their company to improve their English, since many companies were now dealing with foreign countries. English being the universal language intensified their need to speak English.

Classes were two hours long, and when I went to my first class of doctoral students I took photos of my family, a small American flag, and a North Carolina flag. Before I presented my sixty-minute lecture, I had written the following eight sentences on the chalkboard and left blanks for students to complete:

My name is _____

My hometown is _____

There are _____ people in my family.

I have _____ brothers and _____sisters.

My favorite food is _____.

In free time I like to _____.

I am _____km tall.

My greatest wish is to _____.

This seemed elementary to me, almost too easy. When I called on the first young man in the front seat next to the window, he simply stared at me and made no reply. I continued down the entire aisle with not so much as a blink from anyone. The entire fifty students in the class were completely silent with all one hundred eyes on me. My lesson plan was to get them to speak English, but not one single student uttered a sound! What to do?? I had another whole hour with these speechless creatures! Knowing that pictures speak thousands of words, I pulled out the family photos and was grateful for my large family. "My eldest sister is a teacher, and her husband is a minister." On I went through seven siblings, their spouses, their children, my son, his wife, and two children. I told them where each family member lived and what types of jobs they had, and finally the dismissal bell rang. A bell had never sounded so sweet!

On the way back to the guesthouse where I was living, I felt utterly defeated. If this is what teaching in China is like, I'll pack up and go home, I thought. Several weeks later after communications had surfaced and good rapport had been established, I felt comfortable to ask the class, "Why were you so silent on the first day of class?" Almost in unison they answered, "We didn't understand a word you said!" Only then did I understand the lack of response and decide, well, I guess maybe I should continue. The thought of leaving never entered my mind again until thirteen years later when I did return to North Carolina to live out my remaining years.

CHAPTER 4

Worship in China

"...Not forsaking the assembling of ourselves together, as the manner of some is..."
  (Hebrews 10:25a KJV)

Memories of worship stem from my childhood. There was an automatic understanding in our family that on Sunday we would attend Sunday School and church. Dad was an ordained minister and Mom was a strong supporter and role model. My husband and I practiced the same pattern during our forty-one years of marriage before God called him home. Living and teaching in China reinforced this practice, and I looked forward to worshiping with Chinese in their churches.

There are various religious groups in China, Buddhism being the major one with temples available for those who choose the ugly Buddha as their God. Taoism exists to a smaller degree, and some Chinese still practice ancestor worship. Catholic priests were incarcerated because Communist philosophy taught that first allegiance should be to Communism, not the Pope. Cults from other countries, including the U.S.A, are likewise present with their false teaching. This was and is a grave concern I have, since young Chinese seem eager and anxious to know the truth. I prayed for God to thwart the cults' efforts. From my observations, Protestant Christianity was by far the fastest growing group with eager people spilling into courtyards, looking into church windows after all space inside had been taken.

Older people in drab colors of gray, dull green, and dark blue filled St. Paul's in Nanjing in those earlier years. Men and women wore the Mao high-collared jackets and fairly loose pants. Their dress style did not hamper enthusiasm for worship as they came early (7:30 a.m.) for Bible Study led by a "church lady" and stayed on for the thirty-minute song service followed by at least a one-hour sermon. No one was too old or too young to participate in the singing. I often watched as a parent pointed in the hymnal for the child to follow. Many Sundays a parent and child who had no hymnal would be straining to see the words in the book of a person in the pew ahead of them. I would give my interpreter some money and ask her to slip down to the church book store to buy a hymnal. Tears of joy and gratitude followed when these hymnals were presented to the recipients. In all those years, I never saw a Chinese in church who did not participate in singing.

Many blind people attended church and in several churches, the musician was sometimes blind as well. A blind choir from their nearby home in Fuzhou City sang specials every Sunday in the church which the late Bishop Moses Xi attended. The harmony was perfect as male and female voices blended, singing praises to our eternal God, Lord, and Savior. Faces were radiant, eyes sightless, but there was sunshine in the hearts and souls of the vocalists. The light of Christ cannot be hidden even from those who have no physical vision!

Christmas and Easter celebrations were wonderful occasions. Cantatas and dramatizations emphasized the importance of these events. Choir robes, usually made by a good sister seamstress, would be adorned with red paper flowers as the choir marched in singing and completely filling the choir loft. In some of the larger churches with graded choirs, risers were used to accommodate the singers. I also saw senior choir members, too feeble for bleachers, sitting in the front pews and turning to face the congregation when they sang. How they praised our Father and how beautiful their voices were to me!

The Christmas drama with a full cast of Baby Jesus, Mary, Joseph, Shepherds, Wise Men, and angels was given several times in my church in Fuzhou, Flower Lane Church. Each year the people came by, not just hundreds but thousands, such an enormous number making it necessary for several performances. At times I thought that every American Christian should hear these voices as scriptures from Matthew and Luke were read and acted out. How fortunate to be an observer and participant in such great worship services.

Few children were in church back in '88 when I first arrived in China. After all, churches and schools were closed from 1966-76 during the Cultural Revolution. It was only after Bishop K. H. Ting, Religious Affairs Representative in National People's Congress, reminded the Congress that the Communist Constitution stated that "there is religious freedom in China," and then asked, "Why are all our churches closed?" that, albeit slowly, the church buildings were opened to local congregations. Churches soon filled with older Christians eager and anxious to assemble and worship as they had before the days of Mao Tse Tung. As years passed, more young people came to church and by 2001 when I left China, there were Children's Choirs and Bible Studies for children in some churches. My heart would stand up and clap when, during worship sometimes, I could hear those precious children's voices singing among other songs "Jesus Loves Me."

Easter celebrations were mostly cantatas lasting from one to two hours. Decked out in white home-made robes, the choir sang with all their heart and soul. On one occasion, a young mongoloid man, whose mother was in the choir, wanted to sit by me. Since I had been in his church before, he recognized me. His mother had given him copies of the songs the choir would sing, and when they sang, he would sort through the pages and pretend to follow along. My heart reached out to him as he would try to hum along with the choir. Their closing number was "The Hallelujah Chorus." It has never been sung with more enthusiasm than that choir and my mongoloid friend exhibited on that Easter morning. I believe the angels in heaven clapped their wings when it was finished. My tears flowed freely and unashamedly.

Baptisms in churches I attended were done by what I call "symbolic baptism." Those officiating used a small pan of water that had to be refilled frequently because of the number of baptismal candidates. Candidates were required to be a minimum of eighteen years of age and to spend at least one month attending orientation classes. The pastor would dip his/her hand into the water and then place his/her dampened hand on the head of the person being baptized. During this ritual, the pastor prayed, "I baptize you, my brother/sister, in the name of the Father, the Son, and the Holy Spirit." Well over one hundred were usually baptized on Easter and the Sunday nearest Christmas. The largest number I ever witnessed at one time was two hundred and fifty. A friend in Anqing, Anhui Province, told of the baptism of over five hundred candidates on one Sunday.

Membership in the church is allowed only after one is eighteen years old. Prospective members express an interest to the pastor or appointed church leader and register their names after which they attend orientation classes on church membership. Upon completion of the month-long classes, they become candidates for baptism. Personally, I think this a good plan, as it may prevent church membership of those who have not experienced being "born-again." Indeed, it is not church membership that guarantees personal salvation!

Benedictions in churches were impressive. Invitational hymns were sung; however, parishioners continued to sing, and it was only after the pastor and choir marched out that those wishing to respond moved up to the altar rail, knelt, prayed, wept, and talked with the pastor when he/she returned. Sometimes other church leaders would assist the pastor because of the number responding. The musician continued to play the piano as worshipers began to disperse. I have waited thirty minutes or more just to get out of the door and into the courtyard where boards on blocks had served as pews for those who could not get inside.

TV monitors were placed in courtyards of larger churches for those unable to get inside. I sometimes stayed outside feeling a bit guilty taking a more comfortable seat inside. After the benediction, there was congestion as throngs of people tried to move out while boards were being gathered for the next meeting.

Larger churches held more than one service to accommodate the crowds.

The posted hours in my church were from 7:00-9:00 a.m. and another from 9:30-11:30 a.m., but services did not necessarily observe those particular hours. Sometimes it could be after 12:00 noon before the benediction in the later service. My church conducted a 6:00 a.m. prayer service Mondays through Saturdays, with the older members and the strong prayer warriors being the ones who usually participated in these early morning prayer times.

The Bible in English was taught on Friday and Sunday nights. I was invited numerous times to teach, but one of the rules of the Chinese-Christian Council states that the church will be self-propagated. A foreigner teaching anything in a Chinese church is a suspect and could be asked to leave the country. I did not want to risk being deported, so each time I had to decline and suggested they ask a Chinese who spoke English to be the teacher. Bilingual Bibles in Chinese and English are printed by the Amity Printing Press in Nanjing and are available in churches. Getting one could be a problem, however, since those Bibles sold out as soon as they arrived in the churches.

Bible study was an important part of my day, and after getting settled, I invited other foreigners to my room for Bible study. This practice continued for the thirteen years I served in China. On several occasions there would be Japanese, Canadians, Swedes, Germans, Filipinos, Australians, Danish, and Americans sharing scriptures and singing hymns. Sometimes we sang in our native tongues. God didn't need an interpreter!

Nothing replaces personal Bible study, prayer, and meditation. Early morning was my best time for no interference. Keeping a prayer journal as well as Bible notes enhanced my personal time with Jesus. I felt His presence so strongly that at times I would have oral conversations with Him. Sometimes it was as if I could hear Him laugh, cry, and speak words of encouragement. He was there all the time. What blessings were bestowed! Needless to say, this habit followed me back to the U.S.A.

A Revival Service at Fujian Theological Institute, Fuzhou, China, March 1995

Little did we expect what actually happened. Revival is not a word used in Chinese churches; however, this unspoken phenomenon is taking place in many areas of China. I am a happily surprised witness to a one-night "awakening" in Fujian Seminary.

We had been advised to come early so we could find a seat. The performance was scheduled for 7:00 p.m. Five of us left Huanan around 6:45 p.m. to walk the short distance to the seminary chapel where the event would take place.

Piano music was wafting through opened windows as we entered the courtyard. Thinking we were somewhat tardy, we hurriedly climbed the five flights of stairs leading to the chapel. A small sprinkling of people, students, a music professor and a talented blind pianist made up the group. The musician played sacred music including the "Hallelujah Chorus" and many other well-known hymns. A dark blue curtain with "Glory Be to God" in golden Chinese characters had been hung as a backdrop. The music was most pleasant as we took seats and waited.

Where were the Taiwanese performers we had rushed over to watch? The informer had said the service would consist of songs and dances and that was all he knew. Our curiosity was running at an all-time high with our not knowing exactly what to expect. As hymns pealed forth from the nimble fingers of the pianist, people began to crowd in, filling all available seats. Still no sign of the Taiwanese.

Professor Li, seminary choir director, asked students to bring in more chairs, which were soon occupied. Intuitively sensing a growing restlessness, Professor Li summoned choir members to come forward and sing their alma mater. We foreigners could only listen as we sat, surprised that students also sat, since we westerners stand for such renditions. Still, there was no sign of the visitors from across the Taiwanese (Formosa) Strait. Professor Li went into action again by having students place bleachers for the choir to stand on and with the seminary pianist playing, they gave moving selections including "The Old Rugged Cross" and a Chinese hymn with a tune much like "Go Tell Aunt Patsy The Old Gray Goose is Dead"!

People continued to crowd in. Suddenly, I noticed a small hand waving through the doorway and a bright-eyed eight-year-old, wearing a big smile, began to make her way toward me. The daughter of Professor Huang, she had helped in the celebration of my 72nd birthday. She sat on my lap until a seat became vacant nearby.

An eighty-four-year-old was escorted in, making her feeble way just a few chairs from us. My Chinese colleague, who was sitting beside me, moved up to sit with the woman. Immediately, a young man planted himself down almost before my friend stood up! I perceived that the elderly lady was grateful to have a younger lady sit by her.

The young man, a native of Anhui Province, was traveling with the entertainers and knows another CSI teacher, Mimi Moore, who works in Hefei and was my roommate during several conferences. The young man, Yang Hong Yi, is a member of Chinese Christian Council and was appointed to escort the performers. He assists with travel plans and hotel arrangements as the troupe travels throughout China.

Finally, very professional music began, and singers appeared in dazzling costumes while harmonizing in beautiful Chinese lyrics. Most of their songs were in Taiwanese minority dialects, unfamiliar to me. Then with the very Light of Jesus on their faces, the tune of "Amazing Grace" was sung in Taiwanese. It was no surprise to learn that all of them are ministers among the different minority clans in Taiwan. The uplifting and inspirational music was accompanied by dancing, which was simply slight movements of hands and feet keeping time with the music.

After many beautiful hymns, the leader led the singers into the audience shaking hands as they sang 1 Corinthians 13. This was followed by the audience shaking hands and saying "wo ai ni," or "I love you." Many young people shook hands with me, and never have I experienced a warmer feeling of unity and fellowship as we shared a "Oneness in Jesus."

A very moving testimony was given by the leading lady. She told of abuse, rejection, and suffering as a child and young girl simply because she is a minority Chinese. A number of times she considered taking her life until one day, while walking down the street, she heard music which in time changed her entire life.

The music was coming from a church, a place she knew nothing about, and mustering all her courage, she decided to go inside. Quietly, she slipped through, took a seat in the very back, and was enthralled at what the man standing on the platform was saying. Could this include her, this love, this sacrifice, this power? Of course, she kept going back and in time made that all-important decision to accept Christ into her life. What a difference Jesus made in her life. Now her heart and voice cannot sing his praises enough. She is the leader of this Taiwanese Prayer Group.

Scriptures were read of God's love and forgiveness, and many prayers were filled with repentance and thanksgiving. Young people around me were weeping, rejoicing, and praying. Indeed, the Holy Spirit was moving among this mass of people and seemed to envelop the entire audience.

Softly, the pianist began to play "Nearer My God to Thee." Everyone joined in the singing, and I must admit, I've never felt any closer to God than at that moment. Tears continued to flow and I handed out all the tissues I had brought in my purse and pockets. I wish all of you could have experienced that service.

Praise God for "called-out" people. I praise Him for being a universal Father. I praise Him for allowing me to attend this three-hour Chinese revival. In Him there is one great fellowship of love throughout the whole wide world!

Please pray for a continuation of this movement in China. Remember Jesus loves you and I do, too.

Mama/Sue

CHAPTER 5

Survivors

"I must work the works of him that sent me, while it is day:"
(John 9:4 KJV)

Many of the older Chinese told of experiences involving abuse, persecution, and deprivation. Emotional stress, mental anguish, social isolation, and physical hunger were prevalent during those infamous years of the Cultural Revolution.

Siu Tu Tong was president of the Nanjing YMCA when he was taken by Red Guards twenty-five miles into the countryside, where he sowed rice seeds and set out the seedlings in ankle deep water – without boots, of course. Later, he helped harvest the rice, working from twelve to sixteen hours each day.

"I was a good worker," he reported. "I was good at ping pong. You throw rice seeds with the same arm movements used hitting the ball in ping pong," he chuckled.

He felt lucky because the "leaders" recognized his quality of work. They rewarded him by appointing him the deliveryman of food to their camp. "Every two weeks I pulled a two-wheeled cart into Nanjing to bring back oil, rice, and other available staples," he said. "I would run the twenty-five miles to Nanjing because that way I had more time with my wife and two children. I could collect available food items and walk very slowly back to camp," he laughed. This continued for most of the ten years of the Cultural Revolution.

Most of his coworkers were well educated and could speak some English. "When we felt depressed, we would speak in English, and several of us were Christians so we taught others many hymns. 'What a Friend We Have in Jesus' was our favorite," he said. When asked whether he felt anger and hostility toward the guards, he replied, "No, they were just doing their job. We would work hard to try to please them and we often prayed for them," he said in a concerned voice. "On the cross, Jesus said to forgive them because they didn't know what they were doing. That's how we felt toward those young men who were our guards," he explained.

The Revolution ended in 1976, and the "intellectuals," or professionals, were allowed to return to former jobs if they still existed. Siu Tu Tong went back to the YMCA as director and also taught classes at the Jing Ling Seminary in Nanjing. An inspired man of God who shared his faith, demonstrated his patience, prayed for his enemies, and stood true to his Savior through it all – that is Siu Tu Tong!

Four years were not enough as I worked at Southeast University in Nanjing with Professor Gu, dean of the English Department and thus my boss. His salary at that time, 1988, was only one-hundred and sixty Yuan (roughly $20.00 USA currency) per month. He was apologetic concerning the lack of textbooks, which the guards had destroyed, and suggested that I make up lesson plans. This was done basically for the next four years. *The China Daily*, a four-page English newspaper, became my only textbook resource.

Chinese are friendly and hospitable. Mr. Gu was no exception. I was invited to his home to meet his wife, mother, and five-year-old daughter. His house was sparsely furnished; however, I noticed a beautiful dining room table. "It was too heavy for the guards to take," he smiled. "We never have sweet potatoes at our house," he continued. "During my years of 're-education,' I only had sweet potatoes to eat, three times every day. Now I can't stand them," he said with a turned-up nose.

Mr. Gu was only nineteen years old when he was forced to go to the countryside. He was a first-year college student at the time. "I worked from twelve to sixteen hours in the hot, steamy rice paddies. I worked very diligently for two years. Finally, the guards learned I had been studying to be a teacher, so they allowed me to hold class for village children under a tree since schools were closed. We had no paper, no pencils. We made Chinese characters in the dirt. I did that for eight years," he said. "At least, it was easier work than the rice fields."

After being released, Mr. Gu returned to Nanjing and later graduated from Nanjing University with a degree in English. A leader and a survivor still involved in training young minds on the university level – that is my former boss and a survivor, Mr. Gu.

Bishop K. H. Ting and his wife, Siu Mei Gu, were also survivors. Each of them suffered in different ways during those turbulent years. "Guards entered our home, took what they wanted, destroyed everything else including K. H's books," Sui Mei said. Bishop Ting had been swished away by leaders of the Chinese Christian Council and placed in a secretive hiding place in Shanghai. "We must protect him; his leadership is needed," she was told. Later he was brought back to Nanjing and continued to serve as president of Jing Ling Seminary, largest of the seventeen seminaries in China. He also served as president of the Chinese Christian Council and preached on Sundays when churches were allowed to reopen during the late seventies. His book, Love That Grows, occupies a special space on my bookshelf.

Bishop Ting was the Religious Affairs Bureau's representative in the National People's Congress during the late seventies. At one of its meetings he bravely stated, "The Communist Constitution plainly states that religious freedom exists in China. If that be true, why then are all the churches still closed?" After this quite bold remark, consent was finally granted for certain churches to reclaim their buildings, but many problems existed as a result of the use and abuse of church buildings by government forces. Church buildings had been used for offices, storage for all kinds of material, and housing in many cases.

Church members were joyously happy to be allowed use of their buildings. Some had taken pews, podiums, etc., under the cover of darkness years earlier. Those cherished furnishings began to trickle back, and slowly parishioners could have a seat for the two-hour worship services.

In one church, the baby grand piano was covered with hay

and left unmolested for ten years. When permission was given to reopen the church, members hastily removed the hay and the baby grand would still play! This good news was relayed to me by Eloise Cauthen, whose family had donated the piano years earlier. Eloise was the wife of Baker J. Cauthen, once president of the Southern Baptist Foreign Mission Board in Richmond, Va., now International Mission Board. As churches began to open their doors again, people gave praise to Bishop K. H. Ting for his part in achieving this goal. He is highly respected and revered by Chinese Christians for his role in this great accomplishment. I often told him he should be called Saint K. H. Ting, to which he would reply, "I don't think I deserve that." With that, I totally disagree. Chinese Christians would agree with me!

Siu Mei Gu was a small bundle of knots, lumps, and humps with every finger twisted and ravished by rheumatoid arthritis. She had been confined to a wheelchair years before I met her in '88. I never saw her when there was not a smile on her face and a warm glow in her eyes. She had suffered so very much, and never once did I hear a single complaint from the lips of this dear lady.

She was an English teacher in Nanjing University until it was closed in 1966 by the edict of Mao Tse-tung. All other universities were closed as he planned "to eliminate the old and introduce the new." Siu Mei's punishment for being an intellectual was to move iron rails from one location to another. Once the last one was moved, she was required to take all of them back to the original site. "I could feel the strain in my joints and muscles," she told me. This ordeal lasted for eight years. Little wonder she was bound to a wheel chair.

In spite of her inability to walk, she went back to Nanjing University to teach English. "I had no textbooks," she said. "The Red Guards had burned and destroyed all of the books and school supplies." Defeat not being in her vocabulary, she wrote two English textbooks, *Venturing into the Bible* and *Journeying into the Bible*. She began writing a third book but was unable to complete it because of her declining health. She never complained nor displayed the tiniest bit of self-pity. Rather, she radiated sunshine into the lives of those fortunate enough to know this noble lady.

Once she told me about yet another visit by the guards before she was taken away for re-education. They locked her in the bathroom and plundered, throwing books through an opened window in their upstairs library. Later these were burned along with clothes and other flammable belongings. "I could hear them breaking dishes, destroying porcelain vases, and scattering kitchen ware, pots, etc.," she said. My heart and eyes cried as she relayed such experiences to me. "Did you not feel angry with them? How could you remain quiet in such circumstances?" I asked. With the same smile I had come to expect she said, "I was lucky. They did not bodily hurt me. Many others were grossly abused, so I thanked God for keeping me safe and asked Him to forgive them!"

Siu Mei and K. H., as she referred to him, would often visit me and we shared many dinner appointments. I always enjoyed hearing the Bishop return thanks before we ate. He would invariably begin, 'Dear God, Father of Jesus Christ our Savior." The deep reverence, love, and respect for our Lord resonated in his voice. These two great survivors who made a great impact in the fields of Christianity and education will surely receive their just reward in the hereafter. My life was enriched by knowing these two servants of our Father.

He Hui Bing, a beautiful Chinese art and music teacher, is another survivor. She became a Christian when she began to notice the words of the hymns she was singing. "I like to sing so I joined my sister's choir in Guangzhou," she said. "I began to notice the words I was singing and the Holy Spirit brought conviction to my heart," she said. When asked whether she remembered which hymn brought conviction, she answered with a smile, "Amazing Grace!"

She is best known as Ah Bing by her closest friends. She was arrested for being a Christian, a name which classified her as an enemy of the government. She and several Christian girls were incarcerated within a wire fence enclosure because all prisons and jails were full, she said. "Guards were stationed to watch us. We had just a small shelter where we slept. Food, terrible food, was brought twice every day. I prayed and prayed, begging God to let us escape. One day I noticed the bottom nail on a fence post was bent. That night we took turns twisting that nail. We did that for three nights. We were so happy when it came out because then we pushed the wire fence aside as far as possible and the smallest ones could get through. We walked all night without stopping. We wanted to get as far away as possible," she related.

The following morning they saw Red Guards coming toward them. At the same time a group of peasants appeared coming from the opposite direction. He Hui Bing anxiously relayed her run-away experience. "The guards caught up with us and asked, 'Who are you? Where are you going?' We told them we were villagers who worked in the rice paddies. I think the peasants knew we were escapees so they allowed us to work until late evening. They shared their food with us, mostly rice with a few green vegetables on top. After it became dark, we began walking again. Our goal was to reach Hong Kong Bay and swim across to Hong Kong City. There we would be out of reach of those guards." (Now that Hong Kong has reverted back to China, escape would no longer be an option.)

"Did you get to Hong Kong?" I curiously asked. "No, we were able to get back into Guangzhou City and some family members hid us until the revolution ended," she sighed.

This petite young lady went on to share how blessed she was to be a Christian because "It was by God's grace and mercy that we managed to escape. The girls left behind most likely were abused, perhaps beaten, or even worse things could have happened to them," she said as tears trickled down her cheeks. "The guards would blame them for our escape and made them suffer even more," she explained.

After the turbulent years ended, He Hui Bing went to Jing Ling Seminary in Nanjing and upon graduation, she became an art teacher on the faculty. Her artwork was usually biblically based paintings, Chinese paper-cuts, and portraits of Bible characters developed and revealed through her artistic skills. God had even greater opportunities for her as the door was finally opened for her to come to the USA for study. She graduated from Columbia Seminary in Decatur, Georgia, and did further study at an Episcopal seminary in New York. Today Dr. Bing pastors a church on Long Island, N. Y. Her prayers, her faith, and God's purpose for her life are being realized because she is a true example of a survivor working in God's Kingdom on earth.

Dr. Hannah Lin, a retired pediatrician, is another survivor. "My faith in God sustained me and gave physical protection when I needed it most," she said. She and her husband were devout Christians, both of whom served as doctors in Fujian Medical Hospital in Fuzhou. Her husband was deceased when I met Dr. Hannah. Their commitment and participation in church activities resulted in abuse inflicted by the Red Guards.

"Many times I was brought before government officials to confess my failures as a supporter of Mao Tse Tung's regulations," she recalled. "I was classified as an enemy of the government and forced to attend self criticism meetings many times," she said. "The guards were determined to destroy everything related to Christianity, Bibles, hymnals, all Christian literature, and in many cases, people as well. I lost many good friends during those terrible years," she wept.

She told how her pastor was almost burned alive as parishioners were required to watch. The edict went out for all Christians to come to Flower Lane Church on a certain day and bring their Bibles. "We had to follow this order because they would come unexpectedly into homes, confiscate Bibles and anything else they so desired," she said. "The guards were strong young men, but our God proved to be stronger," she chuckled.

The appointed day came and as members arrived, Bibles were piled in a stack in the courtyard. "All the Bibles and hymnals had already been taken from inside the church, and the pile was higher than our heads," she cried. "Then the pastor was made to sit on top of the stack of Bibles and a 'church lady' was forced to kneel beside the Bibles. Petrol was poured on the Bibles and set on fire!" She lamented, "All we could do was to watch and pray."

With an angelic glow on her face, she continued. "Then a glorious thing happened! As the flames leaped up, the pastor called out, 'Father God, you saved Daniel from the lion's den and you saved the Hebrew children from the fiery furnace, please save me and that good church lady,' he frantically prayed. Then a miracle happened. A whirlwind suddenly blew all those burning pages straight toward the guards, who turned and ran away. We hurriedly took the church lady and pastor away, snatching their burning clothes from their scorched bodies. We took them inside the church and when the pastor revived from inhaling the smoke, he called out, 'Father God, thank You, thank You for saving our lives!' We had a praise and thanksgiving service right there around the smoking Bibles. Of course, most were ruined but we salvaged a few pages we could still read!" she joyfully reported.

There were other experiences of torture. "We Christians were made to walk down hot Wusi Road barefooted in August and our feet were almost cooked. We had to wear a dunce cap with 'enemy of the government' printed on it. They herded us into an auditorium where we were required to state our offenses and pledge our allegiance to Chairman Mao. When it came my turn, I refused to give the Mao salute and instead placed my hand over my heart and said that my allegiance is to Jesus Christ my Lord and Savior. The guard raised his rifle to hit me and I said, 'God bless you!' He dropped his gun and ordered me to sit down." Hannah could talk endlessly relaying her stories of suffering, murders, incarceration, sexual abuse, thefts, and destruction of personal property. Sometimes her eyes would overflow with tears and sometimes twinkle with thoughts of how she had outsmarted her enemies, like the time when she hid a small Bible in a cooking pot!

This fearless, retired pediatrician not only is a survivor but continues to witness to young students on the campus of Fujian

Medical University. She attends church regularly and sings in the senior adult choir. What a Christian! What a survivor! Her reward awaits her in heaven.

Dr. Lin, former president of Anglo Chinese college and husband of my foreign affairs officer, was a "reformed" survivor – reformed, not to accept Mao's theories, but a reformed Christian. The persecutors, or Red Guards, came into his school, arrested him, and led him away for "re-education" in the rice fields far from his home. With great bitterness he relayed how miserable and angry he grew as he toiled in rice paddies, with mosquitoes biting, heat rash developing, and disgruntled guards always shouting and barking out orders.

Time moved slowly and he grew more angry and bitter. Then one day as he was groaning in his misery, he thought that if he ever got out of those paddies, he would fill his pockets with knives and go out randomly stabbing to death everyone he saw. He felt some relief with these thoughts of revenge, but they never materialized.

Seething with fury, taking his pent-up emotions out on the rice plants, snatching, jerking, damaging the tender plants, suddenly he had a vision of Christ. "He appeared right before my face with tears streaming down his face and the crown of thorns on his head. He melted my heart with his tender look and soft eyes. 'Xiao Lin,' he spoke, 'You must forgive them. They are doing what they have been ordered to do. I forgave you, you must forgive them!'" Dr. Lin told how he fell on his knees, crying, "Father, forgive me, please, forgive me! I felt a heavy load had been lifted from my back and my whole attitude and outlook completely changed. Now I felt pity and sympathy for my abusers. I began to pray for them. Little by little, life became easier and I even sang some hymns as I continued working in those rice paddies. I no longer hated. Jesus was with me even in the rice paddy!"

Once released, Dr. Lin was allowed to return to Anglo Chinese College in Fuzhou. He told that some of the same students who had abused him on the day of his arrest came back to apologize, and he even taught some of them in his class! Dr. Lin had found forgiveness was a mode of freedom for him. Survivor, also, but now a reformed Christian ready to share Christ even in his communist country.

On my last visit to Anglo Chinese College, I noticed the words from 2 Timothy 2:15 in twelve-inch letters placed on the walls in the auditorium: "Study to shew thyself approved unto God, a workman that needeth not to be ashamed." These words were in English "because those who come to check our school can't read English," was his response when I questioned him. Anglo Chinese College continues to serve students while Dr. Lin lives out his last days in a nursing home facility in Fuzhou. He is truly a survivor who knows the joy of forgiveness.

There are many others who have stories of equal interest. They attended churches I attended and lived in areas where I served as an English teacher. This association gave me opportunities to interview them as we dined together or visited in one another's homes. They were and are a source of inspiration for me and great examples of survivorship.

CHAPTER 6

Weddings

"What therefore God hath joined together, let not man put asunder."
(Matthew 19:6 KJV)

Weddings are very important events in China. Parents and grandparents are eager for their twenty-year-olds to find spouses and to bless them with grandchildren within the next twelve months. To my great surprise one day, I saw an article in *The China Daily,* the English newspaper, with the caption "The Evil in High Costs of Weddings," written by Li Ji Xuan from Chengdu in Sichuan Province.

The writer noted that food for the "countless guests would detail four thousand five hundred yuan, almost $560 USA. That does not include luxurious furniture, color TV, washing machine, and a refrigerator." He stated that more expensive meant more decent. Now computers, digital cameras, and video cameras have increased the "necessities," he said.

"The reform and opening up have entered a crucial stage," he wrote. "We must liberate our brains to promote development in our Motherland." He suggested that ideas be changed and the old custom abandoned. From my observations, few Chinese couples were adhering to his suggestions.

One traditional business in China is that of matchmaking, which provides for young people wishing to get married an opportunity to meet. One such establishment was near the college where I taught for four years. Dim lights and soft music made a romantic setting for those eager to get married. If a couple met and married through the matchmaker, a sizeable fee was due for their introduction.

Many married students attended my graduate classes. After

reading the article about the high cost of weddings, I asked whether any of them had met their spouses through the matchmaker. It was surprising that such a few had gone this route since women far exceed men in the younger generation. The few who had met through this method admitted the courtship was far too short and in some cases they were still paying money borrowed to pay the $5,000 fee to the matchmaker. Too bad a cheaper way was not available for them to find the mates of their choice.

The Chinese expectation seemed to be that a young lady should be married by twenty-five and a young man by twenty-seven. Weddings were quite extravagant and expensive, in my opinion. When a couple married, all of their family and friends were invited for the big wedding feast. This could amount to hundreds of people; however, the less affluent could not afford this expenditure. In their case, the wedding simply meant going to the Public Affairs Bureau in the groom's hometown, signing the legal document which included a photo of the bride and groom, and paying the small fee of forty yuan, or $8.00, and they were then husband and wife!

The first wedding I attended was for Cheng Ming and Su Ren, my "Little Boy Friday" in Nanjing. Cheng Ming told me that he had been engaged at age four by his father to their neighbor's four-year-old daughter. "But I never even liked her, even as children growing up," he complained. When he was in the fourth grade, he met Su Ren, his classmate. "I wanted to marry her then," he said. So on this special day, he and Su Ren became publicly married, somewhat to the chagrin of his father!

Cheng Ming was a very good student and upon completion of high school was accepted at Beijing University, one of the most prestigious universities in China. He received a degree in Chinese literature and wanted to be a teacher. But upon his graduation, there was no teaching job available, so he was assigned by the government to a factory putting bottles of medicine in a box. "I hate my work," he told me many times.

One day while in the university, Cheng Ming received a letter from his father denouncing him as his own son. When

Cheng Ming wrote home to tell his parents that he and Su Ren were engaged, his father became angry to the point of rejecting his own son! "I hope you will have a son and he will make you lose face just like you have done to me!" The father was now embarrassed that his son would not follow through on the engagement made when Cheng Ming was only four years old. "My father still has my letter and said, 'I will show this to your son when he grows up. Then you will know why I am angry with you.'" Cheng Ming will not follow in his father's footsteps and choose a spouse for his child. "I think, if I have a son, he should choose the girl he loves for his bride," Cheng Ming told me. I must admit that I had to agree with his viewpoint.

So it was on February 17, 1990, that Cheng Ming and Su Ren made their way to the Public Affairs Bureau, paid the $8.00 fee, were photographed, and declared husband and wife. Their wedding certificate consisted of a small red book containing their photo with their signatures underneath. They were now legally married but Su Ren, a tax collector, went back to her unit where she lived, and Cheng Ming returned to the unit where he continued putting bottles of medicine into cardboard boxes!

During the following three months, the newlyweds could visit only on weekends. He would come to my room, relay news of their walks and talks, and with great excitement make plans for the next weekend. I never heard him complain because this was just the way the system worked at that time. Nothing lasts forever, so on May 2, 1990, all legal requirements had been met. A small apartment had become available and the young couple were about to celebrate their "public" wedding.

Annette, my German neighbor, and I were among the invited guests to the feast in celebration of their wedding. We went to their assigned apartment only to find Cheng Ming over at the home of Su Ren's aunt. Su Ren was held inside as Cheng Ming begged for her to join him at their apartment. The aunt was saying things like, "Give me ten pounds of rice and a liter of fish oil." He would plead again as the aunt continued making demands before Su Ren would be released. Finally, the aunt shouted, "Give me

200 RMB" (Chinese dollars). We didn't see any gifts or money exchanged as a beautiful Su Ren, dressed in red and looking like a porcelain doll, appeared. We were told that the badgering back and forth was a Chinese tradition meant only for fun.

Once the newlyweds were together, firecrackers began to explode in every corner of the courtyard where the couple's apartment was located. This continued for about thirty minutes as dense blue smoke settled over the area. It was a cloudy, misty day so the smoke seemed to cling to the ground, but this did not deter the hoopla of the couple's young friends and other wedding guests.

Next the proud couple showed us their small two-room apartment, very sparsely furnished. A kitchen with a balcony for hanging clothes and a bedroom which doubled as a living room would be their new home. A public water closet, or toilet, was used by all residents in their building. A royal bridal couple could not have been prouder.

After touring the apartment, we were taken to a rented bus which we boarded to the countryside village of the groom. As we entered the bus, we noticed a large basket of eggs dyed red and sitting just behind the driver's seat. Since Easter had already passed Annette and I puzzled over the meaning of red eggs. Cheng Ming and Su Ren rode in a rented car and none of the other guests in the bus spoke English, so we had to wait for an explanation. The deep tracks of muddy, red clay made the two-hour bus trip seem even longer. Finally, we arrived in the village at 11:30, in time for the big, sumptuous wedding feast.

Word spread quickly that the bus had arrived, and all the villagers swarmed out to greet the couple and their twenty-five guests. Annette and I received more attention than the bride dressed in red with curly hair, or the groom in a dark suit, white shirt, tie and, also, curly hair. Both had gotten permanents prior to this occasion! The villagers, all of whom were cordial toward us, were dressed in the somber blues, greens, and grays usually worn by peasants. We were never introduced to the groom's parents and learned which ones they were when Cheng Ming called them Ma and Bah Bah!

For over three hours we consumed the more than adequate lunch of many meats and vegetables – salted dry duck, roasted chicken, slices of pork, dog, eel, snake, lotus roots, tender bamboo shoots, stir fry greens, onions, rice, rice, rice, mushrooms, potatoes, scrambled eggs, and several unidentifiable dishes I was reluctant to question. Hot sugar water and hot tea were used to toast the bride and groom. The village children were fascinated by Su Ren's and Cheng Ming's hair, because they had never before seen a Chinese with curly hair.

Around 4:00, we began to make preparations to leave. Small children held on to my hand and begged, "Stay longer, don't go," so Cheng Ming interpreted. If I could have been two people at once, I would have honored their invitation! The parents prepared a bag containing two red eggs, candy, and rice cakes for us. We felt the wedding couple should receive any and all gifts, but again we learned another Chinese custom, to reward guests for attending the feast.

Annette and I wondered why the eggs were red. Later we were told that red is the color of happiness in China; thus, the red wedding dress and the red eggs signify best wishes for a happy life with many children. In recent years, however, the one child policy made the "many children" phrase null and void. Our first-hand experiences learning Chinese traditions and customs were exciting, interesting, and in some cases quite unusual.

Following us down the muddy hill to the bus, the villagers stood and waved until we were out of sight. It had been a good way to spend the day with a happily married couple, who now were fully qualified to return to their two-room apartment and begin a new life together.

When summer arrived, Cheng Ming learned I was returning to the U.S.A. for vacation time. He came in one afternoon shortly before I was to leave and asked, "Will you do me a favor in the U.S.A?" Of course, I would be happy to accommodate him in any way possible. "Will you buy a ring with a red stone in it for Su Ren?" When I asked what size she wore, he answered,

"I don't know. Just get a ring with a red stone and if she can't wear it on one finger, she can on another!" Later, during my vacation, I bought a red ruby set in yellow gold and took it back to Nanjing for Su Ren. The Hope Diamond could not have made them happier, but I was even happier because the ring fitted perfectly on Su Ren's fourth finger on her right hand.

A wedding I desperately tried to discourage happened much to my disappointment and later to the bride's. She was a beautiful young lady, about to graduate from Nanjing Pharmaceutical University. We had spent much time together going to the park, having lunch out, and attending church. Elizabeth was a high achiever in her classes, well liked by her peers and professors. One thing was lacking – she had no boy friend and she would soon be twenty-five years old!

She went to her hometown, Shanghai, for a weekend to visit her parents and friends. A group of Christian African students she knew from a university back in Nanjing were holding a gospel sing in the park and she attended. Also in attendance was a tall, young man with blonde hair and blue eyes, a Dutchman. "He spoke to me and bought me an ice cream," she gleefully reported. Two weeks later she received a mushy love letter declaring his undying love for her. This tantalized Elizabeth because no boy had ever "noticed me." The weekend ended too quickly for her and apparently for him.

When Elizabeth came back to Nanjing, she took a part-time job as a cleaning lady in Xu Wu Hotel to earn enough money to rent a white wedding dress. Chinese brides often wore red, but she had seen a church wedding in which the bride wore white. Her scholastic performance did not falter, and she became a model cleaning lady. I saw little of her now that she was working in her spare time, and only when she received another lovesick letter did she come asking what she should do.

The Dutchman had returned to Amsterdam and was working as a dishwasher in a restaurant. "I will get a better job after we are married," he wrote. Living in the Netherlands with a man who loved her so filled her mind that she would hear no words of discouragement. After having known the Dutchman for a total of three months, she graduated as a pharmacist. A few months later, he returned to China, they were married, and then they left for Amsterdam.

Soon letters of disappointment arrived, telling of hard times, little money, angry in-laws, no close friends, etc. These were the very things I had tried to warn her could happen, but all words had fallen on deaf ears. Now they had become realities! Poor, dear, disillusioned Elizabeth!

The last letter I received from her informed me that she had at last found a job as a pharmacist and was also working a nighttime job because Hans, the husband, made a low salary as a dishwasher. I have often wondered about her circumstances and keep her in my prayers. At least, she is a Christian and can call on the Great Provider for help. Hans had told her he was a Christian, too. I hope he was being truthful.

William and Rose discovered each other in my room! He was a constant visitor to help run errands, hang drapes too high for me to reach, and go with me to the market. Rose and Helen, sisters, usually attended the weekend "chat session" when ten or more students would crowd into my small room. William, a student in one of my English classes, was very eager to learn spoken English.

William was the son of illiterate peasants, who lived about two hours away in the remote countryside. Rose lived in Nanjing with professional parents – her father, a dentist, and her mother, a teacher. Different backgrounds did not deter their attraction for each other.

There was little money for outside activities for these two. Rose was a student and William was an honor student majoring in differential equations, a real math whiz! When they came to see me, I would need to go to the shop or to the library, so they could have some private time. Their courtship thrived in my room.

Graduation for William was at hand. On a particular weekend, they did not show up, but I was not too concerned as many others came for the chat session. Surprise! On Monday night they came in smiling and holding hands. William presented me their small black and white wedding picture. They had gone back to his village and were legally married. No big feast, no firecrackers, no fanfare, just husband and wife now happily married and living with her parents. I was happy for them and felt, perhaps, I had become a matchmaker.

Eli and Ann were in an English class for Chinese English teachers. Both beginning teachers, they were quite interested in improving their spoken English skills. Being the same age and moving on toward their later twenties, they began to smile more at each other and on his braver days Eli would sit nearer to Ann. Her parents were teachers, his were peasants, and during the off-season for farming, they ran a small noodle shop in their village.

He was a frequent visitor to my apartment and became an invaluable errand boy. During his college days in Anhui Teacher's College, he was befriended by his Bahai American English teacher. One of his first statements to me was, "I'm a Bahai." However, Eli liked to sing and often accompanied me to church. He discovered church music and after five years decided that Jesus Christ was the correct way to God! He was baptized on Easter Sunday in the church we most often attended. He was hoping Ann would accept his Christ, too, but her father's being a party member made it more difficult for Ann. He said, "I love Ann and want her in heaven with me!" Touching!

Their courtship bloomed and was nurtured as they worked in the same department at their university. Having lunch together, going to the park, window-shopping, and coming over to cook for me were among their activities as special friends. At first there were childlike actions and silly laughter between the two, but later I began to notice a more mature behavior and more serious conversations between them. So it came as no surprise when a wedding invitation was issued.

First, after their legal marriage they went to his village, where his parents held a feast. Relatives and friends came to wish them much happiness and a healthy child. They were gone for only a weekend, and the following week, Ann's parents hosted a feast for her family and friends. This one was attended by several foreign teachers they had met through their English teaching in the Fujian Medical University in Fuzhou.

Upon entering the chosen restaurant, guests were expected to donate at least two hundred Chinese dollars (yuan). This practice was true in other weddings. The foreigners were seated nearest the table of the bridal couple and her family. During the course of the evening, the couple went from table to table, clinking glasses of Pepsi as good wishes were made between all parties present. It was a pleasant and festive occasion.

Ann was dressed in a bright red dress and Eli wore a dark suit with a burgundy tie. Her father proudly introduced them after the dinner as they stood beaming before their guests. There was only one gesture of endearment that we foreigners noticed – she reached over and took his hand. They made a nice looking couple and we were happy for them. They continue to teach English and both have their Master's degrees, two deserving Chinese English teachers, both very dear to me.

Teachers being poorly paid in China, they were fortunate to be assigned one room, which they decorated as best they could. Another small shelter-like room was used as a kitchen, but it was about a ten-minute walk from the bedroom. A red, white, and blue canvas covered the top to keep the rain out. One table, three chairs, a gas cooking unit with two burners, and a cabinet were the furnishings in their kitchen. In spite of the crowded space and no hot water, they could produce a sumptuous meal. Now they were ready to begin life together as husband and wife with hopes of living happily ever afterwards.

Dr. Chen, an oncologist in Union Hospital in Fuzhou, was the father of a lovely daughter, an engineer, engaged to a young cardiologist practicing in Union Hospital. Excitement was rising several weeks before the wedding was to take place. Dr. Chen told me that his parents were Christian and he believed in God, but since he and the young cardiologist were party members, a church wedding was most unlikely.

Friends were invited to the home of the bride where Dr. Chen, an accomplished pianist, played many familiar tunes. Singing, eating, and then more singing and eating created a festive prelude for the wedding. Sometimes the bride was present and sometimes she would be absent and the groom would appear! Foreign friends found this a bit strange, but the father of the bride continued to celebrate the acquisition of a son. The mother of the bride would be present but not always. We learned that work came before pleasure, and this custom explained why the couple as well as the mother missed some of Dr. Chen's joyful festivities.

The couple were legally married several weeks before their public wedding. In a large dining room of a nearby hotel, around two hundred guests were invited and each donated at least two hundred Chinese dollars as a wedding gift. The hall was highly decorated with red banners and red lanterns, and ornate flower arrangements adorned the bandstand, where the couple toasted each other to the pleasure of their guests. They were stunning, she in a gorgeous white dress and he in a dark suit, white shirt, and red tie. Happiness was written on their faces, and proud parents and a glowing grandmother were all enjoying the events of the evening while the newlyweds moved from one table to another, toasting their guests.

"Canned" music was constant and loud. Many guests were asked to give a speech to the couple, and some were asked to sing with no advance warning for any preparation. When the table of foreigners came into focus, it was decided that we would sing "You Are My Sunshine." This song was received so well that we were asked to teach it to the other guests. It didn't matter that none of us considered ourselves vocalists. Fun, food, fellowship, and song were the order of the evening, and at 10:00 the bridal couple thanked the group and bade us a goodnight. Dr. Chen escorted us to a taxi, which took us to our respective universities. The bridal couple was happy and Dr. Chen was even happier. Now he had a bona fide son! It had been a good experience including the loud "canned" music.

Scarlett, one of the most capable students in her class, was employed shortly after graduation by the five-star Lakeside Hotel in Fuzhou. She began as a receptionist but quickly rose to a more executive position in charge of conference arrangements for various businesses using the spacious halls for seminars and in-service training programs. In a specific seminar, a young computer consultant spotted this capable, beautiful young lady. Their friendship developed quickly into a courtship and wedding plans soon became their topic of conversation.

Both of them were Christians, but because the groom was a Party member, they did not plan a church wedding. She explained, "Mike joined the Party so he could get a good job and maybe promotions later on. That is how the system works." Then Scarlett said, "I want to ask you a big favor – will you give us the Christian wedding vows?" Humility flooded over me, but if my former student thought me worthy of this honor, so be it.

The public wedding was to be held in the largest hall in Lakeside Hotel. No feelings of doubt ever crossed my mind, even though I knew there would be government officials among the 250 guests. So I borrowed a white choir robe from my church in order to look official as the vows were given. My good friend, Lynn Yarborough, who was teaching in Shanghai, was visiting me for the weekend. It was nice to feel her support, as she and I were the only foreigners present.

The bride was radiant in a rented white wedding dress. Her groom wore a rented black tuxedo. The bride's sister was maid-of-honor, and the groom's best friend was best man. When it was time for the ceremony to begin, I pulled on the choir robe and stood in front of the couple, now flanked by their attendants. The Scripture from 1 Corinthians 13 was followed by the Christian wedding vows. After I prayed for them to have a long, happy, and productive life together, they began to mingle with their guests as the feast began.

Actually, the couple ate very little, disappearing for several minutes and returning with her in a beautiful red dress and with him in a dark business suit. They continued to move through the room, toasting and greeting the people even while dining continued. Lynn and I were enjoying the feast and did not notice that the couple had disappeared again until they returned with her in a red chipao, a Chinese dress, and with him in the long gown styled like men's clothing hundreds of years earlier. Also, he was wearing a cap with the long plaited queue hanging to his waist!

As people were beginning to finish the elaborate, delectable meal, a bench was brought in and placed about midway the dining room. The bridal couple took their wedding money from a basket conveniently placed at their feet. The atmosphere turned the clock of time backwards for many years.

Lynn and I waited until most of the Chinese guests had made their bows, had given their gifts and best wishes, and were about ready to leave. As we approached them, Scarlett said, "No, no, you honored us tonight so no presents from you." That was not at all what we had expected, but we were forced to obey when Mike joined her in the command. We left feeling somewhat cheated because we would have liked to be accepted as Chinese, too.

It was a beautiful wedding with a lovely couple and 250 of their family and friends. We were honored to have had a small part in this very special day for two very special, deserving young people, Scarlett and Mike. Our best wishes will always be with them.

More and more of the Christian young people were choosing to have church weddings. Those with fewer finances would simply march in after morning worship, repeat the vows, and be pronounced husband and wife. Depending on the pastor, this ceremony could last only a few minutes or sometimes much longer. On one such occasion, I remember the pastor's reminding the trembling bride, her white veil shaking, of her household and maternal duties. He mentioned nothing of the kind to the groom. Her face was not radiant after the ceremony!

The first church wedding I attended was in St. Paul's Church in Nanjing. Rob, an Amity teacher, was marrying Xia Xiu, a beautiful Chinese English teacher, casually dressed as were the maid-of-honor, the best man, etc. A friend sang, "O Promise

Me," a song which brought back memories of weddings past. When the wedding march began, down the aisle came the beaming bride beside her beaming father. An older man in the congregation was heard to say, "It will never work, too much difference in their ages!" He apparently thought her father was to be her husband.

After the ceremony, friends were asked to extend best wishes. Rob's parents spoke first, welcoming Xia Xiu into their family. Several others gave them good wishes for long, lasting happiness. When the wishes ended, the couple left for a nearby hotel for the sumptuous meal which followed. It was a happy occasion for Rob, Xia Xiu, their families, and friends.

The least expected wedding I attended happened on a Sunday morning after worship services. The pastor announced that a wedding would take place and everyone was invited. As the worshipers sniffed the first round of blue smoke from firecrackers exploding outside the church, a mother whose baby became restless took her over to the spittoon and encouraged her to urinate. More people became restless, and I wondered how long they would continue to wait. Suddenly, an air of excitement stirred the people in the back of the church. I checked the time, and it was 12:00 noon. Perhaps the couple wished to be married at high noon. We had waited thirty minutes for their arrival.

There was no wedding march music but there was, indeed, a wedding party. Down the aisle came the bride in a wedding gown escorted by her groom. A small boy held the bride's train. He was followed by two little flower girls, the bride's mother, and then the maid-of-honor. There did not seem to be a mistress of ceremony.

The ceremony was about to begin, but first the government document granting permission for the wedding was read. This was followed by appropriate Scripture, wedding vows, and a prayer. There was no recessional so people seemed to disperse quickly. My thoughts were of Sunday lunch, and I felt that was most likely theirs, too.

As the guests were leaving, friends of the couple issued hard candy. Peng Zhao Deng, a former student now a professor at

Fujian Seminary, and I waited to see the couple emerge and when they did, friends showered them with metallic confetti, not rice! A highly decorated car with streamers flowing on each side and a large bouquet on the hood whisked the newlyweds to a restaurant for their wedding feast. We waved, watched, and wished them good luck and happiness as they drove out of sight.

Upon my return to Fuzhou in September 1994, I was greeted by a seminary student with news that Peng Zhao Deng, known as Alden, would get married in October. Shock and surprise hardly expressed my thoughts at that time. I had known thirty-one-year-old Alden for five years and never once had seen or heard of a girlfriend. One day as we were visiting his seminary colleague, his friend's lovely wife served us tea, watermelon seeds, and oranges. After we left their apartment, Alden self-consciously said, "One day I hope to have a wife and a nice home." This was the closest he had ever come in my presence to expressing any interest at all in young ladies.

The first telephone call I received in September was from Alden. When he came for a visit, one of my first questions was, "Who is she?" He smiled broadly and said, "Oh, you know her. She was my classmate in Nanjing Seminary. You saw her last year in Fujian Seminary. She teaches Systematic Theology." Somewhat relieved and with mouth wide open, I asked, "Beatrice?" "Yes, yes." "When did you discover this interest in each other?" I asked. "July or August," he said. They had been classmates for seven years! They did know each other quite well.

October, November, and December passed. No wedding. After the five-hour Christmas program at the seminary, Alden walked back with me to my school. He confided that on January 11 he and Beatrice would get married in Christ's Church at either 9:00, 10:00, or maybe 11:00 a.m. Because of my teaching schedule, I insisted on knowing the exact time. On Sunday, January 9, he said, "The wedding will be at 9:30 a.m. Can you sing a song for us?" Bewildered and overwhelmed, I said, "But I am not a vocalist." "It doesn't matter. We want you to sing," he implored. At this point I simply said, "No, no way!"

The wedding day arrived. Another teacher from Huanan Women's College accompanied me to the church and we were among the early arrivals, having left at 9:00 a.m. for the short fifteen-minute walk. The seminary car was sitting by, fully decorated with brightly colored streamers, bows, and a big, red, double happiness sign glued on the front. Every Chinese couple uses the double happiness symbol on the doors to their apartment or the one room they will call home, another popular Chinese custom. Everything seemed ready for the occasion.

We went up the front steps and were greeted by the lovely bride and handsome groom. I had never seen her so pretty nor him so handsome. She was wearing a stunning white bridal gown with a beautiful veil and extremely long train. Just enough makeup highlighted her beauty and a delicate lipstick accented her lips. She was as pretty as a "China Doll." He was good-looking with a puffy hair style, popular among young Chinese men, and wore a new suit, white shirt, new shoes, a red boutonniere with red ribbon streamers, and the ever present double happiness symbol. After posing for photos standing between the bride and groom, the vice-president of the seminary appeared and asked the title of the song I would sing. "But I am not a vocalist," I protested. He looked at me with an uplifted eyebrow and in a stern voice said, "You have to. You are on the program." He then proceeded to show me the program. On the spot, I coerced my colleague to help since the printed program had included the foreigner's song. We quickly chose "Love Divine, All Loves Excelling!" My miniature hymnbook was still in my bag after having used it during worship services just two days earlier. Lucky? No, I think Divine provision is better!

We were instructed to sit on the front pew, but thinking that relatives should have the front pew honors, we chose pew number two. A blind pianist was playing the "Hallelujah Chorus" as we walked in. Guests began to fill the large sanctuary, which still held the Christmas tree with its twinkling lights, and large angels cut from heavy plastic-like tag board placed between the windows seemed to smile at the assembly.

People came over to shake our hands and welcome us. Among the guests were pastors from all the Protestant churches in Fuzhou, church leaders, two gentlemen from Taiwan, and an eighty-eight-year-old from Xiamen.

The presider took his place at exactly 10:00 a.m. and began to announce those in the procession. First appeared the choir from Fujian Seminary followed by the senior pastor of Christ's Church, the best man, and the groom.

A close friend of the groom's served as best man since the groom's father was deceased. They came with great dignity followed by the groom's mother, who was dressed in typical Chinese fashion wearing slacks and at least three sweaters. The groom and best man faced the pastor on their right, and the mother took her seat on the left front pew.

The piano music stopped as a very loud recording of the wedding march began. Two small children, a girl and a boy carrying baskets of artificial flowers, came next followed by the maid-of-honor looking like a princess in a long white dress. The big moment for the bride finally arrived. Since her father was deceased, she was escorted by her brother to the left of her bridegroom. The atmosphere was that of purity and love as the very presence of Christ permeated the entire ceremony. It seemed so spiritually approved.

The presider read the government document giving permission for the couple to marry. Pastor Chen then proceeded with the wedding vows and the exchange of rings. After the couple were pronounced husband and wife, they took seats in the front of the choir. After the choir sang, the president of Fujian Seminary, pastors from two churches in Fuzhou, and the Taiwanese pastor gave short sermons. Alden's friend sang, and my colleague and I sang! We fudged by accepting offers of help from two Chinese ladies. One of them was eighty-five years old, a retired Seminary teacher whose English supersedes her singing skills. The other volunteer vocalist said she sang also, when in reality her singing was more like sounds coming from a distressed cat. My colleague managed to move her lips without any sound whatsoever. I was glad the hymn contains only four stanzas, since Chinese sing all stanzas regardless of the number. The audience endured and survived. Surprisingly enough, we were not thrown out!

When the last hymn was announced, "Savior Like A Shepherd Lead Us," the congregation stood and sang as the happily married couple made their exit to the front steps to receive good wishes from their wedding guests and to have more photos made. About to leave, we heard Alden call, "Come back! We want you in our photos, too." Standing between the bride and groom, we kept the cameras and video busy.

The formalities finally ended after two hours, so off to the Seminary and wedding feast we rushed. Ten round tables which seated ten diners each were laden with all kinds of fruit, watermelon seeds, hard candy, and dried plums. Seated with the Taiwanese, Chinese Christian council members, and professors at the Seminary, we watched as individual bags were filled for each of us a take-home snack.

Food was plentiful, with over thirty dishes served and, true to form, I didn't ask ingredients for fear of what I might be told. The blissful couple moved from table to table toasting and thanking the guests for coming to help celebrate their wedding.

I was greatly concerned for the cost of such an extravagance since Alden had told me he made only 180 Chinese dollars per month (just over $22 USA), and certainly his wife made even less. Surreptitiously, I enquired of several Chinese friends about how couples could ever pay such a debt as this celebration would create. "Oh, no worry. All guests are expected to give 200 yuan to the couple. It's a Chinese tradition." This was wonderful news, so happily I contributed the equivalent of $25.00.

After the two-hour meal ended, we were invited to see the one room they called home located in Seminary housing. A Christian friend with relatives in Malaysia and Hong Kong gave them a beautiful white bed, matching desk, and dresser. Two white wardrobes completed the furnishings. Decorations consisted of double happiness symbols, multicolored streamers, and a large cross above the head of the bed. Matching pink curtains and a pink bedspread added a note of daintiness to the décor.

Alden and Beatrice – bound together in holy matrimony, two of God's special servants in Fuzhou. Pray for them as they begin life together in His service. Surely God will bless this union.

That was the most memorable wedding I attended, since Alden and Beatrice were special friends of mine. There were other, more simple ceremonies and many when the couples had only a legal wedding because of a lack of funds for a big feast. My prayers and best wishes surrounded all of the newlyweds.

CHAPTER 7

Funerals

"...Come, ye blessed of my Father, inherit the kingdom prepared for you from the foundation of the world...."
(Matthew 25:34 KJV)

Firecrackers usually announced the passing away of family members, especially in a Buddhist family or in a family of non-believers. This ritual, we were told, was to ward away evil spirits. The loud, smoky explosions could be surprising, startling, nerve-racking, and disruptive.

One day as I was walking by a fenced yard, all of a sudden, loud bursts of firecrackers made me almost jump out of my shoes. A gate I had not even seen opened, and cracking, noisy bunches of firecrackers were thrown almost at my feet. I didn't know whether I should run forward or go backwards. The blue, smelly smoke seemed to form a cloud around me. Maybe they think the foreigner is an evil spirit, I thought. Apparently, the gate was opened to clear any demons present inside or outside the area of the deceased.

† † †

It was a cold, rainy December morning and I snuggled under the warm comforter for the last hour of sleep. Suddenly, a loud explosion almost pulled me from the bed. Explosion after explosion continued from 5:00 a.m. until 10:00 a.m. The exploding firecrackers were joined by a band of fifteen people beating mournful sounds on drums while others clanged tinny sounding cymbals and tooted out-of-tune wind instruments. These continued until 10:00 as well.

A large bus rolled up and the noise ceased. The body was loaded through the side door of the bus, which served as a hearse, and soon it was filled to capacity with family and friends. They were going to the crematorium and would return soon for their neighbors, since more than one trip was needed to transport all of the mourners.

Armbands identified family members. Different colors indicated the relationships to the deceased; some relatives wore red, and others wore white or black. Sometimes relatives wore long sashes, symbolic of kinship to the deceased.

The bus returned as expected. In the meantime, a hired chef with many pots and pans and helpers had arrived earlier and set up large tables for about seventy-five people. Big pots were heated with coal underneath them, and a feast was held for a good three hours. From the jubilant laughter and conversations we wondered whether the deceased left a big inheritance or whether they were glad he was gone to his destination!

The band, likewise, returned with the family and stopped eating periodically to break the sound barrier, or so it seemed, with more of their funeral renditions. This alternation between music and food lasted until sundown, and the band members looked somewhat weary as the final notes died down. They loaded the instruments, climbed into their means of transportation, an opened truck bed, and left our neighborhood. We wondered whether they would have a repeat performance the following day.

Three months later as I was coming in from teaching a class and rounding the curve up the hill, I saw a red dancing image. When the view came into focus, it was a large fire burning in front of the apartment building of the deceased. His family and friends were pitching paper items into the fire for him to use in the other world. Houses, airplanes, clothes, food, and paper money kept the blaze going for a full hour. I only wondered what he could buy.

† † †

Jessica had been in an orphanage all of her four young years. Her mother, no doubt disappointed her baby was not a son, had abandoned her at birth. Her frail little body was that of a two-year-old, yet when she infrequently smiled or laughed, her teeth revealed the age of an older child. Like most orphans, she was quite pale, withdrawn, and very shy, but she eagerly responded to any adult attention.

A young couple from Australia, parents of three small boys, fell in love with Jessica. Wishing their sons to have a sister, they adopted her and no little girl ever received more love and attention than Jessica. She clung to her new parents, held tightly to the hands of whichever brother was nearest, and seemed to thrive with her new family, a happy situation she had never experienced before. The Australian family was happy but little Jessica was happiest of all.

Jessica had not been with the family very long when it became obvious that she had an equilibrium problem. The first time the problem was noticed occurred when she received a broken collar bone when she seemed to stumble and fall while walking in their home. Shortly after that, she fell and broke an arm, and next was a leg. Of course, the parents were highly upset and concerned for little Jessica; however, doctors made no definitive diagnosis. As time went on, the prognosis for Jessica became much darker.

Two years later, early one morning, word came that little Jessica had died. All who knew this precious child wept, yet we knew she was a beautiful Chinese angel now in custody of One who could more adequately care for her. It was a sudden death and a severe shock to her family and friends. Everyone was sorry to lose the little girl we had all come to love.

Since the parents were committed Christians, an appropriate funeral was in order, but because foreigners cannot be members of a Chinese church, no funeral would be held in the church they regularly attended.

Since most bodies are cremated in China, her body was taken to a nearby crematorium. Her family and friends gathered under nearby trees for a memorial service. Jessica's family was grief stricken and when one of the crematorium workers came by with her body in a small cart, similar to a grocery cart, and headed toward the visible furnace, all of us went into shock. We turned our backs as the funeral service began with a pastor friend reading appropriate scriptures and praying. We had planned to sing "Jesus Loves me," but none of us could utter a note because of what we had seen. Dear, precious Jessica was gone but will never be forgotten by those who loved her. We found much comfort in knowing that she was now safely home with our heavenly Father.

The parents were devastated by this traumatic experience and within a few days packed their belongings and returned to Australia. But for sure, they took little Jessica and the too few memories of her with them.

† † †

Another time as a funeral procession was about to pass, two young people marching in front of the entourage carried a large photo of the deceased man. Behind them was a young man carrying a black paper wreath. Two boys on each side of the wreath bearer were shooting strings of firecrackers as they moved along. They were followed by the band, behind whom came sixteen other people scattering paper money for the deceased to use in the next world! Six men were carrying the coffin on poles and then came the family weeping, mourning, and helping each other along. Behind them were mourners to enhance the sadness of the occasion. We watched as they marched up the mountainside to a cemetery and the burial site. Our hearts filled with sympathy for the family.

† † †

One day while I was in class, a Buddhist family nearby received word of a relative who had died. Unable to travel far away to attend a funeral service, they held it in their home. The band came with their noisy instruments and played the entire day from early morning until 6:00 in the evening. The music stopped only long enough for them to eat yet another orange, banana, or apple – among other things. The diners would throw the apple cores and orange peelings out the open windows. Then more music would blare forth. The musicians must have been very tired after such a long day. Foreign neighbors were even more tired of their noise!

† † †

One day while in Yang Ding in Fujian province, my grandson, Matthew, and his friend Marion, both of whom were visiting from the States, and I were traveling to see houses made of dirt. We passed a funeral procession walking along the road in a very poor countryside area. There was no music or paper money being scattered; present were only a few family members with arm bands to denote their relationship with the deceased.

A sizable black box was being carried by six young men holding to ropes, which supported the box, or casket. We had no way of knowing how long they had been walking or how far they would have to go. No gravesite could we see, nor any homes near the highway. Our hearts went out to them, and we offered a prayer for God to take care of them and their loved one.

† † †

Behind the building where I lived, a Buddhist man died one afternoon. Firecrackers exploded until sundown. He was either a very popular person or had a huge family – I could not decide which. It was during heavy rain, and rain capes and umbrellas made a colorful rainbow as crowds came and went. He was not cremated until the following day, so early that morning the band arrived and began their daylong performance.

Cremation was scheduled at 10:00 a.m. Buses and vans came to take the large family and friends to the crematorium. Others stayed behind to erect big sheets of plastic to ward off the rain. Big pots were cooking under plastic sheets as tables came from many directions along with chairs to seat the mourners.

Back they came around 12:00 noon, rain was still pouring, but the feast proceeded in spite of inclement weather. About 4:00 the crowd began to disperse, the big pots disappeared, down came the plastic sheets, and tables and chairs were also removed. This was surely not an ideal day for a funeral, but these dear people did their best in spite of the unfavorable weather conditions.

Three months later, a band returned and more music filled the air to ward off any evil spirits not frightened away earlier. A big fire lit up the night as various items were thrown in for the deceased to use in the other world. Again, it was paper trains, houses, clothes, cars, and always paper money for use in the other world. How I wished they knew about a God who needed and wanted only them, not things!

† † †

April 4th is Ching Ming Day, when families go to cemeteries and clean the graves of rubbish accumulated during the past year. Swarms of people gathered to sweep and to remove unwanted foliage, etc., from their relatives' resting places. Sometimes it appeared that a ceremony was taking place, as one person would be standing in the midst of a circle. Foreigners assumed yet another eulogy was being given for those "in the other world." This custom was strictly a family affair so guests were not included.

After April 4th one year, I was privileged to visit a cemetery with Chinese friends. They were quite proud of how well the graves of their relatives looked. Scattered over many of them still were grains of rice, flowers, and remains of fruits left on Ching Ming Day. "We must never forget our relatives. We want them to be happy in the other world," Chen Min explained. I, too, wanted them to be happy and well fed! More importantly, though, was to share with the living how assurance for happiness could be secured only by a belief in the living God and Father of our Christ Jesus.

† † †

Bishop Moses Xi was in poor health when I first met him, due in part to abuse he had suffered during the infamous Cultural Revolution. His frail body was slowly dying even as he related many of the tortures he endured because of his strong faith in "Christ my Savior."

He liked to reminisce about the English missionary friend who led him to Christ. As a small boy, he was with her in a boat when he fell overboard. She pulled him to safety and said, "Your name will be Moses now, because I pulled you out of the water."

Several times, Communion was taken to him and his dear wife while I was stationed near them. His tears flowed freely and as he took the elements of Communion, he would always say, "He did it all for me!"

Time ran out on the dear Bishop, and God called him home during the winter holiday while I was away attending a conference. A memorial service was being held the day after my return to Fuzhou. How grateful I was to be back in time for his funeral.

Christ's Church was packed to capacity for the service; Bishop Xi had been a faithful leader and was admired and loved by Chinese Christians and even by some of those who were not Christians. Three ministers took turns eulogizing and telling of his life and work. The Fujian Seminary Choir sang "Blessed Assurance" and "When We All Get to Heaven." Also, the church choir sang several hymns among which was the favorite of most Chinese, "What a Friend We Have in Jesus." The Bishop was father of two children, a son and a daughter. The daughter gave an outstanding appropriate eulogy.

There was no body of the deceased as it had been cremated the day he died. The family did not follow the usual customs but had the cremation done with only the Bishop's family present. They felt this procedure gave more dignity and privacy to them and also to the Bishop's memory.

After the church service, the family simply returned home. There was no big feast and there were no firecrackers to ward off evil spirits. They knew Bishop Moses Xi was now free of bodily infirmities.

✝ ✝ ✝

When Ho Ru Ying died, a befitting Christian funeral was held in a small building outside the nursing home where she had spent her last few months. Bodies are not taken to a church for a funeral. Ho was lying in state on a small platform covered with a white sheet. Only her face was visible and even in death she looked like a special agent of our God. Wreaths of paper flowers surrounded the area. (These are burned after the body is cremated.)

A large photo of Ho draped in black was smiling as the residents of the Home for the Blind and her friends came to pay their last respects. Her church choir came and sang several of her favorite hymns, "What a Friend We Have in Jesus," "Over There," "When We All Get to Heaven," and "Amazing Grace." The pastor gave a sermon commensurate with her life. After the hymns and sermon, church ladies distributed washcloths to Ho's good friends as a memory of her. I accepted the cloth but needed nothing to remind me of my dear departed friend. She had written her name on my heart years before.

After the funeral service ended, Ho's body was placed in a long, red cardboard box, which was taken to a funeral bus and slipped into a side door. People filled the bus, vans, and cars for the trip to the crematorium. Few words were spoken but many tears flowed as the entourage made its way for the finality of dear Ho.

Many Chinese friends, non-Christians, awaited the arrival of the group. Armbands identified their relationships to Ho. Several gave emotional eulogies to their old colleague and friend, but foreigners were only observers. After forty-five minutes of praise and memories, the red box was removed to the furnace room.

The group dispersed as one person was overheard to say, "Ho is probably singing alto in heaven's choir!" For sure, Ho now knew the full meaning of God's love. She had been one of His saints on earth. Now she is one of His saints in heaven.

✝ ✝ ✝

While I was visiting friends in India, their pastor's mother died. Since embalming is not practiced there, burials should take place as soon as possible after death. Unfortunately, we were ten hours away when word came of her death. We were attending a graduation ceremony in Madeira, so we could not leave until this entire event ended at 11:30 p.m.

Highways do not equate to those in our country. Some with only one paved lane require oncoming vehicles to go off the pavement to allow passing on each side. This situation makes for dangerous driving, but we had to get back to Madras, if possible, by 10:00 the next morning for the funeral.

The trip back was not pleasant as we were already tired and

sleepy. My friend, David, and his driver took turns as we sped along, at times dodging a wandering cow or even a person. Lois, my friend, and I tried to sleep in the back seat, but the bumpy roads were not conducive to lullabies, snores, or sweet dreams.

We finally arrived at the church where the funeral was to be conducted at 10:30. The body lay in an open casket on a platform in the center of the church auditorium. People were sitting on the floor in every conceivable space. Chairs were brought in and placed beside the casket for us. We had ringside seats!

Ice had been packed around the body, and a white cloth tied around her chin and over her head to keep her mouth closed. A granddaughter used an old newspaper to keep the flies away. The funeral director would come by periodically and spray room deodorant on the body and around the casket. Observing all this, I forgot about being tired and sleepy.

There was much singing, and three ministers gave eulogies to the faithful old matriarch. David was among the ministers who gave reminders of her good life and her devotion to her Christ. Few tears were shed because her family had seen her suffer a long time. Now she could rest in paradise free of the infirmities of old age.

After the hour-and-a-half funeral, six men came in and lifted the casket up and away to the truck, which took it to the cemetery about thirty minutes away. Cars followed, carrying her family and friends to her final resting place.

A tent with an extension had been set up for the mourners to shield them from the hot sun. The shade was a welcome sight to us because I was afraid of sunburn. The area was soon filled as people crowded in, fanning and breathing deeply. We had to walk a good mile after reaching the cemetery.

The casket was placed in a concrete grave over which the grandchildren threw in bouquets of flowers. Boards were placed over the casket, then a layer of bricks was put on top of the boards, and finally dirt was used to finish filling the grave. There were no large wreaths to decorate the grave. Another hour and a half passed before everything was complete. I think Lois, David, and I were staggering from fatigue by the time we reached their home. The dear, departed sister had been duly memorialized and could now rest in the comfort of paradise. All we wanted at the moment was a warm bath and a bed!

Funerals occur daily in different ways in all cultures, traditions, and countries. Chinese are entitled to follow customs established long ago by their ancestors. I, for one, respect their rights and find no fault in their choices. My only prayer is that the departed ones had the opportunity to accept Christ and can hear the words of our Christ, "...Come ye blessed of my Father, inherit the kingdom prepared for you...."

(Matthew 25:34 KJV)

CHAPTER 8

Birthdays

"...A time to be born...."
(Ecclesiastes 3:2a KJV)

Birthdays are important events in China. This is especially true with parents celebrating their child's birthday, even at age one. In some areas in years past, a baby would not be given a name until it was a year old. The reason, we were told, was "the baby may not live for a whole year!" Infant mortality rate was very high during that time.

So when Scarlett, a former student, called to invite me to her one-year-old son's birthday celebration, I immediately accepted. Having never attended a party for one so young, I was greatly surprised to see so many relatives.

Gifts for the little one were piled in abundance from life-sized stuffed animals to a piggy bank, which I took to begin an educational fund for his future tuition needs. A small tricycle would have to wait a few years before the little one could put it to use. Such a variety of presents, while the honoree was showing little interest in the adoring relatives and even less in the stack of gifts!

Proud parents and two sets of beaming grandparents passed the poor baby from one to the other as the parents' "goo-goo's," "ah-ah's," and funny faces provided more entertainment for the guests than for the little one. The long, black, braided pigtail attached to the baby's cap was in constant motion as he was handed back and forth. He was stunning in his little red and gold emperor's suit and seemed somewhat bewildered by all the noise and commotion among so many people.

Chefs had arrived with big pots set up to prepare the birthday feast for the eighty guests of the "little emperor." Ten round tables that could accommodate eight diners each were set up outside in the alley and patio area. The blue sky and bright sun added their gifts for the occasion as well.

Lunch was ready at 12:00 noon. Fourteen different dishes were served including pork, beef, chicken, duck, a variety of seafood, vegetables of every type available, rice, noodles, "sweet biscuits" (cookies), dumplings, eggs, melons, oranges, apples, bananas, and a huge birthday cake. The baby tried to reach for the one oversized candle as it blazed away in his honor.

This celebration lasted two full hours while the little boy began to fret and whine. He had to be tired after all those times he had been hugged, kissed, patted, and stroked. Well-meaning family members were stretching his endurance by many hours!

Cameras were constantly flashing as the celebration continued. Two relatives had a video camera in full action. This was going to be a birthday that would be preserved for future generations. The "little emperor" fell asleep in the midst of all of this and was promptly awakened by his overly zealous relatives. Poor baby! He probably was wishing that birthdays would just go away.

Birthdays are not restricted to just children or young people. Dr. Chen, a hematologist, was about to celebrate his fifty-seventh birthday. We had shared many concerns related to students whom both of us were teaching. From time to time we had lunch together, and he would often bring friends to my place to practice their English. So as his birthday approached, he invited me to his party to be held in the Chinese Air Force Hotel.

Guests were restricted only to his colleagues and the few foreigners he knew. No family member was present, even though he had a wife and daughter living in Fuzhou. His one son was in Munich, Germany, doing cancer research. I had learned from some previous experiences that wives usually did not participate in the social activities of their husbands. This custom seemed very strange to foreigners.

The Fujian Medical University had a car, which could be used by the staff for non-university purposes from time to time.

Since Dr. Chen also taught classes at the university in hematology while practicing medicine, he had access to the car and its driver. On the appointed night, he came by car to take Joni and me to the Air Force Hotel. I felt a little apprehensive going into a place controlled by any phase of Chinese military units. Our birthday celebrant reassured us we would be welcome and safe. This was a little comforting, to say the least.

Two round tables, which could seat ten diners each, were fully decorated, one with a large birthday cake bearing fifty-seven candles winking and blinking at us, and the other with a large flower arrangement fit for a princess. Joni was asked to sit on his left; I was seated on his right – two places of honor for limited guests!

As soon as all guests were seated, a roaring rendition of "Happy Birthday" was sung, and like a small child the honoree made a wish. He made several attempts to blow out the candles before they were all extinguished. Guests received slices of the birthday cake, and the two foreigners received the largest rosettes of all. Although Chinese birthday cakes are beautifully decorated, what they have in looks they lack in taste. But when a jovial atmosphere exists, who cares about taste! The rosettes can be stirred until they appear to be partially eaten. Rosettes are large lumps of sugar that are highly decorated but without flavoring, so they are not tasty though very beautiful.

Birthday cake out of the way, other dishes began to appear: fish, pork, duck, chicken, eels, a variety of vegetables and fruits, the ever-present rice, and long life noodles. Long life noodles are from fifteen to twenty inches in length and are symbols for long life. While calories were being consumed, many toasts were made, not only to the birthday gentleman but also to all of those attending the party.

Two hours later, the group moved to the disco hall for another two hours for singing and dancing. It didn't matter how well either could be done; we just sang to the tops of our lungs, slid around as well as possible, and called it dancing. Everyone laughed, joked, and had good, clean fun.

Dr. Chen's fifty-seventh had been duly celebrated without his family, but with his closest colleagues and two foreign friends. All of those in attendance felt it had been a fun time and hoped there could be many more birthday celebrations for Dr. Chen.

All of my twelve birthdays celebrated in China were different in very special ways! The first one, my sixty-eighth, October 31, was perhaps the most simple but one I shall always cherish along with all others.

The foreign affairs officer brought in a beautiful cake covered with thick, white, tasteless icing bedecked with huge rosettes and "Happy Birthday, Sue Todd" made in red. The five foreign teachers and the four-year-old son of Wendy, an English teacher from England, plus a few very special students came to the one room, which was my home. Warm drinks of Pepsi, Sprite, and hot tea were served to them. No cold drinks were available then, as the Chinese warned us, "Cold drinks cause stomach cancer!" All of us agreed that the birthday celebration thought was better than the cake.

The next year friendships had multiplied so much that on my sixty-ninth birthday the foreign affairs office gave permission for "The Purple House" to be used. It was a small building used by the President of Southeast University on special occasions. Four of the students strung orange and black streamers overhead. Crepe paper pumpkins and black cats and witches cut from tag board were used to create an eerie environment. A few white ghost figures were hung about the party room as well.

The house manager brought a large decorated birthday cake. Guests munched on cookies, peanuts, and raisins, and drank warm Pepsi, Sprite, and orange drinks. The twenty-six people present were like small children having fun at a party. We enjoyed simple games like playing musical chairs, dressing a model like a mummy using only toilet tissue, passing the thimble, attempting tongue twisters (hysterical), and pinning the tail on the Halloween cat. The greatest pleasure was seeing the students having so much fun. Getting older was not so bad after all!

Twelve months slipped by quickly. I celebrated my seventieth birthday mostly with foreigners. I had left the one room and was now in a three-room apartment with a kitchen, a real luxury. The day before Halloween, October 31, I cooked a southern dinner for the foreigners. When the food was available, chicken pot pie, green beans, potatoes, and corn made up our dinner. A variety of fruits, plentiful year round in the areas where I was assigned, were our desserts.

A big surprise awaited me the next morning. When I arrived in class, "Happy Birthday" in huge letters covered the chalkboard. Seven candles, each representing ten years, burned brightly on the teacher's desk. Homemade birthday cards were piled one by one on the desk as each student came up and made a verbal birthday wish in English, of course. They were like cats that had swallowed the canaries, so proud of themselves for surprising the foreign English teacher. They brought tears to my eyes and gratitude to my heart.

Seventy-one follows seventy! Lily Wilson from North Carolina was visiting me, and she and Katie Neal from California made small Halloween bags filled with nuts and candies as favors. These were distributed at the party, attended mostly by my seminary students. A student called in to the local radio station to play a birthday song for his "American English teacher, Sue Todd." The YMCA class and the seminary class made tapes of birthday greetings supervised by Katie Neal.

The living room was decorated with a Halloween motif. Black cat and jack-o-lanterns with a few ghosts hanging overhead added a degree of festivity to the party held on Halloween night. Students were given paper, strings, and scissors, and were asked to make masks for one another. What a riot that created! Dressed all in black, another teacher told their fortunes in such ridiculous ways it sent them into laughing spasms.

Some seniors dislike birthdays, but this writer is not one of them. With imaginative friends like Lilly, Katie, and the fun-loving students, growing older is a blessing. I felt a great indebtedness to all of them.

Birthday seventy-two also brought feelings of gratitude and

happiness. First of all, a surprise Halloween party for my class brought giggles and laughter to all of the students. Seeing them happy made me even happier.

Our classroom was fully decorated with the windows bearing angry black cats, but friendly, smiling jack-o-lanterns and shivering ghosts. Two other teachers, Michelle and Candi, assisted with the celebration. Michelle was the "wicked witch from the west" while Candi painted their faces. Halloween songs were sung in another corner and questions were answered as these young people had never before celebrated Halloween. Along with their questions, I explained "trick or treat," costumes, masks, etc., and when the event ended, each one received a small bag of trick or treat goodies. Their exuberance was contagious.

That night, two of the younger teachers baked a chocolate cake and served it with ice cream for dessert. This special treat added another dimension to my seventy-second year. Dear friends, precious students, cards, and phone calls from family back in the United States had made this a day to remember.

The following night, Peng Zhao Deng, my seminary professor, friend, and former student, invited me to his home for a birthday dinner. His one room was brightly decorated with hand-painted pictures of flowers, long life noodles, the longevity Chinese character, and a 24" x 36" red paper on which each guest wrote a special birthday wish using verses from Psalm 103. This hung in my room for the remaining nine years I was in China.

Peng did the cooking for our dinner of rice, vegetables, chicken bits, and fruits. His income was rather meager, but he would not accept any reimbursement. None of us left hungry! The seminary and the nearby college, where I was a volunteer, donated a three-tiered birthday cake. Besides the large decorative red, yellow, and green rosettes, scrawled on top was "Happy Birthday, Sue Todd." I could not contain my emotions when they sang.

After the dinner, we sang favorite hymns, they in Chinese and I in English. We shared favorite scriptures and made prayer requests. As they discussed their goals and plans, their eyes betrayed the uncertainty of their future. Most would become assistant pastors and work at least seven years before ordination. They had been called by God and He does not neglect His own. I found a great comfort in this knowledge.

So number seventy-two had now passed, and in only twelve short months seventy-three was on the horizon. It could not possibly provide more pleasure than I had enjoyed for seventy-two!

Number seventy-three began in class with students going through the "House of Horrors," which was made by arranging chairs in a kind of maze. Bedspreads concealed this arrangement before each student entered in a crouched position. A cassette tape of Halloween music provided eerie sounds as each one wormed his or her way through the contraption, while blindfolded. Needless to say, other classes in our area heard the commotion and laughter this activity created.

After the "House of Horrors," they could proceed to the fish pond where each fish caught had an assignment printed on it, such as singing, dancing, imitating, making short speeches, etc. When each completed the assignment, that meant freedom to move on to the refreshment counter loaded with pumpkin candy from the United States, watermelon seeds, peanuts, raisins, and a cup of hot green tea. A hot plate and a large kettle provided the hot water. Several students were overheard to say, "I wish Sue Todd had a birthday every week so we could celebrate!" I pretended not to hear because birthdays seemed to come too quickly already.

At this time, six other foreign teachers were assigned to my same college. Two of the younger ones made a big cake and decorated it with a chocolate spider in his chocolate web. Served with ice cream, that dessert topped off our Halloween night.

The following day I had another birthday dinner at Fujian Seminary with a big overly decorated cake as the centerpiece. Several professors and students were present for the occasion. Good wishes and homemade cards joined those which had already found themselves on a wall in my one room. Too much food, fun, and fellowship rounded out number seventy-three. A loving God, wonderful supportive family back in North Carolina, and a host of Chinese friends reminded me of just how much I needed to pay back and how blessed I was and still am!

Number seventy-four centered around the party planned for my class. Early that morning, I went to the classroom building to prepare a surprise Halloween party for students. I set up tables and materials for making masks and a fish pond for producing a small gift for each class member. A friendly "witch" would tell their fortune while cassette music would provide a festive atmosphere for the party. All this was to be my surprise for them.

The second bell rang as I rushed from the downstairs ballet room, site of the party-to-be, to the second floor classroom. Well, when I flew in, shouts of "surprise, surprise" rattled my eardrums. Faces were lit up like Halloween lanterns or pumpkins! Positioned in the center of the room were two large cakes, each bearing thirty-seven candles, all of them winking and seeming to enjoy my astonishment as well. The class president pinned on my jacket a corsage of white carnations. They insisted that I open a beautifully wrapped package, and inside in just my size was a burnt orange corduroy coat trimmed in tan. I could not hold back my tears because I knew that gift was a sacrifice for most, and thus for me it was very special. My true feeling was that they should have kept their money and used it for their own personal needs. But through the years, I have learned that times come when one must be a gracious recipient. I could not destroy their happiness on this day.

That night a group of foreign friends came for dinner, which included another birthday cake. Afterwards, we retired to the TV room and watched the video "Gandhi." How fortunate I felt to have such a wonderful class of young people and good friends to round off another birthday.

The Big Seventy-Five

This year's birthday was one of the greatest yet. It began when Han Hui and Chang Kang, Gu Nian's parents, came with a dinner from McDonald's and a lovely bouquet of roses. Gu Nian is now working on her Ph.D. at Waterloo University in Canada. They also brought along a small amount of peanut cooking oil as a special gift. Little did I know this was just the beginning of birthday attention.

The Fujian Provincial Education Commission, led by Zhang Jiu Yuan, had planned a trip for foreign teachers to Ningde, a city approximately four hours north of Fuzhou. We were to leave on none other than Halloween Day.. When I arrived at the Dong Hu Hotel at 1:00 p.m., two large fairly modern buses were parked awaiting passengers to Ningde. Time arrived for loading, so I casually made my way to the designated bus. A group of Chinese journalists, a TV crew, and special friends were standing near the bus, apparently waiting their turn to load. As I stepped around to get on, I absolutely could not believe my eyes. I was shocked speechless but only for a short time. In bold, multi-colored letters from twelve to fourteen inches tall was taped the caption, "SUE TODD'S 75th ROLLING BIRTHDAY." That wasn't all. Happy Birthday letters were taped over the windshield, green and pink streamers were strung in the top of the bus, and people were asked to make a creative birthday hat because the party was just beginning. Michelle Long and Lisa Ravenhill, colleagues for the past three years at Huanan, had planned games and even composed a song to the tune of "I've Been Working on the Railroad." The title of the song was "It Is Sue Todd's 75th Rolling Birthday," and I include the words here:

> It is Sue Todd's birthday – did you hear?
> It is Sue Todd's 75th year,
> It is Sue Todd's birthday,
> It is Sue Todd's birthday,
> It is Sue Todd's birthday – glad you're here!
> We are going to Ningde on this day,
> We are going to Ningde to – oo play,
> We are going to Ningde,
> We are going to Ningde,
> We are going to Ningde, Hip Hooray!

There'll be minorities' song and dance.
Get up and join if you get the chance.
It might not be the cha cha,
But wait till you see Sue Todd prance.
Ningde's best hotel is two-star,
To find bed bugs you won't look far,
But Suc Todd will kill them
And save them in a peanut butter jar.
Now we've come to the end – nd of our song.
It's been a rousing sing along.
It's Sue Todd's Birthday,
Her 75th Birthday!
Eat long life noodles to live long.

After that rousing birthday song, the group also sang "Everyday in China" to the tune of "Everyday with Jesus."

Everyday in China is sweeter than the day before.
Everyday in China I love her more and more.
Striving hard to serve her,
Helping her to bless the world,
Everyday in China is sweeter than the day before.

The trip to Ningde was to see the She minorities perform in native costumes. The entrance to the stadium was lined with school children waving colorful plastic flowers as they chanted, "Welcome, Welcome." Our group was led to a draped platform and seated just behind the VIP section for better visibility of the performers. I felt ill at ease in such a comfortable position when so many Chinese were crowded in or were sitting in trees to get a view of the performers. Those perched in trees were literally swept out by the police. I saw a policeman with a broom swatting at young men in palm trees lining the stadium. The morning passed quickly, and we were taken back to the hotel and a sumptuous lunch of typically minority dishes, all of which were very delicious. For some dishes, I didn't ask, "What is this?"

A street parade was held at night, but I was delayed in seeing it. The hotel dining room sent a big bowl of long life noodles and a birthday cake to my room. I persuaded our guide, Zhang Jiu Yuan, to help us eat some of the noodles as these are considered a must on birthdays. Later, we were able to join the others in watching the parade.

Mountain climbing was the planned activity for the afternoon. Yes, I climbed as high as the others and passed two dry waterfalls to a Buddhist Temple, which I tried to walk through with my eyes closed. The grotesque figures of Buddha gave me the creeps. I'm glad our God is not depicted in such ugly figures. Could you believe that several American adoptive parents with their darling baby Chinese girls from ages five to nine months climbed that mountain with us? They were part of our entourage. This was an experience I shall always cherish and will pull from my memory bank to enjoy in the days ahead.

Halloween was even celebrated after we returned from Ningde. Eight girls from my class last year and eight young men came to visit me on Friday, November 3, 1995. Two special friends who had been there earlier decorated with orange and black streamers, black cats, ghosts, and jack-o-lanterns. In one game we played, each person was blindfolded and asked to tape the missing eye on the jack-o-lantern, which was taped on the wall. Eyes ended up every place except where they should have been! The celebrants bobbed for apples in a large container of water, and some were quite successful at that. They seemed to enjoy the party because by 11:00 p.m. I had to say, "In one hour it will be tomorrow."

Back in Fuzhou, eleven Chinese teachers of English came to my apartment for oral English class. The dean, foreign affairs office personnel, and the teachers brought a huge birthday cake fully decorated and two more bouquets of roses. Of course, they had several snack-type foods such as watermelon seeds, green olives, black olives, red olives, small gelatin-like cups, peanuts, and white rabbit candy. We stuffed ourselves again as I unwrapped small gifts from them.

Huanan Women's College invited me over for dinner and a

party for all teachers who had birthdays during the fall semester. I was surprised again when I was honored with their group. They will always have a soft spot in my heart, and I appreciated the invitation to participate.

So, being a quarter of a century old is good, half a century is better, but three quarters is best of all so far. Watch out, one hundred – here I come!

Time marched on to my seventy-sixth where four birthday cakes were brought by different groups to celebrate. Classes of undergraduates, postgraduates, foreign affairs office personnel, and a dear Chinese family brought them at different times, thank goodness. Each one was larger and more ornately decorated, and I shared them all with students, colleagues, and foreign friends.

Han Hui, a very special friend, brought over a bouquet of thirty beautiful pink roses. I had helped her daughter with English prior to her departure to Toronto, Canada, for graduate studies.

Prof Li, uncle of another student, Dick, who later went to Fitchburg, Massachusetts, for graduate school, came bringing a lovely arrangement of asters and a container of pork brains, which I happen to like.

Like all past birthdays, cards from family, friends, and students, plus many phone calls made this a very special day. Small, yet unaffordable gifts filled my desk top as in previous years. Feelings of humility and gratitude flooded my total being for where God had placed me and for the undeserved love I felt among these dear people.

My seventy-seventh year had arrived! As in all other years past on my birthday, the Sunday School Class I had taught for many years back at Ross Baptist Church, Windsor, North Carolina, sent gifts and best wishes. This year a greatly needed address book and three Hershey candy bars came, which I didn't need but thoroughly enjoyed anyway. Cards and phone calls from family and friends back in the United States were always welcomed and treasured.

The foreign affairs officer called at 4:00 p.m. to say that a birthday party would be held at 4:00 the next day. Sorry, I had planned to visit a friend who was celebrating her eightieth at that time. I never could get used to impromptu notices, which happened too frequently. Fortunately, the unexpected party could be delayed for another day.

The English Department heads, Professors Guo and Chen, and class presidents came bringing a beautiful basket of flowers and a huge beautifully decorated cake. This was shared with a steady stream of students singing "Happy Birthday" and bringing small gifts they could not afford.

My colleague that year, Shirley Angell from New Zealand, was a barrel of fun. She was ingenious, entertaining, and a little bit mischievous. She planned a surprise Halloween party, which she and the students enjoyed and I tried to enjoy. She was always doing the unexpected with all good intentions. I really missed her after she left at the end of only one year.

So seventy-seven had come and gone after being fully celebrated with students, fellow teachers, and friends.

The Grand Ole 78th began a little early with a whole package of beautiful cards from dear people in Center Grove Baptist Church, Ahoskie, N.C. Others came from cousins in faraway places and special ones from family and friends. I also received a gift from the WMU of New Hope Baptist Church in Williamston, N.C., several telephone calls, and e-mail greetings. Again, thanks to all for your kind thoughts, prayers, and good wishes then and now.

My Kiwi friend in New Zealand sent a kiwi stick pin and included a package of decaf coffee. She was a "solacer" of sorts last year, 1997. Even now, seven years later, I still miss her.

In my diary entry for October 30, 1998, I wrote the following account. "Eli, a former student, took a taxi from the hospital on October 30 to bring me flowers, a money belt, and birthday cake. God is answering prayers on his behalf as his doctor is about to discharge him from the hospital. My school has given permission for him to use the extra bedroom in my flat for a few weeks until he gains strength. He said, 'I'm so weak.' Of course, lying in a Chinese hospital for three and a half months would make anyone weak. Please continue to pray for him. He thanks you all, too."

My former seminary student, now seminary teacher, and his sweet wife invited Betts (my e-mailer), a vocalist, trumpet player, and me to a birthday luncheon in their nice new home. The wife's mother and a nephew were also present. After we had eaten too much well prepared food and another birthday cake, the vocalist sang "I'd Rather Have Jesus" and "What a Friend," accompanied by the trumpet which could be heard all over Fuzhou! All of us sang "Amazing Grace" and all too soon Betts and I had to leave for other obligations, but we left overflowing with the love of God coming through those wonderful people.

The foreign affairs officer came bringing another birthday cake, making it number three. So I was three cakes sweeter and three years past three-fourths of a century! God is so good to me.

Number seventy-nine, which was on a Sunday, proved to be a quieter one. It began by going to church, and shortly afterwards Peter, a young man I had met at church, came in and sat with me. This was his first time and he showed much interest, which filled him with questions I tried to answer to his satisfaction later.

Peng Zhao Deng and Qi Bi, a seminary couple and good friends of mine, invited Betts, Sandy, Kaye from America, and me to their home for a birthday dinner. Sandy was always cooking up special surprises, and today was no exception. She had baked a delicious Betty Crocker pecan cake.

Samuel, the couple's one-year-old son, was most definitely the center of attention before, during, and after the lunch. Every movement, every burp, every grunt caused great excitement among his onlookers. The seventy-nine-year-old lady was his greatest admirer of all.

That night more close Chinese friends, Eli, Nancy, and Wendy brought flowers, instant coffee, and Coffee Mate. After we played several games of cards and viewed the Jesus film again at their request, the day came to a most pleasant end. Cards, an e-mail message from my granddaughter, and telephone calls from several family members added to this special birthday, the seventy-ninth.

Birthdays of institutions are often observed, as well as those of people. On June 6, 1992, Southeast University in Nanjing celebrated its ninetieth birthday. It was established in 1902. The auditorium was packed with former graduates, faculty, and as many friends and students as possible who could squeeze into any available space. Outstanding engineers from various fields filled the stage. Some had to be assisted on stage because of their fragile conditions. The presiding president pointed out their contributions to the engineering industries and presented them with awards and certificates in honor of their achievements. This service consumed three hours from 9:00 a.m. to 12:00 noon.

Two visiting English professors from Elon College, N.C., and I were seated near the head table in a large faculty dining room located near the campus auditorium. We had hardly sat down before more speeches of appreciation were being offered by the university officials – vice-presidents, assistant vice-president, deans of various departments, and the president with a few more words of appreciation.

The hour was then 1:00 and my American friends and I wondered whether any food would be included in the luncheon. Finally, after including us in her speech of gratitude she calmly announced, "Now it is time to eat!" No banquet in China could have been more lavish. If the dishes could have represented all the speeches, no words would have been necessary. Dish after dish came one after the other for the next two hours. Chicken, pork, seafood of every kind, rice, many vegetables, and a large variety of fruits filled the tables as well as the diners. I did not eat any dinner that night.

Birthday Number 80

The celebration actually began on October 30, when I attended worship services from 7:00 – 9:30 a.m. The logic was to arrive early to get a seat, but at 7:20 a.m. the patio was filled and others kept arriving. I found one seat beside the faithful, handicapped, illiterate, odoriferous cripple who sat through both services. This means that he was in church from 7:00 to 11:30 a.m., having attended both morning worship services. His hymnal was well worn, tattered and ragged, and he sang with enthusiasm either ahead or behind the congregation. I don't think God minded, and He must wish all Christians were as faithful as this one. Each Sunday is a celebration within itself to praise and thank our loving heavenly Father whether in a soft seat or on a plastic stool.

Another entry from my diary reads: "On October 31, a telephone call at 7:00 a.m. from the USA to say Happy Birthday came just as I was brushing my teeth. A former Chinese student now in Presbyterian Seminary, Pittsburgh, Pa., rang to say, 'God bless you on your birthday.' He and his good wife had a party for me last year, and he remembered the date! He will be in Pittsburgh for three years. Please pray for him, his wife, and his year-old son."

Many beautiful cards, e-mail messages, and phone calls added to this special day. Family, colleagues, friends, and students have made it a birthday to remember. Students had fun designing their own masks and playing games with balloons, apples, and oranges, and teachers dressed in costumes (I was a witch) made quite a festive affair. So my philosophy is this: Come on, birthdays. Each one is more exciting and rewarding than the ones before!

I can only bow my grateful head with humility and thanksgiving to a loving, protective Provider who has given me so many rich blessings these past eighty years – the greatest of these being His Son as my Savior and Lord. Praise the holy name of Jesus. May He bless you as He has blessed me.

CHAPTER 9

Home Visitations

"...Go home to thy friends, and tell them how great things the Lord hath done for thee...."
  (Mark 5:19b)

More invitations to visit in students' homes were issued than I could accept. The ones I visited were in many ways alike and yet vastly different. All were friendly and hospitable and even though the language barrier existed, the student host/hostess would act as translator. When it was time to leave, more fervent invitations were given "to come back, come back soon, stay longer." Such gracious people!

One student, Kathy, had been accepted by a university in Sydney, Australia, so she needed to improve her English. Each morning after her classes at the university, where her parents were physics professors, she came for oral English training. My having been a speech therapist for several years proved to be quite an asset to us both.

Kathy's birthday was a few weeks before her departure for Sydney in late November. Wanting to buy a gift for her, I asked, "What do you need to take to Australia that you don't have?" She shyly replied, "I don't have a clock," and of course that was my present to her. I learned later that one never gives a clock as a gift in China since the Chinese associate a clock with death. As if that was not enough, I insisted that she open the decorative package. Her parents' and grandparents' faces, as well as Kathy's, clued me in that something was inappropriate. The next day when I told the Foreign Affairs officer of my experiences the night before, with horror on her face, she explained why clocks were never given as a gift. When I asked why Kathy seemed reluctant to open the gift, the Foreign Affairs officer looked shocked and said, "Chinese don't open a gift until after everyone leaves." I had learned two cultural lessons which helped on several occasions during the next several years.

A round table was set up in the living room of Kathy's house, and a chef had been hired for the occasion of her birthday. Each of us had a small bowl full of rice and a pair of chopsticks. I was not at all proficient with chopsticks, but I tried to use them and was successful enough in spite of many failures. Believe me, I did not leave hungry.

The first course was cold foods and since I was somewhat hungry, I was enjoying those calories that didn't drop before they reached my mouth. We consumed dried bits of various fruits, pickled vegetables, peanuts, and small pieces of dried fish as we drank warm Pepsi Cola. After some time, these dishes were removed, and steaming dishes of what must have been some of every vegetable grown in China were delivered one dish at the time by the chef. As we ate, all the diners continued to place food in my rice bowl with their chopsticks saying, "Eat more, eat more!" When I was served an enormous bowl of jiao zi, a pastry-like pie filled with ground meat and green vegetables, Kathy informed me that I should eat at least fifteen servings! Finally, realizing that my capacity for food had long passed, I asked, "How many dishes did you plan for this dinner?" Kathy checked the menu listing and said, "Not but twenty-nine!" (See Appendix.) Surprisingly enough, I was able to waddle back to the guesthouse pushing my overly stuffed stomach in front of me. Did I sleep well that night – you guess!

Kathy's parents continue to teach physics while Kathy and her brother, who went to Sydney later, are now professional engineers in Australia. Both had scholarships and both did well as students. I was blessed to have known this family as they were the ones who taught me some of the first "no-no's" of Chinese culture.

Another student, Steve, is the son of parents who were professors in a university in Missouri. He phoned one day to ask whether he could visit. His father had sent him a Baptist Press article which included my name and my location, Southeast University, Nanjing, China, Steve's alma mater. Upon his arrival, I instantly liked Steve; his politeness, courteous ways, and gratitude were most impressive.

Steve's grandparents had been people of great wealth, with a large compound of houses for the entire family. However, that property was all claimed by the government, and the family quarters were reduced to only four rooms. When I met Steve he lived in two rooms – a bedroom and a small kitchen. His parents and older brother had managed to secure jobs in Missouri, and Steve was the only member of his immediate family still in Nanjing. Working as an engineer, he had been given a scholarship to the University of Missouri, where his parents were teaching. When I saw the sprawling buildings and the obvious care the grounds had been given, I knew Steve came from an outstanding background. One of his first statements to me was, "All of my family are Christians!"

Steve made five trips to Shanghai before the United States Consulate would grant him a visa. He never gave up and pursued his dream of studying abroad until it became a reality.

Shortly before leaving for Columbia, Missouri, Steve invited me to his home for dinner. Although he had visited me many times, I had never been in his home. Since I did not know where he lived, he came for me and as we walked from the bus stop to his place, he pointed out what had once belonged to his grandparents. His voice communicated a note of sad acceptance of his family's losses.

One of Steve's friends, his roommate no less, greeted us on arrival. He was busy running from the bedroom down a long hallway to their kitchen. He was preparing dinner for the three of us – rice, greens, and bananas for dessert. The place reeked with poverty but no complaints were made during the entire visit. I was totally shocked, yet honored, when Steve announced, "Today is my birthday. My family is gone so I wanted you to share my birthday dinner with me." I could have cried!

Despite the small, cramped space, meager furnishings, and a

communal restroom shared by too many, a sense of purpose and determination prevailed during the entire evening. This capable young engineer was eager to further his education and join his family in the U.S.A. My prayers centered around Steve that night. Later he met all the requirements and finally was able to leave Nanjing for Columbia, Mo. What a happy day for him and for me!

Eddie, another student, was teaching Chinese to my next-door neighbor who lived to my right. Just as he arrived one day, I opened my door and with great excitement, he said, "There's a white rabbit on the balcony!" A lady from England and her four-year-old son, Mark, were neighbors to the left of my room. Mark, indeed, did have a white pet rabbit. I took Eddie to the balcony to pet the rabbit, and that was the beginning of our friendship.

Majoring in Chinese literature, Eddie had graduated from Beijing University, a very prestigious institution. Upon graduation, he was assigned to a medical company, putting bottles into a box! "I really want to teach," he told me many times. During the late 80s and early 90s, the government placed students wherever there was a job vacancy with no regard to their education or training. What wasted brainpower, what bored employees! What a waste of four years in one of the best universities in China!

I made nights available for students and friends to visit. Eddie was a regular and led the others in games of Uno, Skip-Bo, Old Maid, etc. He became my translator, shopping guide, and errand boy. His father was the village cadre (Communist leader), so that position gave connections and to some degree prestige. As time passed, I learned a great deal from this young man as he spent most of his free time in my room. One night he said, "A driver is coming tomorrow to take us to my village." Sure enough at 8:00 a.m. Eddie met me in the lobby and said, "We will meet our driver outside the campus."

Two men, who looked like cadres, were in the old model car but were cordial enough for me to feel comfortable in riding the two hours with them and Eddie. As we traveled along, Eddie pointed out where he attended high school. The buildings, including the dorm, were quite old and unpainted. Though Eddie lived three hours away by foot, every Friday afternoon he would walk home. "Sometimes I would run to get home earlier, and sometimes my Dad would come for me on his bicycle if the weather was bad," he explained.

Rural Chinese live in communal villages. Being the cadre, Eddie's father had a large house with a sizable kitchen, a storage room, a coal burning cook stove, buckets of water – no running water and no inside plumbing, a spacious room used for dining on boards placed on "saw horses," stored garden tools, bikes, etc. Two bedrooms opened off the right side with a double bed in each. A TV that didn't work was in the parents' bedroom, but there were no closets and no chests. Homemade narrow benches served as chairs. Most people were relatives and all came to see the foreigner who was the first ever to visit their village.

The mother, with her neighbor assistants, went to the garden and gathered the fresh vegetables of greens, potatoes, carrots, peas, and cucumbers we enjoyed for lunch along with much rice and small pieces of meat, the origin of which was questionable. A female dog was roaming inside and outside the house. Eddie said, "We keep her to have puppies so we can have meat." Pork, dog, or whatever, I found tasty and enjoyed it along with the vegetables and rice.

Eddie suggested that we climb the mountain just beyond the garden. The path up the mountain passed the two-room school in the village. Eddie's uncle was one of the teachers and a cousin completed the faculty. Old, scarred desks built for two students, cracked chalkboard with no chalk rack, and one faded, outdated calendar in each classroom were the furnishings. No bookshelves, no books, only a pencil and a few sheets of paper made up school supplies!

Asked to speak in each classroom, I tried to write on the damaged chalkboard from one to ten and also the days of the week. The students were eager to learn English and tried very hard to pronounce the words correctly. In my heart, I wished to go back as their instructor and have more time to teach them.

A large hole in the floor between the two classrooms was filled with sweet potatoes for the village. I was concerned that students would fall into the opening which had no cover. When I raised that question, I was told, 'Oh, the children know it's there."

Eddie and I made our way to the top of the mountain. From there we could see the stream where our two companions and Eddie's Dad were fishing. The flat area on top was used to grow turnips and sweet potatoes. As we walked, Eddie said, "My footprints are all over this mountain." When I asked how often he came to the top, he replied, "Everyday. I was the goose herder and I brought them up here to eat the grass."

A goose herder uses a long, slender bamboo pole with a small cloth tied on its end to guide the flocks to and from their grazing areas. I often wondered whether there was a lead goose on the ground as when geese are flying in formation. If a goose stepped out of the flock, the herder could dangle the white cloth in front of him or beside him and he would immediately get back in step with the others. It was interesting to see hundreds of them marching along with only one person with a bamboo pole and a white cloth to keep them moving in the desired direction. Chinese are ingenious people!

"Time for lunch," Eddie announced, so down the mountain we went, passing the school, now empty. Students attended only a half day so the older children and teachers could work in the rice fields in the afternoons. As we arrived at the house, the appealing aroma from the kitchen was a pleasant reminder that it was time to dine. And dine we did on all those wonderful vegetables fresh from the garden only a few hours earlier. I hoped the meat was pork, but I didn't ask. It was safer that way.

Dining was a leisurely activity, with much talking, laughing, and joking among the group as food continued to be served by the kitchen team. After the main dishes were consumed, peanuts in shells were placed on the table. They were put into mouths in the shells and with much effort the shells were soon spat out on the table or floor. Nobody, except me, shelled the peanuts before putting them into the mouth. I tried not to show surprise but it wasn't easy.

Mid-afternoon arrived and time to return to Nanjing. It had been a wonderful day, the drivers caught a few fish, and I had met Eddie's parents, grandmother, uncles, aunts, cousins, and neighbors. But our nearly perfect day was shattered when I walked into the guesthouse where I lived. Paul, the young receptionist, asked, "Did you hear about what happened in Tiananmen Square today?" It was the day that students were massacred in Beijing! I wanted to go back to the countryside where news of such tragedies would take weeks, perhaps months, to be made known. Our perfect day was spoiled by this dismal news.

Charles, a second-year student, had literally begged me for months to visit his home in a small village in Anhui Province. This trip required an overnight boat ride followed by a four-hour bus ride, ending with a two-mile hike across rice paddies.

The boat ride afforded several different surprises. I had given Charles money to buy two tickets and make reservations, but on arrival we were shown to a cabin with fourteen other people in it. Oh well, I thought, it's just for one night. I took out the book I was currently reading and stretched out on my bottom bunk bed. The old man sitting on his bed across from me was eating peanuts and spitting shells on the cabin floor. In the meantime, he rinsed his mouth with beer and promptly spat it on the floor. Several others were also enjoying peanuts and rinsing their mouths with beer.

I ceased to be surprised by the peanut beer party when a mother on the bunk over mine held her little girl over and down came a stream of water barely missing my arm! Babies wore bottomless pants and adults relieved them publicly as needed with no apparent embarrassment. Later, diapers became available for those who could afford to buy them.

"Charles, go upstairs and see if there is any other cabin space on this ship," I implored. "But that will cost more," he protested. "Just go, Charles, I'll take care of any extra charge. Go NOW and hurry back," I replied. As he left to seek another less crowded cabin, I pretended to read but in reality I was poised for what could be yet another surprise.

Forty-five long minutes passed before he returned. "There is a cabin for six on the second deck. It has two vacancies, but it will cost twenty more dollars," he announced. Grabbing my overnight bag, I said, "Let's go. Show me where it is." We climbed the narrow steps to the upper level and stepped into a room filled with blue cigarette smoke. A chain-smoking grandmother, her son, his wife, and a two-year-old were the other occupants. It was a reprieve from the former situation in spite of the smoke.

By then it was bedtime. Each one occupied a bunk except the baby was with her mother. My body was ready for a good night's sleep. Our cabin was far removed from the engine noise and the mournful foghorn. I rested well and could have slept except the dear grandmother kept getting up, tucking me in, and puffing away on yet another cigarette. But even so, that was better than being involved with a peanut-beer party and showered by a baby who was relieving herself over my bunk

Morning came and we had arrived in Anqing, where we were met by one of my former seminary students. He insisted that we have breakfast with him, but Charles had previously contacted a cousin who was expecting us. We promised not only to come back and attend my former student's church but also to have lunch with him on Sunday. This we did, even though it meant leaving Charles' village earlier than initially planned. After a night on the ship, it was good to set foot on solid ground.

Breakfast with the cousin, who lived in one room, was pleasant. The watery rice and eggs scrambled with tomatoes were filling and tasty. We had little time to visit with her as the bus to Charles' village was soon leaving. Like most Chinese, she liked to collect stamps, so I gave her several U. S. stamps which pleased her greatly and served as a gratuity from me. We thanked her for breakfast and rushed out to the bus station.

Riding a Chinese bus in the late '80s was interesting and greatly different for me. Besides people, it seemed the bus would transport anything else which needed a ride. We mounted the bus and found that the only two vacant seats were in the very back. Bags of rice, potatoes, boxes containing ducks and chickens, and red, white, and blue striped plastic bags filled with personal items cluttered the aisles. After a few gymnastics steps, we made it to the vacant seats. People stared at me as many had never seen a foreigner before. I smiled and said, "Ni hao," (Hello) and they would immediately think I was fluent in Chinese until Charles explained my inadequacies in their language. We popped, snapped, bounced, and roared for the next four hours on the rickety old bus that I prayed would last until we reached our destination. It did!

Arriving in the village, we were immediately surrounded by onlookers, gaping at the first foreigner they had ever seen. I thought we had arrived at our destination when Charles said, "We have to walk a little ways." No problem, I thought. After four hours on the bus, I needed to walk. It seemed the entire village followed, making a circle around us as if to size up the foreigner from every angle. I had some chewing gum which I broke into small pieces to distribute to them. The dear children didn't know what to do with it until Charles showed them and advised them not to swallow it. The entourage continued to a fork in the red clay road. All of them turned left while Charles and I went to the right. Charles said, "We should be there in about two hours."

There was no road to follow so we walked on rice paddy dikes, jumped a few irrigation ditches, and finally came to a narrow concrete slab which crossed an irrigation canal too wide to jump. My knees trembled as I held on to Charles' arm when we walked across side ways. Reaching the other side, we entered a bamboo forest where we trampled along a path that appeared seldom taken. Finally, we came into an opening where adobe houses with tile roofs stood mostly in a circle. Faces peered from several doors when we entered the circle of homes. Red banners fluttered on each side of one special door. "What do the banners say?" I asked. With great feeling in his voice, Charles replied, "The one on the left says 'Welcome to our home.' The one on the right says 'Happiness dwells here.'" Puffing out his chest, he said with enormous feeling, "This is my home!" No king or prince could have shown more pride in his castle.

As we moved closer to the house, a little lady came toddling out gesturing and chattering, "Come in! Come in!" The interior was dark, unlit with a special fragrance all its own. The dear little lady was Charles' mother, whose face was woefully disfigured from burns she suffered when she had rushed from the rice paddy years ago to save Charles. The thatched roof had caught fire and she risked her life to save her baby. We were hardly inside before she presented us the equivalent of a cup of tea. My container looked like an unwashed mayonnaise jar. I was glad the floor was dirt so I could pour out a little of the beverage when no one was watching, and scrub it into the earthen floor. The dear mother was offering her best and I felt much queasy gratitude.

Bedtime came early because the village generator was shut down at 8:00 p.m. I was assigned to the sister's bed made of boards and covered with a mattress of rice straw that the mother covered with a sheet. I was grateful for the sheet and even the rice-filled pillow. The family "resting pot" was in my bedroom and about ready for emptying. Contents are used to help fertilize gardens.

Soon after stretching out, I realized I was not alone! Squeaks and fast movements through the rice straw on the bed and the straw stored in the rafters above notified me that I had invaded the domain of "Rat City." It was a sleepless but lively night.

Tunnels in the hardened earth floor were storage places for the rodents. I made a big mistake by not giving the peanuts to the mother when I presented her some apples upon arrival. During the night, rats entered my bag and made a trail from the bag to every tunnel in the bedroom. Smart rats! All the peanuts were now in their possession.

Morning could not come too early, but it did. Around 4:00 a.m. I heard water being poured in the kitchen just beyond the wall. I learned later that the residents went early to get water from the village well. It appeared to be surface water, and creepy crawlies were running around the entire upper surface of the water when Charles and I checked it out later. Everyone boils water before drinking, so we survived the infested water.

The next morning Charles asked whether I would like to pick tea leaves. "Of course," I almost shouted. Up the mountain side we went to join those who were busily snapping and putting leaves into their baskets. I eagerly began pulling leaves when Charles stopped me. "No, don't pull the big leaves. The small ones are better for tea," he explained. Another lesson I had learned.

Time for lunch and as we made our way down the mountain, we passed a young teenage boy trying to give directions to a young buffalo. It was hard to say which was unhappier, the boy or the buffalo. The boy was shouting and jerking the reins while trying to stand on the farm implement used to smooth the lumpy, red soil. When I asked Charles what the boy was saying, he replied, "You don't really want to know." I didn't know which one, the boy or the buffalo, deserved my sympathy more.

Shortly after lunch four men and a group of small children appeared. One was the village cadre (or leader), one came to check on young wives to see whether a second child had been conceived, and the other two were their assistants. Since they spoke no English and I spoke little Chinese, much nodding of heads, smiling, gesturing, etc., took place. Apparently, I passed inspection and after about an hour's visit, we shook hands and they left.

The village children continued to walk around and stare when they thought I was not looking. A little girl of around five years of age kept digging and scratching her head. I called this to Charles' attention and he said something to his mother. She went to her bedroom and returned with a bottle of green liquid and a small piece of cotton. Then she called the child over and began to anoint her with the substance from the bottle. When I asked Charles what it was, he nonchalantly answered, "She has bugs (lice) on her head." "Well, isn't it good your Mom had the right medication for the problem," I cautiously said. To this he responded, "Oh, she and my sister had the same problem last week." I had been sleeping in the sister's bed and even now my head itches when I think of that experience! As soon as we returned to my university, I went to a beauty shop and got a perm. I had heard years before that perm lotion would kill lice. At least I never saw or felt any.

Our visit came to a close much too quickly. How to show my appreciation was a concern. I had taken apples and peanuts which the rats stole, so I gave the mother sixty Chinese yuan, or $7.50 in American money. At first, in typical Chinese fashion, she refused to take it, but with my insistence and Charles' explanation she finally tucked it inside a pocket.

I was now ready to leave when the dear lady wanted me to take one of her five chickens as a gift. I was relieved of that when I told Charles that his mom and sister needed the chicken to lay eggs. Furthermore, a four-hour bus ride, an overnight boat trip, and a city bus to campus with a live chicken, I felt was too much hassle to tackle.

After I refused the chicken, the poor lady took the pillowcase Charles had slept on, filled it with her very best rice and forced me to take it. The pillowcase filled my bag so I took my personal items back in a plastic bag. I did not buy rice for several months and gave much of it to married students. She gave of her best and I was humbly grateful.

After lingering good-byes, Charles and I made our way toward the path leading through the bamboo forest. I looked behind and it seemed the whole village was following us. Only when we reached the large irrigation canal did the villagers turn around to retrace their steps back to their homes.

Walking slowly with tears in his eyes, Charles said, "I hope one day to make enough money to have my mother's face fixed. She woefully needed plastic surgery to correct facial burns. Then with more concern he said, "When I graduate, I want to come back home and build a church and tell my people about Jesus Christ because no one has ever told them about God. " His prayer has been my prayer since that wonderful visit to a remote countryside village in Anhui Province.

Through my years in China, I visited more homes, including the poor, rural countryside homes as well as some very well-furnished urban homes of the well-to-do. As the economy improved, more families could buy a comfortable four- or five-room flat. Usually these apartments would have many of the conveniences of modern living – washers, dryers, hot water heaters, and air conditioners. Whether in a poor village home or a well-furnished urban home, the hospitality was always the same. Chinese are gracious hosts and hostesses, and they give their very best to visitors.

CHAPTER 10

Holidays and Special Days

"...but he that is of a merry heart hath a continual feast."
   (Proverbs 15:15b KJV)

China has only three important national holidays: Independence or National Day on the first of October, Chinese Lunar New Year, and Labor Day the first week in May. Labor Day does not seem so important as National Day and the Lunar New Year, and celebrations consist mostly of visiting family during the time off from work. The lunar calendar determines the date of the New Year celebration, which may occur from mid-January to mid-February.

Special Days include the International Kite Festival held in Weifang in March. Tree Planting Day is held during March, when high school students set out small trees. Most trees had been burned for fuel during the reign of Mao Tse-tung. Four students were required to plant one small tree; one dug the hole, one put the plant into the hole, one watered, and one filled in the hole. Through the years, these efforts were making a much greener environment.

Qing Ming Day is observed on April 5th, when families go to their ancestral cemetery to clean off graves and scrub tombstones. Small branches, flowers, and paper wreaths are then left in memory of departed loved ones. Through my thirteen years in China, I visited several Buddhist cemeteries. Stones are quite ornate for wealthier families, and space is saved for others who will join them later in death. It was not uncommon to see evidence of fruits and rice left for the deceased to use in "the other world." The birds and bugs probably look forward to Qing Ming Day – free meal!

Two special days in June include Children's Day on June

1st and Dragon Boat Festival on June 4th. September has two celebrations, Moon Cake when the moon is full in September, and Lantern Festival, the week of September 30th. Moon Cakes are like a good size cookie with a very sweet filling between the two layers. For the Lantern Festival, lanterns of many shapes and sizes line streets and hang from lamp posts and trees. They are quite colorful and create much interest as onlookers compare their shapes and sizes.

Christmas and Easter are not included in the national holidays, but churches plan events with dramas and cantatas. Communist theory teaches one needs only self and the socialist government, so I heard from many Communists who were curious about the need for God.

International Kite Festival in Weifang is held in March. This is a big demonstration of Chinese kites from the long-tailed dragon kite to those as large as the current lunar animal.

The horse was the lunar animal in 1990. Early one morning the Jiangsu Educational Committee invited foreign teachers in Nanjing to board a train for Weifang to see the kite festival. The train left at 9:30 p.m., and we arrived at 2:30 p.m. the next day. Foreigners were allowed a sleeper car, which enabled us to rest some during the night. We could not imagine seeing kites as big as a horse, so we were somewhat excited by this possibility.

We were hardly settled into our hotel when two young men from Yantai showed up after having looked for us for three hours! We had met them earlier while visiting another friend who taught in Yantai. Both are Christians and wished to share some of their witnessing experiences with me.

A walk through the streets gave opportunities to talk undisturbed by those who could be listening. Each had dreams of studying in an American seminary, each one reasoning, "so I can be better trained to help my country men." One of them realized that dream a few years later and went to Southwestern Seminary in Ft. Worth, Texas.

The following morning we were taken by bus and police escort to the viewing stand. Along the way throngs of people stared as the bus moved through heavy traffic, perhaps wondering whether we were criminals or celebrities. Upon reaching the area, we were led not to bleachers like the Chinese but to chairs for a better view of the activities.

An army of flags from many countries accompanied by a well-conducted band provided music for the parade. When the Stars and Stripes came into view, we Americans stood and saluted. As the parade ended, hot air balloons, small kites, and caged pigeons were released. The pigeons seemed to have been well fed and proceeded to "anoint" many of their viewers, cameras, and seats as they chose to fly over the spectators. At least the flags were not affected by their escape.

As the morning progressed and many companies presented decorative fan dances, frilly scarves drills, and military exercises, it was becoming more obvious that the wind was not strong enough to hoist the larger kites, especially those the size of a horse. Disappointment was written on many faces, and finally it was announced that the big kites would be flown the next day in the Yellow River Bed, nearer the city. Years earlier during a flood, the river had changed its course, leaving a dry bed now being used as a market.

Sure enough, the next day, strong northeast winds blew and the sky was filled with kites as big as horses. Many prayers were probably said the night before and the Great Provider answered every one. Spectators who had traveled long distances to see this spectacle did not go home disappointed.

Our bus left under police escort as we returned to the hotel. As we collected baggage and were about to depart, the hotel staff came rushing outside and asked to have photos made with the foreigners. Out of the buses we went and posed for the next forty-five minutes with the manager, assistant managers, receptionist, and housekeeping and kitchen staffs! Chinese are very particular when snapping pictures. Also, they are quite skillful and usually acquire good results; however, the photo session was tiresome and consumed much time before our twelve-hour bus ride back to our individual schools. But they were pleased and that made us pleased as we pulled away for the trip back.

National Day is important to government and the citizens. On October 1, 1949, Mao Tse-tung formally declared the Communist People's Republic of China to be a Communist government. That declaration meant that all people would be treated and would live equally. The wealthy were required to surrender possessions to the government. In turn the government would redistribute to the poor. The policy sounds better than its implementation! As time passed, holidays were increased from two days to at least a full week to celebrate National Day. Families would plan reunions to be held during this time, and every means of transportation would be packed beyond capacity. People standing, sitting, and squatting in aisles of buses and trains were common sights. Fireworks in parks and athletic fields would light up the night skies all over China.

The fiftieth birthday of the People's Republic was an ongoing celebration with buildings, trees, and shrubs overly bedecked with twinkling, sparkling strings of colored lights. The cities looked like giant Christmas trees. Red banners and red balloons added much color to buildings, bridges, pagodas, temples, gazebos, etc.

Performances were held to entertain government leaders. Ballets, dramas, musicals, operas, talent shows, and magician acts were among performances offered. Many of us foreigners enjoyed a piano recital by children from ages five to fourteen during one of the National Day holidays. Their timing was perfect. One hundred talented young children all dressed alike in red circular skirts, white blouses, white leotards, and white caps with red top knots played for two hours without missing a note. Amazing!

Pleasing the government leaders with choices of entertainment seemed to be important for performers. Besides leaders, others could attend if they could afford the price of admission. Foreign teachers were guests of the college or university in which they taught. All of us agreed that we never saw an unprofessional presentation.

Chinese New Year is the longest holiday of the entire year,

lasting for at least four weeks and even longer for schools. This extended time provides travel time for those wishing to explore China and other Southeastern Asian countries. Most Chinese are happy to be with family even though family visits entail travel for many of them. It was during this time that I was able to visit Thailand, Indonesia, Singapore, Malaysia, India, and the Philippines.

Bountiful feasts are a big part of the celebration. Many students with several aunts and uncles are expected to visit each one for yet another banquet. This could include making the dumplings (jiaozi) as a family affair. Talking, laughing, and making jokes always go on during this doughy process. When these feasts are served, it is a contest to see who can eat the most. I was told that fifteen banquets are the minimum for each person. Stand by, emergency rooms!!!

Children always look forward to New Year somewhat as we anticipate Christmas. Each relative is expected to present a small red envelope with money inside to each child still in school. This is true through higher education years, so the youngsters are quite excited and happy when New Year rolls around.

On June 1st, children dressed in their new clothes are seen in parks, in restaurants, and out for a stroll with family. Little girls in frilly dresses and red ribbons in their hair enjoy showing off their new attire. The boys are less conspicuous but nevertheless equally proud of their new outfits. Since the one-child-per-family policy was imposed, from my observations, every day is Children's Day. Too often, the government controls parents and grandparents. It is an exciting time for the children to parade around and enjoy the admiration of relatives and friends.

The rivers and lakes are always busy on June 9th, when canoe-like boats with a dragon head and tail race to a given destination. We saw sixteen young oarsmen, eight on each side of the boat, and one older man beating a large drum on which he had doubtlessly practiced for several days prior to the day of the race. Bright headbands worn by the participants, plus the brilliant colors and design of the long dragon boat, made an interesting and noisy flotilla when the old drummer pounded louder and longer. Laughter and words of encouragement to row faster filled the air from onlookers and the oarsmen. The sun was never too hot and enthusiasm never waned throughout the competition. Business and other organizations sponsored the races. I never knew how the young men were rewarded, or even whether they were. I hope that those responsible expressed their appreciation in an adequate and material manner.

The Lantern Festival is held the last week in September. Generally, lanterns of varying sizes and shapes fill park areas and sidewalks. Bright lights and animation make them seem almost alive.

Each year I attended this festival and enjoyed viewing the skill and ingenuity of Chinese designers. Some designs were more lavish than others. I remember one quite well in Nanjing in 1991. A huge dragon as tall as a two-story building could open his large mouth, blow smoke, and wag his forked tongue. His beard below his chin was a full two yards long and was made with peanuts strung in a row and attached to his jaws. Dinosaur figures were "drinking water" and then spurting it out. Cranes and other animal lanterns were made to look like emperors and empresses with their attendants. A large lotus plant with a lady rising up was surrounded by other "lantern ladies" watering nearby plants. Flashing tiger-eyes from all the figures made a rather eerie atmosphere. This was the largest and most ornate of all those I was privileged to see during my thirteen years in China.

Churches observe Christmas and Easter, and foreigners are always welcome to these very special and long services. The last Christmas program I attended in 2000 began at 7:00 p.m. and finally ended at 11:00 p.m. No one left or seemed bored or concerned about the next day's obligations.

From my letters home and diary, the reports of Easter and Christmas observances are true experiences I enjoyed. Christmas celebrations increased as years evolved. Besides the Christmas dramas in churches, the commercial aspect invaded the business world. Santa Claus figures, reindeer, and Christmas cards became available. My favorite celebrations were with colleagues, friends, and church people.

The following accounts of various holidays come from my letters home and my diary.

National Day -- October 1, 1997

Dear Family and Friends,

Your letters always make my day a lot happier, and even the sun seems brighter on those days when I hear from you. So please just know how much I appreciate hearing from you and knowing about things on your side of the great Pacific!

The Chinese holiday for National Day lasts for seven days. It is duly celebrated with enormous parades in Beijing and every other city and village in the country with songs, dances, and overly elaborate decorations on buildings and walls. Even the trees have upturned lights underneath to give them a freshly washed appearance. Spectacular and extravagant are words too simple to describe the outlay of the extremes which the government takes to praise the glories of the past fifty years of the New China. Unbelievable!

I was privileged to visit two factories with a friend on an inspection team. She works in an export company that deals with many foreign countries, although the U.S.A. is not a recipient of this particular company. One factory is owned by a father-son team; the second one is owned and managed by a thirty-six-year-old who looks more like nineteen to me. Generally, Chinese don't show their age like Americans.

Clothes were being made in each of these factories, and I did not see the first idle person; the machines were humming at very high speeds. An interesting observation about the finished garments was that the label tags read "styled in Italy." A bountiful feast was served, after which I was told that no other foreigner had ever visited these factories before, and I received a hearty welcome to come back. I really appreciate the hospitality of the Chinese people.

Another day, I went to see the blind children and was greatly surprised to see how much they had grown since June. All four are as tall as I am now. I ate lunch in the school and enjoyed the time with the children. They seemed very happy and quite appreciative of the fruit and key rings for the four boys and hair clips and bows for the girl. Little things mean so much to them. I wish more of those unable to attend could also be enrolled because the space is available, but unfortunately many parents cannot afford the tuition required by the school. I met a graduate of the school who looked like a business lady. She and her boyfriend, also a graduate of the school, are working as masseurs in a medical clinic here in Fuzhou. The children were so happy to "see her."

For two days I was escorting an expectant Swedish lady to a local hospital for a checkup and an ultrasound. Amazingly, the doctor allowed me to see the four-month-old fetus. What a miracle to see that little head – I could even see the heart beating and the arms moving. If every pregnant girl could see her unborn child, I firmly believe there would be no need for any abortion clinics.

So my holiday consisted of a variety of activities. Now classes are back in session and I am seeing 165 smiling faces every week. Pray that all may come to know the One who can put a permanent smile in their hearts!

I am looking for your next communication. Peace, grace, and His love. Please keep us in your prayers.

Much love,
Mama/ Sue

National Day – 2000 – Holiday in Fuzhou!
Dear Family and Friends,

"New China" is fifty-one years old as of October 1, 2000. Celebrations began on October 1, 1949, so all employees except food service personnel, clerks, and emergency staffs have a week long holiday. This respite period encourages people to travel, shop, spend money, increase business, and deplete savings. I plan to stay right where I am, however, and help a new teacher, who just arrived last night, to become acquainted with Huanan and Fuzhou.

The new teacher, Jeannie Farrer from Michigan, is well

experienced in working with other cultures. She has taught in Japan, Romania, and Africa and is now in China. Her plane arrived from Shanghai an hour and a half late because of an "unknown cause." I insisted on sitting while the Foreign Affairs Officer, Yu Dao Feng, and I waited for her late arrival. The only seats available in the waiting area were in the snack shop so I bought two coconut drinks, over her protest, just so we could have a place to sit. She kept saying, "Too expensive, too expensive," but the table and chairs were worth the cost.

Tonight (30th) Huanan is invited to a special performance in honor of National Day. It will be a two-hour affair with typical Chinese singing, fans fluttering, girls wearing fancy, flimsy garments with flowing silk scarves – all very colorful, graceful, and beautiful. It will be an elaborate affair! I'll do my best to enjoy and appreciate it. They work so hard to do a good job.

A knock on my door just brought my "foreign expert card." I arrived in Fuzhou on August 30 and today is September 30. It has taken four weeks to collect all information required by the government, including another physical exam, to get back my passport and to be issued a health card, a residency card, and today the foreign expert card. How many officials had to approve all of these are legion! It provides jobs for people but can be very frustrating to foreigners who feel and need protection from their passports. The wheels of rules and regulations in China grind slowly.

My thoughts, concerns, and prayers are with all of you. I hope that daily activities are status quo and that you will enjoy the last three months of Y 2K.

Please give my love to your families, church families included. Continue to pray for the Chinese, for one another, and for me. God loves you and I do, too!

Much love,
Mama/Sue

Thanksgiving – 1999
Dear Family and Friends,
Today is Thanksgiving Day, November 17, and as I reflect

on the blessings of the past year I find them to be countless. At the top of the list, however, is a loving, caring, all-powerful, all-knowledgeable Savior who loves even me. Next are the love and support from my dear family members, friends, and innumerable Christians who are calling my name in their daily prayers. The very privilege of serving our Father in this great country and among these who must be among His chosen people is near the top of my gratitude list. Actually, every day should be a day of Thanksgiving because God is so good to us.

The night before Thanksgiving I was invited to have a dinner with some foreigners and administrative personnel at Huanan Women's College, my first assignment in Fuzhou. No, we did not have turkey or cranberry sauce, but there were really too many dishes of well-prepared food to meet our caloric needs!

Special guests at the dinner were two Amity leaders, one from Nanjing and one from Hong Kong. They were in Fuzhou for official visitations to the universities where Amity teachers work. They had been in Ming Jiang University the day before, and I was able to prepare dinner for them, which provided us more uninhibited conversation time. They are my support team, and I am deeply grateful for their concern and encouragement. Along with the rest of us, they enjoyed the Thanksgiving dinner.

Two special Chinese friends called at 4:30 p.m. today and invited me to have dinner with them tonight. This is typical of Chinese culture – last-minute invitations. I was sorry to decline but a previous commitment made it impossible for me to attend. Two people are coming for special help with their English, and I had assured them I would be available. The would-be host said, "I'll give you a rain check," and then gave a hearty ha-ha because it was raining very hard at that moment.

Another Thanksgiving in a country where they do not celebrate Thanksgiving and yet I have so much for which to be truly grateful, including friends who invite me to last-minute dinners.

Much love, Mama/Sue

Thanksgiving – 1999

Dear Family and Friends,

On Tuesday before Thanksgiving, I had told the Foreign Affairs Officer that I needed to leave for the airport at 6:30 on Thursday morning. No problem, she told me; however, on Wednesday afternoon she said that our president had to be at the hospital by 7:30 the next morning, so the car could take me only to the bus station to go to the airport. That offer proved unnecessary, as my dear friend May called to ask whether I needed any help to meet my flight. Her company's car was going to the airport the next morning to take a gentleman who needed to fly out on the same plane I was scheduled to take. This man was from Hong Kong, spoke very fluent English, helped to get me checked in, and sat across the aisle from me on the plane. I have learned to let our wonderful Father take care of such emergencies.

When we arrived in Guangzhou, my former seminary student, John, was nowhere to be seen, but my new friend did not leave until John came running up, apologizing for being a few minutes late. He is a pastor in Guangzhou and had a call that delayed him. After thanking my new friend, John and I went to the Friendship store, where I bought four boxes of corn flakes and some Campbell's soup. We had lunch at the Friendship Café and were able to talk, talk, and talk! John had been studying at the Lutheran Seminary in Hong Kong. He is working on his dissertation for his doctorate and hopes to complete it by January. Please pray for him, his wife (also a pastor), and their eight-year-old daughter.

John took me back to the airport for the continuing trip to Nanning, where my CBF (Cooperative Baptist Fellowship) leader met me. It was good to see him and his wife again. They plan to retire in September 2000 and are deeply concerned about the need for more people to come over and help with the harvest. Blessings await those who would respond. Please pray that people will feel led to come this way. God loves the Chinese people, too. They deserve to know our Jesus.

Our meeting went well, we spent much time in prayer, and

of course we shared our experiences. I marvel how God answers prayer and performs miracles in the lives of people we know. A young man I know has three children, but the third child had been living in a remote countryside village with his maternal grandparents, so the Government officials would not know of his birth. The child had no birth certificate, but through strong faith and prayer the father was able to immigrate to Canada with his wife and three sons. I do not know the logistics of just how he managed that escape, but today I know only that they are living safely in Toronto. God does work miracles.

While in Nanning, I was able to visit the lovely church where Xiao Li is pastor. He was my student when I taught in Nanjing. We had a great lunch in a restaurant called "Food Street," which is about one-half mile long and serves food from many Asian countries. The most unusual dish was fried honeybees, which tasted like fried cicadas and fried grasshoppers. Pastor Li is doing a great job, and his church is holding a training class for students who will become church leaders. We discussed CBF projects and Dr. Ron Winstead, our CBF leader, showed a video of some of the work, among which was rebuilding a primary school, digging deep wells for poor villages, and providing electrical generators for people who had never had electricity before. CBF hopes to build a church in these areas as funds are available. Pray! Pray! Pray!

The CBF Conference ended too quickly, and it was time to return to Fuzhou. My leader took me to the airport where I met a pretty business lady, who took me under her wing and we sat across the aisle from each other to Guangzhou. I shared the seat with two intellectuals, one an oceanographer and one a civil engineer. They became my friends and treated me for lunch in the airport restaurant. Likewise, they helped me to get to the correct gate for departure to Fuzhou. They were going to Qingdao, Lottie Moon country.

Other reasons for Thanksgiving are family, friends, e-mails, letters, cards, and most of all – prayers of people who care. Please continue to pray for the Chinese, my family, and for me.

God bless all of you!
    In His care,
    Mama/Sue

The following message was included in an Amity bulletin for Christmas:

Christmas Message

Once more we are a short while before Christmas.

The mystery of Incarnation fascinates the imagination of Christ's followers of all generations and of all nations, bringing out old and yet ever new treasures to add to the adoration of the Christ born in a manger.

At this time our thoughts especially turn to Christians and churches worldwide, with thanksgiving for the triune God's loving work of creation, preservation, redemption and cleansing, and for the prophecy and prayer that the whole humankind is to come to worship Him and to become one in Him.

May your Christmas 1992 be a greatly blessed one.

Christmas – 1990

Dear Friends and Family,

Last Sunday at the Christmas carol sing-along, a young, blond, and blue-eyed man walked into our International Fellowship meeting alone. As I spoke to him, he told me that his home is in Moscow and that he became a believer in '89 through his best friend. His greatest need was friendship and a fellow believer. He went with us for dinner, ate like a hungry puppy, and then accompanied us for a second carol sing-along.

After we were given candles in paper cups, we walked for one hour, singing favorite carols and ending up at a clubhouse full of refreshments. Vlado, my Russian friend, stayed right beside me throughout the entire evening.

Last night he came to borrow tapes of the Christmas songs. I gave him a copy of the Bible that had been gift-wrapped. He removed ribbons and paper so carefully the world should have seen his face! Gratitude and astonishment mixed with tears of joy as he kissed the Book, took my hand, and placed a gentle kiss on it. Carefully he wrapped it back and said, "Now I will have it to open as a gift on Christmas Day!" He thanked me profusely, saying, "My sister, my sister!"

What joys there are in His Kingdom's work! My thoughts, love, prayers, and concerns are constantly with each of you. May the love expressed through that first Christmas gift fill your lives with His love, joy, peace, courage, and praise.

Love,
Mama/Sue

Christmas – 1991
Dear Family,

My heart is so filled that I feel it will explode if it isn't shared. Today in class I asked students to write what they had learned about Christmas. The following are some of their comments:

"People have festivals in greeting Jesus Christ's birth, because He brings us happiness and peace, throws off illness and evil."

"Jesus brings love and peace to the world."

"People stay with family sharing the love and happiness given by God."

"I know everyone hopes for Christmas because they will receive a lot of blessings."

"The date of Christmas 25th December when Jesus was born. Students who are interested share this happiness with their western friends. I am one of those students. I wish a merry Christmas to my dear Todd. God bless you!"

"Many people go to church and their faces are happy."

"Christmas is the day that celebrates a universal spiritual message of peace and goodwill to all people."

"There are religious songs expressing joy or a sense of spiritual mystery!"

"Jesus was born in a manger and then slept calmly."

"People sing 'Silent Night' all the time."

"It is widespread that Jesus who is recorded in the Bible is a great man who brings happiness to mankind." Much love,

Mama/Sue. P.S. Rejoice with me! Chinese are learning about the Christ of Christmas.

December Delights 1991

December was a month filled with many exciting, joyous, and fulfilling activities.

In the beginning of the month, we took a trip to Shanghai to buy items unavailable in Nanjing, and we visited briefly with fellow CSIer's Bob Jantz and Shiggy File. We attended the Muan Church and participated in Communion with Chinese Christians including the retired director of the Shanghai YMCA. No sooner had we returned from our short trip to Shanghai than we began celebrating Christmas!

On December 13th, the Seminary class came to my home for a Christmas celebration, which included dinner and caroling.

On December 15th after worship at St. Paul's, six of the Chinese students who attended Church with us went for a brunch afterwards at a western hotel. In the afternoon we attended a carol sing led by Katie Neal at the Seminary. Among the group was a young Russian Christian from Moscow, who shared his faith and belief in God with us. The senior pastor from St. Paul's, Cheng Xi Ming, and Katie sang a duet, "O Holy Night." Later in the early evening, we joined another group in Dong Jiao, a joint venture residential area, for candle-lit caroling through the community. Delicious refreshments were enjoyed while Santa Claus made his jovial entrance for the children present.

On December 17th, Katie presented a musical concert for the Graduate English Club at Southeast University with approximately 300 people in attendance. The room was so crowded that many crawled through windows and went one story higher in another wing of the building so that they could see the words of the transparencies of songs the group was singing. Their participation and facial expressions were our rewards.

On December 19th, the YMCA came alive as students and teachers assembled for carols, skits, recitations, and dances. My class, with their teammates, presented a beautiful and moving

Christmas skit, "Why the Bells Rang."

Just two days later, along with the YWCA secretary, Katie organized and emceed the YMCA/YWCA Christmas program, which included Chinese and foreign participation. This was preceded by a worship service in which a recent Chinese seminary graduate read the Christmas story in Luke and Matthew.

Earlier that day, we attended the annual open house held by Bishop and Mrs. K. H. Ting. She joined us singing "Every Day in China," and with stars in her eyes and a smile on her face, she joyfully sang "Silent Night" with those in attendance.

After worship service on Sunday, December 22nd, we enjoyed a covered dish luncheon with approximately sixty foreign friends. Then Katie and I attended a Christmas worship service sponsored by the African fellowship at Nanjing Pharmaceutical University. Appropriate scripture and carols were enjoyed by Chinese, Africans, and Americans.

A highlight of all Christmas events was a celebration at the Mandarin Chamber Hotel. Katie and I were invited by the management to plan the decorations and a Christmas program for Christmas Eve night. The evening's activities included a delicious complimentary dinner, dance with live music, caroling, and a beautiful midnight candlelight worship service, where the Christmas story from Luke and Matthew was read. As all lights were extinguished, the hotel staff members, Chinese guests, and foreigners held candles and sang sacred carols through the program, ending with Katie and He Hui Bing singing "O Holy Night." Transportation was provided by the hotel to take foreigners back to their respective universities.

On Christmas morning, a brunch was held in my home for an international group composed of Dutch, Russians, Germans, Japanese, and Americans. A breakfast of blueberry muffins, coffee cake, sausage balls, cheese, eggs, hot biscuits, and hot drinks was served. While carols were sung by the group, their wishes for a white Christmas were met as white snow fell silently and gently outside. The spirit of unity was evident as Russians, Japanese, and Americans sang from the same hymnbook. For the Japanese lady, it was her first celebration of Christmas ever.

The next morning Katie and I continued the Christmas festivities by meeting with my foreign trade class of seniors. The last classes before Christmas consisted of an open house to see western style decorations including a small crèche, which initiated many questions about the first Christmas. The biblical account of the first Christmas was shared with each class.

In the following days, CSI staff people, Charlie Wilson and Dr. Vi Marie Taylor, visited us. Opportunities for a longer visit were made possible because of a five-inch snowfall that interrupted traveling plans to visit other CSI personnel.

Katie and I attended a New Year's Eve banquet sponsored by the Foreign Affairs office at Southeast University. Firecrackers exploded on both sides of the Foreign Guest House to say goodbye to 1991 and to welcome 1992.

The December Delights of 1991 are ones that are in my memory bank to stay. They bring back fond memories as I reflect on these various experiences.

From my observation during my years in China, enthusiastic excitement abounded as holidays came. Seeing family and plenty of food seemed to be the most important activities for Chinese. Distance and travel presented hardships for many, but when these were overcome jubilation ensued. It was an awesome pleasure to be included in some of the festivities in families of some of my students. Simplicity often added to these occasions. Perhaps we could learn from them.

Amity conferences during Winter Holidays

Winter holidays, occurring during the Chinese New Year, are also referred to as Spring Festival and can last five to eight weeks. The following experiences came from my diary or from letters sent to family.

Winter Holiday 1993

Excitement filled the air as foreign teachers boarded the Huanan van for the short ride to the long distance bus terminal. Winter break for us had just begun. Though it was January 9, the weather was more like a balmy, bright spring day. Familiar faces of other teachers began to appear as we arrived at the Ming Jiang Hotel and the designated bus station from which to begin our trip.

Xiamen (Sha-mun) was our first destination, a more southern city of approximately 4.5 million people, and an eight-hour bus ride from Fuzhou. After crowding in with heavily laden suitcases, which were stacked in the back of the bus, we settled into the ten seats reserved for us near the front. I personally prefer a seat farther back so that cyclists, pedestrians, animals, and other motorists are not so visible. Guardian angels must be very tired after watching traffic for so many hours! Xiamen had been selected for the Amity Conference site because of its warmer climate and the location of our hotel on a more or less tropical island.

We traveled along until 12:00 noon. The driver came to a rather abrupt stop in front of a typical Chinese restaurant. Although lunch was included in our ticket fare, I chose to munch on crackers and fruit instead of greasy noodles and half-cooked vegetables.

This was considered a rest stop and a lunch break. Several of us sought out the place for "resting," which was nothing more than a hole in the ground well used before our arrival. Feeling more relaxed and somewhat refreshed, we started back to the bus. Suddenly, I spotted a cross hanging beside an open door. Moving closer, I saw an elderly man who through gestures and a mixture of Chinese and English conveyed to us that he was a Christian. Tears filled his eyes as he motioned us to come inside. On a rickety, old, dilapidated table was a well-worn copy of the Bible. He lifted it upwards with great reverence and then pointed to each of us. I was glad to be wearing a cross given to me just the day before by one of my students. He gave me an extra firm handshake as we bade him farewell. I thought of Sam Walter Foss' poem, "The House by the Side of the Road." Surely God is using this old gentleman in his house beside the road. I continue to wonder just how many people's lives he touches with his quiet witness and dedicated devotion to our God. If I return to

Xiamen, hopefully, this old saint will still be there to share his love for our universal Father.

The conference went well, and now I am back in Fuzhou settled in for the second term. Many opportunities are here to share the good news in deed, if not in words. Please pray for the Chinese and me that we may tell others of the God who loves us and can meet all their needs. Blessings, prayers, and love to all of you.

Mama/Sue

Winter Holiday 1995

Final exam grades recorded, we were ready for a different routine until February 20, when spring terms would begin. Marjatta Punkkinen, Mitzi Harris, and I – all three Amity teachers – left Fuzhou for Xiamen and the annual winter conference. The short, one-hour flight took precedence over the seven-hour bus ride because of road construction between the two cities. A feeling of jubilation and relaxation emboldened me after checking in at the Seaview Garden Hotel on Gulangyu Island in Xiamen. Classes, textbooks, papers, and speeches could wait for a few weeks.

Many "biggies" occurred while in Xiamen. First, as Marjatta, Mitzi, and I stepped from the taxi from the airport, we spied Pizza Hut! M-m-m, pan pizza never tasted better, and with real cheese, too. The next biggie was meeting seven of my former students, now business ladies in Xiamen, at McDonalds for a Big Mac, chocolate shake, and apple pie. One former student has been baptized. Another one is attending a required month-long Believer's class in preparation for baptism. Please, pray for Candi and Jessica.

Two days later, after I had eaten again at Pizza Hut, I headed for window shopping and conversation with Jessica, a 1994 graduate. As we were about to pass a bus terminal, a young couple appeared through the mass of people. The young man's eyes sparkled, his mouth fell wide open, but there was no sound. I was also speechless. Moments later, both of us regained our voices. Then he said, "Sue Todd, Sue Todd, Sue Todd." I replied, "Toby, Toby, Toby." He and I had met three years ago while I was attending the Amity Conference in Xiamen. He became a Believer, asked for a Bible, and received the English Bible that he had requested three years earlier. I had seen him only once since then, although he writes and will occasionally call. After the initial shock of our seeing each other, he said, "Surely God planned the timing and circumstances of our meeting." Toby and his girlfriend came for a visit that night and as time drew near for them to leave he said, "Could we pray together before we must go?" More exciting news – his lovely friend is now going to church with him and plans to be baptized! Jessica said, "Don't we have a wonderful God who puts us in the right places at the right time?" I agreed.

This conference ended with worship and Communion Service conducted by various teachers.

One young man mentioned a student who shares a dorm room with nine others, not uncommon in Chinese institutions. He had become a Christian and when asked about relationships with his roommates, he said, "I must get along with them because I am their salt and their light." Should we not remind ourselves of this when dealing with non-Believers?

A friend from a northern province told of a banquet in her honor. The first dish was a fish still struggling to breathe with gills opening and closing and mouth gasping for breath. The poor thing had been scaled and then immersed in hot oil which cooked the body but not the still functioning head. She had the "honor" of taking the first serving.

Now off to Guangzhou, location of CSI's Language Camp. That's correct, I am trying to learn more Chinese. Wish me good luck! While waiting for the camp to begin, I was privileged to stay in the Guangdong Christian Guest House. My host, a former student from Nanjing Seminary, met me at the airport, checked me in, ran out for towels, washcloths, etc., since the house furnished no amenities. He invited me to dine with his family and performed many other thoughtful acts of kind concern.

The former student is now pastor of the Shamin Church in Guangzhou. His church choir was leaving the next day for a concert and visitation to some other churches. I was invited and, of course, I accepted. Pastor John, his five-year-old daughter, thirty choir members, and I left for Zhongsan City in a mini-bus loaded with hymnals and Bibles. On the way we stopped at the Salvation Army Store to leave the books. Until now, I did not know the Salvation Army operates in China. The store reminded me of any American Christian Book Store.

The next stop was to visit a fairly new church facility that had four pre-school classes in session. Biblical pictures were neatly arranged on classroom walls. Selected Bible verses were part of bulletin board displays. Any church would be proud of the work taking place in the young lives attending these classes. I was greatly impressed with teacher enthusiasm and the happy faces of those young children.

A sumptuous dinner was served before we moved on to where the choir would present its concert. I can't report all that was on the menu because, frankly, I was afraid to ask! There was more than enough to satisfy caloric needs.

An elderly pastor greeted us at the next church. He proudly showed us his adopted five-month-old granddaughter whom he had rescued from the front steps of the church when she was only a few hours old! His daughter adopted her and now there are happy grandparents, happy parents, and a happy baby girl. No grandpa has ever been prouder.

The choir did a superb job as their faces and voices blended to reflect commitment, dedication, and praise to our Savior and Lord. What a genuine privilege and blessing to be an observer and worshiper with them. I felt that angels must be clapping their wings after each song

The next morning, a soul-searching by choir members took place. It was like a self-examination of one's relationship with God, other choir members, and other people with whom one works or meets. Each member gave a testimony and a challenge to one another and to one's self as Paul said to fight a good fight and keep the faith (2 Timothy 4:7). What a blessing which lasted from 9:00 a.m. to 12:00 noon! These people sing to the glory of God and with His Spirit filling their hearts and lives. Little wonder they make such beautiful harmony.

We had to return to Guangzhou because the next day was Sunday. I attended Pastor John's church, listened to that wonderful choir again, and participated in the English Bible Study for foreigners who stayed for Bible Study.

After the Bible Study ended at noon, twenty of us went to a typical Chinese restaurant for lunch. The questions and discussion continued all through the meal. One young man, who calls himself Aaron, asked whether I would answer a personal question. In China, nothing seems too personal to ask, but I consented. In all seriousness he inquired, "What is your blood type?" He wishes to find a girlfriend with his type of blood because he feels that they as a couple would be more congenial and happy. He is only twenty years old, so I advised him to keep looking and maybe find a doctor friend who analyzes blood types. Perhaps he could make a recommendation. Aaron was quite serious.

The next day, Aaron came to escort me to see a friend teaching in a primary school. He talked about his fifteen piano students and his great enjoyment playing for the choir at the YMCA. I was sorry not to accept his invitation to go to choir practice that night, but Pastor John had invited me to dine with him and his family. I was disappointed to miss that opportunity, but one must honor previous appointments.

CSI has done some work at a leper colony outside Guangzhou. Pastor John asked Samuel, another of his Bible Study students, to make arrangements for a visit. This effort entailed a long bus ride and a forty-five minute walk to the proper government office for permission. Upon arrival, we were told to come back the next day, but that was impossible for me. Finally, the official asked, "Why do you want to go out there?" I told him my CSI agency had done some work out there and I would like to see it. Then he asked, "Which agency?" When I said CSI, he jumped up from his chair as if maximum voltage had been applied, ran out the door jabbering Chinese, came back in a few minutes, and said, "The car is ready and the driver is on his way." (Only the person licensed to drive a particular vehicle may do so.) He locked his desk, closed the door, took Samuel and me to a white van bearing a red cross on each door, insisted that I ride up front, climbed into the back with Samuel, and we were off. CSI was the magic word!

We were taken to the hospital where pathetic figures smiled as they welcomed us, some without feet, fingers, legs, etc. Many kept their disfigured hands or feet hidden. A nineteen-year-old boy was turning black. He had lived on the streets surviving on food discarded as garbage until he was brought to the colony by a Christian who had discovered him. He kept both hands in his pockets all the time we were near. I could see how gnarled they appeared. A kind nurse from Hong Kong pays a Chinese teacher to teach him since he had never attended school. My heart was heavy as I left this facility.

We made a tour as our guide called our attention to painted doors, repairs, etc. The official said, "College students from Carson-Newman University did all this!" I told him that Carson-Newman was the alma mater of three members of my family – my father, my eldest sister, and her husband. Well, that just about made the official and me relatives. I should explain that, last year, the BSU (Baptist Student Union) from Carson-Newman, Jefferson City, Tennessee, came to Guanzghou and built chicken houses, painted, and remodeled. What better way to spend two weeks vacation than helping these rather isolated people. The chicken houses are to help those who are able to raise chickens for the market and thereby supplement the meager government allowances. These residents will never return home. Families do not want them back. Pitiful human beings.

Lunch was interesting that day: a menu of dog soup, fried snake, and many other tasty delicacies. Samuel was seated next to me and, as we were eating, he said, "I would like to be the next CSI and I will help people like I've seen what your CSI has done." Pray for Samuel; he is a fledgling business man who dreams of giving retired people an easy job making plastic garbage bags for buses, trains, and cars. They are very much needed.

Time for Language Camp arrived, so Pastor John took me to the hotel where CSI forces were gathering. His little daughter patted the pretty floral bedspread in my room and said, "Daddy, can we stay here?" Her drab surroundings in her home made the hotel room seem like a castle to her. It was a contrast from where I had been staying and where she lives.

I'm not sure how much Chinese I learned during those seven days, but this I do know, nobody has ever enjoyed classes more than our group. All of us were over sixty and were not afraid of making the wrong tone. (Chinese has four tones which determine word meaning.) The week was too short and very hilarious and ended all too soon. Maybe a few words were learned.

Packing suitcases and crowding on buses, we took a hydrofoil ride to Hong Kong for our next venture. In two short hours we had skimmed down to Hong Kong for the CSI Conference. Our inspirational leader was Dr. Avery T. Willis, editor of the Master Life Materials. At one time in the Sunday School Department in Nashville, he was a collaborator with Dr. Henry Blackaby and Claude V. King, editors of *Experiencing God,* a Southern Baptist publication What a refreshing experience and how gifted Dr. Willis is in expounding the truths in God's Word! I shall forever treasure this time spent in conference with him, his wife, Shirley, and my brothers and sisters in CSI. What a family to have away from my own biological family. The two families may be easily compared.

All good things must come to an end, and so it was with this conference. My thoughts began to turn to Huanan and Fuzhou, so after bidding my friends farewell, I flew back to Fuzhou and into my little one room which seems like home to me in China. May our God bless and keep each of you in His tender loving care as you continue to pray for the Chinese and for me.

Mama/Sue

Winter Holiday 1996

It began unlike a holiday as I had to get up at 4:30 a.m. to catch an early morning flight from Fuzhou to Kunming. Xiao Wei and Tony, my foreign affairs officer and friend, accompanied me to help with two heavy bags and the check-in process. People are so important in our lives!

The uneventful flight was made in good time, and reliable Amity had a person on hand to meet the teachers from Fujian Province. She took us to the 'Rosy Mansion," a three-star Chinese hotel, adequate but not plush. My roommate, Mimi Moore, a Mississippi Southern Baptist teaching in Hefei, immediately shared events of the last semester as well as updates on reports from her local church in the States. With our two churches many kilometers apart, it is incredible how similar the situation is in her church and in mine, both without a pastor for too long.

Because the conference was well planned, it ran very smoothly. The eighty-three participants are English teachers assigned to various areas of southeast China. Consultants from the sponsoring agencies were present. Charlie Wilson from Hong Kong's CSI office, always a supportive force, was a welcome sight to me. The two events which interested me the most were the Small Interest Groups and the ecumenical worship service.

The worship service centered on Micah 6:1-8 and Matthew 11:25-28. Each passage was read in Chinese, Danish, Norwegian, Swedish, German, and English, since teachers were there from each of those countries. This meaningful event ended with Communion, a reminder of the universal God we serve.

Great anticipation and excitement filled the atmosphere the following morning. We were going to visit projects that Amity Foundation has helped to initiate and support. Four buses took us high into the remotest parts of Yunnan Province, where we visited a village using methanol gas from a plant installed by Amity. Prior to the bio-gas plant, villagers were forced to gather twigs or wood scraps wherever they could be found in order to cook. Such appreciative faces and warm welcome by these grateful people made the rather long trip worthwhile.

Next we visited an area destroyed by the earthquake on

October 24, 1995. At that time Amity immediately sent blankets, coats, food, tents, etc., to help these dear people. Few children were killed because they were outside raising the flag when the earthquake struck. They are presently having school in four flimsy buildings with only two scratched up black boards as equipment. Students sit on the ground. I think God has big future plans for these young people. The residents prepared tofu for all of us as a gesture of thanks and friendship. Tofu is a popular Chinese pudding-like food made from soy beans. The entire population followed us to the buses which took us to the next project.

The mountain we had to ascend next had a single, narrow roadway wide enough for only one vehicle. Our bus could not maneuver this route, so we were put into older, more "tumbled down species," which could not suffer much more from service or looks. However, they struggled their way to the peak. The Mioa minority group who live in this village had made a walkway for us of pine needles, a symbol of honor for their guests. The walk ended on a plateau that was also covered, as though a carpet, with pine needles. Nice, small, good appearance! Various food choices in large containers, along with individual bowls, were neatly arranged for our use. Beautiful Mioa girls dressed in traditional costumes of colorful blue, white, and red stripes distributed new chopsticks as we served ourselves from the bountiful caloric provisions. I never felt more humble and more honored. Luckily, the feeble buses were able to take us down without any mishaps. All of us prayed that the brakes would hold. They did!

Now we were back in the more reliable buses and were hustled through four villages enjoying electricity for the first time ever. Faithful donors had made that possible by purchasing the electric poles that the village could not afford.

The next stop was the campus of both a primary and a high school. Again, caring people have donated funds to pay the required tuition for poverty stricken children to learn to read and write. Another humbling experience! We have so much! They have so little, except for a great big, grateful heart!

The CSI Conference followed the Amity meeting. This year it was held in Chiang Mai, Thailand. Southern Baptists from all over Southeast Asia attended. Missionaries working in Korea, Malaysia, Indonesia, the Philippines, and China made up the 160 people in attendance. Young parents were able to bring their children, sixty in all, because volunteers from the USA came as childcare workers for those ten days. The older children were in DVBS (Daily Vacation Bible School) and gave a commencement on our last night. That brought back many memories of years gone by when I used to help in Bible School at my church.

Dr. James Hampton from the Foreign Mission Board in Richmond was our eloquent, divinely inspired preacher during the conference. This man of God blessed all of us as he "broke the Bread" each morning. He will retire in July after serving as a missionary and a leader in the FMB. What a fruitful ministry and how many lives were changed because of him only God Himself knows! Over forty years of full-time service in winning souls for our Lord to his credit.

We were given one day to visit places of interest. Many went to the elephant farm, rode on elephant backs, and fed them sugar cane and bananas. Did you know that elephants don't peel bananas before eating them? Ha! A favorite exhibit for me was the butterfly and orchid farms where colors were breathtakingly beautiful. The last stop (and one I could have done without) was the snake farm. Trainers handled cobras, an enormous python, and several non-poisonous species. A few daring people posed for pictures with the python wrapped around their necks as the trainer held the serpent's head and tail. That was a photo I chose not to have taken. During the show one of the trainers threw a rope into the section where I was seated. Had you been listening, you would have heard me scream. The day ended with a cone of ice cream, honest to goodness ice cream from Baskin-Robbins. Mmm-mm!

The time to return to Fuzhou arrived. After being gone three weeks, I was ready for the trip back to my apartment. I praised God as I traveled across the southern part of China for people who are serving Him here and for people like you who are praying, caring, and sharing in this field, which is still "white for harvest." (John 4:35 KJV)

In His Care,
Mama/Sue

Winter Holiday 1997

The car from Fujian Medical University and Eli, my Chinese "little boy Friday," arrived exactly at 7:30 a.m. on January 21. We were taken to the bus station near Ming Jiang Hotel, where we met others going to Xiamen to attend the Amity Conference.

Eli handled not only my luggage but also some for other ladies in our group. A thoughtful young man, he was so excited to be going to Xiamen, a seaport city south of Fuzhou and only six hours away by bus. He would visit a friend there while I attended the conference.

One of my former students from Xiamen met us at the bus station. We made a straight line to the Pizza Hut for lunch, a luxury we did not have in Fuzhou at that time. The atmosphere and food were very Americana, with only the restrooms still Chinese. They had water but no soap and no paper towels; however, foreigners learn quickly the importance of Wet Ones or antibacterial lotion.

The Amity Conference was held on Gulangyu Island, across from Xiamen. Eli, Jessie (my former student) and I took the ferry across to the hotel where I would stay. Eli would stay in an apartment assigned to Jessie by her work unit, but she was staying with her parents nearer her job.

The five-day conference was enlightening, informative, and pleasant. Many friends stationed in other areas of China were present. Of course, there were always new faces, and I usually asked, "Why did you choose to teach in China?" Answers varied from adventure to an opportunity to learn a new culture. All were good reasons to be in China.

The highlight to me of the entire conference occurred on Sunday morning. A worship service was always held during these conferences. Many countries were represented and scriptures were read in the language of the persons reading. Nine different people read John 2:5: "…but whoever keeps His word, in him the love of God has truly been perfected. By this we know that we are in Him:…" (KJV) Swedish, Danish, Dutch, German, French, Japanese, Finnish, Chinese, and English all read in their native language, and God could understand them all! A feeling of being one in the Spirit permeated the entire worship service. The Lord's Prayer prayed in one's native tongue ended this service. We do, indeed, have a universal God who made us all and loves us all equally.

Dr. Phillip Wickeri, one of the Amity officials and an ordained Presbyterian who was also ordained by the Chinese Church in Nanjing in 1991, was the minister who spoke. I was privileged to attend his ordination in St. Paul's Church in Nanjing. He and twelve Chinese young men were ordained on the same Sunday afternoon. During his sermon he talked about following God's will and doing what God told us to do. He developed the topic well and left us feeling motivated to seek out and follow God's will for our lives.

Seven Southern Baptists were working through Amity, having been assigned by East Asia China Office in Hong Kong. From Xiamen, we went in a group to Hong Kong for a meeting with our leaders there. Gwen Crotts and Faye Pearson, our leaders, met us at the Hong Kong Airport, and Eli returned to Fuzhou alone when I left for Hong Kong.

This was my first introduction to Faye, who had been a missionary in Taiwan for thirty years. I had met Gwen briefly in Beijing during summer orientation for incoming volunteers. Gwen had served sixteen years in Hong Kong and understands Chinese culture well. They will make efficient and spirit-filled leaders. Our former leader, Charlie Wilson, is on furlough in the U.S.A. and was greatly missed by those who have worked with him in the past.

The one and a half days in Hong Kong were quite profitable and well spent. We shared testimonies, sang favorite hymns, and I learned about a charitable project for remote villages. A supportive church had just sent me $200, which was donated to buy pairs of goats to furnish meat and milk for needy people.

Two days later, we flew to Taiwan for the remainder of the conference. Missionaries from Japan and South Korea joined us and added their prayers and testimonies to those we had already shared. Mark Whitworth from Tokyo said, "I would gladly give up my nice apartment and live as you all are, if it would bring people to Christ." Only 5% of Japanese are Christians. Our missionaries there need our prayers.

Everything that transpired was a genuine blessing and ended on an extremely high note. Thanksgiving, songs, testimonies, and symbolic footwashing to indicate servanthood made a moving experience for all of us. The atmosphere was electrified with the very presence of God. How privileged I felt to be a participant in such a meaningful service.

I came back to Fujian Medical University on February 4. Now I am awaiting a visitor from Xiamen who called and asked to visit. His mother died, his father remarried, and now he has little contact with his son. Toby, my visitor, has adopted me as his surrogate mother and calls and visits whenever possible.

I met Toby five years ago in Xiamen while he was still a student. He directed and escorted my roommate, Katie, and me to the right gangplank to catch the ferry over to our hotel.

When we arrived at our hotel, he accepted the invitation to come in. He spotted the Bible and asked for a copy. He prayed the sinner's prayer that night and we have been friends ever since.

So he came and spent three days eating home-cooked meals, pouring his heart out and sleeping soundly on the sofa. I enjoyed his company and was a bit sad when he had to return to Xiamen. "I do not want to see a daddy who doesn't love me or a stepmother I don't like, because she doesn't like me," he said. I was glad to be available and felt as if my grandson had been for a visit. It was a privilege and pleasure to share time, food, and fellowship with this young man.

Winter holiday 1997 will always have a special place in my memory bank.

In His Care,
Mama/Sue

Winter Holiday, January 28, 1998

With Spring Festival beginning about a week ago, decorations for doors bearing good luck characters were being pasted or taped to entrances of housing units and on door frames of many individual flats. My next door neighbor has included two children in his display. The picture of the rather plump little girl shows her dressed in the traditional bright red, two-piece dress of a floral design, while her head is adorned with an empress-like crown with dangling bangles and high-rise arches. The picture of the small boy depicts him also wearing a traditional two-piece frock in red and gold floral design with a simple round black cap covering his head. Both are holding signs with the Chinese characters for prosperity and happiness. Chinese believe in traditions!

The campus is relatively quiet, so after a rather uneventful day I retired about 10 p.m. on January 27, but my deep slumber was more than disturbed at midnight. I wasn't sure whether Armageddon had begun! The sky has been invisible for over two weeks – gray, rainy, misty, cold, and windy for the weather pattern. Well, at midnight the surroundings were almost like day. Roman candles, firecrackers of various sizes, and fireworks from boats in the nearby Ming Jiang River lit up the sky! My next door neighbor blasted a full string of those explosives on the landing just outside our doors. I held on to my bed thinking if I go into space, I'll take you with me!! The fragmented remains were still on the landing the next morning.

My church had a Thanksgiving service at 9 a.m. on Chinese New Year's Day, January 18. The day again was foggy, damp, and chilly, and as I made my way to the bus stop I thought that the church would not be crowded because of such dismal weather and the BIG Spring Festival meals everyone was planning to enjoy. Wrong! The place was literally packed beyond capacity as whole families came, many from Hong Kong and Taiwan (easily identifiable by their clothes). All were coming to give thanks for the blessings of the past year and to beg God's mercy for 1998.

A dear eighty-five-year-old widow had sixteen members of her family present. When their group was recognized by the pastor, the matriarch thanked and praised God on behalf of her family. The family then sang, "My Jesus, I Love Thee" and "Praise to the Lord, the Almighty." I was deeply touched as smallest sweet child to the dear mother and grandmother blended their voices of thanks and praise to our God. Their radiant faces spoke more than their voices.

The pastor also recognized the church leaders, ushers, Sunday School teachers, choir directors, and the blind pianist, and with kind words of thanks he praised them for their faithful service to God and to the church.

The sermon began at 9:40 a.m. and ended at 10:30 a.m. The pastor spoke in Putonghua, the nationally accepted Chinese dialect, while an interpreter translated the sermon into Fujian dialect. These language variations were done so that all worshipers could understand that "Jesus is our way to the Father; therefore, we thank God for sending Him into the world." I was privileged and happy to be a part of this group and I reiterate what the pastor said in closing: "Now thank we all our God."

Also, Spring Festival means calories, lots of them. Several friends and former students issued gracious invitations to dine with them. No way could all of them be accepted; however, I did enjoy making jiaozi. I was honored and well fed on this special day with far too many dishes. Some I really abhor, such as Chinese lobster which we would call "craw dad" – many legs, crusty shell, little meat, but one must peel and pretend to enjoy this unsightly delicacy.

Several visitors came to my flat "to keep me from being lonely," which I was not.

It was rather nice to be able to read *The Fist of God* by Frederick Forsyth and *The Little House of Allington* by Anthony Trollope. Then with the full knowledge of the love of God and His ever willing Presence, I really felt no loneliness.

My good friend, Betts Rivet, over at Huanan, and I kept in daily touch by phone, visiting each other and dining with mutual friends. Betts and I both chose to vacation in Fuzhou. I'm glad she did.

Soon classes will begin and spring semester will evaporate quickly. Please, continue to pray for the Chinese, my dear family, and for me. May your new year be filled with His mercy, peace, joy, and love.

In His Care,
Mama/Sue

Winter Holiday 1999

This winter holiday began on January 26 when I took a three-hour plane ride to a city near the Burma border known as Kunming. It is called the garden city of China, and rightly so, because of the carefully arranged pots of colorful flowers placed all over the city. It is home for many minority people dressed in loud colors usually with an equally loud head-dress. It makes for a colorful environment, to say the least!

We were housed in the Golden Dragon Hotel, a rather ritzy hotel for poor teachers like us. Wedding parties appeared daily during our stay there, and his Honor, the prime minister of Laos, was staying there as well. When he arrived or departed, a red carpet was rolled from the elevator to his waiting limo. With security guards all over the place, his presence created much excitement. Hotel employees were dressed in the bright colors of the minorities. Those of us in the less noble class became less conspicuous with his presence – a relief in a way.

The highlight of Amity Conference was seeing seven Southern Baptists of like opinions. We enjoyed fellowshipping and it was a little like family. Another special event was visiting the villages where Amity has special projects, such as deep wells for clean water supply, biogas projects which produce electricity for people who never had it before, mountainside terraces for growing corn and wheat. The gratitude of the people was overwhelming. They prepared their best food and took it up to the mountain top, after spreading pine needles on the path where we walked. This is a custom reserved for the highest honored guest. So the Prime Minister hardly had anything on us!

On Sunday a choir made up of the Miao minority group, all

sixty strong, came to the church we were attending and sang very familiar hymns as part of the services. I thought of the words of the hymn "In Christ There Is No East nor West, In Him no south or north but one great fellowship of love throughout the whole wide world!" We were worshiping with brothers and sisters in Christ. It was indeed a very inspiring conference and I told our leader, "The best one yet." He seemed pleased. While there I met the United Board leader who is responsible for my being in China today. It gave me an opportunity to give her a personal expression of gratitude.

On February 8, I was taken by taxi, bus, boat, and a three-wheeler to an island where a young man has an English Training Center with twenty-five students eager to learn English. He is quite proud of the learners and of the classroom which would break your heart to see. The unpainted walls were very dark with age, a faded U.S.A. map hung on one wall, and a 1999 calendar completed the furnishings. A rather flimsy blackboard hung in front over a too narrow stage, which I would surely tumble off if it were in the classrooms where I teach.

Few foreigners have been to this place, so small children hid behind their mothers and older people stared so hard that I think I know how the pandas in the Washington zoo must feel. We were almost blasted into outer space with firecrackers celebrating two weddings and a huge funeral procession with about nine three-wheelers with young men exploding whole rolls of firecrackers to scare away the evil spirits. Too bad they don't know that our Lord can do that in a more peaceful way.

On the way back to Fuzhou the teacher and I were discussing Darwin's theory of evolution. He was quite interested in the creation story as recorded in Genesis and was so ready to hear the truth. He promised to share his new found faith with his students. Please pray for Walson, his English name. There are a few Christians in a nearby village, and I hope to return soon to attend church with them.

The trip to Sanming was not really to Sanming but to You Xi, a smaller town near Sanming. My hostess and her family live about forty-five minutes from You Xi over very narrow roads around hair pin curves and rough countryside mountains. They live near the top of the mountain, so we had to walk up, up, up a narrower path to reach their home. No one could have been treated more royally that I was during the three days I was there. The house was built of wood unlike Fuzhou homes made of bricks and concrete. It was quite spacious with eight rooms divided by a wide area used to hold family gatherings, and most of them had tables to place incense sticks and fruits for Buddha. A small can was placed on the table to burn candles and, of course, incense sticks.

A somewhat small Buddhist temple was well visited by the village people as they shot firecrackers and placed incense sticks in front of the statue of Buddha. I did not go to the temple because my God does not need firecrackers to drive away evil spirits! Neither does he need incense. He wants people to come to Him through His Son Jesus Christ. How I pray that one day these dear people can know our God, too. Please help me to pray this into reality. It was a good experience and I hope the daughter will soon make a decision to become a Christian. She has been to church recently and she also asked me to say the blessing before we ate. Pray for her – her name is Cindy. She may help her family to know Christ, too.

Back in Fuzhou, I plan to do some serious studying for the next few days in preparation for classes which begin March 4. Spring term always flies by and one of my classes will graduate, so I must try to reach as many students as possible for our Father in these next few months. I will need your prayers and please pray that they will be responsive. God loves them, too.

In His Love,
Mama/Sue

Winter Holiday 2000
Dear Family,
Teachers look forward to a longer holiday during Spring Festival in China. This year the special day was on February

5. The Amity Conference is held prior to Spring Festival. My vacation began on January 25, when I went to Xiamen for the Amity meeting. It is good to see old friends and to meet new ones. The meetings are for sharing ideas and experiences as well as being updated on Amity projects. Emphasis this year was on earthquake victims, school-less children, and goat projects, all worthy of prayers, concern, and financial support. Amity means "love" and that is what we are asked to share. I know another Person who taught His disciples to love. His name is Jesus.

In Xiamen we visited a church shaped like an ark. It was designed by an architect who was given a Bible by the pastor there. The architect read about Noah and the ark, was converted, designed the building, and brought the plans to the pastor, and the result was this unusual structure. It has over 2,000 members and multiple programs for young people, quite an impressive, active group of Believers.

After the conference, a thirty-nine-year-old friend from Austin, Texas, visited me for a week. A Southern Baptist, she works in another province and needed to share concerns; we were able to spend undisturbed time discussing prayer needs, future activities, etc. It was good for her and also for me.

Holiday time is now winding down, classes resume next week, and all too soon this school year will become history. Please, pray for more people to feel the call to come over and help us. Pray for the young Christians, the church leaders (more are needed), and please pray for my sick family members. God has been so gracious to them. I can't thank Him enough.

May all of you find His grace, mercy, peace, and love as you serve Him by serving others!

In His care,
Mama/Sue

Winter Holiday 2001
It was restful, peaceful, pleasant, refreshing, and just right for me. I enjoyed Christian tapes from the USA and from Chinese choirs and a full cassette in tenor by a former student, now a

pastor. My heart clapped several times as he sang. Living in a house with seven other ladies, active ones, I might add, makes one appreciate opportunities for undisturbed time for meditation, quiet prayers, and just praise and thanks to our Father for His adequate provisions and love.

Many former students came to visit and I was invited to several homes, some quite poor and some very wealthy according to Chinese standards. One affluent family came for me in their private car and took me to their home, tastefully furnished with shiny floors, gleaming chandelier, a modern kitchen and real china dishes. The father has his own investment business and from outward appearances is doing well.

My dear brother David, whom you have prayed for, was called home on January 9. I could not be sad even though earthly separations can be sorrowful. I could almost see and hear family members, gone on before, greeting him with "Welcome home, Ballman (his nick name). Welcome home." What a happy reunion there will be one day!

Opportunities were made available to share the Good News with several who visited. I wish I could say all responded and perhaps they will. They showed great interest and for some it was the first time to hear about God's plan of salvation. Please pray that seeds will bring fruition. Two Japanese girls from Fukuoka, Japan, have joined our staff. One is a new Christian, and we are praying for the other one, Mariko, to accept Christ. Please help us pray for her. We have quite an international staff: one teacher from Australia; two teachers each from Japan, the Philippines, and the USA; another lady soon to arrive from the Philippines; and for this week a teacher from Finland who had taught here in 1992-1996. We all speak English in order to communicate.

Please continue to pray for the Chinese, my family, and for me. God is listening and He is answering. Do stay in touch.

In His Love, Mama/Sue

Chinese Christians cherish special days to honor and to show reverence and appreciation to our risen Savior.

Blessing of Easter 1993

On Palm Sunday Peng Zhao Deng and I left at 7:45 a.m. for Flower Lane Church, a good twenty-five-minute ride on crowded bus #20. We were forced to wait for the third bus, as the first two were so packed that people were standing on the steps and made it impossible for the doors to close. When the third bus arrived, we elbowed and jabbed our way in, as did "umpteen" others. We couldn't move an inch in either direction, but at least we were on board.

The horn blew constantly to alert cyclists, taxis, and pedestrians of oncoming #20! At the next ten stops, people dismounted as others pushed in even as departing passengers tried to exit. At our stop, the vehicle was so packed that my shoe laces were pulled loose, and I was afraid of losing my only decent pair of black slippers. Peng Zhao Deng was pulling my left arm while an unknown behind me pushed so hard that I finally squeezed through. I felt like a wreck but was reluctant to check for fear that I would look like one, too.

As we walked the short distance from the stop to Flower Lane Church, beggars shook empty cups in front of us for a handout. Down the narrow street and through the courtyard where stools had been arranged for the overflow congregation, Peng Zhao Deng and I made our way to the reserved seats for foreigners. That Chinese must forfeit space in their church for us makes me uncomfortable. There was no electricity so an emergency PA system had been put into use. Pre-worship hymn practice was in progress with great fervor and enthusiasm.

After the forty choir members wearing white robes marched in singing "All Hail the Power," Pastor Huang preached on "The Way of the Cross." A three-year-old boy, bright eyes shining, kept moving closer and closer and when offered a mint, he came over and sat with me. Both parents smiled their approval and I felt like a proud nai-nai (grandmother).

Communion followed worship, and bread was passed as in western churches. The fruit of the vine came in a large plastic cup placed on a tray accompanied by small plastic spoons.

Parishioners dipped their spoons into the cup, and then placed it on the tray following the one with the cup. God does not care about the procedure so long as the observance is done with reverence and dignity. Flower Lane Church, which can accommodate 1,000 people, was filled to overflowing, with people sitting on the stools in the courtyard; however, Communion was completed in good time as ushers and usherettes assisted with the distribution. I left with a deep sense of gratitude for the sacrifice our Lord made at Calvary and for the privilege of partaking with these dear people, who so deeply appreciated the opportunity for worship. For years, church services were prohibited by their government. Tears were shed. Silent lips whispered prayers as the elements were distributed. Chinese take Communion with great seriousness and much gratitude.

On Thursday, April 8, my dear musician friend, Ho, ate lunch with me. Beef noodles, peanut butter, apples, steamed bun, and Ching Ming cake (made of glutinous rice filled with seasoned turnip strips) was our menu. After lunch, we took a taxi up the mountain to the home of the elderly blind. We soon learned that over half had gone to church, yes, church on Thursday afternoon.

A young Christian man pushing his bike up the mountain offered to take us to the church, so off we went arriving forty-five minutes later as an eighty-one-year-old lady was preaching on "The Resurrection." The church is so small that the congregation divides into thirds. On Friday, the next third would come and the others would come on Sunday. The pastor, Mao, explained the plans for enlarging the building so that all could come on Sundays. Even though it was Thursday, the building was crowded with people of all ages.

The blind people waited until all the others left. Then Ho gave gloves, dresses, hats (caps), and shirts to them. Two men with perfectly bald heads left with one wearing a white cap with colored dots. The other was proud of his hot pink cap and pulled it down to his nose. After all, he couldn't see and had probably never worn a cap before. My heart was deeply blessed, my spirits lifted, and I felt an overwhelming sense of gratitude that God allowed me that special privilege with those special people.

A couple from a nearby school, parents of two little blonde heads with blue eyes, invited the Huanan teachers for a Good Friday celebration. A worship service was held followed by Holy Communion. My heart was blessed again as people from different countries, denominations, and backgrounds united in the fellowship and in the Spirit which make all Christians a part of the one body of Christ.

Easter Sunday arrived and off I went in the rain to a smaller church near Huanan. The lack of electricity on Sunday did not prevent the people from coming to church. The usual practice of hymns before worship took place by lighted lanterns. Red flowers being a symbol of happiness, choir members marched in wearing artificial red carnations on their white robes. The choir presented its Easter Cantata, followed by a sermon entitled "The Good News of the Resurrection." These dear people were endorsing the elderly pastor with head nodding and almost a chorus of "Amen." Services were scheduled from 8:30-10:00 and were still in progress when I had to leave at 10:00 for Huanan.

Huanan ladies had invited all of the foreign teachers in Fuzhou for brunch at 10:30 a.m. Back I rushed to assist with the last minute preparations. Candles and lanterns had been placed in strategic areas; however, electricity came on about midway through the meal. I think it's safe to mention that no one left hungry. All present had contributed so a feast fit for a king was consumed. One diner of Chinese origin brought Hall's cough drops! Only a Chinese would think of that. I even shared a treasured block of American cheddar purchased in Hong Kong. It quickly disappeared! Cheese is unavailable here and most of us miss it.

Following brunch, two of the teachers conducted a worship service. Again we were reminded of the greatest sacrifice ever made for mankind. Music was enhanced by a new piano donated to Huanan by Fujian Fine Arts Council. The couple who did the service was well prepared and did an excellent job.

Previous arrangements had been made with the Fujian Seminary to have Communion for foreigners. A newcomer to

Fuzhou, Reverend Harry T. Maclin, served the Lord's Supper in a most reverent and dignified manner. He and his wife are retired Methodist missionaries and make their home in Atlanta. We were blessed again as this part of our Easter Day reminded us of the magnitude of God's love.

Back at Huanan, we watched a video, "The Inn of Sixth Happiness." This is a moving true story of Gladys Aylward and her work as a missionary in China in the late 30's. Please get a copy and watch it with plenty of Kleenex handy. Her life story is available in book form entitled *The Small Woman* by Allen Burgess. I strongly recommend it; you can see the manner of Chinese life and lovely scenes which depict today's society.

Easter wasn't over yet. Four of us accepted the invitation to hear the Seminary Choir on Sunday night. In typical Chinese style, we were asked to sing. None of us claim to be vocalists but with grim determination we belted out "Amazing Grace" to the apparent approval of our audience.

The students attending my English class were asked to sing "Everyday in China." We sang it twice and then persuaded the audience to join us. I was very proud of those who sang so well in English.

Easter 1993 – a week I will always cherish and preserve in my memory. More importantly, I renewed my vows to serve, honor, and obey the One whose death on the cruel cross gives us the sweet assurance that we shall, also, experience resurrection.

In His love,
Mama/Sue

Hallelujah! What a Savior!
Easter 1994

Easter celebrations began early at Huanan, because some of us were eager to attend Chinese worship on Easter Sunday. Our Foreign Fellowship celebrated this special day on the Sunday before, March 27. Among countries represented were Sweden, Holland, Finland. Australia, Canada, and, of course, the USA. In all languages, the message was the same, "Christ the Lord is risen today! Hallelujah!"

The following Friday, the English class at the Fujian Seminary "lifted the rafters" with "He Arose, "Were you There," and many more hymns related to Easter. The teacher assistant slipped outside as we sang and hid the duck eggs they had carefully decorated with felt tip pens. Small children have never enjoyed finding eggs any more than these young men and women did on that day!

Good Friday night was dark, dismal, and rainy. Holy Communion was being observed at the church nearest Huanan. In spite of the inclement weather, my Chinese-Australian friend and I joined a church crowded with people who came to partake of the elements of the Last Supper in appreciation of the sacrifices Jesus made for us at Calvary. What a blessing to see the gratitude on the many faces of those who treasure the opportunity to participate in this ordinance of our Lord!

Easter Sunday sunrise services were held at many Protestant churches. Choirs and congregations sang again of the risen Savior. People came for their 6:00 a.m. service and were back for the 9:00 a.m. regular worship. Cups of Chinese Christians are never filled. The "Good News" is never too long or too tiring for them.

The regular service at the church I attended began at 8:30 a.m. Words are inadequate to describe the feelings of joy and ecstasy as fifty choir members marched in behind twenty small children singing a Chinese hymn, "Hallelujah Morning." The words and music were written by a pastor and professor in Nanjing Seminary. It was a happy privilege to be able to sing along with these saints of God.

The Easter Cantata was conducted by Professor Li from Fujian Seminary. The children's, youth, and adult choirs all joined to sing hymns related to the Resurrection of Christ. Pastor Chen preached a moving sermon on "How Deep the Love of God."

Baptisms are held in many churches on the Sunday nearest Christmas and Easter Sunday, but in this church, they are held periodically. Thirty-one candidates were admitted this day into full fellowship, and all were young people except three middle-aged men. My cup was filled and continues to run over.

Easter Sunday night I attended the celebrations at the Fujian Seminary. The choir filled with strong young voices again blessed my soul as they sang of "Victory in Jesus"; solos, duets, quartets, and short dramas, all telling of God's love for man, began at 7:00 p.m. and ended two hours later. Chinese Christians love our Lord and never seem to tire of celebrating His birth and Resurrection.

What a privilege to be an eye witness to this depth of devotion! Easter 1994 – I'll never forget it.

The Baptist World Alliance, Southeast Asian Directors met at Nanjing Seminary April 7-12, 1994. Yes, I was able to attend and met wonderful Baptist leaders from the Philippines, Malaysia, Korea, Japan, Indonesia, Singapore, Australia, some European countries, Canada, and the USA. One leader, Dr. Denton Lotz, now president of BWA, had visited Nanjing in 1991 and eaten dinner in my apartment with several others on his team. I felt humbled to be a listener with such a group.

My weekend was doubly blessed by seeing former students now working, visiting Southeast University, enjoying lunch with former colleagues, attending St. Paul's Church (my home church in Nanjing), and meeting YMCA friends and seminary staff which now has several former members of my English classes as faculty members. Many reports given at the conference were made by some of "my boys." I rather felt like a proud mother hen of her brood of chicks!

A very special person among the delegates was Sam Way, a friend and neighbor of former President Jimmy Carter's. President Carter wants to help Chinese students study at Mercer Baptist University, Atlanta, Georgia. We hope to get scholarships for a few deserving students to further their education. Please, pray for this endeavor.

My life has been so blessed by God. How fortunate to have a Spiritual Father who cares for me. Praise, glory, and honor all go to Him! Please, continue to pray for the Chinese and for me. I only wish you could be here to see the great things He is doing.

Easter 1996

The sky was overcast and gray, but when I walked into Pu Chen Church, the environment took on an immediate change. The church was packed with people filling every inch of space, crowding even the aisles, and overflowing the three balconies. I had to weave through worshipers to reach Emmanuel, my statistician friend who had asked in January, "Can you tell me how I can become a Christian?" Now my interpreter in church, he spotted me as I entered and eagerly waved his hand from about midway in the sanctuary. I wondered why all of the frenzy. When I finally reached him, he said, "The lady from Huanan is waiting for you up front." Services were to begin at 8:30 a.m. and it was already 8:15. I was led to the platform where the pianist and the Huanan lady both tried to dress me in a white robe bearing a big pink posey (flower). Being properly dressed, I took a seat and suddenly realized a big, red plastic empty cross to my right had been electrified. From this position, I could look directly into hundreds of expectant faces just waiting for the forty-five robed choir members to march in as everyone sang "Christ the Lord Is Risen Today." Emotions overwhelmed me and tears trickled down as I watched the young, the middle-aged, and the elderly sing of our risen Lord. The expressions of praise and gratitude filled my heart and soul.

The choir did a superior job with the Easter Cantata. Three young musicians – a flutist, a violinist, and a pianist played several numbers. I felt a tinge of nostalgia when the notes of "The Old Rugged Cross" filled the air. Soloists, duets, trios, quartets, and the youth group – all did a great job as they sang of the sacrifice Jesus made for us. What a great blessing to see and hear Chinese raising their voices to their risen Savior.!

Near the end of the two-and-a-half hour service, I was programmed to sing with a group of four others. They chose "Softly and Tenderly" as the special. Actually, it was appropriate as an invitation hymn. I felt very humble and honored to participate in a small way in this service of wonder and praise.

Pastor Chen gave a fairly short sermon of only forty-five minutes, during which usherettes distributed hard-boiled eggs to everyone present. I was a bit surprised when ladies with big buckets filled with eggs began to circulate throughout the audience. Pastor Chen used this symbol as an illustration for new life in Christ, impressive and different.

Services finally ended with many people kneeling around the altar weeping and praying. I wish all of you could have been a witness to this great occasion.

When Emmanuel and I were about to leave, the choir director said, "Wait a minute." Photo albums were presented as a gift of appreciation to all those who did specials. Chinese are like Christ in that respect – they never stop giving, even when they can't afford it.

My heart continues to rejoice in a God who loves us so much that Jesus gave His life for us, and for the privilege of seeing how Christ brings peace, joy, and love into hearts who accept and worship Him. Hallelujah! What a Savior! We must share this Good news.

Easter 1998

Easter had a wonderful prelude at Flower Lane Church on Palm Sunday, the third Sunday. Communion is observed each third Sunday as well as on the first Sunday. Chinese Christians dare not miss Communion.

My interpreter friend, Eli, was waiting in the narrow street outside the gate that opens into the courtyard of the church. Because of the masses of people, we squeezed through the emerging crowd and were literally pushed along with those trying to enter for the 10 a.m. service. Finally, we made it to the vestibule and spotted places for two people, so we took our seats as the elements of Communion were still being distributed inside the sanctuary.

I had not really noticed the rather tall Chinese man sitting to my right until he greeted me in English. I learned that he is from Auckland, New Zealand, a business man and a very happy Baptist. He and his wife became Christians six years ago, and his knowledge and love for our Christ just blessed my heart as he talked about his Chinese church in New Zealand and about God's many blessings. I felt I had had a visit with a close relative after conversing with him. We are relatives, indeed, in our heavenly Father's family.

After hearing a moving sermon about the triumphal entry and the praise due our Jesus, Betts and her interpreter, James, joined Eli and me for a delicious lunch of identifiable food at a Chinese restaurant. Surprise! Surprise! My new friend and brother from New Zealand came to the same restaurant with a pastor from Malaysia and Alden, my former seminary student in Nanjing. Alden, their acting host, enjoys the food at this particular restaurant. I counted this fortuitous meeting an additional blessing as they ate very near us.

Saturday before Easter, I received from Cooperative Baptist Fellowship (CBF) in Hong Kong an e-mail message informing me that the United Board would support me through CBF and Amity Foundation. Hallelujah! PTL! Rejoice with me! This means that I can stay in China and continue to work through Amity and be affiliated with Southern Baptists whose platform I totally accept and endorse. My heart overflowed with gratitude to all the officials in Nanjing, Hong Kong, New York, and Atlanta who worked through this for me. What a wonderful time to receive this reassuring news. If God is for us, who can be against us? (Matthew 12:30 KJV)

Easter morning was overcast and gray but not in Flower Lane Church. A huge empty cross covered with greenery and lined with small white lights was placed in the center and back of the choir loft behind the pulpit. Three choirs in white robes with red stoles marched in with young people leading, followed by the children's choir and then the darling cherubs with strips of purple metallic over their robes. A precious five-year-old boy sang in English "I'm so Glad God Made Me." I needed Kleenex after he finished because it reminded me of my grandson, who has black hair and brown eyes and who sang a solo part when he was four years old in the Christmas Cantata at his church. The childish, innocent voice brought back a precious memory. All the music was well done with solos, duets, and choruses. I think Jesus was pleased with this service.

The pastor used Matthew 28:1-7 and John 20:19-21 as scriptural texts. He did an excellent job as he preached on the resurrected Christ and the peace that comes to those who put their faith and trust in Him. My heart was blessed again when I saw the interest and attention of the worshipers as the scriptures were explained. As usual, the altar again was surrounded by those waiting to rededicate or make a profession of faith. Surely the Spirit was at work in this place.

My good friend from Mississippi, now teaching at Huanan, invited her "housemates," her Foreign Affairs officer (a good Christian lady), and me to have lunch in a nearby restaurant. Again the food was delicious, the fellowship sweet, and everyone spoke English so that all conversations could be understood by all. It was a wonderful way to conclude a special season of the year, Easter.

Easter 1999

Jesus is alive, and many Chinese in Fuzhou filled churches all over this city and publicly were baptized, acknowledging their faith and trust in our living Lord. Easter Sunday was a joyous occasion among the Christians. Hallelujah, what a Savior!

In my church alone, 150 people were baptized. After the services the altar rail was crowded with others kneeling as they were asking Jesus into their lives. Tears flowed freely and prayers were audible as the very Spirit of God touched the hearts of these dear people. What a privilege to be a witness to such a movement of the Holy Spirit. During the worship service two choirs sang many of the familiar Easter hymns. A small child sang "Because He Lives," and the hymns ended with the Hallelujah Chorus. My emotions ran from tears to exultation. Intense humility filled my heart to think that He did it all for me.

On Good Friday, a former student rang and asked whether I would come to her company. Her manager had suggested this idea. I was a little suspicious of such an invitation, but since I had some free time, I consented. One of the employees was having a birthday, and the staff was going to a very nice restaurant for lunch. Because my student had told the manager that I am a Christian, I was invited so that a blessing could be asked before we ate. This took place in a public restaurant in Fuzhou. In spite of what you may hear or read about Christian freedom in China, I have never felt fearful or threatened by saying grace before eating out, no matter which place we were dining.

Also, many churches held Communion services on Good Friday. The atmosphere was one of humility and gratitude as the elements of Communion were shared. Surely the Spirit of God was in this place. I believe Jesus was pleased as He observed from His heavenly home.

A new friend and a former Buddhist was among those baptized in my church. She told me that as a Buddhist she had never experienced such a deep peace and joy before. She shared the Jesus film with her husband, also a Buddhist, and the next day he told her that Jesus appeared to him but that he had never seen Buddha. She is praying that he will accept Jesus as well. You help us pray for his salvation, please. Many more Chinese are ready to know the plan of salvation but the workers are too few. Pray that others will feel the urge to come over and help with the harvest. Blessings await those who respond.

In three months classes will end. Pray that all of my students will come to know and accept Christ into their life.

In His Loving Care,
Mama/Sue

CHAPTER 11

Chinese Angels

"For he shall give his angels charge over thee, to keep thee in all thy ways."
   (Psalm 91:11 KJV)

Webster's New World Dictionary defines the word angel as a messenger from God, a guiding spirit or influence, and a person regarded as beautiful, good, or innocent. From biblical times to modern day, many people have felt, if not seen, these supernatural spirits we call angels. In Genesis 24 one can read of Abraham's encounter with God and the very promise of God in verse 7 (KJV) where it is written, "...Unto thy seed will I give this land; he shall send His angels before thee...."

Billy Graham and others have written books containing stories of encounters with God's messengers and guides (angels). To these I would like to share times when angels seen or unseen influenced, protected, and helped me or one of my students.

On September 11, 1990, two Chinese friends, Wen Lin, Wei Wei, my brother Joe, and my son, Glenn, came to see me off at Raleigh Durham Airport, Raleigh, N.C. I was returning to Southeast University in Nanjing, China, to continue teaching duties with the English Department. As handshakes, hugs, and tears abounded, my son slipped an envelope into my hand. "This is from my church," he said. My big luggage had been checked, and the carry-on was locked, so I dropped the envelope into the only available bag, my pocket book, and thus caused an uneasiness I had to endure for the next twelve to fifteen hours, while en route to Hong Kong. From the feel of the envelope, I knew it contained money. Later, my son explained why it was cash instead of a check. "You are going back earlier than our pastor and missions chairman realized, not leaving enough time to get the money in the bank and a check written." The donation was collected on Sunday; I left the very next day!

Throughout the trip from Raleigh-Durham Airport to Hong Kong via Chicago O'Hare and Los Angeles airports, I checked periodically to see whether that envelope was still in place. From time to time, I would nap while hanging onto that pocketbook under the blanket furnished by the airline. Another surprise awaited me in Hong Kong!

Following the other passengers from that 747 flight, I made my way to luggage claim only to discover that mine did not arrive on that flight. Two airport attendants, whom I had asked for assistance and advice, said, "Let us see your tickets!" Of course, I carefully opened my pocketbook to reveal the ticket and just as carefully closed it. "Your luggage is either lost or will come in on another flight. You should go over to Lost Luggage and report this," they advised.

Looking around for Lost Luggage signs, I passed several carousels and lo and behold beside one of them, which had stopped, were my two large bags. No need for Lost Luggage Claim now. Obviously, they had been sent on a different flight from mine. This confusion often happens when transfers must be made on longer trips.

My hostess, Ava Shelby, wife of the CSI (Corporate Service International) leader working in Hong Kong, met me and by taxi we were soon in their flat, where I was to spend the night. Jet lag made bed time sound very inviting. Retiring to the designated room, I opened my pocketbook to get the envelope containing the money, but it was not there! I dumped its full contents on the bed. Still no envelope! When? Who? Where? The last time I checked on the plane, it was there. What should I do? Call my son and tell him I had lost an amount of his church's money, and I still did not know how much? Scream? Cry? Call the airline? Airport? I did not tell the Shelbys of this dilemma. There had to be an explanation. Oh, so, it must have been one of the baggage men at the carousel. As I opened my pocketbook one of them inched a little nearer, I thought. Could he have in a split second and with a swift movement picked the envelope out of my purse? Pondering these possibilities through my mind, I unlocked and unzipped the carry-on bag to remove my diary to record the day's events. Now it is September 12, 1990. I had lost a day crossing the International Date Line. I opened the diary to September 11, words failed me, tears blinded me! There was the envelope in my diary with the $631.00 my son had given me.! It was tucked between the pages where I was to write the activities of September 12. The unseen hand of God or His protective angel had miraculously taken it from my pocketbook and placed it where I would be certain to see it. After reporting that miracle and rejoicing with my friends, I slept well that night. Believe in angels? You know I do!

The first Sunday that I rode the bus to church without a friend, I felt like a sixteen-year-old who had just received his driver's license. After worship, a group of foreigners had lunch at Jing Ling Hotel, a fairly western hotel in Nanjing. Now to get back to campus by bus alone was the next endeavor. Number 3 bus stop was near the hotel, so I had no problem in boarding it. Peter, a young man from Oregon, wrote Si Pai Lu in English and in Chinese for me so I could show it to the bus conductor. She would tell me when to get off; however, another passenger saw the note and argued with the conductor. In the meantime, the bus continued to discharge passengers, and I was concerned we would pass my stop. At the next stop, I got off and began walking the direction that seemed right to me. Nothing familiar came into sight. After walking some distance, I came to a street on my left and decided this must be the way to campus. It was Sunday afternoon and Chinese take naps after lunch. The street was desolate, not one person in sight.

I walked and walked for several more minutes, when suddenly it was as if someone pushed me from behind, and stumbling to keep from falling, I reached out to touch the wall I was passing. Suddenly the gate a few feet in front of me opened and a young girl came through. She did not close the gate and when I arrived there and looked through it, my heart skipped and clapped. There was the big green dome of the auditorium on the campus of Southeast University, the university where I was stationed!

I did not see who pushed me, and when I turned back to see the young girl who came through the gate, she had disappeared! The push caused me to look to the right and the girl (angel) appeared through a gate I never knew existed. Angels are beings sent by God to help when we least expect them. Yes, I do believe in angels.

During a weekend trip to Shanghai with three of my foreign colleagues, we met Matthew Ying Teng. He had been a medical student and was editor of the school's newspaper. He had been expelled for some of his comments related to Christianity. He told us that the Party leader on campus was responsible for his expulsion. Once expelled, students are not allowed to enter another university regardless of the dismissal charges. He told us that he is the fifth generation of Christians in his family.

His family had suffered much because they would not denounce their Christian beliefs. His mother spent two years in prison for allowing people to worship in their home during the Cultural Revolution (1966-76). Churches and schools were all closed during these infamous years. One uncle had been in prison for many years because he continued to maintain his Christianity. His father had been a pilot with the Chinese Airline but was fired because he would not refrain from attending church. "But in all of our troubles, we know that God loves us and we plan to continue worshiping Him," Matthew said. Nanjing was only a four-hour train ride from Shanghai, so from time to time I would go back to see this devoted Christian family. "We would like for you to visit our home," Matthew said, "but we are under constant surveillance. It would not be safe for you or for us." So I would spend the nights in the Conservatory of Music, and we would meet for meals in a nearby restaurant.

Feeling concern and deep compassion for them, especially for Matthew, I contacted my family and church friends, as well as Campbell University, Buies Creek, N.C. After learning of his situation, all were willing to help. A fund was begun, Campbell was considering a scholarship, and plans were taking shape for him to continue his education in the U.S.A.

A few months later, I went to Shanghai alone to give an update on the possible scholarship at Campbell and the fund being established by my family and my home church, Ross Baptist, Windsor, N.C. Again I checked in at the Conservatory of Music. Matthew and his parents came over and took me out for dinner, which we thoroughly enjoyed.

After arriving back at the Conservatory of Music, Matthew's mother took a double jade ring and insisted on placing it on the fourth finger of my right hand. It was her mother's wedding ring and very expensive at that. I had it appraised in a jewelry store in Hong Kong, and the jeweler wanted to buy it! No way would that be the case.

When I left for Nanjing the following morning by train, Matthew accompanied me to the train station and stayed with me until boarding time.

The waiting room for all passengers wanting soft, cushioned seats is on the second floor of the train station. To get to the train, one must go down many steps. I had a carriage cart to move my luggage. While I was standing at the head of those steps with the carriage cart folded in one hand, luggage and pocketbook in the other, people literally almost ran over one another to get to their cars. I learned later that more tickets for hard board seats were sold than there were seats available. This accounted for the mad rush not only to get on board but also to get a seat. Hard seats were not numbered as were soft seats.

Looking helplessly around as throngs kept rushing by on each side, I prayed, "Father, how will I ever get down these steps and to car #12, where my seat number is 14A?" Suddenly, out of that unruly crowd, a young Chinese man wearing a white shirt and dark pants appeared before me. "Show me your ticket," he said in perfect English. He picked up the luggage, took the carriage cart, and almost ran down those steps. In the meantime, I was scrounging for some money to tip him as we trotted to car #12.

When we reached the car, he handed luggage and cart to the attendant. By now all other passengers had boarded. I looked down to get the money and turned to give it to my helper. He was nowhere to be seen! God had answered my prayer! He sent a Chinese angel who could speak English to my rescue. Believe in angels? You must know that I do.

Pam, a teacher from N.C., was having a church wedding in Zheng Zhou. Since she was an Amity teacher, several of us from Fuzhou went to see her wed a Chinese English teacher, a very handsome one at that. Franklin and Jean Woo from California were in the area visiting Amity personnel. Pam planned the time for her wedding around their visit so that the Reverend Franklin Woo could give the vows in Chinese and in English.

The wedding and reception went well. The bus trip back to Fuzhou was pleasant, and we arrived there around 4:00 p.m. that Sunday afternoon.

To return to Fujian Medical University, my school, I first arrived at the central bus station and then took another bus. I knew that bus Route 51 would pass nearest our school, so I was on the last leg of the weekend journey.

After I got off the bus at the right stop and was walking by the hospital on campus, a young man I did not know came up and said, "Let me take your bag. I know where you live." I had never seen him before. Reluctantly, I let go of the bag, and we passed through the gate toward my building.

Two more surprises awaited me. I told him as we reached the building that the bag was not heavy and I could take it upstairs. "No! I know you live in flat number 403 and I will take it for you," he insisted. Up the four flights he went with me tagging along behind. When we reached #403, he set the bag down. As my back was turned to him while I was unlocking the door, I turned around to tip and thank him. He was nowhere to be seen, not on the landing, not going down the four flights which were visible from my location. Another Chinese angel dressed as a young man had been sent by God to help. Believe in angels! You must know that I do.

There were other occasions during those thirteen years when at my greatest point of need, the right person (angel) would appear out of the mass of people to offer the exact assistance needed. Yes, there are Chinese angels!

CHAPTER 12

Experiences with the Blind

"...Inasmuch as ye have done it unto one of the least of these my brethren, ye have done it unto me."
  (Matthew 25:40 KJV)

I had been in China only a short time when many blind people captured my attention. Many were in churches, several were pianists, and a choir in one church was made up entirely of blind people. It was not unusual to see blind beggars in busy sections of the city. Poor lighting in homes, inadequate diet, and lack of needed medical attention probably accounted for many of the visually impaired. My sympathy always went out to them.

The Fujian School for the Blind in Fuzhou was built by the United Nations and could accommodate three hundred and fifty students. There are enough blind to fill the school, but too many parents are financially unable to pay the two thousand Chinese dollars per semester. The building is well built and designed for easy access and maneuverability of students. A wing of the building unoccupied by blind residents was rented to students from a nearby university. It concerned me that many who needed this kind of training and care were unable to enroll because of the lack of needed funds. A building designed for three hundred and fifty students never enrolled over eighty during my nine years in Fuzhou. My reaction was typical of a Chinese expression heard frequently, "What a pity!"

A young Chinese English teacher, a devout Christian, became my close friend. Her husband is blind and teaches music at the school for the blind. Through them I learned of a widowed mother with three blind children. The older son is totally blind, and the daughter and younger son have very little vision. The mother could not afford both clothing and food as her job was removing oysters from the shells. I was told she earned less than $5.00 (USA) each week.

The older boy, age nine, had been in school but when the father died, the poor mother could not meet tuition requirements. The sister, age eight, and the younger brother, age seven, had never been enrolled in school. Pan Yi Ling, a teacher friend, informed me of this family and their needs. My heart was deeply touched by their circumstances.

In 1996 when I learned of their situation, I shared it with my family and friends in the States. Concerned hearts made funds available to get the three siblings in school. Their happy faces and broad smiles were our reward!

Another student was brought to my attention in 1997. He was enrolled in the school but when his father died, the school was about to send him home because his mother could not pay the tuition cost of 1,500 Chinese yuan per semester at that time. (It has risen to 2,000 Chinese yuan per semester now.) This student is a high achiever in all of his classes, learning Chinese Braille and the beginning skills of massage. Once again, my brother Joe and his close friend, Lib, provided the funds to keep him in school. The four students are doing quite well. The eldest is quite proficient with the accordion, the sister plays the piano, and the youngest brother enjoys playing the trumpet.

The fourth child shouted, "I like sports more than music!" Though legally blind, he won first place in handicap track competition on the local as well as the national level. He is an albino, a good student, and a skilled track star.

Pan Yi Ling and I made periodical visits to take needed items and small gifts to the four. On one such occasion, the track star presented me with one of his four gold medals won in the National Competition. My first reaction was to refuse it. He earned it, he should keep it! Through Pan Yi Ling, the translator, he said, "Please take it. I wouldn't be here if it were not for you!" At that, I was obligated to accept it but later gave it to my brother Joe, who considers it one of his greatest treasures.

The music teacher had become a Christian. Besides teaching music, he decided that students needed to know about God's love, so in his classes he was sharing the Good News with them. Formalized Bible classes are not allowed in schools; only in the seventeen Protestant seminaries can Christianity be taught in China. God inspired Chen En Jun, the music teacher, to tell his students about the plan of salvation through Christ. Now they know the song, "Jesus Loves Me."

The presence and background of many students were heartbreaking. A three-year-old girl, deserted by her parents at the gate of the school, immediately won my heart. A very intelligent, excellent student, who did not know her surname, lived in the school. She knew of no family member, so Pan Yi Ling became her surrogate mother. She spends holidays and summer vacations with Pan Yi Ling and her family.

As time passed, the girl matured rather quickly and excelled in Chinese Braille as well as massage classes. She craved acceptance and attention so on my visits, I would take a special gift to her. She liked jewelry very much.

Shortly before I left China permanently, she gave me a full-body massage such as I had never had! I was wearing a friendship ring on my right hand. As she massaged my arms, hands, and fingers, she kept going back to the fourth finger on my right hand. She twisted the ring and mumbled in Chinese. From her tone of voice, I knew she was admiring the ring. When the hour-long massage ended, I removed the ring from my finger, and I think God must have shrunk it some. I placed it on the fourth finger on her right hand over her squeals and tears of delight. She danced for joy and almost broke my neck with her tight squeeze of gratitude. What a privilege to share such a small thing which brought her so much happiness! She filled my cup to over flowing many times.

A small, malnourished five-year-old boy stole my heart the first time I saw him. He had just recently been placed in the school. He had a little vision but his eyes rolled and thus focusing was difficult. He was craving for someone to show him affection. One day as he sat in my lap, he reached up, stroked my hair and face, and said, "Ni piaoliangde" (You're pretty.) Had my circumstances allowed it, I would have adopted him on the spot! Each time I visited the school after his arrival, he was my personal guide, holding my hand as we toured living quarters, classrooms, and the dining room. At times he almost seemed visual as he led downstairs and upstairs. In his future, I hope a young lady will capture his heart, and he can guide her as they establish a home together. He is a deserving student.

A ten-year-old boy had been abandoned and left to beg on the streets. A Christian Chinese rescued him and brought him to the school. He was twelve years old when I met him. His interest and talent were in music and the different musical instruments. He was learning to play guitar, mandolin, flute, trumpet, accordion, and piano, but his favorite was the erho, a two-stringed instrument played with a bow. His face would light up at the very mention of an erho, and no one could resist tapping or clapping along with his music. I pray that he can teach one day and share his skills as well as his love for happy musical tunes. His students would be fortunate to have such a talented one as their teacher.

One of the foreign teachers donated a badly damaged suitcase to the school. It was given to a young teenager, an orphaned boy. He had previously used plastic bags and cardboard boxes to store his belongings. The lid was lopsided and could not be closed, the handle was loose on one side, and the buckles were bent out of shape, yet he was so very pleased to have a real suitcase for his clothes. It was good that I am a Christian; otherwise, my disappointment would have been expressed to that donor, probably in not a very kind way. Actually, I was furious, so much so that I went to a store and bought a suitcase on wheels for the young teenager. I could hardly wait to take the new suitcase to him. He couldn't see it but he "looked it over" with his hands, tracing the inside pockets, lining, zippers, etc. After he removed his belongings from the bedraggled old suitcase and almost with reverence put them into his new suitcase, he said, "No one ever gave me such a nice gift before." His tears and facial expression of gratitude melted my heart. Little did he know how he had blessed me!

Each spring the children gave a performance for parents, friends, supporters, and interested parties. How proud they were in colorful crepe paper costumes they could not see as they sang, played instruments, and did simple drills in time with the music! Their pleasure and happiness in performing were well worth the time required to practice and perfect their musical exhibitions. I always looked forward to this special event as it was obvious how much it meant to them.

My departure was nearing and I had to return to say good-bye to the precious students and staff. On previous occasions, I had looked forward to visiting but this would be a final farewell. Emotions were running a mile high as my grandson and his friend accompanied me to the school. They sensed the stress I was experiencing. It was good they were with me.

The van pulled into the parking area of the school. Word soon spread that the Americans had arrived. Soon the grounds were filled with students eagerly waiting, knowing a surprise bag would be given to each.

Next we moved into the large conference room where they presented a "Farewell Musical Program." Many solos in songs, musical instruments, group singing, and words of thanks from staff and students consumed the afternoon. Earlier, I had taught them "You Are My Sunshine," which they sang tearfully. My grandson, his friend, and I were then asked to sing it back to them. Our voices cracked with emotions as we tried to reciprocate in song.

The mother of the three siblings and the mother of the fourth recipient had been brought in for the occasion. Receiving their hugs of tearful gratitude brought a flood of tears to my eyes. The director, president, staff, students, my grandson, his friend, and I were almost drowned in the tears that flowed so freely. No funeral could have produced more tears.

It was time to leave and the four students I had supported clung to me as if to say, you can't go. They followed us to the van which was waiting to take us to my college. One of the hardest experiences of my life was to pull away but not before assuring them and their mothers that financial support would continue until they graduated. With my brother Joe, his friend, Lib, and me, and with God's help, we will see them through graduation!

Ho Ru Ying was piano teacher in Huanan Women's College when I met her in 1992. Her warm smile, gentle spirit, and soft-spoken words endeared her from the start. Like many others of her age group, she had experienced hardships during the Cultural Revolution (1966-1976). Her faith in God and concern for others did not allow her to harbor feelings of hostility and hatred. Rather, like many other Christians she told how she felt sympathy, pain, and sorrow even for the abusers. Often I heard her quote the words of Christ, "Love your enemies...do good to them that hate you, and pray for them which despitefully use you, and persecute you." (Matthew 5:44). Ho Ru Ying practiced Christ's words along with prayers for her enemies. Sometimes she would sing hymns which "became one of my favorite pastimes," she said. She had a beautiful alto voice that was most pleasant to hear

Ho Ru Ying, director of a home for blind people in Fuzhou, obviously loved all the residents and worked for their best interest. Many blind pianists in the thirty-two Protestant churches in Fuzhou were trained by Ho years earlier. Besides teaching them to play piano, she taught hymns and explained God's plan of salvation to them. God used this dear lady to share His love with them. How they respected and loved her!

One afternoon after I walked over to Ho's home, she and I went to a factory where blind employees were making paper bags for a cement factory in Shanghai. Hands were in constant motion, measuring, cutting, gluing, pressing together and smoothing the sides of the bags. No conversations were heard, only the sounds of the bags being made by these sightless people. Ho explained that each had a daily quota, so there was no time for them to converse on the job. If quotas were not met, deductions would be made in salaries of those who had failed to meet their required number. As we turned to leave this beehive of activity, Ho turned to me and with sheer joy in her eyes and voice she said, "Sue, they are all Christians!" She made sure that all of them knew of God's love for people!

This dear lady enjoyed cooking delicious Chinese dishes and inviting friends over to dine. One of her specialties was a rice, raisin, nut pudding served as a dessert. She liked greens very much and usually served them at every meal. Her income was quite limited, so as she grew more feeble, I would go by McDonald's or Kentucky Fried Chicken and take a lunch to her. So many times I heard her say, "I don't deserve this." To which I would reply, "You deserve only the best, nice lady." She would smile and in a most humble voice say, "Thank you so much. You are too kind to me." I disagreed with her and after the blessing, we would enjoy our fast food lunch together. A good cook, a kind soul, a great prayer warrior, and a Chinese angel on earth was this wonderful lady.

A friend in Stokes, N. C., sent a box of scarves, gloves, and warm caps to be given to these people. Ho was notified and at the appointed hour, we met at a church which many of the blind attended. They could be heard singing as they came with a sighted leader bringing them to the church. Each one had his/her hand on the shoulder of the person in front of him/her as they marched like small children obeying teacher's orders. Caps, gloves, and scarves were distributed to these precious women and men. In appreciation for their warm gifts, they showed gratitude by singing several hymns taught to them by none other than dear Ho. One man, who was completely bald, had an outstanding tenor voice. He received the last available cap which happened to be pink. When they lined up to leave the church, the "pink cap" was still singing in that wonderful tenor voice "How Great Thou Art." Ho had taught them this magnificent praise song, one of my favorites, too. How blessed I was and how grateful I felt to those dear Baptists in Stokes, N.C., who cared and shared!

Dear Ho became disabled in her last years and was moved to a nursing home. She lived only a short time before God called her home. I'm sure Christ must have met her at the gates of heaven to welcome this great lady in to enjoy the fruits of her labor. Ho is now resting peacefully and enjoying the heavenly rewards of labor while on earth. The four blind children whom I had supported and come to love have realized their goal and are gainfully employed as masseurs. When I returned in 2004, I saw them and they seemed quite happy to be earning money "to help their mother." What a blessing to help four underprivileged, deserving, peasant children to become self-supporting!

CHAPTER 13

Special Moments

"...for the hand of God hath touched me."
(Job 19:21b KJV)

Browsing through diaries I kept while in China reminds me how those precious comments made by students blessed and encouraged me daily. This chapter includes direct quotes from some very special students who enriched my stay in China (1988-2001). Also, some special moments are included.

May 20, 1989: "I was a child just walking along and suddenly the words just came out of my mouth, 'God bless me,' and this great feeling of love and peace came over me!" I think this was an election of John by the Holy Spirit since no relative of his was a Christian then.

May 23, 1989: "We should dress properly to visit you." Johnson and Sammy came to visit, dressed in white shirts, ties, and dark pants.

June 5, 1989: Esther quoted Romans 8:38-39 saying, "I am convinced that nothing can ever separate us from His love. Death can't, and life can't. The angels won't and all the powers of hell itself cannot take God's love away. Our fears for today, our worries about tomorrow, or where we are high above the sky, or in the deepest ocean – nothing will ever be able to separate us from the love of God demonstrated by our Lord Jesus Christ when He died for us." This happened the day after Tiananmen Square Massacre.

June 23, 1989: Eddie asked, "Will you teach me to sing 'Because He Lives'?"

June 24, 1989: Paul said, "When I listen to the minister, my heart feels so full." He was the first young man to tell me he was a Christian, having been led by a Canadian a few months before.

December 8, 1989: The Jing Ling Seminary English class sang Christmas carols today, "Silent Night," "It Came upon the Midnight Clear," etc. In my classes at Southeast University, we can sing only secular songs, as hymns are forbidden.

December 10, 1989: Don Whitehead, a friend from Vancouver, Washington, said, "You don't have students, you have disciples." I was humbled and flattered by his statement.

December 11, 1989: In a Christian Fellowship Meeting with Africans, Russians, and Caucasians, testimonies were being shared. One African said, "I was jailed in Russia for having a Bible. There was no need to call family or the embassy. I rang God's telephone!" Another Russian said, "I read my Bible and prayed, too. I was given back my Bible and released from jail." A tall African reported, "I found Christ in China, and even though I was reared in a Christian home I didn't really know Him until I came to China." A small African told of being knocked across the street by a motor bike. "God healed my broken bones and helped me to pass the examination so I could study in China."

December 16, 1989: Eight students helped to decorate my foot tall Christmas tree. They cut out small snowflakes and candy canes. Red crayons made the candy canes more realistic.

December 17, 1989: I received a gift package from my Bible class back home in Ross Baptist Church, Windsor, N.C. Among other things was a pair of much needed bedroom shoes.

December 19, 1989: William went shopping with me to buy Christmas supplies – pens, handkerchiefs, fruits, and large decorated candles.

December 21, 1989: The Foreign Language Department held

a Christmas party tonight. Santa Claus came in on a bicycle! The tree was surrounded by candles, and colored paper was put over the lights to create some color. The words "Merry Christmas: had been cut out along with snowflakes. These adorned the walls to make the occasion more festive. Each class was asked to perform, and my students sang "Jingle Bells" and "We Wish You a Merry Christmas."

December 22, 1989: Amity Office, my sponsoring organization, invited its foreign teachers to a party at Jing Ling Seminary. A small Chinese boy played Christmas carols on a keyboard, a little girl sang "Jingle Bells," and two daughters of an American couple did a typical Chinese dance using hand movements with fans. All of us enjoyed a nice meal.

That night I had a party for my seminary students. Li Yen played the flute, and we sang many Christmas carols. No gifts as the students are too poor and need to keep their small change. Each received a pad of paper and pen donated by a church group of young girls in West Chowan Baptist Association in northeastern North Carolina.

December 23, 1989: Today is Saturday and I spent it in a primary school. I told why people call themselves Christians and celebrate Christmas. I taught them "Jingle Bells," "Up on the Housetop," and "Santa Claus Is Coming to Town." No Christmas hymns are allowed in schools. The children seemed interested and responded with great enthusiasm.

December 24, 1989: He Hui Bing sang "O Holy Night" at church this morning. It has never been sung more beautifully in my opinion. She has an angelic voice to accompany her angelic face.

December 25, 1989: I taught classes for four hours today. China does not recognize Christmas as a national holiday. I talked with my family tonight. They were having a nice Christmas, and I was – until my precious grandchildren sang, "Away in a Manger." How I miss them!

December 31, 1989: I attended worship with African friends today. With their African drums and in strong voices, they sang and asked God to bless their motherland. I was deeply impressed and moved by their prayers and songs.

January 17, 1990: Jonathan happily exclaimed, "I feel joyful tonight. God's hand touched me! I feel power from Him. It was my birthday so I had two birthdays on the same day!" Later Jonathan was admitted to Southwestern Seminary in Ft. Worth, Texas.

January 28, 1990: Mark said, "God broke my heart but saved my soul!"

February 17, 1990: Chang Hong Wu said, "Would you give me a Bible, please? My grandmother is a Christian and my boyfriend is one, too." She accepted Christ soon after receiving the Bible.

February 18, 1990: John came and asked, "Could you give me three Bibles? I want to give them to my colleagues. I have told them about Jesus and they believe in Him, too!"

April 8, 1990: Alexander, Mike, and his wife, after experiencing baptism, explained, "We feel so clean on the outside but more clean on the inside!"

April 21, 1990: Bubba, a North Korean, upon making a profession of faith, said, "I am so happy. I will take God back to my country."

April 25, 1990: Today after church, a young man came up to me and began singing "Into My Heart." He was so proud to have remembered the words. He had sat in my seminary class on Friday and we sang many songs. He said, "I will teach this to children and older people in my village."

April 27, 1990: Dick prayed, "Thank you, God, for accepting me as your son."

April 29, 1990: A young lady minister, Wei-Li, just released from jail, said, "Now I have a deeper understanding of Ps.23:1, because God has proven to be a good Shepherd for me"

May 6, 1990: A ninety-three-year-old man, with his grandson on the back, rode his bike for one hour to get to church. "I want my grandson to know about the Jesus that has put peace and joy in my heart," he explained.

May 7, 1990: Betty made a profession of faith and said, "I feel raptured!"

May 9, 1990: Tonight Tom reported, "The road has a new light. I am a new man. Jesus Christ has given me peace."

May 10, 1990: Xiu Peng said, "When I was seventeen, my Christian mother persuaded me with these words, 'Trust in the Lord with all of your heart and do not rely on your own insight. In all your ways acknowledge him and He will direct your paths. (Proverbs 3:5-6 NRSV) I had accepted God in my head and in my thoughts, but this morning I invited Jesus into my heart and I know He loves me and will take care of me."

May 27, 1990: Li Ming reported, "My family is Christian but for a long time I didn't want to be called a Christian, but my family never gave up. They prayed for my salvation and now I finally realize that their faith and salvation could not save me, so today is the happiest day of my life! Jesus has saved me! My parents are happy but I am the happiest of all! "

May 28, 1990: Si Tu Tong, president of the YMCA in Nanjing, was sending a representative to a conference relative to YMCA affairs. The representative said, "I am a Christian inside but a Communist outside; I could not be a leader, unless I joined the Party. My faith is in Jesus Christ, not Communism."

June 1, 1990: At a speech contest, one student finished with, "Good night and may God bless you all." Then he pointed at me and said, "I see this judge at St. Paul's Church every Sunday." Neither of us suffered any repercussions.

June 2, 1990: After receiving Christ, Qin Mei said, "Now I have God as my father, Jesus is my brother, the Holy Spirit is in my heart!" She continued, "I will tell others about God and Jesus. I can't stop reading my Bible. I read it until 12:00 midnight!"

June 3, 1990: A young man reared as a Catholic joined a Bible study group and found Christ as his Savior. "The Holy Spirit is my constant companion," he said.

June 11, 1990: William had been sent to Beijing on business for his university. "I thought about you when I saw all of those churches. You had given me a Bible and I read John 3:16 and realized 'whosoever' meant me! Now I am so happy and at peace with Jesus in my heart."

June 18, 1990: Dick had an argument with a good friend who he thought was trying to "steal my girlfriend." After much dialogue, he prayed, "Thanks, God, for removing the anger and hurt from my heart."

June 18, 1990: Phillip, a new Christian, called to ask for a Chinese Bible and closed by saying, "God bless you on your trip back to see your family, but, please, come back to our University."

September 20, 1990: Ab De, a Moroccan and Muslim, came asking for a Bible in French, his native language. "If I change from Muslim to Christianity, I'd be executed if they knew," he said. He had accepted Christ and his family did not excommunicate him. "God is looking after me," he said.

October 19, 1990: Rebecca asked how to pray for a better understanding of the Bible.

October 21, 1990: On a very stormy night, riding back to our campus, Xiao Yu said, "God is my refuge and strength. In Him I put my trust!" How reassuring!

October 25, 1990: Patrick said, "It is a good treat to be in church."

November 8, 1990: Jim returned for a visit tonight. He was almost walking on air. "I am so happy. I don't have words to express how I feel. I want my wife to know Jesus. I want to go to church but I must go in plain clothes. In the military, we are told not to talk with foreigners. We are ordered not to go to church."

November 19, 1990: Jim came to keep me from being lonely! "How I wish someone had told me about Jesus earlier," he said. He was a captain in the People's Liberation Army and had been in the military for seventeen years.

December 1, 1990: William and Rose announced, "We went to William's village and got married last week!" There was no wedding, only a photo of the two and their signatures on the little red certificate.

December 7, 1990: Jack and Charles came asking if they could decorate my Christmas tree before the "Christmas Goody Man," or Santa Claus, came

December 9, 1990: Rebecca sat with me in church today. She said, "Jesus is like a bridge to God!"

December 17, 1990: Glenn's ears were frostbitten. I gave him a woolen scarf sent from Stokes Baptist Church in Pitt County, N.C. He said, "No one ever cared about my sore ears before." He later took fifty Bibles to his village.

December 25, 1990: As David remarked, "You are a good mother to everyone," he presented me a pin with the word "love" inscribed in gold letters. The gift and his words brought tears to my eyes because David could ill afford to buy the pin.

December 26, 1990: James Theodore said, "I am ready to

accept Jesus and I want my own Bible!"

December 27, 1990: Jim proudly reported, "Some of my military buddies want a Bible like mine!" Bobby said, "My Dad reads my Bible every day. Will you help him to become a Christian, too?"

December 30, 1990: James Theodore celebrated his first Communion today. "I feel so clean and pure inside," he smiled with tear-filled eyes.

January 2, 1991: Patrick's thesis and calculator were stolen today. He was given money to buy another calculator. "With my calculator and God's help, I will get my thesis rewritten before the term ends," he said. And he did!

January 3, 1991: Temperature was 0 degrees today. Mark received a warm scarf and gloves from those sent by friends in the USA. "Why do people who don't even know Chinese buy such nice gifts?" Expressions like this opened doors for sharing how God loves through others.

January 5, 1991: "Do you have any more Bibles? I have been telling my friends about this wonderful Book and they want to have one, too," Zheng Wei asked.

January 6, 1991: James Theodore squatted beside my chair in church and said, "Thanks for making a new man out of me!" To this I replied, "Not I, James, but the Holy Spirit of God made you a new man."

January 19, 1991: Jefferson became a Christian through a teacher he had in Beijing. "I saw Jesus last night. He told me I would be successful if I could go to Idaho University. Jesus will help me," he told me. He actually went to Idaho University and is still there as a doctor in the engineering department!

February 6, 1991: Robert from the English Department came to discuss his schedule for the spring term. He asked, "Can you get me a Bible and tell me how to be a Christian?"

March 9, 1991: Joanne came in tears saying, "I was fired by my boss because I am a Christian." She had won her boss' son to Christ.

April 2, 1991: Amos was quite excited when he came tonight. "My roommates asked why I am so happy and don't fret when I have problems. They want to be like me," he said. He went on, "They asked what kind of tonic I am taking and why I keep reading that same Book!" Then with a far-away look in his eyes he said, "People in my village are mostly illiterate but when they became Christian, robberies and disputes among angry neighbors have decreased. My roommates say, one day they may believe that Christian propaganda." Then he asked, "Will you help me pray for them?" Of course we did, even before he left my room.

April 3, 1991: Zhou Zhang left with the Spirit of God shining on his face and a Bible in his hand tonight. "Now I am God's child," he said.

April 20, 1991: As we left Charles' village, he turned back for one more glance and said, "One day there will be a church in my village, so my mom and sister can learn more about God."

April 25, 1991: William was very happy for two reasons today. "I will be baptized on Sunday and I got my visa to study in the USA today." Later, in 1995, he graduated from Kansas State University with a Master's in math. Today he is Superintendent of Chinese Sunday School in Kansas City, Kansas, and a consultant with H & R Block.

May 7, 1991: Elizabeth was reading Luke 2 and when she finished, she said, "I would like to see Mary, Joseph, and Baby Jesus!" The Bible is new to her and she is eager to know more about its teachings.

May 10, 1991: Huang Yin said, "I can't read the Bible fast enough. I read until 4:00 this morning."

May 12, 1991: Wade was waiting for me at church with a bouquet of flowers. "Today is the American Mother's Day, so I brought these to you!" Tears filled my eyes as I accepted them.

May 13, 1991: Edmond was very disturbed this afternoon. He explained, "One of my classmates is pregnant and doesn't even know who the father is. If the pregnancy is too advanced for an abortion," he said, "she will have the baby and then be put into prison, probably for life. The baby will have no identity and be placed in an orphanage." I was told this by several others as well as by Edmond, who is a Christian and is very much concerned for the classmate's future.

May 21, 1991: Jefferson prepared many documents for various universities in the USA and asked whether I would post them when I came home for summer vacation. "Of course, I will be happy to do that," I told him.

"My colleagues say I can't do this because it is too much trouble. I just ask God to help me and ideas just pop into my head and time flies as I work," he smiled. "Now I have finished the experiments and also my papers. I'll present one at the Conference for Chemical Engineers in Beijing in June. God helped me," he reiterated. He was admitted to Idaho University and now has a Ph.D. in Chemical Engineering.

May 22, 1991: Amos reported that his friends want to know why he has changed so much. They say, "You are more friendly and kindhearted now." Amos said, "I just smile and tell them, 'Jesus makes the difference' and then I explain about God and Jesus to them!"

May 26, 1991: A group of Campus Crusaders were on the streets tonight near Jing Ling Hotel. They were singing "I Surrender All" and "When I Survey the Wondrous Cross."

Patrick and Guo Ling, who were with me, asked, "Why are those people so happy?" This question opened the door to witness to them. Both became Christians that night!

June 7, 1991: "Can God understand Chinese? I want to talk to Him," asked Huang Yin.

June 15, 1991: "I wish you were not going back to America for the summer. I need your help to understand more about the Bible. Jesus is in my heart and I want to know more about Him," Jack said pleadingly.

June 20, 1991: "I will never forget December 1, 1990. That day you told me about Jesus and now I am telling my colleagues about Him. Some are ten years older than I am. They want to know more about how to become a believer," Jim reported. He went on, "I feel so pure when I go to church. People there are so friendly and kind. Scriptures give me courage and help me to love others more!"

June 21, 1991: Tom, Jack, and Wade came to see me off as I was leaving for summer vacation. In unison they said, "Do you have to go! Please come back before September. We need to know more about Jesus."

September 27, 1991: Huang Yin had made a list of questions from Bible reading during summer vacation. "I could hardly wait for you to return so you could help me understand the Bible better," she said.

October 11, 1991: Liu Su waited after several others had left and when we were alone, he said, "Please tell me how to be a Christian." After receiving Christ, he said, "I feel like a new person. I am so happy."

October 21, 1991: Patrick's father, the town's communist leader, said, "Please come and teach in our town. We need a teacher who cares about the students."

November 11, 1991: Shen Zheng Qun was so happy and excited as he made a profession of faith tonight. Through tears he said, "I feel happiness inside me, beside me, and around me."

November 17, 1991: Mike and Xiao Kong are Party Members but asked to become Christians. They agreed, "It is not safe as far as our government is concerned, but in God's care, we are even more safe."

November 19, 1991: Wade asked for two Bibles tonight, one for his girlfriend and one for a roommate. "They want to know about the Jesus I have told them about," he said.

December 4, 1991: Jim telephoned from Shanghai to inform me that he had celebrated his second Spiritual Birthday.

December 5, 1991: "I thought of killing myself when my girlfriend left me. I felt so defeated and then God came into my life and filled my heart with joy. Now I can see her and it doesn't hurt any more," Jimmy said.

December 6, 1991: "Please help me pray for the police. They encourage deceit and lies," Wade reported.

December 7, 1991: Paul, the pianist at St. Paul's Church in Nanjing, said, "When I play hymns, God controls my fingers. When I try to play secular music my fingers don't seem to do right. "

December 8, 1991: As Neil was given a hymnal this a.m. at church, his eyes sparkled. He had been given a Bible earlier. "I just can't read it fast enough. It makes me feel so peaceful and pure," he said.

December 15, 1991: Among the 150 candidates receiving symbolic baptism this a.m. were several of my students. Six joined me for lunch at Jing Ling Hotel, where I answered questions until 3:00 p.m.

December 18, 1991: Vlado, from Russia, opened his Christmas

present so very carefully. When he saw the Bible, he kissed it, kissed my hand, and with tears streaming said, "How can I ever thank you enough for this very special Book?" He went on to say, "I won my mother to Christ and we are asking God to help us to win my dad."

`December 22, 1991: It was raining as we left the African Fellowship. James ordered me, "Get on the back of my bike. I will take you to the bus stop!" The bike wobbled with the heavy load, but we made it without even a tire going flat.

December 25, 1991: I served Christmas brunch in my apartment for a Dutch couple, a German lady, a Russian, a Japanese, a Canadian, and four Americans. After the meal, all of us participated in a worship and praise service. "Silent Night" took on a deeper meaning for me that day as this international group using their native language celebrated the birth of our Savior for all peoples of the world.

January 10, 1992: As Matthew looked through a Life Magazine with pictures of what heaven is like, he said, "I want to go there when I die." After reading Genesis I and Galatians 5:22, he made a profession of faith.

January 16, 1992: Mike and Vlado came for dinner. Mike told of giving his heart to Christ last night. Vlado responded, "Now you are my brother!"

January 25, 1992: Lillian told about how she became a Christian through Campus Crusade. Her family rejected her as part of their family when they learned she had become a Christian. "But now I am a member of God's family and I will pray that my family will come to know my Jesus," she said as her tears flowed freely.

February 29, 1992: A well-known eighty-five-year-old communist leader was quoted as saying, "Communism will fall before Christianity," according to Si Tu Tong, President of Nanjing YMCA.

March 15, 1992: James Theodore said, "I've been reading I Corinthians and writing my thoughts in a journal. It really fits me! Today I feel so clean and peaceful."

March 19, 1992: After Jiang Bao accepted Christ and was given a New Testament, he said, "Oh, this is the Book I dreamed about a month ago. Even the picture on the front is the same as in my dream. (A butterfly was on the front cover of the New Testament from Hong Kong.)

March 20, 1992: Jiang Bao's friend came by to talk about Christ. He said, "Earth is short. Heaven is long. I want to go there! He made a profession of faith and received a New Testament.

March 22, 1992: After hearing "O Worship the King," Jeremy asked, "What does defender mean?" My response: "Defend us from Satan." Later after hearing, "No turning back" from "I Have Decided to follow Jesus," he said, "I will never turn back!"

March 26, 1992: George phoned today to say, "Thanks for giving me a new direction in my life."

April 1, 1992: Millie was confused by false teaching. After hearing about the plan of salvation, she asked for a Bible and said, "I want this Jesus in my heart."

April 6, 1992: Mark, a pastor from Anqing, asked for help to attend the University of South Shawnee, Tennessee, because "The voice of God and a big flock of people are calling me to help them."

April 7, 1992: Xiao Wang prayed, "Jesus, we speak different languages, but in You, we have one heart, one love, one Savior."

April 9, 1992: Neil came in depressed but after reading Psalm 23, he said, "I need to ask God to be my Shepherd." After doing so, he tearfully exclaimed, "I feel so much better now."

April 13, 1992: During an imaginary trip through Washington, D.C., Xiao Wang said, "Over to our left is the Imperial Palace (the White House). Does Jesus live there?"

April 24, 1992: Clara reported that her friends say she has changed so much and they would like to know why. "They don't feel the Peace in their hearts yet. I am so happy since I became a Christian," she continued.

May 10, 1992: Michael said, "When I am depressed, I get on my knees and cry to God to help me. I'm reading Job and it is helping me to grow."

June 7, 1992: Our farewell party with seminary students consisted of favorite hymns and precious comments. "You helped me to see Christ on a higher level." "You are my best friend." "I'll never forget you." "Your kindness has made me happy." "I asked permission to leave Systematic Theology Class to come and say good-bye to you."

October 9, 1992: Madam Su, an elderly Christian said, "You are like the missionaries used to be." Humility overwhelmed me.

October 31, 1992: For the birthday dinner at Fujian Seminary in celebration of my seventy-second birthday, the students had printed, "He fills my life with good things. My youth is renewed like the eagles. Psalm 103:5." Each wrote a birthday wish and then signed his or her name.

November 14, 1992: Julie accepted Christ after which she said, "This is the grandest night of my life!"

November 15, 1992: As we walked to church, Julie held onto my arm and said, "I am your disciple and I am now a disciple of your Jesus." When the invitation was given after worship, Julie went forward "to thank God for saving my soul."

December 27, 1992: A dear lady at church took off her volcanic rock necklace and placed it around my neck. My Chinese friend said, "You must accept it." I was embarrassed and would like to return it to her, but my interpreter said, "Absolutely NO!"

January 1, 1993: Ho Ru Ying told of a dream relative to two of her colleagues. Both had embraced Christianity before 1949. During the Cultural Revolution (1966-76), both denounced their Christianity for protection from Communist officials. In her dream, two sheep came to the gate of Huanan Women's College. The white one went inside, the black one turned away and left. "The white one came in and announced her Christian belief. She is the president of Huanan and represents the white sheep in my dream." She continued, "The black one came back as the treasurer of Huanan but has never reclaimed her faith in Christ." Then with a sad voice she said, "I think she is the black sheep in my dream."

January 2, 1993: Zheng Fu Gui, President of Fujian Seminary, told me that his mother committed him to Christ before he was born. His favorite hymn is "Nearer My God to Thee." His wife's favorite is "What a Friend We Have in Jesus."

January 3, 1993: I visited Bishop Peng Xi, who as a child was saved from drowning by an English missionary, Eleanor Harrison, who pulled him into the boat. She gave him the English name Moses, "Because she pulled me from the water," he said.

January 8, 1993: Ho Ru Ying was so happy today because her sister had asked for a Bible. "Our cousin in Taiwan, you, and I have been praying for her," she said. She continued, "I told her that both of us would soon die and she must get ready to meet our parents in heaven,"

March 2, 1993: After returning from Nanjing to Huanan, Jeanne, a fellow teacher and professing atheist, said, "Look at her face. You can tell she had a good time."

May 3, 1993: Dr. H. T. Maclin, Director of the Evangelistic Mission Board of the United Methodist Church, shared his conversion experience with our Foreigners' Bible Study tonight. An Afro-American navy buddy shared Psalm 107 with him. Until then, "I had never heard God's name except in vain," H. T.

said. He and his wife, Alice, had spent many years in Africa as missionaries for the United Methodist Church.

May 30, 1993: Hai Chun hugged the hymnal tightly as he said, "Now I can sing the Jesus songs, as well as read about Him in my Bible."

June 5, 1993: "Come, sit where I can see you mouth the words in English," Peng Xiao Deng begged. He was to interpret a sermon given in English by Warner Burklin, an American evangelist from Boca Raton, Florida.

September 16, 1993: "A church nearby wants you to preach to them," Peng Zhao Deng reported to me.

October 26, 1993: Suzette said, "Please don't ever leave us. You are so thoughtful toward all of the students. You tell us Jesus stories."

October 27, 1993: Ho Ru Ying had a friend who recently died. "She will have a high place in heaven," Ho said. (Ho herself is now in heaven sitting near Christ, I believe.)

November 9, 1993: During lunch with Dr. Lin he said, "Loving others is the greatest need in all the world."

November 25, 1993: Jessica called to say, "Thank you for helping me to have peace in my heart."

December 6, 1993: Xiao Guo from Amity Foundation visited my class today. She said, "Their English is better than their Chinese!"

March 27, 1994: Nancy attended church for the first time today. She asked for a Bible and hymnal. "I felt rejoiced and happy," she said.

May 29, 1994: Finona closed worship with this prayer: "Grant us, O Lord, light adequate for each stage of our journey, companions enough to brighten our way, and grace sufficient for our pilgrimage through time and eternity. " Finona is from Belfast and a devout Christian.

September 14, 1994: An elderly lady walking by our building stopped to chat this afternoon. She had seen me in church, "So I knew you were a Christian," she said.

October 8, 1994: Laurie is so happy tonight with "peace in my heart," she said after accepting Christ.

October 10, 1994: I met John Tsren, a trustee of Interdenominational Chinese Church from Los Angeles. "We have a mission budget of $800, 000," he said.

October 17, 1994: "I close my door and talk to God every night," Debbie reported.

November 14, 1994: "Why are you so high spirited and always smiling?" asked Nancy. She went on, "My life and mind are empty." After being given the plan of salvation, she readily accepted Christ and left feeling high spirited and happy, too.

November 15, 1994: Joni asked, "May I copy these words for my grandmother?" She was reading Galatians 5:22, the fruits of the spirit passage.

December 7, 1994: Ho Ru Ying said, "During the Cultural Revolution, I sang 'I Know That My Redeemer Lives,' but I had to sing it in my heart. The soldiers would not allow me to sing it out loud."

December 17, 1994: Franny asked, "Can you get me a Bible? I want to be a Christian."

January 2, 1995: My grandson Matthew, on his birthday, kept repeating during our phone conversation, "I love you, I love you." Whitney Sue, my granddaughter, joined him in their declaration of love!

January 15, 1995: I met Toby and his girlfriend, Li Qin, tonight. Toby said, "I believe God brought us together. Can we pray before we must go?" He was leaving on business for Tianjian and Beijing.

January 18, 1995: A Christian student living with nine others said, "I must get along with them because I am their salt and light."

March 2, 1995: Susanne came for a visit. As we talked, she said, "Thank you for telling me about God. I always want to keep in touch with you."

March 3, 1995: Susanne came back today reciting Matthew 4:4, "Man shall not live by bread alone, but on every word that comes from the mouth of God!"

March 7, 1995: Zhang Hua and her husband are interested in knowing about God and Jesus Christ. PTL! She is head of the English Department and could have a great impact on students.

March 9, 1995: I met Xiu Ping's Christian grandfather who was held prisoner from 1958-78 and forced to do hard labor because he would not denounce his Christian beliefs. "I survived because God helped me," he said. He went on to say, "I am of the seventh generation of Christians in my family. "

March 16, 1995: After reading Genesis 1-2, Lauren asked for a Bible.

March 25, 1995: Jimmy is an avowed Buddhist. "He can do anything for me that Jesus could do," he bragged. I still pray for him.

April 4, 1995: Jimmy and Josie had shared their faith with Debbie and she became a Believer. Debbie asked, "Why don't you tell all of the class about Jesus?" "According to Chinese law, I cannot," was my reply, "but you can!" And she did!

April 24, 1995: As we traveled back by bus from Ningde

to Fuzhou, Karen, a Scottish teacher in our group, summed up the experience with these words. "This was a day out of time!" Goats on the roadway, workers using hand held tools to construct a highway, huge rocks to be avoided on the road, etc., all contributed to a hectic trip to and from Ningde.

April 29, 1995: Will, a new Christian, said, "I want to make enough money to help people, old and young!"

June 8, 1995: While singing with a group, Dick said, "Music is the language God gave to all the world!" I had to agree with him.

June 11, 1995: Jimmy, the avowed Buddhist, came and gave me his Buddhist bracelet saying, "I want to know your God. Please take this – I don't need it anymore."

June 12, 1995: Alice showed me her old Bible in Chinese characters, "I can read it and my parents can, too." She, however, requested a new bilingual Bible in simplified Chinese and in English

September 24, 1995: This morning Pastor Chen spoke about the Holy Spirit, God's Power on earth. "When I was a primary student, a Chinese evangelist came to our village, just beyond Ningde," he said. "On a Saturday morning he held a healing service. Villagers not attending the services reported seeing fire and thought the church would burn down, but there was no fire, only the healing of many people through God's almighty power!" he said.

September 27, 1995: Tonight we watched "The Dying Room," a video of life in a Chinese orphanage. It was a heart breaker and all of us left horrified and tearful.

September 29, 1995: Dr. Wu and Dick are interested in Christianity. Dick said, "Foreigners who are Christians act differently. They are kind and care for us." Each was given a Bible with the plan of salvation underlined.

September 31, 1995: Dick came to escort me to Dr. Li's for dinner – delicious food, pig stomach included. Dick told us of his special experience. "As I was reading my Bible, a wonderful feeling came over me, such a calm peace I had never felt before. It was too late to call you, so I called Dr. Li and he told me to come to his house. We live near each other. Dr. Li, a great Christian and retired pharmaceutical professor, told me that the warm, peaceful feeling was the Holy Spirit of God coming into my life." Dick and Dr. Li wore radiant faces as he shared this experience with us. One more for the kingdom, I thought!

October 10, 1995: The class was discussing how to prepare a live chicken for dinner. Elizabeth said, "First, you murder the chicken, then anatomize it. Next, put it in a hypertension pot to cook!" The fact that she is a medical student could account for her description.

October 15, 1995: Tom asked, "Is it O.K. for me to go to church? People who believe in God seem more peaceful and happy!"

October 20, 1995: The Woos came and the husband asked why Americans celebrated Christmas. The discussion went from Santa Claus, which he knew, to the birth of Christ. After checking out the living Bible, he asked, "May I borrow this? I believe I will let Jesus come in. I'll open my heart's door to Him." He also requested a Chinese hymnal. Later, he became a Christian and is sharing his newfound faith with others.

November 8, 1995: Eli brought two fish that had been prepared for cooking from the market. "They are fresh," he said. "Their mouths are still moving."

November 10, 1995: Dick was ecstatic tonight! He had received an invitation to attend an International Nutritional Conference in Boston. A local pharmacy will finance the trip. "I am so happy because in the U. S. I can go to church. The Party doesn't allow that here," he explained.

November 14, 1995: Eli was so pleased to get a bi-lingual Bible today in Chinese and English. "Now my parents can read about God," he said.

November 28, 1995: Chen Feng raced after me when class was dismissed. "Would you please tell me how to become a Christian?" he asked. We made an appointment, he came, and he left as a Child of God!

December 6, 1995: Cheng Feng came to go shopping with me and announced that his name has been changed to Emmanuel. When asked whether he knew the meaning, he replied, "Yes, it means 'God with us' and now I know He is with me."

December 20, 1995: I gave the taxi driver a 50 yuan, which he tried to get changed. When he was unsuccessful, he returned the bill to me! In English he said, "Welcome to my country!"

December 28, 1995: Flower Lane Church was giving its Christmas Cantata. Eli came over and said, "I know you want to hear those fifty-six people singing so I have come to go with you."

December 31, 1995: My heart stood up and clapped when Eli said, "I have started praying every night."

January 4, 1996: Eli is being wooed by the Holy Spirit, I believe. Tonight he came over and asked, "Will you go for a moon walk with me! The moon is round and beautiful in a clear sky." We talked about Genesis 1-2.

January 9, 1996: While I taught a class tonight, Eli came and took a shower and watched a video, "The Fall of the Roman Empire." On my return he said, "I think God arranged for you to come to Fujian Medical University because I need a grandmother and you needed a grandchild in China!"

January 22, 1996: A mother came with her daughter who is studying English. We sang several hymns. The mother said, "Tonight is the first time I have felt any happiness since my husband died. For a long time I have been praying to meet someone who could help me," she said.

January 23, 1996: Xiao Wei reported that "I want to invite Jesus into my heart tonight!" Now she is safely in the fold.

January 28, 1996: Emmanuel asked, "May I come and talk to you about Matthew 5-6 (Beatitudes and the Lord's Prayer) this afternoon?" What an excited young Christian gentleman!

February 22, 1996: Emmanuel and Woolworth asked, "May we watch the Jesus film?" They had seen it in the video collection near my TV.

February 25, 1996: Eli went to church, then came back, and cooked cabbage and noodles for our lunch. While eating, he looked up and said, "The church songs have such nice words and sound so peaceful."

February 26, 1996: "Do you know an American girl I can pay money to marry me so I can go to the USA?" asked Paul. He seemed desperate to leave his country.

March 4, 1996: Dear Paul prayed, "Dear God, my English is poor but I hope you will accept me as your child. I am almost thirty years old and feel sorrow that nobody had told me about Jesus before. Please, take me, forgive me, and help me to live for You." I could not contain my tears.

March 8, 1996: Paul called from Beijing, "Thanks to God and for your help in English, I passed the immigration test to go to New Zealand." He was ecstatic!

March 16, 1996: Lisa, Sue, Thomas, and Eli came to play Skip Bo. Thomas, a medical student training to be a surgeon, was winning and enjoying the game when suddenly he blurted out, "What a fun place. Before you came we had no place to go to have a good time." Dear, young people with little or no provisions for entertainment! My heart breaks for them.

March 22, 1996: Eli's English teacher colleagues surprised him with a jiao zi luncheon in honor of his birthday. The state of my kitchen was chaos but worth it to see his pleasure. "No one ever gave me a birthday party before," he said as tears trickled down his cheeks.

April 1, 1996: Whoopee! Woolworth called and asked about the resurrection of Christ. All he needed was a simple explanation. "Now I understand and can believe I will go to paradise when I die," he said.

April 12, 1996: Eli, Yang Feng, Xiu Ding, and Daniel ate dinner prepared by Eli and Xiu Ping. Menu was fish soup and dragon-eyed soup. Dragon eyes are a sweet grape-like fruit with a hard skin, which must be removed. Peanuts, dates, and rice are added to make a sweet soup. They played scrabble until 10:00 p.m. "Your flat should be called party time," Yang Feng announced as he was leaving.

April 15, 1996: Lincoln is very sad. He wants to be a Christian. "My sister and grandmother believe in Jesus and I want to, but I must respect my mother," he said. Dear God, save him and his mom.

April 23, 1996: Woolworth called and asked, "May I come tonight? I have many questions about the Bible."

April 24, 1996: Rachel, a violinist, lives near me. Her mother is my seamstress. Rachel said, "The string on my violin is made from the tail of a white horse."

April 28, 1996: Lincoln now has a bilingual Bible given to him on request. "What does 'lo, the star in the east' mean?" he asked. Thank you, Father, that he is reading and believing your Word.

April 30, 1996: Ray Hill visited from Shenzhen, and I had not seen him since 1992. He is the proud father of two-month-old Tammy Sue. "She has part of your name because you introduced me to her mother," he said. Her mother was the receptionist in the guesthouse where I lived from 1988-92 in Nanjing.

May 6, 1996: Xiao Wu and Lin Feng came asking, "What should we do, stay in Fuzhou or go to Vancouver, Canada?" Both are considering becoming Christians. It was suggested that they accept Christ into their lives and then seek His will and follow His guidance. Both had tears in their eyes as they left. Today they are active members of a Baptist church in Vancouver, British Columbia, Canada!

May 7, 1996: Allene brought her sister for an introduction to an English teacher. Then she asked, "Can my sister live with you and attend your class?' The response was, "If the Foreign Affairs Office gives consent, it's O.K. with me." They did not ask the Foreign Affairs Officer because they knew the answer already.

May 19, 1996: Emmanuel had to translate for a Brazilian friend and his Chinese girlfriend. He can't speak Chinese and the girl friend can't speak English. "I had to pass their words for them," he told me.

May 26, 1996: Emmanuel gave his Bible to a man sitting in front of us in church. Emmanuel was given money to go buy another one for himself. The man had been trying to follow scripture by leaning over and looking into the Bible of a person sitting nearby. Emmanuel smilingly whispered, "I asked God to bless the man and my Bible which I gave to him."

June 2, 1996: Lin Yin Xiang confessed, "After studying Buddhism, Confucianism, and Christianity, I felt confused because each claims to be right and each had someone who lived on earth. Buddhism had Buddha, Confucianism had Confucius, and Christianity had Christ." Then he went on to say, "Today as I was coming from class, I heard a voice. The voice said, 'Who made the earth?'" He was so happy and excited as he said, "I know the voice of God had spoken to me and now I believe in Him and His Son, Jesus Christ!"

June 3, 1996: Dr. Li, Dick, and his wife brought pork brains. Dick explained, "I know God has opened the door for me to go to Boston to attend an international meeting on calcium research."

June 16, 1996: A Buddhist, a researcher, an atheist, and a Christian were visiting to watch a movie. As we were about to have watermelon and some cookies, Dick asked, "Will you, please, pray before we eat?"

June 20, 1996: Shi Yin and Li Hui had dinner with me. Shi Yin said, "We don't eat until the blessing is asked."

June 24, 1996: Tom said, "I sat behind you at church and I am telling my friends about Jesus!"

June 29, 1996: Dick said, "God worked through those five offices to get my passport to the USA!

June 30, 1996: "If you will teach a class for us," a business official said, "we will send for you." They did send a motorcycle, and I got on behind the driver more easily than I got off!

July 7, 1996: Pu Chen baptized 150 people this a.m. Lincoln was in church looking pale and forlorn. "My dad went to sleep forever last Sunday," he said. "Do you think he had a chance to go to heaven?" he asked. A minister family had given the father a Bible, and Lincoln hopes he accepted Christ. "God loves all people and your dad could have invited him into his heart," I said to try to reassure him.

July 8, 1996: Ava, an atheist, said, "You can't hear God speak so how can you know what He wants you to do? To this I responded, "You can't hear your parents speaking now, but you know when they would approve or disapprove of your decisions." She did not respond to that.

July 9, 1996: The taxi driver sent by Amity to meet me at Beijing Airport asked, "Do you know 'Edelweiss' and 'Auld Lang Syne?'" We sang them over and over all the way to the hotel where the Amity summer team was gathering. Those were the only two English songs he knew, and he did not tire of them for the forty-five minute drive!

July 10, 1996: The tour guide to the Great Wall and Ming Tombs told me, "The Bible is a myth." He asked, "What does Amity mean and does it come from the Bible?" After hearing that "Amity" means love, friendship, and peaceful relationships, he said, "Because you say it is true, I will believe it."

July 25, 1996: Tom, a Chinese English teacher, wishes to study in the U.S.A. "Since I met Christ, I think He will help me," he said.

July 30, 1996: Eli phoned to say, "We miss you in Fuzhou. Please hurry back!" I was in Jinan helping in the Summer English program at Shandong Institute of Education at that time.

August 4, 1996: A ninety-three-year-old lady with feet which had been bound asked me, "Will you pray the Lord's Prayer with me?" She truly blessed me.

August 16, 1996: Julie, a former student, phoned from Cairo, Egypt, today. "Would you please help me?" she implored. "I need a recommendation from my foreign English teacher so I can enroll in college here," she explained. Julie is a beautiful Chinese girl married to a foreign businessman twice her age. Of course, I will write a letter of recommendation once she sends the address.

August 17, 1996: Dick and his wife were at dinner at Dr. Li's tonight. "God has finally opened the last door for me to attend the International Conference in Boston," he reported. Our emotions were mixed, as Dick's wife would be left behind. We had prayers asking God's blessing on this young couple. Dr. Li, Dick, his wife, and Dr. Li's son are all Christians.

August 25, 1996: I flew to Nanjing, arriving in time for

church at St. Paul's. Jun Hua, William's sister-in-law, and Little Joe, Wei Wen Bin's young brother, met me. Little Joe had never attended church. He was puzzled by the singing, prayers, and the many people. "They must really believe in God," he marveled. We must pray him into a salvation experience.

September 24, 1996: Hong Hua from Fujian Educational Commission complimented me as we were eating lunch. She said, "I forget you are not a Chinese because you are like us."

October 6, 1996: Michael's girlfriend was at church and told me, "I have peace in my heart, and I am glad to take part in the bread and wine." It was her first Communion as a new Christian.

November 13, 1996: Eli watched the Jesus film tonight with me. With a trembling voice and tearful eyes he said, "I want Jesus, not Bahai, to be my Savior." This is a BIG answer to prayer. He was under the tutelage of an American Bahai believer while in undergraduate school.

November 22, 1996: Dick phoned from Massachusetts, "Please have Professor Li at your telephone at 11:30 p.m." John raced out to find Professor Li. I kept my phone off the hook until Dr. Li came. Right at 11:30 the phone rang. It was Dick. "God has worked out all of the necessary arrangements for him," Dr. Li reported to us. He plans to study in the USA so his wife must surrender the room provided by Fujian Medical University. Dick has a sister in Fuzhou and his wife can live there until she can join Dick in Massachusetts. God will work that out, too," Dick said. He is really exercising his newfound faith!

November 30, 1996: John had been showing an interest in Christianity. Tonight he asked, "Who is God? Where is He? Have you ever been robbed? (He knew my wallet had been taken on the crowded bus.) Why did God allow you to be robbed?" My response to John was, "God is a Spirit and lives within the hearts of Believers. Yes, my wallet was stolen on a crowded bus, God allows people free choice, and thieves choose to steal because the evil spirit of Satan controls them." I hope this explanation will clarify any doubts he has about God.

December 9, 1996: Hai Chun prayed the sinner's prayer tonight as he invited Christ into his life. He kept repeating, "I am so happy! I am so happy!"

December 12, 1996: Whoopee! Xiao Xu got his visa to go to the University of Louisville, Kentucky. Thank you, Father, for helping him.

December 24, 1996: Three thousand people packed Pu Qian as Christmas music filled the air. Pastor Chen preached, "You are the star, moon, and reflection of God's Son in the world. Take the candle offered to you and go out, taking the light of the candle and the Light of God's Son into Fuzhou wherever you are." The service ended at 10:30 p.m. Every person left carrying a lighted candle.

January 19, 1997: Charles Huang preached a moving sermon from John 14:6, "Jesus said, 'I am the Way, the Truth, and the Life!'" The altar rail was two deep with people waiting for Pastor Huang to pray with them. What a moving sight! After the service ended, Charles joined Eli and me for lunch. Charles said, "God's power can do what Communism will never do!" Charles has studied at a Presbyterian Seminary in Philadelphia, Pennsylvania, for three years. His use of English is good.

January 24, 1997: Joni Wiggins, an Amity teacher from Texas, is teaching in Heze, a remote Chinese village. A church member asked, "Can you bring that preacher back from Hong Kong! If you can't, please bring all of his videos." His name is Billy Graham! The parishioner had seen a video of Billy Graham preaching.

February 7, 1997: Toby spent Spring Festival with me because his father's wife is unkind to him when he visits his father. Toby is a Christian. "I will keep asking God to save their souls," he confided.

March 2, 1997: Dr. Hannah talked about her abuse during the Cultural Revolution (1966-76) and said Matthew 10:28-30 was a great comfort to her. Her paraphrase: "Don't be afraid of those who can kill your body but can't touch your souls. Not one sparrow can fall to the ground without your Father knowing it! And the very hairs on your head are all numbered! I know my heavenly Father took care of me then and is still taking care of me now," she said.

March 17, 1997: Dr. Hannah has so many horror stories of life during the Cultural Revolution. Today she told me, "After a woman gave birth, people were eating the placenta, saying it tasted like beef!" Although she never participated, she knew of others who did engage in that practice.

March 21, 1997: Ava and Doris came to help celebrate Eli's twenty-fifth birthday. He was somewhat shy and overwhelmed while opening his packages of new shoes he so desperately needed, shampoo, pen, and men's cologne, something he had never had. Ava and Doris are his colleagues in the English Department.

March 26, 1997: Lin Jin reported, "My company exports democratic candles," meaning decorative candles. We must admit both words look somewhat alike!

April 6, 1997: I gave a copy of *Experiencing God* to Xiao Wang. "I have been a Christian for four years and I just love reading the Bible," he said. "I will enjoy working through this book with my wife. She is a Christian, too," he pointed out.

April 20, 1997: As Roy and Catherine were leaving, he turned back and said, "You believe in God, don't you? A friend gave me a Bible and I believe in Him, too."

May 2, 1997: Johnson and Zilpha watched the Jesus film and

then listened to a praise tape sent from another foreign teacher. When the words "Jesus, you are beautiful" were sung, Johnson tearfully said, "I want that beautiful Jesus. Tell me more about Him." Later on in the tape the vocalist said, "I love you, Lord." Zilpha was touched by the music. Both Johnson and Zilpha became Believers tonight.

May 18, 1997: Xiao Xu called from Kentucky to tell me, "My wife is here and we are headed to church. Keep praying for us," he said.

June 11, 1997: Eli told of his dream about Mary and Samson. He said, "The dream revealed to me that the only way to God is through His Son, Jesus." He is reading his bi-lingual Bible daily and thriving on his new-found faith in Christ.

June 21, 1997: I spent six hours at the hospital with Eli, who kept begging for prayer. He is suffering so much pain, and pain medicine is very scarce. He kept repeating, "Please ask God to help me."

September 8, 1997: I could not believe my ears when the Foreign Affairs Officer and Dean of the English Department came and informed me that two beginning Chinese teachers would move into my four-room flat. "You are entitled to only one bedroom and they can share one. All of you will use the one bathroom and kitchen," they informed me. The kitchen was a small-sized room hardly big enough for one person. Amity Foundation came to my rescue again so the two beginning teachers were housed elsewhere.

September 21, 1997: Si Di had gallbladder surgery because "I had a lot of dirt in my stomach," he explained.

October 8, 1997: When I requested a textbook for Class 2, I was told by Dean Wang, "Perhaps it has not been published yet. The company can't tell us when it will be available or how much it will cost." I was left wondering why an unpublished book with an unknown price would have been chosen! I'm still wondering because I never was given a text. Improvisations became a necessity.

October 20, 1997: I took Diane to get larger shoes today. Her toenails are all bruised from wearing shoes too small. When asked why she had shoes too small, she simply said, "They are cheaper. My parents didn't have enough money for larger ones."

January 2, 1998: Xiao Jun, a physicist and one of my former students, came for a short visit tonight. He said, "I am reading the book of John and Jesus called Himself the Son of God. Does that mean I can be God's son, too?" He was told that people become children of God when they accept Christ and since he is a "baby Christian," he can be one of many of the earthly sons of God.

January 25, 1998: Emmanuel took a half-day's leave to come to church. "The week is all wrong if I don't come to worship on Sunday a.m.," he said. He, Kathy, and I had a nice lunch at the Metropolitan Financial Center.

January 30, 1998: While I was having lunch with three couples, one wife whom I had met before asked, "Are you a Christian?" The remainder of the visit was spent answering questions about God, Jesus, and the Bible. Two of the wives have Bibles and all three couples plan to immigrate to Canada. Almost in unison they said, "We will attend church when we get to Canada." Dear God, may this become a reality.

February 22, 1998: Winnie called Eli on my phone and asked, "Are you a Christian?" "Of course," Eli answered. "Yes, I am and I hope you will become one, too." Winnie confided that she is sincerely thinking about it. Please, Holy Spirit, convince her.

May 11, 1998: In a discussion group, the question was asked, "What is something foreigners should not do in China?" A confident young lady said, "Don't be bloated!" (Boastful)

May 14, 1998: Wilhelmina went shopping and then to the

bank, where she withdrew $500.00 and 4,500 yuan. When she returned by taxi, she took her purchases and left her pocketbook in the taxi. Her money, passport, and glasses were in the pocketbook. As she was trying to decide what to do, the driver came back, returned all of her belongings including her money and said, "It was my duty to return it!"

May 25, 1998: Xia Ming donated 50 yuan to the blind children tonight. "I was a Buddhist but now I believe your God and will rear my son to believe in the living God," he said.

May 27, 1998: "You will have no classes on Monday, Tuesday, and Wednesday because your students will be pulling grass," was the announcement of the day!

September 12, 1998: Tyson and Stevie came tonight. Tyson was very excited. He had passed the required interview to immigrate to Canada. Stevie said, "We prayed for Tyson and God answered our prayers."

September 20, 1998: Woolf and Freeman came to tell me, "We went to church this a.m. and it made us feel piety!"

October 8, 1998: Poor Eli was in awful pain and cried out, "Please pray for me." He continues to be in excruciating pain. I feel so sorry for him.

October 22, 1998: I had lunch with Dr. Chen, a hematologist, who told me his parents were Christians, and "I am, too," he admitted, but he is a Party member and as such is forbidden to attend church.

October 25, 1998: I took Woolf and Roy for eye exams today. Both have very poor vision. The doctor who examined them said, "I was not supposed to come today but I felt a need to come in. I guess it was to examine these two boys." God works out details for us when we are His children!

October 27, 1998: "My husband is reading the Living Bible

you gave me and he finds it very exciting," Xiao Wu said. She is a Christian and we are praying that Lin Feng will accept Christ soon.

December 20, 1998: Christmas music was beautifully sung by thirty-six young people. Pastor Chen preached about Peace. "Only Christ in the heart gives peace," he said. He symbolically baptized 223 people today!

December 21, 1998: Scarlett and Robin came requesting that I give them the Christian wedding vows on January 2 in Lakeside Hotel, where Scarlett works. They are Believers, but Robin is a Party member so they cannot have a church wedding.

January 4, 1999: Wade came in tears tonight; he has serious girlfriend problems. When he was told that he was not being fair to himself, he said, "I can't help myself." After hearing who could help him, he prayed the sinner's prayer and left with a smile on his face.

February 4, 1999: May brought an e-mail from my youngest sister, Kappy, tonight. She asked, "Can I go to church with you next Sunday?" I was delighted to see her interested in our Spiritual God.

February 25, 1999: Leslie, who is a Chinese English teacher, a practicing Buddhist, and a policeman's wife, came to Flower Lane Church today for the first time. In the courtyard after worship, she said, "I heard a voice that spoke to me. It said, 'You are a sinner!'" Then she asked, "May I come and talk with you some more?" Of course, I shall be happy to talk with her and will pray that she will respond to the call of God's Spirit.

February 27, 1999: Candi, who hopes to study in Australia, ate dinner with Eli and me. While dining she asked, "What is the purpose of life?" She is a Christian so I gave her a response I felt she would understand. My answer was, "To grow a soul and to be a servant for Christ to others." She thought for a moment and then commented, "That's a very wise answer and I will try to do that."

March 11, 1999: Some officials from Hadley School for the Blind in Chicago had a big dinner at Lakeside Hotel. I was seated by an official from Foreign Services in Fuzhou. As we were about to take our seats, she asked, "Do you know Sue Todd?" She was somewhat taken aback as I reached out to shake her hand and said, "I am Sue Todd.' She had heard my name from Xia Rong Qiang, the blind man I had escorted to Boston in June 1998.

March 16, 1999: Xiao Wu phoned me saying, "I would have had an abortion the day I called you last week, if you had not discouraged me." This gave me chill bumps and gratitude. Abortions are murder, I think.

March 26, 1999: Leslie asked to borrow the Jesus film to show to her husband, a policeman. She had a quarrel with a Christian neighbor which she reported ended "when I turned my other cheek!" I knew then she had been reading her Bible.

March 27, 1999: Leslie said, "When my husband saw the Jesus film, he said Buddha never appeared to me like that." Dear God, please speak to his heart and help him to receive Christ into his heart. Later, he did!

April 2, 1999: May finally asked the key question tonight, "What must I do to be a Christian?" In recent days, she has been coming to church more frequently. Her boss asked whether I would say grace before we ate. We were in a large restaurant with eleven people in our party. After lunch we did tongue twisters, such as "Sister Susie Sitting on a Thistle," "Six Slim Six Saplings," etc. We ended by singing "Edelweiss," "You Are My Sunshine," and "Auld Lang Syne." Our closing song was "Jesus Loves Me!"

April 21, 1999: Alan from Fujian Medical University phoned to say, "I would like to return the Bible you gave me two years ago. I have bought a bi-lingual one and am reading it." I suggested that he pass it along to a friend who did not have one.

May 9, 1999: Milton called from Manila to say, "I passed the interview. I went to church and asked the pastor to pray for me. I felt a strong Spirit as I answered all the questions. God helped me. Now I can take my wife and three children to Canada," he said with jubilation! Government officials never learned of the third child because his wife took leave from her job. She returned to her parents' countryside home, gave birth to her third son, and left him there. He is now five years old. They did not believe in abortions.

May 15, 1999: While I was teaching the Canadian National Song, a young man asked,"Did that come from the Bible?" When he heard the line "God keep our land glorious and free," he thought it sounded scriptural when in reality it is a prayer.

May 21, 1999: A student asked in class, "What do you think is the future for America?" This took me by surprise. My response was, "Only the God of heaven and earth knows that answer. I cannot predict the future!"

May 30, 1999: Pan Yi Ling will bring a blind Buddhist friend to church. She recently opened her heart to receive Christ as her personal Savior. She is a professing Catholic but says now, "I pray to my Father through Christ."

June 13, 1999: Peng Zhao Deng and Qi Bi became parents today of a baby boy. Customs have changed in maternity hospitals. The father, who was allowed to stay in the room with them, was quite excited when he called to report the baby's arrival. "We want you to give our son an English name, if you will, please," he almost begged. So after a few moments, the name Samuel seemed appropriate, so baby Samuel Peng he became.

June 13, 1999: Seated beside a lady from Penang, Malaysia, I asked how she became a Christian. "The Holy Spirit of God just came down and possessed me. God chose me and I responded," she said.

June 17, 1999: Jim, a cardiologist from Fujian Medical University, is back from Australia for a short visit. "I took a correspondence course in Bible because you had told me about Christianity four years ago while I was your student," he said. My heart clapped! He is a happy Christian now.

June 18, 1999: Hans, who works in the airport, called to say, "I will come and take you to the airport and help you get checked in!" Another one of God's angels to assist me!

June 20, 1999: Roy reported leaving his Bible at home so his father can read it. "I am reading the bi-lingual Bible you gave me," he smiled.

September 5, 1999: Leslie, her husband, and precious little daughter came apologizing, "We cannot invite you to our home because it is a military unit and foreigners are not allowed!" I wondered what secrets the government thought I might steal.

September 8, 1999: "I saw you on the bus. You were wearing that necklace with love on it," a student reported during class break time. My necklace and earrings are the Chinese character for love. The ring on my left finger has the characters from Galatians 5:22: "love, joy, peace, patience, kindness, goodness, faithfulness, gentleness, and self-control."

September 25, 1999: "Last year you told me about God and Jesus. I want to know more about them. May I go to church with you on Sunday?" Jackson asked, "Why don't you meet me at Flower Lane? I will wait for you at the gate." "O.K" was my response. If a student is genuinely interested in Christianity, he will come and oftentimes bring a friend. Jackson did, in fact, meet me and later made a profession of faith in my room.

September 30, 1999: "A big parade in Tiananmen Square to celebrate National Day can be attended only by those with special invitations," so a friend told me. Fuzhou looks like a gigantic Christmas tree with all of its glittering lights. I think every tree and shrub has been decorated.

October 7, 1999: Mary Wang, a Quaker from London, England, at one time the wife of a Chinese, ate lunch with me today. "My husband's family never accepted me because they had chosen a Chinese girl for his wife," she told me. She had taught at Huanan Women's College last year.

October 24, 1999: Peter was in church for the first time today. "I felt the Holy God in my heart. I will bring my wife next Sunday," he said.

Also, an Afro-American from Chicago was in church. He had met a Chinese girl on the Internet and had come to Fuzhou to marry her. He is at least six feet tall and she is a very petite young lady maybe five feet five inches tall. She was wearing a cross which I was grateful to see. "When is your wedding?" I asked. "Oh, we don't know yet," he replied. Then he went on, "It will take awhile because of Chinese laws." My heart trembles for her. He looks fifty years old or more, and she may be twenty.

November 4, 1999: Emmanuel came from Vancouver, Canada, to visit. He is back to see his family and repay loans he borrowed to immigrate to Vancouver. He brought photos of his baptism, the choir in which he sings, and the young people's group of which he is a member. "God is blessing me and I was able to get a job with Marsk, the same company I worked for in Fuzhou," he said. I am so pleased for him, such a deserving young accountant.

November 25, 1999: May and her driver came at 6:30 a.m. to take me to the airport for a trip to the Cooperative Baptist Fellowship meeting in Nanning. At the stop over in Guangzhou, John Yang, a former student and now a pastor, met me in the airport. He took me to the Friendship Store for Kellogg cereal and several cans of Campbell soup. After shopping, we had lunch and then he took me by taxi to the airport. The plane was delayed to Nanning for about two hours. The announcer was speaking over the loud speakers keeping passengers informed. When a flight finally materialized, the voice would break through again, "Flight no. 215 is now loading at Gate No. 8. Peas go to the boarding gate and we wish you have a peasant journey!"

January 1, 2000: Dr. Zhi Zhe Chen insisted that I don a white coat and follow him on rounds through the oncology department. Many were awaiting a bone transplant from available donors; others were waiting for a donor. One fifteen-year-old girl was in a ward with five male patients who were suffering from leukemia. Each one gave a grateful smile when he or she was greeted. My heart went out to all of them. Dr. Chen would be leaving for Germany soon, so he needed to practice his English. I felt that was his motive for my invitation.

After making the rounds, we returned to Dr. Chen's office. His future son-in-law, a cardiologist, came in and flopped down, obviously very tired. "I have just completed a heart transplant," he said. "Where do you get hearts for transplants?" I asked. Without hesitation he responded, "From criminals who are executed!" The government denies this.

February 7, 2000: Dr. Thomas, now a surgeon, came for a visit. He was dressed in a dark business suit, new shoes, white shirt, and tie. "I bought it all myself," he boasted. I've watched him mature from a freshman in college to now a practicing surgeon. A fine, young Chinese man who will do well in his field, I think.

February 13, 2000: A seventy-six-year-old lady preached in Flower Lane Church this a.m. "My biological father deserted my mother and me, but our God never forsook us," she stated. The congregation applauded her on the conclusion of her sermon.

February 20, 2000: During baptism services this morning, two grandfathers and a young girl were among the many candidates. The young girl's grandmother stood behind her praying, "Thank you, Lord, thank you, Jesus, thank you, God."

For attending church today, Leslie's husband was reported to his Communist leader. "They reprimanded him and forbade him to attend again; now he will go to Bible Study with me at Pan Yi Lin's home," she reported.

March 4, 2000: "My parents refused to help us when our baby was born because I had become a Christian," Timothy tearfully told me. They are Buddhist and now refuse to see me, my wife, or my two children," he said.

March 19, 2000: While I was having dinner with Adam and his family, his nine-year-old daughter whispered to her mother, "Does she know her eyes are blue?" She had never seen a blue-eyed foreigner before.

March 22, 2000: As we were walking downstairs, a student unknown to me asked, "Are you a servant of Jesus Christ?" Whoa! Needless to say, I was more than a little shocked.

March 31, 2000: William was reared by his grandmother, who died last year. At lunch today he said, "You remind me of my grandmother. I will go to clean her grave and talk to her on Ching Ming Day." He needs a maternal figure for support, I think.

April 20, 2000: On the way to the airport, the driver pointed out two churches. I asked, "Do you believe in Jesus?" In response, he made the sign of the cross. To him, in Chinese, I said, "You are my young brother. I am your older sister. God is our Father." His reply was, "Yes! Yes!"

Along the way we saw a man slowly riding a motorcycle while leading a cow tied to the motorcycle. I didn't realize any motor would move so slowly, a speed which was good for the cow!

I arrived in Nanjing for the celebration of Amity's fifteenth birthday. It was so good to see Bishop Ting, Stephen, Brenda Lisenby, Faye Pearson, and Gwen Crotts. Also, I met Ann and David Wilson and Joni Wiggins' father. How good to see all of them! Twenty-two different countries had representatives there.

April 26, 2000: Kent and Michael came tonight after I had undressed. I quickly put on my bathrobe before opening the door. Kent asked, "Is that a Christian dress you are wearing?"

September 24, 2000: Peng Zhao Deng left for Presbyterian Seminary in Pittsburgh, Pennsylvania. He was denied studies in Switzerland and Japan by his superiors, even though scholarships were available in both locations. "God has opened this door for me," he smiled.

October 1, 2000: May was baptized today with more than two hundred other people. "I thought about this all day yesterday, and I had such a wonderful, peaceful feeling," she said through her tears. After she was symbolically baptized, she turned to me and said, "Help me pray that my parents, sister, and brother-in-law will become Christians, too."

October 27, 2000: Amy asked, "May I read this book, *Christian Soup for the Soul,* and this magazine, *Guideposts?*" She had been scanning both and, apparently, liked what she saw. She was a new Believer and needed nurturing. "This kind of reading makes me feel peaceful, calm, and relaxed," she said.

October 30, 2000: Jeremiah phoned and said, "I went to Bible Study on Sunday p.m. and will go back every Sunday. I like what the minister said." He had never attended church before. May God open his heart to receive his Son!

December 5, 2000: Students made deviled eggs, a new dish and a new experience, one they seemed to enjoy. Pepsi Cola and crackers were added to the menu and were quickly consumed. "When can we do this again?" they asked.

December 9, 2000: Eli has been a Believer for some time but has not joined the church. Today he called and asked, "What must I do to be baptized?" Hallelujah! His Bahai beliefs had to be discarded and this transition had taken quite some time. His decision was an answer to prayer!

January 7, 2001: "Life is so different now that God is my guide," Amy reported. Her family was atheistic. This decision was a great step for her Amy, a Chinese English teacher, I pray will influence her students to believe in God.

January 22, 2001: Fifty-eight bodies of people from Fujian Province arrived at the airport today from England. They had smothered to death last July in the back of a truck loaded with tomatoes. One of my friends from Cheng Le, the location of the airport, told me, "They paid the snakehead (illegal smuggler) $60,000 each to escape." He knew two of them and also knew a lady who paid 2,000 yuan to claim her husband's body and 2,000 yuan in addition to have him cremated. "About 200 extra police were sent to the airport to advise people not to talk about this tragedy," he said. He has neighbors who work in the airport and they were his source of information.

February 2, 2001: Wei Wei asked, "How can you know God's will?" The answer she received was WWJD (What Would Jesus Do). A married man has asked that she be his mistress. She wants to end the relationship but doesn't know how. She has shared this before and is now deeply troubled. I must try to help her to understand God's forgiveness and His concern and love for her.

February 27, 2001: "My best friend is interested in becoming a Christian," Amy told me today. Amy is sharing her faith and finding much joy in doing so.

March 5, 2001: Ann, a Chinese medical trainee, was taking me to see a neurologist for a check of the trigeminal nerve on the left side of my face. Thinking she was using the right term, she said, "Do you want to have your nose checked? Oh, I mean your nerve," she apologized. Sometimes it was hard not to laugh.

March 14, 2001: Lin Ming Jiang and his girl friend came to

tell me how much they are enjoying the Bible, especially the New Testament. "We feel so relaxed and peaceful since we believed in God. We know it is His Book." I wish all my students could say the same.

April 2, 2001: The couple who came tonight asked about the resurrection! They read the account of Christ's resurrection from Matthew 28. This was proof enough for them. It is always such a privilege to share the gospel and a Bible with the new Believers. They were so grateful for the bi-lingual translation. Now our parents can read about this in Chinese," they said.

April 8, 2001: The windows were foggy and the bus very crowded on the way to church. A small boy accepted the challenge to write Chinese numbers up to ten. I was surprised when he also wrote them in English. Then he drew Bah-bah (Daddy) and Mama. When I got off the bus, he patted my arm and said "Goodbye" in English. He was very proud of himself and so was his mom.

April 10, 2001: Isabel comes from a very poor village in the remote countryside. Her class was giving talks on "My Early Childhood." "My parents gave me to my aunt when I was very young. She was very poor, too, and we had only a little rice to eat. I was always hungry and dirty. There was no water near our home except in the holes when it rained. My aunt would boil the water and save it for us to drink." The whole class gasped when she said, "My feet were never washed until I was seven years old." Amity Foundation had drilled a deep well in her village. Now they could have an adequate water supply. This made me proud to be an Amity teacher.

April 16, 2001: A visit to a communal restroom in a Japanese restaurant furnished a new surprise. Besides the western style commode, the urinal attached to the wall was filled with crushed ice! Surely, this is not where ice is stored for cold tea or ice water, I thought. My friends had no explanations, so mustering up my courage, I asked to see the manager. He came bowing politely asking, "Is everything O. K.?" In unison the five of us said, "Yes, sir!" "Then what may I do for you?" he questioned. Someone had to be bold and perhaps brazen, so I asked, "Why is there ice in the urinal in the restroom?" "Oh," he said, "Many of our male customers don't flush the urinal so we keep crushed ice in it so it can drain itself!" Well, now we knew. Our curiosity had been satisfied.

May 2, 2001: Sophie is an excited new Christian. "My mother was hospitalized for a full year and she got well because church people prayed for her," she reported. "Now I can't read my Bible fast enough. Jesus gave so many good promises, and I want to tell all my friends about them," she said. "That is how Christianity spreads," I replied.

May 12, 2001: My good friend, Hunter, said, "When you are ready for airline tickets, just tell me." He worked with Fujian Airlines and knew the process well. I realized that I would need him soon.

May 14, 2001: Dear Danny wept today as he talked about the corruption and bribery among some local top officials. "Sometimes I want to stop living," he cried. We talked for another two hours and since he had already accepted Christ, he prayed, I prayed, and he left with "Come unto me all you who labor and are heavy laden and I will give you rest" (Matthew 11:28) in his heart and a smile on his face. Father, comfort and guide this, your child, please, I prayed. He is living in Burnaby, British Columbia, now and attending church every Sunday.

May 24, 2001: Matthew, my grandson, Marian, his friend, and I went for shampoos and a massage. Matthew told the masseur, "I think I will take you home with me!"

On the way back we stopped by a Buddhist temple, where we were warmly welcomed and invited to eat lunch, which we declined. Each of us was given a yin yan pin by one of the leaders. My heart goes out to them as all were older people and may never learn of Jesus.

May 31, 2001: Amy took us to see two old Chinese homes near her village. One was 247 years old, one was 205 years old, and both were made of earth. Floors were made of a mixture of rice and clay. Many sections on each side of hallways led to the courtyard between the sections. Today they are tourist attractions with guides to show interested parties through the maze. A museum in one with displays of life in the past captures one's attention.

We returned to her home where we ate lunch with Amy's parents and grandparents, who live in an adjoining house. Amy's home is fairly modern with indoor plumbing and sinks. To get to Amy's home, we had to step on posts driven into a small stream as there was no bridge. The posts were about eighteen inches tall and about four inches in diameter. She waded and held on to me as I stepped from post to post. When we asked why not a footbridge, Amy said, "It gives us protection. Nobody can get a truck or car in to steal our things!"

That afternoon we visited Amy's church and were warmly welcomed by the church staff. Her father went with us and on the way back to Fuzhou she said, "My daddy had never been to church before. I hope he will keep going back." We join her in that wish.

June 2, 2001: Lunch with May and her family and then across town to help celebrate Samuel's second birthday. He has a horrible rash on his face and head because, as his mother said, "I ate shell fish before he was born." He is miserable, scratching and whining. We felt so sorry for him.

It would be too voluminous to record all of the memorable experiences which were evidence of God's spirit at work among these special people. Each, however, was greatly appreciated and added much pleasure and happiness to my tour of duty in China. My mind and heart overflowed as I re-read these comments from diaries kept during that time, 1988-2001.

CHAPTER 14

Treasured Memories and Comments

"...Write this for a memorial in a book...."
   (Exodus 17:14a KJV)

Multiple special moments and events blessed my life, sometimes surprisingly so, during this experience in China. I have chosen to share them as recorded from my diaries. Reading them again brought chuckles and tears, but they will always be special moments to me.

November 14, 1989: Sung Wen came today and said, "I want to know about God. I was taught by Communists, who said we did not need God. I've just heard about God and I want to know more about Him." He was given a Bible with strategic passages underlined and later became a Christian.

November 27, 1989: The YMCA class asked about the origin of Christmas!

March 28, 1990: Edmond from Congo, Africa, told about how he and another Christian were able to command an evil spirit from a Chinese man in Beijing.

October 5, 1990: Zeke asked for five Bibles to take to his village. Only one was available and it was being shared by the Christians there.

October 11, 1990: Mesa and Edmond, Togonese students, requested some Christian literature. Since both of them are Christians, they have Bibles.

November 1, 1990: Jim was ecstatic when he read Genesis 1. He asked to take the Bible home with him to read some more! He was given a personal copy with strategically marked passages.

December 16, 1990: Amos requested baptism today! Jack and Tom made professions of faith today and each received a Bible.

January 20, 1991: James reported that he had won four of his friends to Christ.

March 17, 1991: Paul has begun Bible studies in his home for nearby neighbors.

March 19, 1991: Sammy, from Ghana, came this afternoon just to talk about God's love.

March 27, 1991: Patrick asked to borrow materials for his Bible Study Group tomorrow night.

April 20, 1991: On the bus today, Charles and I met a young lady who said she is a Party member, but she believes in Christ more than in the Party. She was reading her Bible on the bus!

May 30, 1991: One housekeeper, who speaks no English, stopped me in the lobby and presented a Popsicle filled with black-eyed peas. Since she could speak no English, all I could say was, "Xie, xie, ni "(Thank you).

November 20, 1991: After Fan Yin celebrated the birthday of his grandmother, he said, "Please spend the night with us. You can sleep with Nai Nai (grandmother). She sleeps on a cot."

December 24, 1991: Christmas celebration at Mandarin Hotel consisted of carols, the Christmas story read from the Bible, and a prayer of praise and thanksgiving. Candles had been given to hotel employees and those participating in the program. Lights were dimmed; candles were lit as each person passed a candle to the next person. Foreigners present sang "Silent Night" as the candles flickered all over the lobby.

December 26, 1991: A snowy day! Jack trudged through the

snow to come for help on a paper he was writing. Earlier he had heard the foreigners singing, "Nothing but the Blood of Jesus." He said, "The snow is so white it hurts my eyes." Then he added, "Does the blood of Jesus really wash us until we are whiter than snow?" After hearing the explanation of Christ's sacrifice for us, he said, "Jesus is a catharsis!"

December 27, 1991: Wei Wen Bin (Wade) ran through snow and ice to return his friend Katie's camera, as buses were still unable to run on icy streets.

December 29, 1991: Activities are all cancelled because of snow. Wei Wen Bin called to see whether I needed anything. He is such a thoughtful young man.

January 4, 1992: Jack accepted Christ today!

January 5, 1992: Frances accepted Christ tonight and told me that Sharpeno, one of her roommates, had become a Believer, too.

January 12, 1992: Forty-five young Chinese men and one American, Phillip Wickery, were ordained by the Jiangsu Chinese Christian Council today.

January 21, 1992: Today we worshipped in a church just given permission by the government in Guangzhou to reopen. It was packed with Chinese. How they did sing!

February 25, 1992: Jim, the military captain who had resigned, came tonight, happy that he can now attend public worship.

March 27, 1992: Ah Bing's colleagues and the Seminary Choir had an hour and a half sing-along as a farewell celebration for her departure to the U.S.A.

March 29, 1992: A six-year-old was helping her three-year-old brother to hold the hymnal as both joined in congregational singing.

April 4, 1992: Alfred and Edmund from Togo, Africa, asked for prayers for themselves and their countrymen.

April 5, 1992: Katie and I rode in bumpy pedicabs to Eddy's home to help in the one-year birthday of his son. Grandmother, aunts, uncles, cousins, and friends – all were present. Eddy placed a microphone, pen, piggy bank, book, and some cards in a tray. The baby picked up the pen signifying that he will grow up and become a scholar according to Chinese prediction. The items were intended to signify the baby's future: cards, he would become worthless; the microphone, a performer; the piggy bank, a very wealthy person; and the pen or book, a scholar.

Today is Qing Ming Day, when people clean graves of ancestors and decorate with green branches and flowers. Buses could not operate because of crowds headed to cemeteries.

April 17, 1992: I went on Easter egg hunts with the Seminary class. Students were like small children racing around finding the eggs.

April 18, 1992: I went to my 8:00 a.m. class only to learn it had been cancelled for Sports Day!

April 29, 1992: John, a monk, called about attending Bible Class. He was directed to join the group at St. Paul's Church in Nanjing.

September 6, 1992: Xiao Mao said, "I believe in God, not Buddha." He will be baptized soon.

September 6, 1992: I visited Fujian Seminary in Fuzhou, met the faculty, and enjoyed the choir singing familiar hymns, such as "Take the Name of Jesus with You" and "The Old Rugged Cross."

September 28, 1992: Steve Hsiung wrote of his arrival in Missouri; he went five times to the Consulate in Beijing before his visa to study in the U.S.A. was granted.

October 3, 1992: The choir in Xiamen sang "The Holy City." It brought tears to my eyes and memories to my mind!

October 6, 1992: Lisa, who had lived in Togo, Africa, gave me a tape of African children singing Christian hymns. Precious, childish voices!

October 18, 1992: After church, the choir director asked whether we could sing "How Great Thou Art" from my hymnal. Then she asked to borrow the hymnal to teach songs from it to her choir. I was pleased to donate it as a dear friend, Anna Belle Crouch from Murfreesboro, N.C., had sent several for me to use on just such occasions.

October 29, 1992: Peng Zhao Deng got his suit today. It had to be altered. How proud he was of his very first dress suit! Now he can look like a minister as he preaches.

November 1, 1992: A blind man singing in a beautiful tenor blessed many in church today.

November 2, 1992: I met Gu Nian, granddaughter of Bishop Xi in Fujian Province. She is a talented and beautiful pianist hoping to study in Wisconsin.

November 8, 1992: Four TV monitors were set up in the courtyard of Flower Lane Church to accommodate the overflow congregants unable to get inside the building.

November 11, 1992: I visited an exhibit of prominent Chinese structures made of wheat straw. Unbelievable!

November 22, 1992: Peng Zhao Deng preached about talents from Matthew 25 at Christ's Church today in Fuzhou.

November 24, 1992: Gu Nian shared how God had helped in the lives of some of her friends who wished to study abroad.

November 29, 1992: In Guangzhou today the Reverend John

Yang, one of my students from Jing Ling Seminary in Nanjing, preached about "Becoming Fishers of Men." Both he and I were equally surprised and happy to see each other. He is teaching in the Guangdong Seminary and pasturing Shamian Church in Guangzhou.

December 15, 1992: Two boxes from Anna Bell Crouch arrived today containing miniature hymnals, cards, etc. Very useful!

December 16, 1992: Sixty pianists, a tenor, and one soprano vocalist presented an excellent concert tonight. The pianists were ages five to twelve and were dressed in red and white outfits. They gave a talented performance.

December 20, 1992: Seventy-four people gave a moving Christmas Cantata in Flower Lane Church today. The angels in heaven surely clapped their wings!

December 25, 1992: We had lunch and a Christmas party at Fujian Seminary today and afterwards everyone enjoyed the carols and small gifts. Around twenty-five foreigners were present.

December 26, 1992: A telephone call came from Glenn and family. It is always good to hear the voices of my loved ones. I miss them very much.

December 29, 1992: While I was visiting in a home for the blind, a thin, little old lady, who could speak in broken English, asked whether I would pray for her. She almost squeezed my hand off as prayer was being offered.

January 6, 1993: Professor Li Jun Biao, Peng Zhao Deng, and I had lunch at California Fried Chicken. Afterwards, we toured Foreign Trade Hotel, which neither had visited before. It was still decorated for Christmas. Both were like small children walking around looking in wonderment at the ornate sights.

Professor Li spied a can of butter for twenty-eight RMB (Chinese money), which he obviously wanted but could not afford. What a pleasure to present a can to him! Tears of gratitude in his eyes were my pay.

January 9, 1993: Nancy asked for a copy of "that Book" about Jesus.

January 11, 1993: Candi asked whether I would read 1 Corinthians 13 at her wedding. I borrowed a jumper from Norma Foskett of Texas, and Edith Seiling from Gatesville, N.C., had sent hose, which came to Nanjing to my old address. Katie Neal from Nanjing brought the hose to Xiamen, where we were holding Amity Winter Conference. Norma and Katie are Amity teachers, too. Then I was dressed more properly to participate in Candi's wedding. God continues to provide in unexpected ways.

November 12, 1993: Katie and I met David Zhou, who helped us onto the right ferry back to our Island Hotel. He saw the Bible on the table beside my bed, asked for a copy, made a profession of faith, and promised to "See you tomorrow."

February 21, 1993: Over one hundred people gathered around the altar as the pastor sang, "Nearer My God to Thee."

February 28, 1993: Many former students came to the guesthouse at Jing Ling Seminary as I came back for a short weekend visit. We sang hymns and prayed before they left at 9:30 p.m.

March 14, 1993: Hai Chun asked many questions as he read my Bible. He believes in God and was grateful for the Bible and a copy of "Guideposts" he had received.

March 16, 1993: Candi came asking for dry socks. Her shoes and socks were soaked. She left in dry socks and dry shoes, a bit large but dry.

March 17, 1993: Candi brought ornate rhinestone earrings in gratitude for the dry footwear yesterday. She retrieved her now dried shoes and socks.

March 27, 1993: We enjoyed Fujian National Acrobatic Children's Show today. Performers were from five to ten years of age. There were skillful and scary acts.

March 28, 1993: As the pastor sang, "Pass Me Not," 150 people crowded around the altar rail and the front of the sanctuary.

March 31, 1993: Patrick, a former Southeast University student, called to ask whether he should marry a girl taller than he is! Patrick works as an electrical engineer in Shi Hong but is eager to get married to please his parents.

April 2, 1993: Gu Nian gave us a mini piano concert tonight. Her grandmother was her piano teacher and did a super job teaching her piano skills.

April 4, 1993: People filled streets going to family cemeteries to decorate graves of deceased relatives. Small branches and flowers were being carried on bikes, on motorbikes, and by hand.

April 8, 1993: We distributed caps and gloves to blind people in Shan Do Church today. These were sent from Stokes Baptist Church, Stokes, N. C.

April 9, 1993: According to Chinese culture the five "happinesses" are health, wealth, longevity, virtue, and peaceful death in old age.

April 11, 1993: Our Seminary class learned "Every Day in China," a transliteration of "Every Day with Jesus." They liked it. "Every day in China is sweeter than the day before. Every day in China, I love her more and more. Striving hard to serve her, helping her to bless the world, every day in China is sweeter than the day before."

April 23, 1993: Chen Jian Zheng used Matthew 25:40 in his thank you note for his eye exam and glasses: "Inasmuch as you did it for one of these, you did it unto me."

April 26, 1993: Revival services at Fujian Seminary were conducted by the Taiwanese Prayer Group. A spirit-filled thanksgiving! Great!

April 17, 1993: Tiffany read Genesis 1; John 3:16; Philippians 4:13, 19; and Galatians 5:19-22. She was converted and left carrying a Bible!

May 7, 1993: A seventy-year-old man sat up front in my class of English students today. He was so proud to be taped along with the seminarians.

May 19, 1993: I visited Anglo-Chinese College today and was pleasantly surprised to see "Ye Are the Light of the World" in large letters on the auditorium walls. The goal of the college is to teach morality and self-development, according to the president of the college.

May 20, 1993: I wore cut-off blue jeans with a tank top for my first swimming lesson today.

May 23, 1993: Two little girls held my hands as we walked from church this a.m.

June 4, 1993: Seminary class ended for the term with students singing their favorite hymns, "Safe in the Arms of Jesus," "Oh Happy Day," "Abide with Me," and "What a Friend."

September 4, 1993: I gave Peng Zhao Deng a bilingual New Testament and hymnal, which will help him in teaching English at the Fujian Seminary.

September 14, 1993: I sang "Happy Birthday" to my son,

Glenn, at 6:00 a.m. U.S.A. time!

September 25, 1993: Patrick called and requested that I come to Shi Hong, his hometown, to teach. He asked for a description of the ideal girl for him to marry!

October 3, 1993: Two outreach church leaders took the elements of communion after worship to shut-ins. They had small containers for the bread and bottles for the wine.

October 10, 1993: After being approved by the local Chinese Christian Council and Religious Affairs Bureau, I consented to speak at Dong Mein Church. My topic was "The Riches of God's Grace."

October 13, 1993: From my right hand I removed two rings and gave them to two Chinese ladies who had been pointing at and admiring them.

October 24, 1993: Jessica went to church for the first time. She was most impressed and asked for a hymnal and Bible. She went back at 2:30 p .m. for choir practice. She enjoyed all of it and had many questions about those symbolically baptized.

October 31, 1993: Flora and Candi brought a birthday gift, which read, "Love is another name for mother."

November 1, 1993: I had another birthday celebration at the seminary. Too much food was followed by sweet fellowship, hymns, and prayers.

November 4, 1993: Laurie, who graduated last year, came and took home a Bible, "Upper Room," and "Open Windows" with the prayer calendar removed. She asked for a picture of Christ. I gave her a Madonna and Child pin.

November 7, 1993: Church was inspirational as I observed a grandmother with a three-year-old, both kneeling at the altar; many people praying at the altar before worship; young mothers teaching children the posture of prayer; and a young man praying and singing beside me. Diana, a new Believer, took a New Testament home today.

December 5, 1993: I gave used greeting cards to children as we walked back from church. They liked the bright colors and beautiful pictures.

December 14, 1993: The Holy Spirit was busy in Christ's Church today!

December 16, 1993: I attended a piano recital by Ho Ru Ying's students. She was so proud of them

December 17, 1993: I bought and deviled 116 duck eggs for a staff Christmas party. All eggs were consumed!

December 18, 1993: The Christmas party for the seminary class included a big dinner, simple games, carols, the Christmas Story, and distribution of socks and handkerchiefs to all of them.

December 19, 1993: We had a wonderful Christmas service in Tian An Tun Church with full participation by all worshipers. The choir was outstanding!

December 23, 1993: Our Christmas dinner with the seminary staff was followed by a performance which lasted until midnight.

December 24, 1993: The five-star Lakeside Hotel gave a big dinner for the foreign teachers. We sang "Angels We Have Heard on High" when called on to perform.

December 25, 1993: Worship in our living room included scripture, carols, and prayers. Afterwards we exchanged simple gifts with each other. Wang Ling came at night and asked questions about the Bible.

December 26, 1993: Worship was held at San Do Church with an overflow crowd. A luncheon was enjoyed at a nearby restaurant by church staff and foreigners.

December 27, 1993: Elderly ladies are showing up with black wigs, which they call one-hundred-year-old hats!

January 2, 1994: Twenty young people, fifteen to sixteen years old, attending a weekend spiritual retreat at Fujian Seminary, came to Flower Lane Church today. Each was armed with a Bible and hymnal.

January 9, 1994: The wedding of a couple who sing in the choir at Christ Church took place after worship. The groom wore lipstick and rouge, as did the bride. Hard candy was passed out to their guests as we left the church.

January 16, 1994: A lady whom I met at Peng Zhao Deng's wedding and who is married to a Party member invited me to her home for lunch after worship today. Although her husband is a Christian, he is not allowed to attend church because of his party membership.

January 18, 1994: Toby asked for a Bible for his girl friend today. She is now attending church with him in Xiamen.

January 21, 1994: Today I enjoyed a wonderful bath and plenty of warm water in a heated room! I stayed in the Guangzhou Hotel attending Amity Winter Conference.

January 22, 1994: Charles, a former student studying in Guangzhou University, rode a bike for two hours in 6 degrees temperature to visit me today. He would like to study theology instead of sociology. May God grant his wish. He asked for more Bibles to share with classmates.

January 26, 1994: I left my money belt at the last security check point. I ran back and the official was counting my money when I returned. I hugged him impulsively and frightened him as he stiffened like a corpse!

February 2, 1994: Prayers in Kowloon Baptist Church were prayed in English, Filippino, and Cantonese. A Chinese man thanked God for opening his eyes to what is most important in life, a saving knowledge of Christ!

March 4, 1994: I taught "Old Time Religion" to a seminary class today. I ate jiaozi, a pastry filled with ground meat and vegetables, and 1,000-year-old eggs with Peng Zhao Deng and his wife, Qi Bi, afterwards. Thousand-year-old eggs are those covered with a clay-like mixture and set aside for several weeks. They do not spoil but become somewhat like a pickled egg. Not bad!

March 6, 1994: Collections on first Sundays at Christ Church are put into the bank and used to pay countryside ministers whose salary is around 20 yuan per month ($2.50 USA).

March 8, 1994: Huanan Women's College gave the foreign teachers gifts for Women's Day. I received a hand towel and two pairs of knee-highs.

March 13, 1994: Jessica and Chloe joined the choir at Christ Church. Chloe asked for a Bible and hymnal today. Christianity is a new concept for her.

March 15, 1994: Patrick called to report that his father, a Party leader, is going to church with him. Also, his girl friend is attending worship with him.

March 20, 1994: There was another mournful Buddhist funeral, with incense burning, sad music, and relatives wearing identification bands to denote kinship to the deceased.

March 23, 1994: Dolly says she can't eat from 8:00 a.m. to 8:00 p.m. on the 1st and 15th of each month because her Buddhist goddess, Guang Ying, does not allow it. She says Guang Ying was a man in the former life. Poor misinformed girl needs our prayers.

April 1, 1994: The seminary class colored boiled duck eggs with crayons. The Cross, Jesus Christ, and God were scrawled on all of them.

April 3, 1994: The choir made up of 50 adults and 20 children sang praises to the risen Christ of Easter this a.m. There was a symbolic baptism.

April 7, 1994: Wade and Zou Lin met me at Nanjing Airport. I came to attend Baptist World Alliance held in Jing Ling Seminary in Nanjing.

April 8, 1994: Many countries were represented, and we enjoyed great fellowship and wonderful singing with the Holy Spirit obviously present. A former Jing Ling Seminary student asked, "Will you please come back and teach us?"

April 18, 1994: Yvonne has requested baptism.

April 24, 1994: McDonald's opened today. People stormed it and broke plate glass windows, so it had to close for repairs and then reopened at 9:00 p.m. Huanan foreign teachers went for a hamburger – foolish ones we were!

April 29, 1994: We took the seminary class to McDonald's for their first hamburger, French-fries, apple pie, and Coke. They were not sure how to eat them so had to be shown!

May 1, 1994: While crossing the bridge, I saw Gu Nian's father. Gu Nian will go to York University in Toronto, Canada, to pursue her higher degrees.

May 11, 1994: A dear, blind Christian lady gave me a wonderful back massage today. She could tell by feeling that she was given a twenty-yuan rather than a ten.

May 13, 1994: Hai Chen came with a TV crew and filmed my family's photos to be shown in late June. I will be in the USA for summer vacation then.

May 17, 1994: Two blind sisters sang "Jesus Loves Me" after the message today. There were smiles on their faces and a light in their sightless eyes.

May 24, 1994: Ho Ru Ying told me that Vice-President Chen is often called the Great Wall. She tends to be "quite stubborn, according to the other teachers," she said.

May 26, 1994: Toby came asking prayer for God's leadership in helping him to get proper documents to study abroad.

May 27, 1994: Sandra visited tonight to learn how she may become a Christian. She understood! She is!

May 30, 1994: Sandra asked for an explanation of the Holy Trinity tonight!

September 4, 1994: A fiberglass coffin with a Red Cross on one end was thrown into the trash bin in front of our housing unit. After the cremation some people came and beat it to pieces. I just hope the Red Cross means the deceased was a Christian.

September 5, 1994: Peng Zhao Deng and Qi Bi brought longyans, a grape-like fruit sometimes called dragon eyes, which were shared with other teachers. They were sweet and tasty.

September 19, 1994: The bridge over Ming River closed so we ferried across to the bank and McDonald's.

September 21, 1994: I spoke at the Fujian Seminary about "Churches in the USA." Students asked questions after the lecture. They wanted to know whether churches ordained homosexuals and whether they were allowed to have church weddings. Many other questions were asked as well.

September 28, 1994: The Fujian Education Commission hosted a banquet at the Lakeside Hotel for foreign teachers. Ling Jia Lin, a governmental official, asked whether I would make a tape of Christmas music for him. Of course, I would and I did.

September 29, 1994: A dance performance to celebrate the 45th birthday of the People's Republic of China was held at Fujian Cinema. The school van took twelve of us. It was a colorful and talented group of dancers.

October 2, 1994: A little boy joined others at the altar for prayer after worship at Pu Chen Church this a.m.

October 16, 1994: Fifty people responded to accept Christ in Tian An Tun Church this a.m.

October 19, 1994: McDonald's played "Country Roads" for fifteen of my class today and also gave us free French fries.

October 22, 1994: Sandi and Amy were so happy to get Bibles today.

October 31, 1994: Students sang "You Are Our Sunshine" in every class today for my 74th birthday.

November 3, 1994: Birthday cake and pomelo were served at Ho Ru Ying's birthday celebration today. Green tea was the beverage served.

November 6, 1994: Kentucky Fried Chicken opened another restaurant in Fuzhou today. Now there are two!

November 8, 1994: Twelve of my girls will teach English at a nearby primary school on Friday afternoons.

November 16, 1994: Don McGinnis, first director of Amity Foundation, told of finding a day-old abandoned baby girl under a bush as muddy water washed over her. He took her to a nearby hospital, where she was adopted by a nurse. He had come back to Fuzhou to visit her again. Before 1949, he and his wife worked as missionaries in Fuzhou.

November 24, 1994: I received a letter from the North Carolina Women's Missionary Union that said $75.00 from the

Heck Jones Offering had been deposited into my bank account. A big surprise for which I was very grateful! This meant more Bibles, eye exams and glasses, food for the hungry, and clothes for the needy.

December 4, 1994: Eighteen former students came for a Christmas party. They decorated one another like a Christmas tree.

December 11, 1994: Two small girls helped feeble grandparents to the altar rail for communion. A young boy led a blind man by the hand to the altar so he could partake of the bread and wine.

December 15, 1994: I went to Nanping with Peng Zhao Deng to attend the dedication of the new church building. The pastor is one of my former students. Great singing by the congregation consisted of "I Would Follow Jesus," "Now Thank We All Our God," "What a Friend," and "He Leadeth Me."

December 21, 1994: Fuzhou Community Choir gave a wonderful Christmas Cantata at Tian An Tun Church tonight.

December 23, 1994: Christmas Dinner at Fujian Seminary was followed by performances which lasted until 10:30 p.m. Chinese Christian Council Members, Religious Affairs Bureau, several pastors, Seminary staff, and students jammed the auditorium.

December 24, 1994: I sang with the Choir at Christ Church tonight. The program was made up of Christmas carols.

December 25, 1994: I attended church with my Foreign Affairs Officer, Xu Dao Fang. Foreign teachers sang "Silent Night" and "Away in a Manger."

December 30, 1994: I provided a Christmas dinner for the English Seminary class tonight. They were very hungry!

January 1, 1995: A two-year-old tried to sing along with his parents today in church. A four-year-old kept repeating "Amen" during prayers. Many Chinese endorse audible prayers with Amen throughout the entire prayer.

January 20, 1995: I watched a skit of a man with a swollen stomach full of foreign objects because his life was not dedicated to Jesus. (Galatians 5:19, sins of the flesh.) He found relief by accepting Christ into His life.

January 20, 1995: A pastor in Zhong Shen found a baby girl on the steps of the church a few months ago. His daughter adopted her.

January 23, 1995: I worshiped with the Guangdong Seminary staff. John Yang, a former student, is Vice-Chairman of Guangdong Christian Council.

January 24, 1995: Thanks to John Yang, I was taken today to a leprosy colony, where Baptist students from Carson-Newman College in Jefferson City, Tennessee, had built chicken houses so residents could raise chickens for the market. They also did repairs and some much needed painting both inside and outside buildings. Pitiful people, those lepers, with limbs missing and trying to play board games, their only recreation outlet!

February 1, 1995: We saw a singing Christmas tree video of Bellevue Baptist Church, Memphis, thanks to Gerry Bowen, a member attending the Amity Winter Conference in Guangzhou.

February 3, 1995: I took hydrofoil from Guangzhou to Hong Kong to attend CSI (Corporate Service International) Winter Conference.

February 12, 1995: I attended a fitting memorial for Bishop Moses Xi at Christ Church. Services began at 2:00 and lasted until 5:30. Gu Nian, his grand-daughter, is in Toronto. Han Hui, her mother, gave a beautiful eulogy for her father. Fujian Seminary and church choirs sang several hymns while three pastors reviewed the Bishop's life and his ministerial accomplishments – very appropriately done for a very special Christian gentleman.

February 14, 1995: Wei Wen Bin phoned from Nanjing to inform me he had been invited to a University in Lausanne, Switzerland, because of scoring in the top 5% of those who took the GMAT (Graduate Management Admissions Test)!

February 22, 1995: Joni's boyfriend lost his father today. He died of a heart attack on Wu Shan Mountain. Joni's mother died when she was quite young. "Thank you for understanding and caring about me and my boyfriend," she sobbed.

March 8, 1995: The foreign teachers marched in the Women's Day Parade wearing Huanan Women's College T-shirts. Fun!

March 17, 1995: Joni and Jessica requested and received a New Testament today. They are both excited about knowing Jesus.

March 18, 1995: We visited a museum where a mummified lady buried 400 years ago is on display! Her bound feet with broken, twisted toes hurt me just to look at them.

March 22, 1995: Classes went to Xiao Pu village for an outing and a picnic, a cookout of pork, chicken, jiaozi, and fish balls. They were excited and enjoyed it.

March 24, 1995: I received a letter from Dr. Jerry Wallace, Campbell University, Buies Creek, N.C., offering $1,200.00 for room and board for Wei Wen Bin. The student now has a Ph. D. in Civil Engineering from the University of Berkeley, California. He did not come to Campbell because of his major.

March 27, 1995: A baby girl, abandoned at the hospital, was sent to the nearest ill kept orphanage today. My heart bleeds for her.

April 8, 1995: Ho Ru Ying, almost blind now, walked a full

hour to come and ask when we could go to Beijing for her eye examination. She is a Chinese saint.

April 12, 1995: I went to Project Hope's office today and learned that 300 Chinese dollars will send a poor child to school for five years. Betts and I made donations to help in this project.

April 15, 1995: We had no water until a hail storm and heavy rain came and provided enough water to fill buckets from drain pipes and enable us to flush toilets.

April 16, 1995: We attended a sunrise Easter Service at Fujian Seminary and an Easter drama tonight. "Hallelujah! What a Savior!" was the theme for both.

April 20, 1995: The pastor at Pu Tian reported 150 baptisms on Easter Sunday in his church.

April 22, 1995: We made a trip to Ningde over rough roads as people were using pick axes to chisel and break rocks from the mountain sides. Many peasants in mud up to their knees were working in rice paddies.

April 23, 1995: The swine keeper donned a white apron as he prepared to feed the pigs in a nearby compound. The stench was overpowering. I felt he needed nose plugs rather than a white apron.

May 15, 1995: I was notified of my transfer from Huanan Women's College to Fujian Medical University for next year. Word came from Stephen Ting, Educational Consultant for Amity Foundation, in Nanjing.

May 19, 1995: Xiu Ping gave me an electric fan which sounds like a big Mack truck taking off!

May 21, 1995: Wei Wen Bin called to report a fax he had received from Carnegie Mellon University in Pittsburgh,

Pennsylvania, to apply for a research assistantship. What rejoicing and praise at this unexpected opportunity! The efforts to attend Campbell University were not in God's plans, but our gratitude prevailed for his having being considered.

May 24, 1995: I spent three hours in a TV studio talking about houses in the U. S. A. It was very tiring and the lights were very hot and bright.

May 28, 1995: Wei Wen Bin and Zou Lin met me at Nanjing Airport and escorted me to the Jing Ling guest house for overnight lodging. I went to St. Paul's Church, saw the Jing Ling Seminary staff and many students, and gave Wei Wen Bin needed funds to come to the U.S. A.

May 29, 1995: I visited Siu Mei Guo in the hospital. She is a dear, dear Chinese sister who will soon go to heaven. Her husband, Bishop K. H. Ting, was in the usual place beside her bed reading, two of God's special Chinese.

June 2, 1995: I moved to Fujian Medical School today. A friendly lady and four men came on a van to assist. I have been busy unpacking and settling in since my arrival.

June 7, 1995: The bedroom has air conditioning – no noisy fan needed anymore. I am so lucky!

June 10, 1995: I took Charles Huang, his wife, and two daughters to McDonald's. The girls ordered only French fries and a sundae, and when eating the fries, they dipped them in the chocolate on their sundaes. It was their first trip to McDonald's.

June 21, 1995: A great privilege was afforded me to give the graduation speech entitled "A Time for Everything." It was well received and I was grateful.

August 31, 1995: I used a Chinese washing machine for the first time. Those washing machines are not equipped with an agitator. I wondered how clean my laundry would be.

September 3, 1995: A man on the street had a mouse trap shaped like a hook. A small mouse dangled from the hook and made passers-by sorry for the victim.

September 10, 1995: Observations at church today included seeing: a man with a twisted body the size of a small child, a grandmother seated between twins and sharing the hymnal with them, a husband pointing to scripture references for his wife, people taking notes on the sermon, and a brother helping his sister remove one of five sweaters she was wearing.

Nearby, a hearing impaired man removed his hearing aid with a faded blue cord, removed the battery from his shirt pocket, and carefully placed both in a worn plastic bag. Next the plastic bag was put into a blue velvet box, which was placed into a very old and well used black bag. What care he was giving to his "ears."

September 14, 1995: I had a good telephone conversation with my son, Glenn, today. It is his 50th birthday.

September 16, 1995: I met retired president, Dr. Chen, of Fujian Medical College today. His wife, Nancy, and I shared a taxi to and from Pu Chen Church.

September 19, 1995: Xu Dao Fang entertained the foreign teachers with a big dinner in her home. The building is quite large and was her home before Communism. After the government took all personal property, it was divided into several parts. She and her husband now have only two rooms – a bedroom and a living room. The kitchen, dining area, and bathroom are communal with several families using them.

September 22, 1995: Rachel and her mother, a retired pediatrician and now a seamstress, came to take my measurements for a dress. Because women retire at age fifty-five and men at age sixty, they are able to find a second job.

September 23, 1995: Eli, one of my students in the class

for English teachers, announced that he has an American grandmother! She was his English teacher in Anhui University and influenced him to become a Bahai. I must pray diligently for him.

September 24, 1995: Dick bought iodized salt and 100 packages of calcium, of which he advised me to take ten packages each day to prevent loss of bone and protect my teeth. A generous offer, but for fear of becoming "calciumified," I took fewer than he recommended.

September 25, 1995: Jain Li brought 200 packets of Anchor butter tonight. Whoopee! She stayed and ate jiaozi with me.

September 26, 1995: I sat through eighteen speeches this afternoon. I had tutored Yan Ling Mei; however, she was not a winner, but the experience was good for her.

September 29, 1995: National Day celebration included an acrobatic show sponsored by the Fujian Provincial government. Some of their stunts were breathtaking and quite dangerous, I thought.

September 30, 1995: Frances Wang, a confused eighty-five-year-old, brought a cooked fish, head included, as a National Day gift. She asked for a T shirt and was given my black Campbell University shirt. She was so proud and happy.

October 1, 1995: Ava, a young Chinese English teacher, came to talk about Christianity and requested a Bible. She later accepted Christ and attends Pu Chen Church, my church.

October 2, 1995: Dear Siu Mei Guo in Nanjing was finally released from her distorted arthritic body today. God is merciful. A Christian funeral will be held tomorrow in Nanjing. So sorry I will not be able to attend. She was like a sister!

October 3, 1995: I was invited by Huanan Women's College to visit eighteen streams with them in the pouring rain, a fiasco.

I ate a picnic lunch in the van and returned by taxi to the Fujian Medical University campus.

October 4, 1995: Dr. Wu has a meat grinder and brought ground pork which Eli made into patties for dinner. He is a good cook!

October 8, 1995: A great tenor blessed me as he joined in the singing of "I Need Thee Every Hour" and "God Will Take Care of You," always the last hymn sung in Pu Chen Church.

October 13, 1995: I ate dinner with Birgitta, a friend from Sweden teaching nearby. She made burgers from tuna, carrots, onions, and apples. Tasty! Eli enjoyed them but wondered why no rice was served!

October 14, 1995: I attended the Romanian Trio Concert at the Fine Arts Center, where three talented musicians played piano, drums, xylophone, saxophone, clarinet, trumpet, and flute.

October 17, 1995: I met Skylar and Yvette, who speak good English. He studied at Oregon State, his father at Cornell. Yvette is a retired organic chemistry professor and now teaches piano. Skylar is a wonderful tenor and sings with a group, with Yvette as their pianist. They are devout Christians, as well.

October 18, 1995: Wei Ming's boyfriend is studying at Duke University, Durham, N. C. His parents live in #301, and I live in #401.

October 19, 1995: Eli helped to cook dinner for Lin Hai Chen and Birgitta. Creamed potatoes, cauliflower, tomatoes and egg dish with cooked pears for dessert composed the menu.

October 22, 1995: Li and Chuck came asking, "Please, tell us more about your God!" They needed only a clear explanation of the plan of salvation. Party members, but now Believers!

October 25, 1995: Eli and I ate pizza at Hot Springs Hotel. A happy surprise occurred when I found Del Monte pickles for 25 yuan ($3.00 U.S.A.). Also, cheese was available for 78 yuan per kilogram. No thanks! Too expensive!

October 28, 1995: I received many birthday remembrances by friends and students, my 75th! Wei Wen Bin called from Pittsburgh, Pa., to say, "Happy Birthday!"

October 31, 1995: English teachers and foreign affairs officers came with flowers and gifts. My son called to say, "Happy Birthday, Mom!"

November 3, 1995: We had a delayed Halloween party with sixteen guests. Eli had decorated with orange and black crepe paper streamers. Bobbing for apples, pin a nose on a Jack-o-lantern, and other games filled the evening from 7:00 to 11:00 p.m.

November 4, 1995: Dr. Li came for help on his questions about immigration to New Zealand. He is trying to help a grandson who has a job offer in Wellington, N.Z.

November 18, 1995: I took an overnight train from Fuzhou to Longan to see a three-hour performance in the hot sunshine. Two children collapsed from the heat and from standing so long. The performance was colorful and well done. Foreign teachers were given straw hats, a bottle of water, and a package of cigarettes, which I trashed even though they are considered a nice gift.

November 19, 1995: A van took us over unfinished mountain roads to Yong Ding to see circular houses made of dirt. One three-story building will accommodate 350 people.

November 21, 1995: A covered dish luncheon for the English teacher's class was a pleasant affair today. Since it is near Thanksgiving, I told them about why America celebrates this holiday. As I prayed, they repeated each word of my prayer.

November 24, 1995: Eli's brother is studying in the Economy College, so Eli sends him one-third of his salary each month, about 25 yuan.

November 26, 1995: While making an apple pie for some foreign teacher friends, I discovered that the flour brought by a student was corn starch, so I made toast and crumbled it on top. At least, it was eaten.

December 3, 1995: Eli went to church for the first time today. He continues to talk about his Bahai grandmother.

December 8, 1995: Yvette promised to give Eli piano lessons. He is very excited and happy.

December 14, 1995: I took Eli to Ho Ru Ying's to practice piano.

December 15, 1995: I gave a Christmas party with eighteen students in my apartment. We cut snowflakes, passed an orange from leg to leg, placed a pear between our knees for a race, dressed a boy and a girl like Christmas trees, and sang Christmas carols – such was our entertainment which lasted until 11:30 p.m.

December 19, 1995: We attended Pu Qian church after which 250 people enjoyed a delicious Christmas luncheon. As usual, the foreigner was asked to perform, so I sang "Silent Night" and taught them the song and words to "We Wish You a Merry Christmas."

December 23, 1995: Anglo-Chinese College invited me to see their performance of Charles Dickens' story about the Scrooge who stole Christmas. Performers enjoyed their roles and put their hearts and souls into the performance.

December 24, 1995: Eli and I went to Pu Qian Church at 8:30 and on to Christ Church at 10:30. Wonderful Christmas music in each! At 12:00 we took a taxi to San Guan Church for the Christmas luncheon. Since foreigners are regarded as special guests, I was seated next to the pastor and the president of Fujian Seminary along with officials of the Religious Affairs Bureau.

December 25, 1995: Our post-graduate class today was turned into a Christmas celebration. Dr. Li sang "Silent Night" in his beautiful tenor voice. Soon the students joined in and the harmony brought tears to my eyes. Phone calls from family and friends made this a Christmas to remember.

January 15, 1996: A lady directly across from my building was playing the piano this morning. Suddenly, I heard "Crown Him with Many Crowns," "That Will Be Glory for me," "I Need Thee Every Hour," and several more. Little did she know how she had blessed my heart this morning. I sang right along even though she could not hear me.

January 20, 1996: Pretty little Dolly is coming for English class on Saturday morning. She is the precious eleven-year-old daughter of the Fujian Provincial Governor and his wife, who have dreams of her studying abroad.

February 1, 1996: I visited a bio gas plant in a remote village out of Kunming. Gas forms from waste collected from pigs and public toilets and placed in a pit. It provides enough gas to operate a generator which produces some electricity for the villagers.

February 2, 1996: During the earthquake today in Li Jiang, the children were outside raising the national flag at 7:30 a.m. The school building was totally destroyed, but no lives were lost!

February 14, 1996: While in Chaing Mai, Thailand, I went to elephant, butterfly, orchid, and snake farms. Python and cobras are scary and dangerous. A few people were photographed with the python around their neck, but not I, no way!

February 17, 1996: It was a privilege to share my testimony with the CSI and Global Missions Group today during Winter

Conference.

February 19, 1996: Skeet, my brother, and Lib, his friend, sent several boxes of Jiffy cornmeal. Yum! Yum! Yum!

March 9, 1996: Two nights ago a mild earthquake occurred, but I slept through it.

March 10, 1996: At Hai Sun Hotel we enjoyed a big dinner, courtesy of Dolly's family. Her father's office in Foreign Trade Plaza on the 31st floor is fully equipped with four TV screens, video equipment, table tennis, and an exercise room. A stereo system provides music for the dance hall. He is city manager, but how much business takes place in this environment may lead one to wonder.

March 23, 1996: John and Rachel heard about Jesus today for the first time. They are interested and I hope will soon return for more information.

March 24, 1996: A Pu Qian quartet asked whether I would sing "Softly and Tenderly" with them on Easter Sunday. I am flattered and humbled they would invite me to participate.

March 31, 1996: Eli and Emmanuel were in church with me. Eli is still confused with Bahai as opposed to Christ. I must keep praying and show patience with him. God is able.

April 2, 1996: A noisy Buddhist ceremony for a deceased man is taking place just outside my building. A bus with large paper wreaths attached, two vans, and a big flatbed truck with the band on board pulled off around 4:00 p.m. to the crematorium. All of them returned for a big dinner in the court yard below. Noisy mourners!

April 5, 1996: During our party tonight, Rachel and Jim were the perfect candidates to drink Coke through baby bottles.

April 7, 1996: A white robe and pink flower were presented

to me as I walked into Pu Qian Church. Then I was put on display on the right side of the platform. The reason for all of this – I was going to sing "Softly and Tenderly" with the quartet. Boiled eggs distributed to the congregation signified "that Christ is alive in you," according to Pastor Chen. A photo album was presented to each member of the now quintet as a gift of appreciation.

April 14, 1996: This morning sixty choir members at Flower Lane Church sang about the resurrection of Christ. My heart rejoiced with them as every face reflected their faith and joy in our risen Savior.

April 19, 1996: A package containing a chocolate bunny and an Easter card came from "my girls" in the Sunday School Class I had taught for many years at Ross Baptist Church in Windsor, N.C.

May 3, 1996: I attended Pam Whitfield's church wedding in Zhang Zhou. The Reverend Franklin Woo conducted the ceremony in Dong Bang Hou Church. Pam is from Winston-Salem, N.C., and the groom is a Chinese English teacher from Zhang Zhou.

May 8, 1996: Warner Berklin, an evangelist from Boco Raton, Florida, and Ed Lyman, his vocalist, were in Flower Lane Church tonight. I could understand the entire sermon and thoroughly enjoyed the tenor solos.

May 16, 1996: Paul brought anti-aging tonic, "to keep you from getting old," he said. "Take 4 capsules 3 times daily and you may double the dose for faster results," he explained. I shall continue the aging process as I didn't take the capsules.

May 27, 1996: It is pouring rain. A dear family with their earthly possessions passed by on an open bed truck, all the while holding umbrellas over the furniture not covered by a much too small ragged piece of plastic. I felt so sorry for them.

June 11, 1996: Sam took me to see the monkeys in his Family Life Control Center today. There were 150 monkeys of many sizes.

June 27, 1996: Xu Guo Zhong and his wife accepted Christ tonight!

July 5, 1996: We went to see the snakes milked for their venom, which is used for anti-aging tonic, cancer tablets, and antitoxin for snake bites. Venom is processed in a clinic upstairs above where the snakes are kept.

July 12, 1996: I met Texan Ann Hudgens; a friend of a former college classmate of mine, Lona Boatwright; and a friend of my sister's, Kappy Goslee from Wilmington, N. C. Ann is here to teach English in the summer program at Jing Ling Seminary in Nanjing. Coy and Betty Privette, good N.C. Baptists, are here as well. It's a small world.

July 15, 1996: Our team finally settled in at Shandong Institute of Education in Jinan, Shandong Province. Doris Burden from Missouri, Edna Cain from Virginia, Jean Eads from Indiana, Betty Cummings from Tennessee, and Libby Smith from Alabama were my team members. All are retired and capable ladies.

July 19, 1996: Jean has a swollen eye. Libby suffers from blistered feet and has a fish bone in her throat. The doctor at the school clinic removed the fish bone.

July 20, 1996: Eleven people loaded in the school van for the trip to Yantai to visit Lottie Moon country. The six foreigners, two assistant teachers, dean of education, assistant dean of education, and his girl friend crowded into the vehicle for the journey. The driver took us over a bumpy dirt road for one hour to avoid construction sections!

July 21, 1996: In Penglai, we attended the same church

where Lottie Moon worshiped. A baptistery is located under the pulpit and 200 people were scheduled for immersion. The congregation sang "Jesus Loves Me" and "Wherever He Leads I'll Go" as the benedictory hymns.

July 27, 1996: Mr. Song, our director, took us on a field trip to Qifu, home of Confucius. We saw his grave and his son's, both of which look like giant ant hills. Doris' glasses almost slid off her face as the temperature was very high. She was in a precarious position in the public restroom when this happened. What a trauma and chaos that could have been!

July 28, 1996: In Jinan Christian Church, I met David Tye from San Bernardino, California. He is involved with Campus Crusade and received his education in Taiwan and Canada.

July 31, 1996: An American style wedding with dear Tom as acting groom was a smashing hit tonight. I was very humbled to act as minister and used 1 Corinthians 13 and Christian wedding vows. The students enjoyed it as well as cookies and soft drinks afterwards – no wedding cake available!

August 1, 1996: I was almost blinded from flashing cameras. Shandong officials, school staff, students – everyone showed up at photograph time. Outside photos were made as we sat in metal chairs in the blistering hot sun. My legs had a bad heat rash tonight so my team members shared their remedies with me.

August 3, 1996: Professor Song took our team to Yellow River which was flowing west to east, an interesting phenomenon. From the river we were taken to Bao Tu Springs, natural springs in a resort area with water almost as cold as ice water. Both the river and spring are near Jinan in Shandong Province. The Yellow River is known for having changed its course a number of times through the years.

August 7, 1996: Each of the four classes decorated a classmate as a Christmas tree during party time today, Christmas carols were sung, and teachers gave small gifts to her students. This will be the last party since classes end tomorrow.

August 8, 1996: Our summer school assignment ended today. The team held our last prayer meeting. Blessings were received and gratitude to God for this experience was repeated by all five of our team members.

August 9, 1996: I returned to Fuzhou this p.m. Eli and John met me at the airport. I am expecting my brother, Joe Stroud, to arrive from Garner, N.C., tomorrow. It's good to be back in my flat.

August 11, 1996: Eli, Joe, and I went to Pu Qian Church this a.m. Eli cooked fish for our lunch unlike any Joe had eaten before – fish soup with head included. Surprisingly enough, Joe liked it.

August 15, 1996: Sam took Joe to Jin Qiao Park to ride a camel and then to Sam's lab where he researches family planning with the use of monkeys. Joe was impressed.

August 18, 1996: Eli and I saw Joe off at the airport in Fuzhou bound for the USA via Hong Kong. He will be greatly missed by my students and friends. They enjoyed showing him places of interest in Fuzhou and the surrounding area.

August 20, 1996: I gave Xiu Ping clothes Lib sent by Joe. She was quite happy with them. Rachel, daughter of my seamstress, came and took the pants and shirts that Joe gave to Eli to alter for him.

August 23, 1996: I faxed a recommendation to Cairo, Egypt, for Julie today. Hope she can continue her studies.

August 26, 1996: Eddy, whom I had not seen in three years, came by to visit today. He is now working in Guangzhou for a company selling large Chinese characters for businesses.

August 28, 1996: A big rat ran across Mitzi Harris' foot,

causing her to scream so loudly that Su Di, the cook, dropped all the dishes he was carrying and scattered food and broken bowls in many directions.

September 1, 1996: I went to the School for the Blind and paid fall tuition of 4,500 Yuan (Chinese dollars) for three children.

September 9, 1996: The four flights of stairs leading to my fourth floor apartment looked as if they had never been swept, so I began sweeping them. Glares were cast my way as residents moved up and down the stairwell; however, I continued to sweep to the ground level.

September 24, 1996: I received a letter from Dick, informing me that a friend of Dr. Li's had helped to get a scholarship for him, and he will remain in Massachusetts to study for a master's in Business Administration. Good news for him!

September 25, 1996: Dr. Yu, president of Huanan Women's College, died yesterday. I attended a memorial for her at Huanan today. She had been ill ever since I arrived in Fuzhou in 1992.

September 27, 1996: Today is Moon Festival Day. I plan to share five big boxes of Moon Cakes with sixteen young people tonight.

October 1, 1996: I visited Panda World with Mary, Kathy, and Eli. The ticket clerk tried to charge me thirty-five yuan while others were paying only five yuan. After seeing my residency card and passport, she agreed that I could enter for five yuan. The giant pandas were good performers riding a bike and a motorbike, playing basketball, and baby-sitting. Very entertaining!

October 2, 1996: Mary Hardy, a Bahai believer, and Mary Carol had lunch with me today. I hope to be able to help Mary see that Christ is the only way to God.

October 5, 1996: Jiaozi and fruit salad were the menu tonight as Eli, Ted, Winnie, and Doris dined with me. Making jiaozi for a meal is a family affair, as one member rolls out the dough, others grind meat and place it and vegetables into small dumplings, and another then crimps the edges with the fingers. Someone else places them into the pot and adds cool water as needed to keep them from boiling over until done. Much joking and laughing goes on during the entire process.

October 18, 1996: Peng Zhao Deng asked for help in filling out an application for higher study in Japan. I must pray that the officials will approve this endeavor.

October 23, 1996: Xiao Xu decided to take the $13,500 offered by the University of Louisville, Kentucky. He was hoping to enroll at Cornell.

October 26, 1996: Peng Zhao Deng talked to the Amity teachers about "How Foreigners Can Help the State Approved Churches in China." He suggested prayers, church attendance, and participation as approved by the Chinese Christian Council and Religious Affairs Bureau.

October 28, 1996: My Sunday School class at Ross Church, Windsor, North Carolina, sent Hershey candy bars for my birthday. Yum! Yum!

November 2, 1996: Five birthday cakes this year! Twenty students attended our hot dog and French fries dinner topped off with cake and ice cream My house was full as was my heart.

November 3, 1996: An invitation was issued to me to sing Christmas carols with the Pu Qian choir. I'm brave. I'll try!

November 7, 1996: David, a businessman from Australia, sent me a fifteen-inch tube of salami today. I've taught some English classes for his company. Now I have something different to share with hungry students.

November 17, 1996: Xia Rong Qiang, the blind director of Fujian Services for the blind, brought two pomeloes, which I dearly like. They are like a grapefruit only sweet and larger.

November 28, 1996: I spent Thanksgiving with nineteen foreigners at Huanan Women's College tonight. We enjoyed good fellowship and food including chicken dressing and pecan pie.

December 4, 1996: My upstairs neighbor died of a massive stroke early this a.m. John and I went upstairs to pay our respects. Candles, incense sticks, a large portrait of him, and four huge paper wreaths decorated the living room. I knew him only as my neighbor upstairs since he was a retired professor in Fujian Medical College.

December 7, 1996: I listened to a tape of Glenn, my son, speaking in his church, First United Methodist, in Henderson, N.C. It really blessed my heart!

December 10, 1996: Dana Hughes from Georgia called, asking for help to get $30,000.00 to a congregation in Ningde. The church had burned from faulty wiring. I will assist as best I can.

December 19, 1996: VOA announced the death of Deng Zhao Peng today. Chinese TV did not announce it until much later. He had died in October.

December 21, 1996: I gave a lecture at the provincial library about ways Christmas is celebrated in the USA. Participants asked many questions. I wish all of them believed in the Christ of Christmas.

December 22, 1996: I sang Christmas carols with the Pu Qian Church choir. Violin and saxophone solos added to the occasion.

December 23, 1996: We ate a big Christmas dinner at the Fujian Seminary and attended long performances afterwards. Solos, readings, choir music, and dramas made a great observance.

December 31, 1996: Xiao Xu phoned to bid me farewell. He is leaving tomorrow for Louisville, Kentucky. May God go with him.

January 3, 1997: I finally got through the lines to the U.S.A. to sing Happy Birthday to Matthew, my grandson. I could not get through yesterday, his special day.

January 7, 1997: I received $30,000.00 in checks for the church in Ningde. I will bank it tomorrow and send the deposit slip to Dana Hughes, the person who sent it to me.

January 9, 1997: Peng Zhao Deng is helping to contact the pastor in Ningde about the donation to rebuild the church.

January 16, 1997: The school for the blind refunded 750 yuan today ($80.00 U.S.A.), which I gave Ho Ru Ying to distribute to blind residents near her home. Twelve blind ladies will receive eight to ten yuan depending on their needs as dear Ho Ru Ying determines it.

January 23, 1997: With our group Eli went today to Xiamen, a city he had never visited before. He enjoyed the bus ride. Jessica, a former student from Xiamen, met us, took us to Pizza Hut for lunch, and by ferry to Seaview Hotel on Gu Lang Yu Island. Amity's Winter Conference will take place there. Eli will stay in a flat assigned to Jessica's family in Xiamen. He is so excited to be in Xiamen, a poplar tourist city in China.

January 26, 1997: Jessica took Eli and me to see a "Combination Home," which was adequately but sparsely furnished. One section was for the handicapped and one was a hospital. We were not allowed to see the children, as a new rule had just been passed forbidding foreigners to tour orphanages. This was just after the international report of dying rooms in orphanages for the severely handicapped.

January 27, 1997: A great worship service indeed took place

this morning during Winter Conference. Scriptures were read in French, Finnish, Swedish, Danish, English, and Chinese. The Lord's Prayer was prayed in one's native language. God does not need a translator! East Asia personnel flew to Hong Kong this afternoon. I went to a jewelry store and bought a pendant with matching earrings made like the Chinese character love. They will help relay a message of love and concern, I believe. Also, I ordered a Fruit of the Spirit ring, which has the Chinese characters of Galatians 5:22 – love, joy, peace, patience, kindness, goodness, faithfulness, gentleness, and self-control.

January 28, 1997: I received two books from North Carolina WMU, *Soup for the Soul* and *Hand in Hand*. I am so indebted to them for thinking of me in such a nice way. I had to go to Star House, East Asia Office location, to get them. Personnel from Korea, Japan, Macau, Hong Kong, and only a few from China made up the East Asia Personnel. Other Baptists working in China have a different platform unacceptable to the Chinese Christian Council. This is breaking our hearts and destroying the trust Chinese Christians once held for Southern Baptists.

January 29, 1997: I flew from Hong Kong to Taipei, Taiwan, for a meeting with East Asia personnel. Gwen Crotts and Faye Pearson from the East Asia office in Hong Kong led the conference.

January 30, 1997: I met Virgil and Ann Cooper, parents of Jamie, whom I have known for some time. They have worked as missionaries in Korea for many years. They led a devotional time entitled "Intimacy with God," very meaningful and inspirational.

February 3, 1997: Mimi had to remove batteries from her small clock at Hong Kong Airport, even though it had been going through security for five years.

February 15, 1997: Boxes came to me from Nanjing, where Chinese friends had spelled my name Sue Tool and Sue Toll. I received them because the address was correct.

February 19, 1997: Unknown teenagers threw kisses at me in McDonald's today as Eli and I were having lunch.

February 20, 1997: The $30,000 donated by Alex Kemp, a successful businessman from Georgia, for the rebuilding of the church in Ningde has finally cleared the Bank of China. Eli and I went to withdraw the funds, which in Chinese money amounted to 248,422 yuan. It was placed in my backpack in bundles of 10,000 each, and I felt uncomfortable as the cash was being stuffed into the backpack. But God protected us – not a single customer came into the bank until the now very heavy backpack was zipped closed. Taxis are not allowed on the street where that bank is located, so Eli and I walked three blocks with him carrying the money with me on his heels as if I were a protective guard. We hailed a taxi and rode to the campus. What a relief when he set that bag of money on the dining table! A telephone call to our contact person was made and the pastor and assistant pastor from Ningde came the following day to get the money, enough to rebuild the burned-down church. God provided!

February 24, 1997: Tomorrow has been declared a Day of Mourning for Deng Zhao Peng, who died of Parkinson's disease and lung infection. He is being almost deified by the government.

February 26, 1997: I took Gwen Crotts and Faye Pearson, East Asia officials, to Fujian Seminary to meet President Zheng, local Chinese Christian Council members, and the Agape House leaders. East Asia is offering volunteer services for a summer English program. Time will determine whether this plan materializes.

March 1, 1997: Fan Shi wrote that he is enjoying Chinese Bible Studies on Thursday and Friday nights in Cincinnati, Ohio. He has graduated from the University of West Virginia and now lives and works as an engineer in Cincinnati.

March 4, 1997: Eli trimmed the callus on my right foot; it feels much better.

March 7, 1997: Gwen Crotts called from Hong Kong to say the yearly medical exam could be given in the Provincial Hospital here. Dr. Hannah Lin, M.D., will accompany me. Good!

March 23, 1997: A Palm Sunday service in my flat today was held with Believers present from the Catholic, Friends of China, Bahai, and Christian persuasions.

March 30, 1997: My heart rejoiced at Pu Qian Church as the choir sang of our risen Christ – "Christ Arose," "Loyalty in Christ," "Christ the Lord is Risen Today"— and the rafters were almost lifted with the Hallelujah Chorus! I'm so blessed to see and hear Chinese Christians sing. How they enjoy singing!

April 10, 1997: I accompanied the post-graduate class to Bird's Paradise, an aviary recently added in Forest Park. It was drizzling rain but we went anyway, slopping through mud and puddles and pretending to have fun. Trained birds took only ten yuan bills from spectators and then flew back to their trainer. A few people held up one yuan bills, which the birds ignored. Smart birds! (One yuan bills are brown; ten yuan bills are grayish green.)

April 13, 1997: A young lady bought a picture of Christ and gave it to an elderly lady standing nearby. The recipient was overjoyed, as she obviously could not afford to buy one. The picture is sold along with Bibles, hymnals, and Christian calendars in church bookstores.

April 14, 1997: Peng Zhao Deng asked for help to translate into English a fifty-eight page book entitled *Questions and Answers for Seekers.*

April 28, 1997: Westfield Baptist Church, Dunn, N.C., sent forty pairs of glasses, which I gave to my ophthalmology students for use with poor village residents who cannot afford to buy corrective lenses.

May 4, 1997: I went with Peng Zhao Deng to a Meeting Point Church, which began four months ago with twenty members. Today, 150 people crowded in for worship.

June 9, 1997: Dragon Boat Festival Day and all visitors brought the sticky rice with meat (pork) or bean curd inside. Zongzhi is a specialty food for Dragon Boat Day in honor of a poet who drowned himself because he was considered an enemy of the government. Each year people throw zongzhis into lakes, rivers, etc., for him to eat in the "other life."

June 15, 1997: The youth choir did a beautiful arrangement on "What Would You Do with Jesus?" Their faces and voices reflected what they are doing with Jesus.

June 16, 1997: Dear Eli is in the hospital with serious colon problems. He has a temperature and little appetite. Friends and family must bring his food as the hospital does not serve meals.

June 17, 1997: My heart bled for a mother bringing her seventeen-year-old son in on her back to the hospital. He was diagnosed with tetanus. Oh, please, God, in your mercy, please, heal him. The mother is a widow and needs her son.

June 25, 1997: I visited two countryside village schools today south of Ma Wei, port of Fuzhou. The mountains were beautiful as I passed through three tunnels and met a motorcycle parade celebrating Hong Kong's return to the mainland. The schools have too many children in too small a space, each student paying 200 yuan to study English during summer vacation. A funeral procession met us with mourners in various costumes and headdresses, and several others walking on stilts!

June 30, 1997: When I was nearing the hospital to visit Eli, coming toward me was a man with an IV hookup sitting on the back of a bike holding up the bottle of glucose. His wife and brother were pushing him along. I felt sympathetic but helpless to assist him.

July 1, 1997: Hong Kong returned to China today! TV coverage, newspaper articles, parades, and loud music were included in the celebration. Eli came for a short visit and watched the televised activities with Xiu Ping, Mary Logsden, and me. He had to return to the hospital for further treatment.

August 27, 1997: I arrived at Ming Jiang University to an almost empty flat on the sixth floor. A non-functioning toilet, no stove, no telephone, no living room furniture, no cabinet space, no desk – what a surprise! A friend called Amity Foundation in Nanjing and authorities there phoned the Fujian Educational Committee, who in turn contacted the Foreign Affairs office of Ming Jiang University. That created some actions and soon the flat was furnished and livable.

September 3, 1997: My telephone extension continues to change, but at least the assigned phone number hasn't changed. Where will this end???

September 5, 1997: A young man was standing in the rain at the bus stop. I shared my raised umbrella with him. When the bus finally arrived, he grabbed my hand and led me to the only empty seat and refused to take the 1.50 yuan for the fare. When I got off at Fujian Medical University, he smiled, waved, and in English said, "Good-bye!" This was probably the only English word he knew.

September 6, 1997: I watched the funeral of Princess Diana with my New Zealand colleague, Shirley Angell, whose TV works. Mine doesn't and the promised replacement hasn't arrived yet.

September 20, 1997: Maintenance came to increase the height of the low slung dining table. He adjusted it too high, but he will need to return anyway and lower it some more because the screws are falling out of the legs.

September 28, 1997: Shirley Angell's shower and toilet do not work. She has been coming to my flat for two weeks. She lives on the third floor in a different section of the building. I live on the sixth floor far removed from her. Maintenance personnel could use some additional training, she and I have decided.

October 6, 1997: I went to class expecting to meet Monday Class 1, but because of the National Day Holiday on Wednesday, Class 2, which regularly meets on Wednesday, was assigned to meet Monday to make up for missing a class on National Day. But no one bothered to inform me of the change!

October 11, 1997: After a meeting in Hong Kong with International Mission Board leaders, Dr. Jerry Rankin, Bill Fudge, and Don Gardner, I knew it was time for me to resign from the Southern Baptist IMB. Others in our group who likewise could not support the difference in philosophy either resigned or found other means to stay in China. Needless to say, this was a painful but for me a necessary decision.

October 28, 1997: The Foreign Affairs officer inquired of my teacher colleague friend whether I was holding religion classes in my flat. Many former students came periodically to visit. My friend told her we were having a dumpling party, and that was quite true. The groups made jiaozis (meat and vegetable dumplings) and then we ate them.

October 29, 1997: Flower Lane Church was packed full. Elements of Communion were being passed to the early church worshipers. An elderly man, wearing a well worn cap, was standing on the very crowded steps with many others. After being served the bread and wine, he removed his cap, bowed his head, and prayed before eating the bread or drinking the wine. I knew not his name, but I knew he is my brother.

October 30, 1997: Xiu Ping took Jean Phillips, Betts Rivet, and me to her childhood home by a car with gears which gave out, and the driver had to phone a friend to come for us. We, however, enjoyed seeing the compound of many flats of a one-time very wealthy family. Only a few of the flats are now suitable for occupancy. The government did not keep them repaired – such a waste.

October 31, 1997: Several birthday cakes and many visitors made my seventy-seventh a birthday to remember.

December 5, 1997: Wendy, my Foreign Affairs Officer, seemed impressed with the Jesus Film. She asked many questions and plans to attend church. Since she is my Foreign Affairs officer, I felt it wiser to suggest that she attend church regularly and participate in Bible Studies at church on Friday and Sunday nights. I hope she will.

December 20, 1997: Toby, now a businessman, took me to a tea house for special Chinese tea in dainty china cups. Then he took me back to Ming Jiang University by taxi. He enjoys his new-found fortune as an employee of a cooking oil company.

December 21, 1997: I attended the performance of a beautiful Christmas cantata by fifty-six adults in Guan Lan Church. Small children blessed my heart as they sang "Away in a Manger" and "Jesus Loves Me." A lady who had recovered from a serious car accident gave her moving testimony and then with her daughter sang "The Love of God." There were few dry eyes after that.

December 24, 1997: Our seminary Christmas dinner followed by a lengthy program reminded me yet again of God's Gift of His Son for all mankind.

December 25, 1997: Another wonderful Christmas cantata tonight at Flower Lane Church after a good day with foreign friends made yet another Christmas to remember.

December 26, 1997: Oliver and Su Hui asked for Bibles and advice about how to become Christians. After accepting Christ, they were advised to enroll in Bible studies at Flower Lane Church and to attend worship services. May God bless both of them.

December 29, 1997: Gu Nian and Han Hui, her mother, were in church this morning. Gu Nian is back from Toronto, Canada, for a visit with her family. It was good to see her again.

December 31, 1997: At a big New Year's party sponsored by the school, Shirley, my colleague, and I sang "Old Lang Syne" as our contribution. Chinese dances and Karaoke music filled the remainder of the program

January 8, 1998: Kathy helped me shop for gifts to take to the four blind children supported by my brother Joe and our good friend, Lib Roberts. We chose toothpaste, toothbrushes, soap, towels, and underwear for the four of them.

January 11, 1998: Peng Zhao Deng celebrated his fourth wedding anniversary with me at a Taiwanese restaurant after church. His wife, Qi Bi, is studying in a seminary in Singapore. Tears ran down his cheeks as we dined and chatted.

January 13, 1998: As I was going to class this a.m., one of the maintenance men picked up a broken commode, which had obviously been sitting by the building for a long time. He threw it over the fence and I cringed for fear it would strike someone on the other side. Apparently no one was passing by at that moment, or else there would have been a fatality!

January 17, 1998: Melissa Powers, a foreign teacher, attended the wedding of a friend, who insisted she spend the night with her at her home. The bride and Melissa slept in the only bed while the groom slept on the sofa.

January 18, 1998: Dr. Ewing Carroll of Amity Foundation and David Harrell from the United Board will try to gain support for me through the United Board of Christian Higher Education in Asia. The Board's support would mean that I can remain with Amity and continue teaching in China. Please, dear God, may it be so!

January 28, 1998: Fireworks on Ming River blasted away from 12:00 midnight until 1:00 a.m. Skies were lit with bright colors, and Chinese observers sounded like excited children as blast after blast shattered the otherwise quiet night.

February 11, 1998: The streets, walls, and buildings are decorated with lanterns shaped like fish, birds, bears, and children were dressed in the fashion of the Chinese Lunar New Year.

February 14, 1998: Pizza Hut music consists of "Silent Night" year round. The owners apparently like the rhythm of the song.

February 25, 1998: Dr. Ron Winstead e-mailed that United Methodists would support those Southern Baptists wishing to work through the Chinese Christian Council and Religious Affairs Bureau. I was comfortable with sponsorship through the United Board of Higher Education.

February 26, 1998: Wei Wen Bin e-mailed that the three blind children and I were on internet, a fact I knew nothing about. Later, a fourth child was added to the group Joe and Lib support.

February 27, 1998: The Foreign Affairs Office sent twenty rolls of toilet paper as a gift for Women's Day! At least it is practical.

March 11, 1998: Poor Eli was admitted to the hospital for more colon surgery today. Dear God, please be with him.

March 17, 1998: James, a surgeon friend, had lunch with Betts, Eli, and me. He shared medical advice with Eli. Let's hope and pray it is helpful.

March 22, 1998: The bus passed a family of three on a bike; the father was pedaling, the mother was sitting on the rack over the back wheel, and the two-year-old boy was standing in her lap. I prayed they would not hit a bump.

March 28, 1988: Feelings of gratitude resulted in the

following: praises to my Father, my Jesus, and my Savior for His love and guidance; for His care of me; for His knowledge of my needs; for His promises; for good health, energy, strength; for opportunities to share His love; for the privilege of serving Him in China; for Christian brothers and sisters in the U.S.A. and in China; for family and their belief in Christ; for His Holy Word; for time to read, meditate, and talk to Him; for a comfortable place to live (in spite of the sixth floor apartment); for opportunities to attend Christian worship; for Chinese who pray after worship ends; for familiar hymns in the Chinese church; for answered prayers; and for a secure future in His presence!

March 30, 1998: Sonny offered to give me a ride on his motor bike back to campus. I accepted his offer. The wind was brisk but the ride was better than a ride on an overly crowded bus.

April 1, 1998: Dear Emmanuel leaves for Vancouver, Canada, tomorrow. Dear God, go with him. You are His, he is Yours.

April 6, 1998: The doors to our classroom were locked as the man with the keys had gone to political studies. I brought the students to my flat and discussed geographical locations, using the large world map on my wall. They enjoyed all of my candy corn, cookies, and crackers.

April 11, 1998: Dr. Ron Winstead e-mailed that the United Board of Christian Higher Education will support me through Cooperative Baptist Fellowship. Now I feel home free! PTL!!!

April 17, 1998: Lucy invited Eli and me to see The Titanic movie on her new CD. Very interesting film.

April 20, 1998: A courtship seems to be brewing between Eli and Ann, also an English teacher at Fujian Medical School. She is a smart young lady but not a Christian, my gravest concern. I must pray diligently for her salvation.

April 26, 1998: Winnie showed up at church for the first time.

She requested a bilingual Bible and a hymnal, good indicators of her interest in Christianity.

April 27, 1998: A man, nestled in an inner tube, was sitting in a large plastic pan in the pond under the gazebo this morning. He was using a long handled dipper to remove debris from the water. The rubbish was lifted to a cardboard box on the bank. A ladder was used for his descent and ascent. He was using only his hands to paddle around as the pan tipped back and forth and from side to side. I had to stop looking for fear he would topple over!

April 30, 1998: The new buses, including number 20, were fully decorated with red bows and bright tinsel hanging in the front.

May 2, 1998: Wilhelmina and I decided, on the spur of the moment, to get our hair trimmed. We understood the price was 15 yuan per haircut and 25 yuan for shampoo and styling, all total about $5.00 U.S.A. This included neck and back massage. Surprise! Surprise! Wilhelmina's cost was 170 yuan, and mine was 150 yuan. She enjoyed a full back massage, whereas I only sat in the chair and was charged 20 yuan less. Next time we will take a translator who can help us better understand the explanations.

May 5, 1998: A dear lady got on the bus with half of a dressed pig and at least a dozen dressed chickens. The driver ordered her off the bus. I hope she had enough money for a taxi.

May 10, 1998: A young lady presented a long stemmed rose to me as the youth choir marched out today. It brought tears to my eyes. This was a Mother's Day gesture which I greatly appreciated but for which I felt unworthy as I don't even know the young lady.

May 24, 1998: Our newest blind student won the Fujian racing event today. He will be sent to Nanjing for additional training in hopes that he can win the national track record for handicapped people. I'm proud of him.

May 31, 1998: After worship, the music today included hymns my parents and grandmother used to hum and sing. Included were "Since Jesus Came into My Heart," "What a Friend," "Sunshine in My Soul," and "Heavenly Sunlight." I think, perhaps, they were singing along with the music.

June 4, 1998: I canceled my trip to Russia with Betts as Xia Rong Qiang desperately needs someone to escort him to Boston, Massachusetts. He has a four-month scholarship at Hadley School for the Blind in Administration. He is the Director of Fujian Blind Commission and, of course, is blind himself. He needs a friend.

June 11, 1998: Hadley School is sending flight tickets from the U.S.A. to Xia Rong Qiang for him and for me, a nice surprise.

June 19, 1998: Students still pull grass, no lawn mowers or weed eaters being available. This student activity gave Eli and me time to pack my belongings which will go to Fujian Institute of Education for the next assignment.

June 25, 1998: At last, I bade farewell to Ming Jiang University as the move was made to the Fujian Institute of Education. I spent tonight in Huanan Women's College as Xia Rong Qiang will come tomorrow morning to begin our trip to the U.S.A.

June 26, 1998: I posted a check to the East Asia Office for the stated allotment made to my living allowance account. Xia Rong Qiang and I were met in Shanghai by Boaz, a young man now living in Shanghai and one of my former students from Jing Ling Seminary in Nanjing. He took us to the YMCA for the night.

June 27, 1998: Boaz returned to help us check in at the Shanghai Airport. A young Christian from Japan asked the clerk whether we could board first because of Xia Rong Qiang's blindness. This request was granted and we settled in with the help of attendants for the long flight to Boston via Tokyo and San Francisco. Wei Wen Bin, now a student at the University of California in Berkeley, met us and assisted Xia Rong Qiang as we went through customs, etc., and found the gate for our departure to Boston. It was wonderful having Wei Wen Bin's help. When we arrived in Boston, Hadley School had a representative to meet Xia Rong Qiang, so we said farewell and I went on to the nearby Ramada inn for the night. The warm bath and clean bed were welcome delights.

June 28, 1998: My flight from Boston via Washington, D.C. to Raleigh, N.C., seemed so short. My son, Glenn; grandchildren, Whitney Sue and Matthew; and brother, Joe, met me. They were a beautiful sight to me!

August 29, 1998: Poor Eli is still hospitalized but was granted permission to meet me at Fujian Airport. He has been getting treatment for colon problems since July 14th.

September 10, 1998: Eli had a third colon surgery today with NO PAIN medicine. He walked to and from the operating room with the help of two friends. I hurt for him.

September 16, 1998: A video was being shown on the street leading to my campus. A TV monitor was set up in the middle of the street. People were everywhere.

September 17, 1998: The man in the bed to Eli's left is a Christian who reads his Bible and listens to Chinese Christian tapes on his Walkman tape player.

September 25, 1998: Dr. Chen, Eli's doctor, told me that Eli's continuing problem is due to colon fissures, not cancer. I was quite concerned as he is in the oncology department of the hospital.

September 29, 1988: Clemmons, an English teacher from Germany, and his wife, Corinna, a Chinese, came for Bible study tonight. We had a good discussion and plan to meet on a weekly basis.

October 2, 1998: Dr. Chen came on his motorcycle to take me to the home of Cheng Tao. The flat was well furnished with tile floors and nice furniture; however, the plumbing left much to be desired. Water had to be drawn from the bathtub tap to flush the commode. The pipes leaked and the tub was obviously not being used. The sink could not be used because it could not drain.

October 10, 1998: Julie Dennison and I attended Crystal's wedding at a nearby restaurant. She was in my first class at Huanan Women's College in 1992. She looked pretty in her red wedding dress.

October 12, 1998: Oh, oh, oh! I sprained my ankle while leaving Union Hospital today, where Eli is still a patient. It is so painful.

October 17, 1998: A dirty, retarded-looking man tried to grab my backpack as Betts and I were walking to Han Hui's. He grabbed an empty Pepsi cup from my hand. It didn't frighten me because we had just seen several former students collecting money in the street to pay tuition for school-less children. I really thought one of them was playing a trick on me until the man stared in my face. I was glad Betts was with me.

October 24, 1998: Eli's father, brother, and brother's wife came to see Eli today for the first time. He has been in the hospital since July 14th.

October 31, 1998: Xiao Wei, a wonderful tenor, was at my birthday party at Peng Zhao Deng and Qi Bi's tonight. My tears flowed as he sang "I'd Rather Have Jesus," "What a Friend," "Amazing Grace," and "Oh, Happy day" all in English and in Chinese. This is a birthday gift I shall never forget.

November 1, 1998: Betts and I went to Xiu Ping's wedding

this a.m. Her home was decorated with red plastic flowers and tinseled ropes, and she was dressed in red. The groom and Xiu Ping's family attend a registered House Church; otherwise, she would have had a church wedding. The hymns, "Love Divine All Loves Excelling," "Jesus Shall Reign," and "Joyful, Joyful, We Adore Thee," were sung by her guests. Her pastor preached a sermon on "God's Love and Servanthood." It was a sweet ceremony for a fine Christian couple.

November 4, 1998: Toby, Li Qin, and I ate at Beijing Restaurant tonight. Among other things, the menu included frog soup, cow udders, and very private parts of a pig. We did not leave hungry.

November 15, 1998: I received word from my family that our youngest brother, Thomas Pierce Stroud, is being ordained into the ministry today in Englewood, Florida. How I would like to be there with my family.

November 24, 1998: Dr. Chen was able to get my airline ticket to Nanning to attend a CBF weekend with Ron Winstead, Ina Winstead, and Brenda Lisenby, CBF leaders in China.

November 26, 1998: I spent Thanksgiving with like-minded Baptists, sharing experiences at Guang Xi University in Nanning, where the Winsteads and Brenda Lisenby teach. Judith Richards from Guangzhou is my roommate. Singing favorite hymns and reading favorite scriptures enriched the experience.

November 30, 1998: Eli was finally discharged from the hospital today. He asked for a pillow to use as a cushion. He has endured torture too long.

December 11, 1998: Dick's wife has arrived in Massachusetts. Praise the Lord! This is an answer to prayer.

December 24, 1998: About 250 of us enjoyed our seminary dinner, after which I took a taxi to Flower Lane Church. It was so packed that Eli, who was waiting for me at the gate, and I could not possibly squeeze through the people. We went shopping to get a much needed pair of shoes for him.

December 25, 1998: I taught class this morning. Our Christmas party lasted from 7:00 to 9:30, with stunts, games, and Christmas songs greatly enjoyed by students and staff.

December 26, 1998: A man got on the bus carrying two red chicken roosters upside down. They let it be well known that they were not happy!

December 31, 1998: Lynn Yarbrough, teacher from Nanjing, will come for a visit and return on January 3rd. She is such a nice lady, an inspiration to have as a visitor. Eli and I will meet her at the airport in the school's car.

January 2, 1999: Lynn and I went to Panda World just across from campus. She was impressed with the trained giant Pandas. Next, we went to another park where the exhumed body of a fossilized woman with bound feet is encased in a glass tank. Her long, black hair is still present.

January 10, 1999: When I got on the bus, an elderly man offered me a seat. He had a well-worn Bible and was headed for the 7:30 a.m. worship. Even though he cannot understand English, we walked together but had trouble finding seats in the church. It was packed from the 6:30 a.m. Bible study. We took seats in the patio area and watched the service on the TV monitor. He took careful notes throughout the sermon in a well-worn notebook. I felt he was one of those who had been deprived of public worship during the Cultural Revolution (1966-76).

January 15, 1999: Helen needed some advice about whether she should continue loving her boyfriend if he does not respond to her attention. She hasn't seen him since May but plans to see him while he is home for the Chinese New year. Young people are pressured by parents to marry – girls by twenty-five years of age and boys by twenty-seven. They are an embarrassment to the parents otherwise. This kind of pressure, I feel, is a contributing factor to the rising divorce rate in China.

January 17, 1999: Our hearts are heavy but glad today. Betts is taking Jim, an orthopedic surgeon, to Mayo Clinic in Minneapolis for a year's scholarship to learn new surgical skills. A farewell luncheon was held at the Park Restaurant for them. My feelings of their departure are expressed in this "Ode to Betts":

> 'Tis the week before Betts' departure,
> And all through Fuzhou
> Is a feeling of sadness to see her go!
> Although her leaving is causing a great stir;
> New people are coming in just a few days –
> Huanan ladies may need to alter their ways!
> Betts is so understanding and kind,
> Do your own thing, she doesn't mind.
> Versatility is her God-given talent.
> Next thing will be her very own patent
> On how to assist young men like Jim.
> The world could use more doctors like him.
> Poor Sue is now in deep distress
> Cause Betts sent Sue's e-mails by express!
> Words are woefully inadequate to say
> How much you will be missed every day.
> Our heartfelt gratitude for all you've done
> To make life interesting, as well as fun!
> And when you and Jim come back to Fuzhou,
> We'll be the happiest people you ever did know.
> Bon voyage! God speed! Best wishes with love to you,
> Your sister, colleague, admiring friend, Sue.

January 19, 1999: Pan Yi Ling and I went by Ho Ru Ying's home after we left the School for the Blind. They need to know each other as both are involved in helping blind people. Ho continues to visit the Home for the Blind and assist ladies there.

Pan Yi Ling's husband is blind and teaches music at the School for the blind.

January 24, 1999: Toby and his wife came from Xiamen tonight. He is feeling much better since establishing his own cooking oil company. He boasted of having twelve employees and of the number of orders his company was able to fill. I am happy for him as he was unable to get his visa for studying on a scholarship offered to him. His former boss disappeared after custom's officials were about to arrest him, leaving poor Toby in charge of a company which folded because of unpaid custom fees. Toby needs a break! God will help him as he is God's child!

January 27, 1999: Our flight to Kunming was relaxing and fun. Southern Baptists in the Amity group met tonight in sweet fellowship. Small in number, the only ones present were Stan and Norma Foskett, Mike and Kitty Wilson, Jon Hilton, Lynn Yarborough, and I.

January 29, 1999: Amity took us to Wu Dong County to visit projects Amity supports. Included in the visits were a medical clinic, bio-gas project, deep well project, and a remote village school where several Amity teachers pay fees for children otherwise unable to attend. There is evidence of much poverty in the area.

January 30, 1999: Surprise! Surprise! A long, sleek limousine wove its way to the entrance of Golden Dragon Hotel, where Amity is meeting. A red carpet stretched from the entrance to the elevators. When the entourage passed us, our translator said, "The Prime Minister from Laos is staying here." He got a warm welcome according to Chinese standards.

January 31, 1999: The pastor at church recognized and prayed for the three foreigners – Ian, Gary, and me. We chose a different church from the one attended by other Amity teachers. I had previously attended the church where they were going while in Kunming on another occasion.

February 1, 1999: A kind man in the airport paid 10 yuan for me while I scrounged for my money. After getting boarding passes, we went to the waiting area. A shop was near so I went over and bought a small Chinese doll in order to get change to reimburse the kind man. Then I gave the doll to his little girl. She liked it very much. Her smile and giggles were my pay.

February 4, 1999: Charlie, Dr. Hannah Lin's nephew, ate dinner with me and joined in the discussion about Jonah with Clemmons, Eli, Michelle, and me. He is an engineer and a strong Christian young man hoping to marry his sweetheart soon.

February 8, 1999: Weng Hua escorted me to Lang Qi Island School by bus, ferry, and a three-wheeled taxi. He has 100 students, 50 in the a.m. and 50 in the p.m. His classroom is too small and poorly furnished, but he is to be admired for trying to help his students. I was asked to give a lecture about American young people.

February 11, 1999: A couple I had helped with English brought two blocks of cheese from Hong Kong. They plan to immigrate to Canada.

February 13, 1999: Han Hui and Xiao Kang brought a beautiful bouquet of flowers and a gallon of oil for Spring Festival gifts. "We should visit older people and give them gifts," they smiled. Suddenly, I was made aware of my seventy-nine years!

February 20, 1999: Ho Ru Ying's only sister is seriously ill in a cardiac unit in the hospital. Ho is unable to go by herself to visit her. After we ate lunch at Kentucky Fried chicken, we went to visit her sister. Both were very grateful and seemed happy to see each other.

February 28, 1999: Franny, who has been in Vietnam for two years, and May met me at church this morning. I had not seen Franny since 1995. A mature business lady in textiles, she was sent back by her company to Fuzhou. She is happy to be back, too.

March 3, 1999: Californian Marie Melrose, whom I knew in Nanjing, is teaching at Huanan this term. She attended the Saturday a.m. Bible study for foreigners in my flat while in Nanjing. We had done some traveling together during that time – 1988-1992.

March 8, 1999: In celebration of Women's Day, lady teachers are invited to Zho Hai Park for amusement. Many others went. I hope they stayed dry!

March 12, 1999: After I took Ho Ru Ying back to the hospital to visit her sister again, Thomas, a former student and now a practicing surgeon, gave me the grand tour of "his hospital." He is conscientious and cares about his patients. If I need surgery, Thomas is the doctor I would choose.

March 14, 1999: May asked for a Bible today. Woolf and Cindy came to church, her first time. She seemed awed by what she heard.

March 17, 1999: An e-mail from Julia now living in Cairo, Egypt, requested more information about Jesus. Leslie, the professing Buddhist, prayed to receive Christ today.

March 18, 1999: Leslie removed her altar to Buddha, then threw away her incense sticks, and is literally dancing with joy and singing "Jesus Loves Me." PTL!

March 20, 1999: We celebrated Eli's birthday with six friends who came and made jiaozi. Afterwards, they put puzzles together and played card games. He felt honored, I think.

March 31, 1999: Clemmons was shocked while writing on a chalkboard. He thinks it was caused by exposed wires from an electrical outlet. He teaches at the Banking University near the School for the Blind.

April 3, 1999: Simon wanted to know why Easter is an important holiday, and the door was opened for a full explanation in a class where all members showed an interest. Dear Lord, may they accept and believe.

April 4, 1999: Hallelujah! Leslie, the former Buddhist, was baptized today. She is one of the happiest and most enthusiastic Christians I know right now. May God bless her and use her.

April 10, 1999: An elderly lady preached for seventy minutes this a.m. Not one person seemed restless or aware of the time. The dear lady was a good speaker who held the attention of the people.

April 22, 1999: Xiao Gong, a Party member, said, "I can't claim to be a Christian because of restrictions of the Party." I feel sorry for him because in his heart he believes in God but is afraid to practice his faith openly. "I could lose my job or be put in prison," he explained. Americans are blessed!

April 23, 1999: We made a two-hour bus trip with the Amity teachers from Fuzhou to Ningde for a weekend retreat. After checking into the hotel, Sandy, my roommate, and I spied a rat on the headboard of my bed. We chased him as he ran into the bathroom and disappeared in a smelly open sewage pipe. We put a glass over the pipe and then put a fairly heavy ashtray on the glass. We saw no more of him and we got no backup from the plumbing that night!

April 25, 1999: Sandy and I attended the church rebuilt from the $30,000 sent by the gentleman from Georgia. We were asked to sing and chose "What a Friend" as our duet. Warm handshakes and smiling faces made us feel very welcome.

May 1, 1999: Dr. Chen is leaving for one month's additional training in Beijing. A party given by his piano students and an accordion player was held in the fifth floor flat of one of the students. After their recital a big lunch was served including blocks of pork blood, resembling cubes of brown Jello, and stir fry pork kidneys. The Chinese have learned not to waste anything. In years past, many people starved to death. Some of those present had relatives who died from malnutrition and lack of food.

May 2, 1999: May and I were invited to the home of the man in charge of Tree Planting Day in Fuzhou. An elevator took us to the fifth floor flat, our first time to use an elevator since most flats use only stairs. The floors were a beautiful polished blond, the furniture was nice and well arranged, and the living room was very comfortable. A bathroom with plumbing that worked separated two nicely furnished bedrooms. I was glad to know that some Chinese are beginning to enjoy a more comfortable lifestyle.

May 6, 1999: Leslie has decided to begin Bible study at her home. It is unlawful for me as a foreigner to conduct formalized Bible studies, but she can. She is such an enthusiastic Christian and wants everyone else to know the Jesus she has found.

May 8, 1999: When I arrived at The Old People's University for an English class, a choir was using our assigned classroom. We were finally directed to the second floor. The entire class held forth as musical notes flowed loudly and clearly throughout the whole class. Retired people attend this "University" to learn other subjects of interest to them, such as art, music, and writing.

May 9, 1999: The U. S. Consul in Guangzhou notified all Americans to be cautious because of the unfortunate bombing of the Chinese Embassy in Belgrade. The Chinese TV is showing this incident over and over, proving "the ugly Americans cannot be trusted." This coverage makes me very sad for our image in a country that needs to know the meaning of "In God we trust."

May 14, 1999: Leslie's house was packed with her friends tonight. Charlie played "Ye Must Be Born Again" among other well known hymns. Leslie has become a real missionary and wants all her friends to know her Jesus. China needs more witnesses like Leslie.

May 16, 1999: Sandy, Kaye, Helen, and I accompanied Peng Zhao Deng to a suburban church built by eighty-five families in private enterprises. They had contributed over 250,000 yuan ($31,000)U.S.A to construct a nice building with indoor rest rooms. It was a good worship experience as we listened to Peng Zhao Deng's sermon and observed the grateful faces of Chinese worshipers.

May 28, 1999: International news has been discontinued on TV. The anniversary of the June 4, 1989, Tiananmen Square Massacre is drawing near. The Chinese government is reporting that the U.S.A. is accusing China of stealing nuclear secrets. Adverse criticism of China is prohibited, if at all possible. Before every broadcast, government appointed editors screen the news.

June 6, 1999: Heading to the bank this morning, I was in desperate need of a translator. Praying as I walked along, I suddenly saw Zeke, a first-year student who went not only to the bank but also to the market with me. Galatians 5:19 came to my mind. My God shall supply all of my needs.

June 11, 1999: Mark Stone reported that government officials in Anhui Provinces told people to worship at Buddhist temples, not at any house church. A registered house church has the approval of the government, but some Chinese are too ill informed to follow through with this requirement.

August 29, 1999: Back in my flat after the summer holiday in the U.S.A. with family and friends. Whoa! What a sight! What a total mess! Electricity had been off, food left in the freezer section of the refrigerator was totally spoiled, and the kitchen floor looked like a moving blanket. It was completely covered by small termite-like flies moving lazily along. Liu Jin, from the English Department, and Eli helped me sweep and gather the little varmints. After so long a time and so many bugs, they left and I showered and tumbled into bed.

September 4, 1999: Alan, a Christian friend from Flower Lane Church, has asked for help in his English class. If my class schedule permits it, I would like to help him.

September 10, 1999: A proud grandfather strolled by my door, pushing his small grandson this afternoon. He was strutting like a royal barnyard rooster. Pride was pushing him right along!

September 21-22, 1999: More rat problems – a big one sitting on the stove when I came in from class. Robby, Wint, Charles, and Hugh came armed with metal poles and a supply of poison. We left the two doors open so we think he escaped when the "four-man army" began moving furniture while trying to locate him. Poison is carefully placed throughout the flat. Please, dear God, if he gets poisoned, let him die outside.

September 24, 1999: Lynn brought white roses and moon cakes today. She joyfully told me, "I go to church for Bible study every morning from 5:00 to 6:00. Jesus came into my heart when I heard the scripture 'It is not I but Christ who lives in me.'" She went on, "How happy I was on the bus going home from church. I could hardly sit down I was so happy." What a beautiful testimony!

September 28, 1999: Hugh moved the dining table over, stood on top of it, and cleaned the dusty blades of the overhead fan. Now dust bunnies are fewer.

October 1, 1999: Dr. Chen took Leif, Annki from Europe, and Li Li, their adopted two-year-old Chinese girl to the People's Governmental Hospital for Annki to have an ultra sound given by an ob-gyn doctor. What an amazing experience to see a four-month-old fetus moving lips and fingers. My thoughts were if every pregnant woman could see her unborn child, she would never submit to an abortion.

October 17, 1999: A troubled young man came into church this morning and made his way to the platform. He tried to get to the microphone but was wrestled off and out of the church by ushers. I never learned of his cause and so was left wondering.

October 30, 1999: Today I received an invitation to Gu Nian's wedding in Honolulu. She will marry a young man from Fuzhou. Wish I could attend.

October 31, 1999: Flowers, cards, phone calls, e-mail, and a birthday dinner at Peng Zhao Deng's made my 79th a very special day.

November 8, 1999: I found broccoli for the first time at the market today!

November 21, 1999: I gave balloons to children playing at the croquet court today. They were so excited and happy. Brother Joe sent a huge box of balloons donated by BB&T.

November 23, 1999: I gave *Son of a Prophet* to Xiao Deng, who plans to use it with his seminary English class.

November 24, 1999: I took a KFC dinner to Ho Ru Ying, who thought her refrigerator was out of order. The dear soul had disconnected it when she tried to pull it from the wall.

November 26, 1999: We had dinner with Pastor Li and his family at Food Street Restaurant. Brenda Lisenby and I were so glad to visit them. There were too many food choices from a restaurant that stretched for a good mile featuring food from many countries.

November 27, 1999: I met the Webbs from Texas. They know Ann Hudgens and Lona B. Ruffin, the Sunday school teacher of the Webb lady's mother. Lona was a classmate of mine our first two years of college. Ann Hudgens worked in the Amity Summer Program in 1996. These associations gave me an additional feeling of friendship among the ladies from Texas.

November 28, 1999: It is amazing how God brought interesting people into my return trip to Fuzhou. An oceanographer and a geological engineer shared their seat on the plane. They treated me to lunch and saw me to the correct departure gate. A family from Singapore with two children allowed the children to sit with me. We played word and finger games, making the flight seem shorter.

After my arrival, May met me with her driver and took me to Huanan, where I enjoyed a Thanksgiving dinner with the foreign teachers there. The driver returned at 8:00 p.m. to take me to my school. It has been a wonderful day, and I have much for which to give thanks.

December 2, 1999: Some parents sent three children after me as I came from class. They wanted money, but I gave them each a piece of hard candy in their cup. We were advised to give food, not money, to beggars as many are fakes!

December 4, 1999: Eli and Ann were legally married on November 26 but didn't tell me until today. They looked nice and seem happy. I wish them long life with much happiness.

December 6, 1999: Leslie's policeman husband has become a Christian. Prayers on his behalf have been answered.

December 12, 1999: Between the early worship and later worship services, Rachel's mother, my seamstress, measured me in the vestibule of the church. She is to make a suit for me.

December 15, 1999: In English Corner tonight, we sang Christmas carols and talked about the first Christmas.

December 21, 1999: Xiao Wu and Lin Feng are back from Vancouver for a visit. Lin Feng has become a Believer, and he asked the blessing before we ate. They are attending a Chinese church in Vancouver. PTL!

December 22, 1999: Students enjoyed the Chinese version

of "The Twelve Days of Christmas."

December 25, 1999: Betts and I visited Ho Ru Ying in the hospital. Also, we saw ninety-eight-year-old Dr. Lin, who told us he had been seeing his mother long since departed from this life. Both patients are pitiful. Turkey, dressing, and macaroni were big items on our Christmas Day lunch. A former teacher sent the Stove Top stuffing and macaroni.

December 27, 1999: I hardly recognized Skylar as he and Yvetter joined Fin Zheng and me while we were walking to Guan Lane Church. He has gray hair but today he was wearing a very obvious black toupee. The adult and children's choirs blessed us with their enthusiastic Christmas music. The children always bless my heart. Dr. Hannah Lin was there, having just returned from a two-year visit with her son in New York City. Hannah, Fin Zheng, and I were seated first at table #1, moved to table #2, and finally table #3! Governmental officials must occupy tables # 1 and 2! Church leaders were seating us, so we just obeyed them.

December 31, 1999: Dr. Chen invited several medical students and friends to his home for a celebration. His son, who has been studying in the USA, is back and Dr. Chen's future son-in-law, a cardiologist, was among the guests. The son offered me a book he had purchased in New Orleans. It contained the most important events of the past century, but I could not accept his book. I felt he would probably need it in the future. The gathering was a nice affair, and the songs, accordion, and piano solos along with a high pitched soprano made for a good morning.

January 1, 2000: This p.m. I went with the Huanan teachers to Wu Yi Auditorium for a New Year's celebration – dances, songs, fashion show with music so loud I put tissue wads in my ears, as did my friends! Fireworks and firecrackers lit up the night skies, welcoming in the new century of 2000!

January 3, 2000: Tyson is back in Fuzhou from Toronto,

Canada, for a visit. He has been baptized since going to Canada. PTL! I hope to see him soon.

January 10, 2000: The blind track star gave me one of his gold medals today, but in reality I did not want to take it. He won it. He should keep it.

January 13, 2000: Teacher's Game Day! Rewards included two bars of soap, toothpaste, a liter of soy bean oil, a box of mushrooms, soybean salad oil, and a box of oranges! I needed help to take the prizes to my flat.

January 14, 2000: A vocalist in Guang Lan Church works in the Bank of China, where I have an account. He smiles and nods his head when I come into the bank. I feel honored that he recognizes me.

January 19, 2000: May invited me to visit two companies which produce products for her export business. In Xiamen we met two buyers from Orlando, Florida, who order from her company. One factory we visited was making toy submarines and replicas of the Titanic. Skillful production was taking place in spite of deplorable working conditions.

January 20, 2000: I attended the Christian funeral of my dear Chinese Christian sister, Ho Ru Ying. I could not be sad as she could not get well and was ready to meet our Christ.

January 25, 2000: Amity teachers are having Winter Conference in Xiamen. Toby came and took me to the Holiday Inn, where I bought sauerkraut. It was stored in quantity so a plastic bag was used to fill my order of three pounds. So glad to get it! Amity leaders are very much concerned about the future of Southern Baptist teachers in China. God's will is going to be done in spite of opposition!

January 28, 2000: This afternoon, we were taken to the Ark Church built in the shape of an ark. The pastor had given a Bible to the architect, who, after reading about Noah, decided to design the church as a boat. Even the balcony of the church is shaped like a boat, railing included.

January 31, 2000: Joni Wiggins, another Southern Baptist teacher, came for a few days. She teaches in a remote village school in Guangxi Province. We will celebrate New Year's Day with other foreign teachers and visit places of interest in Fuzhou, such as Dr. Zhi Zhe Chen's hospital. Dr. Chen is eager to practice English with all foreigners.

February 5, 2000: The timing was perfect! The driver's son came to my door just as Joni and I returned. Joni needed to go to the airport tomorrow at 1:00 p.m., and when we asked the driver whether he could take her, without any hesitation he said, "Of course, I'll be glad to take her." His wife is the post office manager on campus, and she had sent her son with a package notice for me. His arrival and our appearance were simultaneous!

February 6, 2000: An embarrassed young girl was seated on a busy sidewalk with a sign meant to humiliate her. This form of punishment was used for certain misdeeds. Neither Joni nor I could read the characters but from her looks, we knew her behavior must have been very bad. Our hearts went out to her.

February 10, 2000: Dragon's brother works at the TV station. He came home with me after dinner and adjusted my TV so that I can now get CCTV4, which carries international news.

February 12, 2000: Tyson, from Toronto now, came telling how Jehovah's Witnesses were appealing to the Chinese immigrants. A Mennonite pastor has told him that they are a cult. Tyson is advising his Chinese friends to look for a Christian Church. I'm so proud of him!

February 14, 2000: Eli and Ann celebrated their public wedding in a cheap hotel tonight. She was dressed in red, he in a dark business suit. One basket of flowers with double happiness characters was the only decoration. They looked happy and made short speeches thanking their guests for coming to their wedding dinner. An earlier one was held in his village so all of his relatives could attend. Both are English teachers in Fujian Medical University.

March 6, 2000: I learned today that Xu Xun Yu (Robert), a cardiologist, is in Harvard Medical School in Boston, Massachusetts. He was one of my very special students at Fujian Medical University.

March 9, 2000: Wheels are turning for me to teach in Huanan Women's College next year under the umbrella of CBF with support from the United Board of Higher Christian Education. God continues to provide.

March 17, 2000: I took Luke and Skeet to Pizza Hut. Neither had ever been and neither had used silverware before. They ate soup, salad, and three slices of pizza. Hungry boys!

March 24, 2000: What a joy to see hungry Luke and Skeet devour fried chicken, mashed potatoes, and cole slaw for their first visit to Kentucky Fried Chicken.

March 25, 2000: We learned today that Dr. Zhi Zhe Chen is the "Senator" from Fujian Province in the National People's Congress.

March 26, 2000: A police van pulled up beside me, doors flew open, and uniformed men jumped out and began to grab peasant women who were awaiting shoppers to buy their garlic buds and vegetables. They were shoved into the van as their produce was tossed and thrown into the street and walks. I felt like weeping for the peasants, who probably had no legal permission to sell on the street.

March 30, 2000: Liu Jian told me that students who failed exams twice must pay their school system 6,000 yuan. Students here are English teachers back in their local villages. Poor teachers! Poor English!

April 1, 2000: As we ate steaks today, I was able to share God's love with Luke and Skeet. Both are very poor and are always hungry.

April 11, 2000: Love gifts from several friends, family members, and churches were sent to Amity to help meet needs in projects in remote villages. Projects include rebuilding churches and schools; installing poles for electrical power to villages, deep wells, bio-gas projects, and orphanages; providing tuition for children whose parents could not pay; establishing medical clinics; retraining for the unemployed; and buying Bibles and hymnals, among other things. Amity's purpose is to help meet human needs.

April 12, 2000: I had dinner at Lakeside Hotel with leaders from Hadley School for the blind. Xia Rong Qiang and his wife were in attendance. Hadley School seems to send a group each year as they provide training for blind services in Fujian Province.

April 16, 2000: Candi has finally met all legal requirements and is headed to Melbourne, Australia.

April 18, 2000: Joe came to ask me to lead him in the prayer "to make me Christian." He has been seeking for a long time.

April 27, 2000: I gave the VCR and PAL movies to Eli. Since I will teach at Huanan next year, I will not need them. Huanan has a big supply.

April 29, 2000: MacDonald's manager allowed me to buy ten sausage patties at $1.65 each. He also sells cheese when there is an ample supply. Rachel, daughter of my seamstress, was baptized with many others.

May 2, 2000: Eli and Ann are so proud to have a bedroom and a kitchen. The kitchen is in a shack with a canvas top to keep out the rain. He had whitewashed the walls to make it look cleaner. The two rooms do not connect, but they are so happy and proud to have a place to call home.

May 3, 2000: May became very distraught and began crying because of parental pressure to get married. They have arranged boys for her but none are appealing to her. She is twenty-seven years old and should have married by age twenty-five according to Chinese tradition. We read scriptures dealing with anger and depression. She requested a Life Application Bible when I return from the U.S.A. Indeed, I will oblige!

May 7, 2000: Americans Dr. Miller, a dentist, and his wife were in MacDonald's this afternoon. They were utterly amazed to see the bi-lingual Bibles that Kevin, John, Matthew, and I had. Bibles printed in China came as a total surprise to them.

May 15, 2000: A small girl wearing slippers that squeak and light up was walking with her fingers in her ears.

May 16, 2000: A very narrow escape and a nudge from God saved me from being robbed of travel money for a trip back to the U.S.A. A thief slipped behind me and unzipped my backpack when suddenly I felt the need to pull it from my back to the front left side of my body. When I checked it, the zipper was completely open. My passport, residency card, bank cards, and 10,000 yuan to buy my plane ticket, and my money belt were still in place. I stopped in my tracks and gave a prayer of thanksgiving that my guardian angel had alerted me just in time. The man and woman following me suddenly changed directions and disappeared.

May 19, 2000: A performance by the deaf, blind, and retarded children was held on the fifth floor auditorium of a primary school. The blind children whom I have befriended were playing the accordion, trumpet, and piano. A milk company donated boxes of milk to the individual schools. Track outfits were donated to the blind. Officials from Beijing gave small red envelopes with money in them to the deaf and blind students. The performance was well done, and the children had been well trained.

May 23, 2000: The purchase of my round-trip plane ticket was finalized today. I leave Fuzhou on June 15th and return on August 30th. It is a relief to have the ticket in hand.

May 29, 2000: Thunderous fireworks woke me up at 10:00 p.m. and lasted until 10:30 p.m. The completion of a new addition at Lakeside Hotel called for a celebration. This was the explanation I received the next day.

June 1, 2000: Fei Tong asked for a Bible. He wanted to read Genesis 1 and the Book of John. It is always a happy privilege to donate Bibles on request.

June 6, 2000: Dragon boats are practicing on West Lake with twenty-four boys in each boat paddling as fast as possible. The drummer up front is encouraging them to paddle faster as he beats the drum faster.

June 8, 2000: God's power is stronger in crises! Huanan Women's College will get a letter of invitation for me to send to the Chinese Consulate in Washington, D.C., to get my re-entry visa. My foreign affairs officer had told me that a re-entry visa is impossible. The United Board of Christian Higher Education will send support money for next year upon receipt of a letter from Huanan Women's College requesting my services. The letter is on its way! Now I can relax as I go to visit my family and friends in North Carolina.

June 11, 2000: Taiwan had a 6.7 Richter Scale earthquake which made Fuzhou tremble, but there was no damage here. How strange to feel the bed vibrating! No harm otherwise.

June 13, 2000: Maria Drumm from Ft. Myers, Florida, who was involved with Teen Challenge, an organization for troubled youth, was on the flight from Detroit to Beijing. She is a delightful and interesting lady.

September 2, 2000: A city block near Huanan Women's College burned today. The cause is unknown still, and much smoke polluted the air.

September 3, 2000: I saw two handicapped friends at church. One was in a "put together cart" he rolls by hand since he is unable to walk; the other one can't talk and gets around on crutches. Both have big smiles when we meet. I look forward to seeing them on Sundays.

September 7, 2000: Dodie and I were interviewed by a Fuzhou journalist for a women's magazine. Fujian Women's Federation gave us a cleaning liquid as gifts.

September 8, 2000: We were required to go to quarantine center for more blood work to be recorded on our health reports. Urine and blood samples were taken and then without any labeling placed on a shelf with many others. All of us checked as worthy of teaching in China!

September 9, 2000: At the red light stops back to our bus stop, the bus driver ate from a plastic container and used chopsticks without mishap. He seemed quite hungry and was almost inhaling the contents of his container.

September 10, 2000: Cell phones have become very popular. Passing the market today, I observed a peasant pull out his cell phone probably to check with another unlicensed merchant to see whether police were in their area. May overheard the conversation from our end, and she told me the jist of the conversation.

September 16, 2000: Qing Hua called to tell me he will study at the International Seminary in Los Angeles, California. I'm sure he will do well.

September 18, 2000: I bought dried beef pieces in small packages to give to beggars.

September 26, 2000: A Fujian TV crew came and televised the National Day Celebration at Huanan Women's College. A big bonfire and decorated courtyard made a colorful background. Balloons, twinkling lights, and ropes of tinsel added to the festive occasion. Songs, dances, a fashion show, and happy students were included in the noisy celebration.

October 4, 2000: Eli and Ann have moved to a nice apartment which has a kitchen sink and a bathroom with plumbing that actually works. They have a computer and will get a phone soon. I'm happy for them. Scarlett and Robin brought tea, which is good for "aged" people as it helps digestion, I was told.

October 10, 2000: Class A enjoyed the "Hokey Pokey," "London Bridge," "Farmer in the Dell," and "Do, Ra, Me" from "The Sound of Music."

October 14, 2000: Police were confiscating vegetable carts, display boards, and produce from peasants again. They were pushing and yelling at the peasants, probably because the peasants are unlicensed. It still troubles me to see their livelihood destroyed.

October 28, 2000: Jeremiah, father of a four-year-old son, cannot afford to send the child to kindergarten. The mother is working, and Jeremiah is a student. Funds were made available for the son to attend kindergarten. It was hard to tell who was the happiest – the mother, the father, or the child.

October 29, 2000: A birthday party for Scarlett's one-year-old son included seventy people. He was dressed like a little emperor and was loaded down with life-size stuffed animals as gifts. A fourteen course lunch was served and would be followed by a bigger dinner tonight. Poor baby will be worn out!!

October 31, 2000: What a happy Halloween Day! It was so much fun to dress in a witch costume and visit the classes, all ten of them this a.m. Students screamed and hid behind desks and one another. They never knew who the witch was as she was in full costume, including a witch's mask. Fun! Fun! Halloween should come more often.

November 1, 2000: Birthday cakes, flowers, phone calls, cards, and visits made a happy 80th birthday. I am a fortunate person to have so many wonderful friends and a loving family.

November 11, 2000: Wu Jien Ming, a Chinese English teacher, said, "After reading *Son of Faith*, I learned that Buddha is not a god. Now I am sharing my book with other friends who are Buddhists." Please, God, please, open their spiritual eyes to Your Truth.

November 12, 2000: May happily reported that her mother is asking questions about Christianity. She hopes her other family members will become interested.

November 14, 2000: Firecrackers exploded so loudly at 9:00 p.m. that I almost fell off the side of the bed, where I was seated checking papers. A Buddhist neighbor had died, and the firecrackers "ward off the evil spirits."

November 19, 2000: Five thousand people worshiped in Flower Lane Church this a.m. Several students and two friends from Samming – Mitt, and Kammy – attended with me. The singing was great, and my heart rejoiced.

November 23, 2000: May and Daisy took me to the airport in Fuzhou for the flight to Nanning and the CBF meeting. When Brenda Lisenby met me, I accompanied her to Guangxi University. Brenda had cooked black-eyed peas and cornbread, good Texas style. Ken and Lu Ann Lock, Ken and Le Nell Webb, Brenda, and I are the CBF'ers in China right now. May God multiply our number quickly is my wishful prayer.

November 25, 2000: The sharing of CBF concerns and updates on CBF projects filled the morning. A delicious Thanksgiving lunch of chicken and dumplings, dressing, mashed potatoes, green beans, Jello salad, and cranberry sauce was prepared by the Guangxi ladies. Mm-mm! I ate too much before leaving for the airport to return to Fuzhou. Lin Feng and May met me in Fuzhou in his car and brought me to Huanan Women's College. We arrived here at 7:30 p.m. God has provided so many nice surprises. I thought the trip from the airport to campus would have to be made by bus fairly late at night. What a relief to see two smiling friends awaiting my arrival!

While in Nanning, I met Stuart and Peggy Milliken, who serve through Wycliffe Bible Society. They are busy developing a dictionary into the Huan dialect with plans to translate the Bible as well, so that this ethnic group may have access to scriptures in their native Chinese dialect. My best wishes and prayers are with them

November 26, 2000: Through the use of her digital camera and computer, May e-mailed my photo to family and friends today. It will be a surprise to them.

November 27, 2000: A student fainted in Jeannie Farrer's class today. She was taken to the hospital but later returned to campus. The diagnosis: "She has a small problem in her brain." Any brain problem would be monumental, I would think.

November 28, 2000: Our taxi acquaintances said they could not come at 6:00 a.m. to take our visiting Amity teacher, Georgina, to the airport. She and I went out on the street, and after a short time we were quite successful in hailing a taxi. The driver, besides being very friendly, also spoke English, another one of God's provisions!

November 29, 2000: Peter Chen, an ABC (American Born Chinese) from Baltimore, Maryland, went to class with me today. The students were fascinated with his account of "Life in the U.S.A." He is back to visit his father, who was living in Baltimore but was deported because of illegal immigration practices. Peter is a strong Christian and is diligently praying for his father's salvation.

November 30, 2000: My seamstress has scripture verses tacked to a shelf in her sewing room. She has a thirst for God's Word!

December 1, 2000: Dodie, Gwen, and I attended a farewell party for Dr. Zhi Zhe Chen in a swanky dining room in Tai Jiang. Much fun, food, and fellowship abounded as we wished him bon voyage to Germany, where he will have advanced studies in hematology. One of the guests is a Christian history teacher at Xi Da University. He provided a good laugh when he gave a hearty sneeze just as his photo was being snapped.

December 3, 2000: A field trip to see an unearthed Buddhist Temple near the airport was incredible. Down many steps we tramped, not believing what we were seeing. The colorful, rotund Buddha was on his throne, while other figures were still in place. No one knew just how long the site had been buried, and I found it difficult to believe what I was seeing.

Gore and Jeanne came tonight and we had a good talk about God, Jesus Christ, and Christianity. They asked to read *Chicken Soup for the Christian Soul*, a good step toward asking for a Bible. May it be so, Father!

December 4, 2000: I worked several hours proof-reading the Fujian Seminary description, so poorly written. They hope to get it published soon.

December 10, 2000: Wei Wei confessed her relationship with a married man. I showed her appropriate scripture and asked her to read it aloud. She was obviously shocked and promised to end the relationship.

December 14, 2000: The Foreign Affairs officer took me to the dentist and insisted on paying the 100 yuan dental bill.

($11.00 U.S.A.) A back tooth had chipped and needed to be repaired. I am so grateful for Xu Dao Feng and her generosity.

December 15, 2000: Christmas is in the air! Our tree is decorated as are the doors to our individual rooms. "Jingle Bells" and "Silent Night" are filling the air. It's sad that the true meaning is not known by all who hear the music.

December 19, 2000: I went to Bird and Flower Market to buy a fish bowl for Dr. Zhi Zhe Chen's fish. He is leaving soon for advanced study in Germany. Foreign teachers will miss him as he is the resource doctor for all ailments of the foreigners who know him.

December 22, 2000: We enjoyed the Christmas dinner at Fujian Seminary tonight. Xu Dao Feng, Amy, and I left after the dinner. The program which followed would last until 11:00 p.m.

December 24, 2000: A beautiful Christmas Cantata at Tian An Tun Church tonight was well attended. It ended with an impressive candlelight service which seemed sacred and holy to me.

December 25, 20000: I met classes as usual but had my students dress as Christmas trees with bits and pieces of crepe paper, ribbons, tinsel, and Christmas bells. Each made up a story of a Christmas gift he or she would like to give to a special person in his or her life. I was moved by some of their "gift giving."

Eli, Amy, and I attended Flower Lane Church tonight at 7:30 along with hundreds of other people. We were seated by an usher up front on a pew only long enough for the three of us. The music and the drama of the first Christmas made it worthwhile. An invitation resulted in 150 people responding to become Christians. God's Spirit is at work in China!

December 28, 2000: Foreign teachers entertained the faculty

with a dinner followed by child-like games, which they seemed to enjoy. One is never too old to enjoy silly children's games. (Example: Inflate a balloon and sit on it until it bursts; walk with an orange between the knees.)

December 30, 2000: Hunter invited Jeannie and me to a special dinner at a new restaurant tonight. It was the first time I have eaten ostrich, a rather bland meat which resembled sliced lamb. Oh, well, that beat cow udder served on other occasions.

December 31, 2000: A TV review of last year's events showed a Catholic Church service during its worship hour. I was told this was to prove religious freedom in China.

January 5, 2001: Brenda Lisenby and I went to visit the blind children today. She offered to handle their tuition for me since I will return to the U.S.A. next year to live.

January 8, 2001: We are so excited. Wal-Mart opened a few days ago and Sam's is under construction! Now I can get good pickles and sauerkraut. Whoopee! The products are the same as in the U.S.A. What a blessing!

January 11, 2001: Amy set up her computer in my room. It is equipped with a dial pad so I talked with Glenn, Doris, Max, Mildred Dawson, Dottie, and Joe today. Our brother, David, went to heaven. His funeral will be tomorrow. He was sick with aplastic anemia for nine years and was ready for release from his sick body.

January 15, 2001: Amy and I went to visit Xiu Ping and her new baby boy! His grandmother wanted to wake him up, but I insisted she not disturb him. Poor little guy was under so many blankets and quilts that he could hardly wiggle. A small jar was being kept close by to catch his urine. Why? They had no explanation.

January 16, 2001: We are on Spring Festival Holiday. I

chose to stay here as I expect to travel with my grandson when he comes in late May. I have had many calls from students with invitations to visit them. Actually, it is rather nice to be alone for awhile.

January 18, 2001: Gore, a successful business man, came for me in his car. He and his wife live in a new, modern flat with nice leather furniture attractively arranged. He is interested in Christianity but hasn't accepted it yet. I must continue to pray for them. The dinner was quite tasty including the dog stew and turnips. Too much MSG caused my stomach to react violently. Most Chinese use MSG to enhance the flavor of food, especially meat dishes.

January 20. 2001: Dear Charlie, a long time friend, has lymphoma and has been in the hospital for a long time. He called to say he hopes to be out by March 1. Dear God, may it be so! Charlie, a young engineer, is a devout Christian. He is doing well now and is back on his engineering job.

January 23, 2001: It is the Year of the Snake, according to the Chinese lunar calendar. The gatekeeper and his wife invited me to join them for dinner. He brought a round table into the living room of the teacher's dormitory. Neither of them speaks English but the teenage son knows a few English words. There were much gesturing, pointing, and smiling! Many well prepared dishes were served. The menu included fish, pig feet, chicken feet with nails included, fish balls, noodles, boiled eggs, carrots, glutinous rice cakes, watermelon, and pomelo. None of us were hungry after the short thirty- minute dinner. They were very gracious and made my evening quite pleasant in spite of the language barrier. It is a Chinese custom to take gifts to one's host and hostess. I gave two sweaters to the wife and fruit and candy to her husband. Children get money in a small red envelope. The son was pleased with his monetary gift of 100 yuan, which is his to use as he pleases.

January 25, 2001: Leslie and her husband were so happy to get a copy of *Streams in the Desert*. Leslie translates the sermons given in Flower Lane Church into English. She grabs anything available in English.

January 26, 2001: I enjoyed another big lunch with May in the home place of her boss, Sister Lin. A modern bathroom looked out of place in the big, rambling house. An automatic washing machine was sitting near the bathroom. The eighty-four-year-old grandmother and I sang "What a Friend," she in Chinese and I in English. She had only one top tooth on the left side and one on the right side. Her granddaughter had to feed her because of her Parkinson's disease. The dear lady is loved by her family. We kissed as we said good-bye. I expect to see her in heaven.

January 28, 2001: Lona read the Creation Story from Genesis 1-2. Her family is Buddhist and does not want her to convert to Christianity. She has a Bible so I must pray that God may have His way with her and her family.

February 8, 2001: Kaye Grimmsey sent a wonderful fruit cake, which we have enjoyed so much..

February 13, 2001: Two Japanese girls, Mami and Mariko, have come to teach English. They have recently graduated from a college in Japan and both speak very good English. Mami is a Christian. We are praying for Mariko.

February 15, 2001: I received word that Matthew, my grandson, will come to visit me in late May when his semester ends. Happy Day!

February 19, 2001: Dear Marjatta from Finland is back for a visit. She was here for my previous three years in Huanan Women's College. She is a committed Christian lady.

February 24, 2001: Eli invited me to his home for lunch. His mother is visiting and we had never met before. Ann, his wife, is studying in Shanghai for her Master's. He looks very much like his mom. Our communication was done by gestures and smiles after Eli left us to go to the market.

March 4, 2001: A young man expecting to go to the University of North Carolina in Chapel Hill, his wife, and infant son were in the restaurant where May, Charlie, Mami, and I were having lunch. He left his wife and baby to join us so "I can practice my English," he explained. His wife did not seem to mind.

March 8, 2001: Today is Women's Day and William and Lona brought a huge bouquet of roses. We placed them on the dining room table so all of us could enjoy them.

March 11, 2001: Ten young people, including four ladies, were recently ordained. The minister in Flower Lane Church today was one of the young men. My prayers are with all of them. Flower Lane baptized 700 candidates last year. It also has an Outreach program which assists in several meeting points by sending more qualified leaders and teachers to train and instruct the local leaders. Also, a committee takes the elements of Communion to shut-ins in the church family. Flower Lane is reaching out to share God's love!

March 18, 2001: Several young people were in the Flower Lane bookstore buying Christian books after worship today.

March 20, 2001: What a treat! Pan Yi Ling and I went to a clinic where seven blind students are practicing massage skills. One of the girls gave me an hour-long massage. There was no muscle or nerve in my body that was not stimulated! I gave her the friendship ring from my right hand as she kept going back and stroking my finger and feeling the ring on it. She was very happy, and I was happy that the ring fitted.

March 21, 2001: The United Board helps to fund a kindergarten we visited today. There are 270 students in well built and well furnished classrooms, unlike many others in Fuzhou and elsewhere. The children led us to the different areas and then favored us with a typical performance of dance and music. I wish all students had such good surroundings.

March 22, 2001: The restaurant known as the Dumpling Shop is near our campus. Tonight we dined there along with many others. Diners are able to see the bakers as the dumplings are being prepared. All are dressed as chefs, white caps included. Twelve people knead the dough and then roll it into small pastries about five inches in diameter. These are passed down the assembly line where another team spoons ground veggies, ground meat, or a combination of both into a pastry. The next team pinches the pastry around its contents in fluted like patterns. Now the pastries are dropped into the pot of boiling water, and they are passed into the kitchen. In short order, they are served piping hot to the customers. The rule of thumb is that each diner will eat fifteen, but I had to stop after the fifth one!

March 25, 2001: Professor Li was in Flower Lane Church today. He told me that Dick, now working in Boston, has two daughters and has completed his computer training in Fitzburgh University. The University hired him as its computer engineer. Dick is professor Li's nephew and both are devout Christians.

April 6, 2001: Easter cards from friends in the U.S.A. have opened many doors to a discussion of the meaning of this holy day. When my visitors see the cards posted on my door, it is easy to identify the Christians by their expressions. A discussion of gratitude always follows, while with others uncertain in their faith a simple explanation is more appropriate. The Spirit must do the convincing!

April 14, 2001: Dr. Huang, a medical doctor in the Provincial Hospital, invited me for lunch in her nicely furnished home. Her husband is the editor of the Fuzhou newspaper. Their ten-year-old spoiled son was the center of attention from the time of my arrival to my departure. We could not carry on a conversation because of his interruptions. He literally shoved his toy motorcycle in my face, but not one word of correction from either parent was uttered. The father set a dish of freshly washed strawberries on the table as hor d'oeuvres. Junior insisted on feeding them to me. There was still no word from either parent. While I was eating lunch, he constantly replenished my rice bowl with his chopsticks. My thought, what does the future hold for this child?

April 25, 2001: Ellen said, "Foreign teachers are warmhearted. They don't just teach English. They teach us how to live." What a compliment! What a grave responsibility!

April 27, 2001: Classes ended. Students are going out for on-the-job training. We will visit them on site and evaluate them with their employers. Most are in secretarial positions, but a few are acting as interpreters and translators.

May 4, 2001: Skeet and Luke came to watch the movie "Out of Egypt" tonight. They completed the two-year course requirement at Fujian Institute of Education, where I taught them for two years. Now they are students at Xu Da University working toward a Bachelor's Degree. May God help them to achieve their goal.

May 7, 2001: Bruce Michael from Canberra, Australia, and his wife, Faye, are in our Bible Study group. His eighty-three-year-old mother and sister, Margaret, had lunch with us today. All are devout Christians.

May 20, 2001: My boarding pass to Beijing had 24A listed as my seat number. Just before I could board, an official came, took my pass, and marked it 4D! Hunter had called and told the officials to "put her up front." They did, almost in the cockpit. I was in Beijing only forty-five minutes before Matthew, my grandson, and his friend, Marian, appeared from Henderson, N.C. We took the next flight back to Fuzhou with tickets Hunter had secured. Arriving in Fuzhou Airport, Hunter met us and took us in a police van to Huanan Women's College. Matthew and Marian have come for a three-week visit to China.

May 21, 2001: Matthew and Marian could not believe the traffic as we made our way by a crowded bus to the bank. This afternoon Mariko and Mami took them on a walking tour ending at McDonald's for ice cream.

May 22, 2001: Matthew and Marian spoke to students in English classes about the life of young people in the U.S.A.

May 27, 2001: Our friend, Hunter, came with a driver to take us to Yang Ding, site of the earthen houses. Rough roads through coal mining and bamboo country provided eye openers for us. Hunter's friend provided a big dinner of snake soup, pig feet, buffalo intestines, cow udder, and several vegetables. My guests were somewhat picky about what they ate but did not leave hungry. There is always safety in rice! Besides the large earthen houses, we visited an open market where live baby snakes were being sold. Two men came by with a shoulder pole carrying two most unwilling pigs in a basket. A tire blew so a new one had to be found for the seven-hour trip back to Fuzhou. Matthew and Marian had seen much in just a few days.

May 28, 2001: The farewell trip to the School for the Blind was a heart breaker. The school had planned a musical program for us, and tears flowed freely from the officials, students, and us as they followed us to the school van, which brought us back to Huanan.

May 30, 2001: Han Hui brought roses and a beautiful chipao as farewell gifts. I shall miss this dear lady. Tonight eighteen students, Amy, Matthew, Marian, and I enjoyed fun, food, and fellowship in a nearby restaurant. Many toasts and good wishes were shared among the group.

June 1, 2001: Down to Ma Wei, the port of Fuzhou, we were taken for dinner. Matthew, Marian, Carrie, and some of the others in our group climbed the pagoda to get a better view of the big ships and harbor area. A big farewell dinner with speeches and songs followed after gifts were distributed to all of us by the school. I felt the money should be used to help students or the school, not the foreigners. But it is a common Chinese practice to bring gifts when one visits and gifts to friends when they are leaving.

June 3, 2001: Communion at church was different for Matthew and Marian. First, a tray with plastic spoons is passed for worshipers to take a spoon; next, bread in small cubes is passed; and last, wine is passed in a glass and each person dips out a spoonful. Another tray is passed to collect the used spoons. They found this procedure different but interesting. There were many tearful goodbyes, and poor Eli sobbed so much that he could not join us for our last Sunday's lunch. All of us were weeping, and we were not very hungry.

June 4, 2001: We are packed to leave. Amy and Hunter have made our flight arrangements and hotel reservations in Xian and Beijing. Amy is so happy to go along as our guide.

June 5, 2001: Our last goodbye at Huanan was very emotional and sad. May and Sister Lin, her boss, came for us on the company van. May cried all the way to the airport and so did I. Matthew and Marian were too tired to cry, I think. Sister Lin got us checked in and she told May, "Stop crying and I will send you to the U.S.A. in a little while to visit Sue and her family!" I hope that will materialize.

June 6, 2001: Since I had visited Xian before, I rented a car, put Amy in charge, and sent Matthew and Marian off to see the museum, mosque, and the Terra Cotta Warriors. They also visited Banpo village, where evidence of life 6,000 years ago can be seen. I was physically tired and emotionally drained, so it was good to have a quiet day without tears.

June 7, 2001: This a.m. we flew to Beijing and rented a car for Matthew and Marian to see Beijing with Amy as guide. She has a tourist guidebook and has made good choices of places to see. They were tired but pleased when they returned.

June 8, 2001: Off to Ming Tombs, the Forbidden City, and Tiananmen Square for a viewing of the Chairman Mao wax figure. They were amazed at the flowers being thrown in honor of Mao Tse-tung. It was a busy day and they saw much in one day.

June 9, 2001: A car took us to the Great Wall, where we spent a good part of the day. They climbed while I enjoyed a small child in his dad's shop as I waited for them. The Wall was a highlight for them, I think. We returned in time to check in for our 6:00 p.m. long flight back to the U.S.A. It had been a good three weeks to have them with me, thereby helping at least two members of my family better understand my devotion and concern for Chinese. Through God this was all made possible.

***

Great blessings, great experiences, great people, and a greater God await anyone wishing to serve Chinese people in their "Motherland." My only regret – that my years in this land of witnessing opportunities could not have been longer.

My constant prayer is that the Holy Spirit will motivate more and more dedicated Christians to heed the call of the Chinese to go over and help them. The hearts and minds of the young people are seeking for that which is the only Source to fill the vacancy felt by those who have never heard of God's plan of salvation through faith in His Son, Jesus Christ. Will you go? Please do!!!

CHAPTER 15

From Rice Straw to Ph. D.

"Trust in the Lord with all thy heart; and lean not unto thine own understanding. In all thy ways acknowledge him, and he shall direct thy paths."
(Proverbs 3:5-6 KJV)

It was mid-May 1989, prior to the infamous massacre of students in Tiananmen Square. A tall, thin young man stuck his head into the classroom empty of students and asked, "May I come in and talk with you?" I had never seen him before and since students were out on the street marching, I was rather glad to invite him to come in and chat.

His English was good compared to many of those in my classes. One of his first questions was, "Will you give me an English name?" "What is your Chinese name?" I asked. "Wei Wen Bin," was his reply.

"Wei is my last name," he explained. "Well now, that sounds like the English name Wade," was my response. "What does it mean?" he quizzed. To that I said, "Tall and handsome!" He was very pleased and said, "From now on, call me Wade." And I have done just that!

Most Chinese students wanted an English name along with the meaning of the name. When I didn't have access to the *Book of Baby Names* and their meanings, I would fudge and make up a name; not really honest but they didn't object when I would say, "Someone borrowed my *Book of Baby Names* but I think it means 'so and so.'" This explanation seemed to satisfy them.

As our friendship grew, Wade began to tell me of his deprivation and poverty circumstances of his family. "When I was a primary student, I cried myself to sleep every night because my dad could not afford to buy a pencil that cost 3 fen

(1 cent). I had only a stick of lead, which would break so easily. This made it very hard to do my homework. I picked up rice straws from the rice paddies and would brace the stick of lead against the straw. This kept it from breaking so easily." He went on, "I had two pairs of socks. My mom saw a little boy without any socks. She gave him a pair of mine, and she would wash mine every night."

This poor young man graduated from high school and came to Southeast University, Nanjing, China. Southeast is a well known school for engineers, and at that time the government paid tuition for students. Wade enrolled in the civil engineering department, where he won the academic award each year through the achievement of his master's in Civil Engineering. His projects in graduate school were to design an international airport and a four-lane freeway leading into Nanjing. The day he submitted his projects he came to see me. "I turned my projects in but they are worthless," he dejectedly reported. "Why are they worthless?" I asked. "Because the government doesn't have enough money to build them," he replied. (In the mid-nineties both the international airport and the modern four-lane highway were opened from the city of Nanjing to the airport.)

Wade became like a grandson from that time on. He was my errand boy riding a bicycle he had put together out of parts from a junk yard. From 1989-1992, Wade came regularly to my room to offer his assistance and to discuss his many concerns and dreams. He ate almost daily with me and went to the market with me. There I desperately needed him to bargain with the peddlers and act as my interpreter. In cold weather, he was allowed to use my bathtub, which he would fill to the brim, and spend the next hour luxuriating in the warm water. After all, he had become my Chinese grandson!

One spring morning he and I took the 7:30 train bound to his hometown of Zhen Zhang. He had a package of crackers for breakfast. We climbed two mountain peaks, had our photos made, rode three buses, took a ferry across the river, ate snacks for lunch, but went to a restaurant near the train station for dinner.

Both of us were hungry, and we enjoyed the meal. We finished the meal just as the train arrived for the trip back to Nanjing. It was a wonderful day with my Chinese grandson!

One day Wade came for his daily visit and was somewhat depressed and downhearted as he talked about the future for young people. He felt so helpless and was deeply concerned for his country. Hungry, discouraged, and sad, he still remained a conscientious student with top grades. "To be successful and become a leader in China, people must have no conscience and give money or cigarettes to get needed information," he blurted out. Cigarettes were often given to guests and a pack was usually placed at each place setting at wedding dinners.

When my brother, Joe, and our good friend, Lib Roberts, came for a visit, they wanted to see a countryside village. So Wade, Joe, Lib, and my "little girl Friday," Doris, went to Wade's home in a car sent by Southeast University, where I was teaching. What an experience for Joe and Lib!

The manager of the Foreign Guest House where I was living and where my guests were staying became very angry with Wade and Doris. His fury was directed at them because he was not invited. The following day the Foreign Affairs Officer gave them a blistering lecture about making plans without his permission. Communist leaders appear power hungry and have an ironclad will for control. It was easy to understand the frustration of people who were capable of making their own decisions.

After going to the market with me, Wade, Doris, and Alfreda from Togo, Africa, liked to come over and make jiaozi (meat and veggie dumplings) for dinner. Much jolly chatter ensued as ingredients were chopped, pressed, and squeezed into small dumplings and dropped into boiling water. More fun as the group enjoyed the "fruits of their labor."

Another young man, William, soon became a frequent visitor along with Wade. Between those two, going to the market was a pleasure. They could spot and identify items I did not recognize, and thus they discovered our first frozen chicken. How convenient for me, since the way it was packaged was beyond my level of recognition. These two came from similar backgrounds and were similar in academic achievements.

During our leisure times, Wade and I would take walks in the parks, just stroll on campus, and browse through the shops and outdoor markets which sold a variety of items from food products, cheap jewelry, clothes, and furniture. Many were the unusual and interesting sights we saw on these frequent walks.

One day we saw a man carrying a shoulder pole with a basket hanging from each end. A toddler was in one basket and an unhappy pig in the other. The peasant father was having a rough time trying to keep the pig in and not dump the baby out. We felt pity for the three of them.

Soon we saw a calf tied onto the luggage rack on the back of a bicycle. The animal was rebelling, but the cyclist was wobbling along in spite of the erratic behavior of his passenger. We uttered a silent prayer for them to reach their destination.

Evidence of Wade's interest in and concern for others was revealed in his many acts of thoughtfulness stemming from his kind heart. My friend Katie, a teacher from California, was stationed near Southeast and frequently visited me. On a cold winter day, Wade spotted her camera as she was leaving for her campus. He ran through ice and snow but missed her when she took a three-wheeler, a buggy-like taxi moved either by man on a motorcycle or on a bicycle. He walked four miles in freezing temperatures and on icy walks to give it to her.

The following morning he walked through five inches of snow at 7:30 in the morning to escort me to the classroom. "I was afraid you might slip and fall," he said. Only twelve of the thirty members showed up, but we had class anyway. Wade was never registered for any of my classes but would audit all those which did not conflict with his schedule.

One day he came to apologize for being so busy. "I was afraid you might need to go to the market, and I must carry the bags for you," he said. I knew he was working on a rather complex transportation pattern. I surely understood, but another American teacher had come to visit me. The dear boy took time from his hectic assignments to escort her to places of interest in Nanjing. "I knew you were too busy and I wanted to help you,' he said. A very considerate and warm-hearted young man seemed eager to be of service!

It took some time before Wade expressed an interest in church. He had never attended a worship service since his village had no church or Buddhist temple. Neither his parents nor his grandparents knew about Jesus Christ. He knew I was going to St. Paul's Protestant Church every Sunday and when I invited him, he was busy with assignments. One day he picked up the Bible on the table in my room and asked, "What is this book about?" After hearing my explanation, he asked whether he had to pay to get into church. From then on, he would meet me at church and the looks of wonder and surprise on his face during the sermons, prayers, and music helped me to know that his empty soul was being nurtured. After every service, he was full of questions about God, Jesus, and the Holy Spirit. One day he asked, "How can I become God's child?" He continued, "I want to be warm-hearted and kind like people who go to church. The people in church are so friendly and happy. I want to be like them." The time had come to explain the plan of salvation to this special young man. He joyfully and tearfully invited Jesus into his heart and asked for a Bible so "I can learn more about God I never knew before," he said. He could hardly wait for Sundays.

Zou Lin was his girl friend and an English teacher in my department. She knew nothing about Christianity and showed no interest in attending church. While Wade was away on an assignment, she dated another boy. When Wade learned of this, he told her he was going to take his life. She ran over to my room, asking for help. I had to meet a class, so I insisted that she attend it with me and after class we would go to his room. There we found him all red eyed and sniffling, yet grateful to see us.

After much encouragement and persuasion, he consented for them to have lunch with me. Among other problems, he was hungry! Once his appetite was satisfied, he began to talk. "Zou Lin went out with another boy," he moaned. The custom in

China seems to be to marry the first person one dates. Multiple dates were unheard of in this culture! To Wade, Zou Lin had committed adultery by going out with another young man. He felt betrayed.

Talking proved therapeutic. Another big concern was the pressure from Party members to join the Campus Communist Party group. He was depressed as he explained, "I do not want to join the Party. It does not practice good living, but I may have to in order to get a good job after graduation. Only Party members get the good jobs and the promotions. Besides, they bribe leaders and don't tell the truth. I am not that kind of person." I knew Wade had good moral values and sterling principles. Now he was God's child and God rescued him from himself.

Wade was concerned about Zou Lin's spiritual future since she knew nothing about Christianity, and he felt inadequate in explaining to her about his new-found faith. "I want my girl friend to experience the contentment and peace I have inside since I became a Christian," he told me. "Will you please tell her about Jesus Christ for me? Now Zou Lin thinks people have to be in a temple before they can pray," he said. To this I replied, "Come to dinner tonight and then we can talk."

I had found beef on my last visit to the food market. After a dinner of stew beef, canned green beans, cucumbers, and ice cream, Wade took the same Bible from my table and said, "Zou Lin, this is the book that tells about Jesus Christ. Sue can tell you more about it." So as clearly and simply as I could, I explained the creation story from Genesis 1 and 2. Next I presented Jesus' birth, life, crucifixion, resurrection, and ascension. By now Wade had read his Bible enough to ask questions for clarification. Zou Lin was mesmerized and continued to listen with great interest. Suddenly, it was as if Christ reached out and took her into His arms. "Oh, I want to be His child. I want Him to be my spiritual Father. Will He accept me as I am?" "Of course, this is the only way. You come just as you are," Wade blurted out. He remembered this from his own conversional experience. Heaven came down in my room that night and glory filled her soul, Wade's soul, and mine.

Graduation was coming in a few weeks. Wade seemed restless when he came to help me or just to visit. Zou Lin was coming more often with him now. "I am going to graduate but I really want to study in America. I 'd like to learn more about airport designs and freeways," he said. Right then we prayed for his future hopes and dreams. These were reinforced with actions. While in the U.S.A., I had bought a World Almanac in which all accredited colleges and universities are listed. He began by choosing those he had heard of, such as MIT, Cornell, Harvard, and Yale. I advised him to study and take the required TOEFL, Test of English Foreign Language, which all foreign students must pass for admission to any USA university.

He and Zou Lin began their study of the TOEFL, and during this time, he began to make inquiries of scholarships available and admission policies to many U.S.A. universities. All this required much time and some days he was impatient and upset. I could understand his frustration and anxiety.

Graduation came without much pomp and circumstance for Wade and Zou Lin. He had a Master's in Civil Engineering and was assigned to the Transportation Department in Nanjing. Zou Lin had a BA in Linguistics and was placed in Southeast University as an English teacher. Time moved along and major changes were on the horizon. The year was 1992, I had been at Southeast since 1988, and in 1995 Amity transferred me from Southeast University in Nanjing to Huanan Women's College in Fuzhou. Wade was working, Zou Lin was teaching English at Southeast University, but Wade refused to give up his dream. He began to study for the GMAT, Graduate Management Admissions Test, but kept it a secret from me. During this time he would phone to say, "Happy Birthday," "Have a good Easter," and "Enjoy a very happy Mother's Day." He remembered all of the American special days as I always gave him an up-to-date calendar, which included American holidays.

Time moved slowly for Wade but seemed to vanish in thin air to me. I would return to Nanjing when my schedule would permit. He and Zou Lin would meet me in the airport, hail a taxi, and escort me to the guest house at Jing Ling Seminary, where I had taught English part time before transferring to Fuzhou and while I taught full time at Southeast University.

Wade spent much time in 1994-1995 sending applications out and in turn sending forms to me to be completed hopefully by a generous American willing to be his sponsor. On May 19, 1995, I received a jubilant phone call, which nearly deafened me! He had been sent a fax from a university in Berne, Switzerland, offering him a full scholarship because of his high score on the GMAT. That young man had scored in the top five percent of all those who took it at the same time he was tested.

Excitement filled with fear was prevalent as we phoned back and forth. "Should I accept this since I had really hoped to study in the U.S.A.?" he asked. "Accept the offer and hopefully while you are there a university in America may accept you and provide a substantial scholarship," I advised him. Exactly five days later, May 24, another call came from Wade. "What do you know about Carnegie Mellon University in Pittsburgh, Pa.?" he asked. Actually, I knew only that it was noted for its engineering training.

It is great how God provides answers before questions are even asked. Another foreign teacher from Pennsylvania, who was in our English department, was passing by as I chatted with Wade. I eagerly asked her, "What do you know about Carnegie Mellon University?" "It is one of the best," she answered. That was what I needed to advise him.

"You must tell me where to go," he pled like a small child. "Where do you want to go? Do you want to study in Berne, Switzerland or in the U.S.A.?" I asked. "U.S.A., always U.S.A.," he literally shouted back. "Then accept the $30,000 scholarship that Carnegie Mellon is offering." "Thank you, thank you. I thought you would say that," he said with a deep sign of relief and a great big, hearty chuckle. His desire to study in the U.S.A. was no longer a dream and was about to become a reality!

My summer vacation in North Carolina with family and friends was coming to an end. I would return to Fuzhou to assume teaching duties and Wade was coming to the U.S.A. to earn a Master's degree in Civil Engineering. He arrived at Raleigh-Durham Airport on August 23, 1995. My brother Joe and I met him as he came through the corridor with arms outstretched, a big smile, and tearful eyes. "I finally made it. With God's help and many prayers, I am really in the U.S.A.," he beamed.

I returned to Fuzhou on the following day, while Joe and Lib took Wade to Carnegie Mellon University. On arrival, they discovered that Wade would have a Chinese roommate. "This seemed to reassure him and he relaxed more as luggage was brought inside," Joe reported to me. A new school in a new country and a much different culture would require more than a few adjustments.

Wade had work to do, so as Joe and Lib were about to leave, he called out, "Wait a minute, please. Let's pray together before you go," he said. This request touched Joe and Lib very deeply. "We looked back as we were about to leave the campus," Joe wrote, "and he was still standing watching us out of sight. We breathed another prayer for him," Joe said.

All went well at Carnegie Mellon but during his first year there, Wade discovered Princeton University in New Jersey had a better curriculum in transportation, so he applied there and received the same scholarship Carnegie Mellon in Pittsburgh, Pennsylvania, had offered. He maintained his academic record in both universities, achieving honor roll status. After one year at Carnegie Mellon, he transferred to Princeton, receiving yet another $30,000 scholarship.

In the meantime, Zou Lin had received a scholarship at the University of Utah to study for her Master's in Linguistics. Both of them were grateful to be in America and to be given an opportunity to study in their field of expertise. Before Zou Lin left for Utah, we had a serious discussion about remaining true to our Christian faith. And she did!

Wade graduated from Princeton but decided he needed a Ph.D. He applied to the University of California in Berkeley, was accepted, and was awarded a teaching fellowship as well as an adequate scholarship, which enabled him to realize his goal of a doctorate in Civil Engineering.

Zou Lin excelled in her studies at the University of Utah, where she received her Master's in Linguistics. Like Wade, she applied to the University of California in Berkeley, was accepted, and was given a scholarship to earn a doctorate in Linguistics. After the completion of their degrees, she and Wade were united in holy matrimony in Berkeley, California, in 2002.

Joy filled and continues to fill my heart for them. "God is able," they said in unison when I called to congratulate these two Ph.D.'s on their marriage.

Dr. Wei Wen Bin was offered a job with American Airlines in Dallas. Dr. Zou Lin was hired at the University of California in the field of Linguistics. Both were employed, but with him in Texas and her in California, the situation was not satisfactory. An unexpected offer brought them back together when the University of California hired Wade to teach in the Civil Engineering department and Zou Lin to teach and do research in the Linguistics department. They hitched their wagon to a star and it finally reached its zenith.

Their latest blessing is a darling baby girl, Yi Yen, which means "beautiful cloud," Wade proudly boasted. These two know what it means to trust in the Lord with their hearts, and He has surely directed their paths. He did bless them and still does! Both moved from rice straw to Ph.D.'s with God's help. They give Him all the credit for their successes. "We must help others now to realize their dreams," they told me.

May it be so for them and for others.

CHAPTER 16

Unusual Cuisine

"...For I was an hungred, and ye gave me meat...."
    (Matthew 25:35a KJV)

Very delicious! Have some more! These were five words of admonition always when eating with Chinese families or friends. Meals are served in a bowl filled with rice, and all other foods are placed on top.

Using their chopsticks, all family members – grandparents, parents, and children – will keep the bowl of their guest supplied with no questions asked. This is a form of being courteous to the visitor and means the guest is welcome to their home.

So eat more! It's very delicious!

One of my first introductions to unusual foods was during Amity orientation. It was breakfast and a nice platter of what I thought were frog legs was placed on our table. What I discovered were not frog legs chopped to bite-sized pieces but chicken feet along with the nails! My chopsticks decided not to risk trying to pick up any part of this very delicious dish.

Pigs' feet were often served, but they were recognizable. Besides, I had eaten those back in America and would sometimes buy the pickled ones. Likewise, souse made from the feet, ears, and head of the pig I knew well. My son and I still enjoy the pickled feet and sometimes a slice of souse meat with a soda cracker. They make a different snack. Some people would find these equally distasteful, but not I!

I had heard of the 1,000-year-old eggs but could not imagine how anyone could consume an egg that had been laid a thousand years ago. Neither could I fathom how an egg could be preserved for that long unless it had fossilized. Shortly after arriving in China in 1988, I was invited to a home for dinner. Among the foods on the table was a platter of large, very dark green, unrecognizable "somethings." In the center of the dark green was a lighter, yellowish green something. The student explained, in great detail, how very delicious these thousand-year-old duck eggs are and how they are made. The process intrigued me more than the eggs themselves!

In reality, the eggs are not 1,000 years old. Preferably, the larger eggs from ducks or geese are more desirable than chicken eggs. The eggs are covered with a thick coat of what looked like red clay and then placed, some people said, in a hole dug nearby. There they can stay for an indefinite period until they are preserved from the clay coating. Not being a physicist, I can neither deny nor support this claim.

As for taste, it was somewhat like a pickle, perhaps a bit stronger. At any rate, I never ordered one from a menu but was polite and consumed a few when visiting with students and their families.

The blood of ducks, geese, and chickens is saved when one is being butchered, it is then heated, and a corn starch or flour substance is added during the cooking. This causes a thickening which can be cubed or sliced. It is used in making a soup which is extraordinary, especially when the dried intestines of the fowl are added. This can be ordered from menus, and many families make their own. It is considered a very exotic dish and can be enjoyed best by foreigners when the ingredients are unknown!

Starvation in years past has probably accounted for many of the unusual foods, or those considered so by foreigners in China. All parts of animals are used to help feed one-fifth of the world's population. The pig is no exception. Everything but the squeal is cut, cleaned, scraped, cooked, and eaten, including the most private parts. Foreigners often react with shock and surprise when they read in the menu the names of some of the available dishes.

A farewell dinner at Fujian Medical University included my introduction to the most private part of a pig. Actually, the dish was tasty and easy to manage with chopsticks. But when I asked the teacher sitting by me, "What is this? I like it very much!" her reply caused my chopsticks to drop, and suddenly I was not hungry anymore. Sometimes, I learned, it is better not to ask.

Students planned a Spring Festival outing prior to the actual holiday. They would be home during that special time. They were quite proud to have planned and paid for this surprise for their English teacher. I was notified that morning of the luncheon at Park Restaurant for that day.

After classes, we climbed the mountain where the view looked over Ming Jian River and to Fuzhou City beyond. They had made a reservation and requested tables nearest the windows so we could enjoy the sights better.

Because Fuzhou is a thriving seaport city, many different varieties of seafood are available – oysters, crabs, clams, mussels, shrimp, turtles, and fish. At every meal, some form of seafood is served. They were showing their teacher just how efficient they could be, so I thought.

Many dishes were served including shrimp, oysters, and fish. The entire fish, with a sizable head included, was placed on each table. Near the end of the meal, a commotion arose at two of the tables. Students were trying to decide which one at their table was most worthy to eat the eyes of the fish! That day, I learned that fish eyes make one more intelligent. Bring on the fish eyes! Among the many fables and traditions in China, some are quite different from ours but interesting.

Foreigners were invited to Weifang in Shandong Province to attend the International Kite Festival. Coming back, the group stopped in Xuzhou for the night. The university which was our host provided a big banquet that evening. The food was well prepared and enjoyed by the foreigners. We were hungry since we had been on a bus about all day.

At the dinner, we were seated by universities, so my roommate and I were not at the same table. When we arrived back to our room, she asked, "Did you eat any of that pink meat tonight?" "Yes," I replied. "It was quite good." "Do you know what it was?" she quizzed. "Yes, it was corned beef, and I had been wanting some for a long time," was my answer. "Oh, no, that was not corned beef, that was Fido (dog)," she chuckled. "Well, I guess from now on, I'll bark instead of talk. But I would knowingly eat it again," I retorted. And, indeed, I did on several occasions, with full knowledge, order a very delicious serving of dog meat and found it to be "very delicious and good for me." I haven't started barking yet!

China is known for its beautiful silk. Seeing small mulberry trees with peasants in wide brim hats snapping the leaves from the higher branches was a curiosity. After harvesting, the leaves are sent to a silkworm farm or hatchery where they become the diet of the worms.

Small cages hold the worms, and mulberry leaves are dropped into their boxes. After a given time, the worm spins itself into a cocoon made of pure silk threads. Once the cocoons are completed, they are taken to processing plants.

After processing, worms can then be saved for yet another "very delicious" dish. People will usually deep fry them before eating them. They become very crunchy in the hot oil and are considered "very good for you."

To my knowledge, I was never served rats; however, in some markets, big rats, lying in repose, awaited hungry shoppers. These rats were those which live in grain fields and rice paddies. Scavenger rats were not considered safe for food, so no rats were included in any cuisine I enjoyed. Infant mice, however, are a different story!

One family had a very nice home with a newly installed telephone, their first. Four rooms are spacious for most families. Colorful drapes, made by the mother, were a cheerful addition in the combination dining-living room. Appetizing aromas floated in from the kitchen. The ever-present rice cooker was plugged into a receptacle in the living room.

Greens, tomato and egg combo, corn, fish, shrimp, duck, and chicken were other offerings on their menu. Soup was very popular so when it was served piping hot, it was different in appearance, smell, and taste. Small lumps floated on top. When an inquiry was made, which I later regretted, I was informed that the small lumps were baby mice! I did not want to insult or hurt the hostess and was relieved to learn that the lumps could be swallowed whole! I never learned how delicious a baby rodent would taste!

It was not uncommon to see small toad frogs for sale at the markets. A chain around one leg would hold the frog until it was purchased to become someone's dinner that night.

Frogs, like baby mice, were usually put into a soup. On several occasions, I was considered the lucky diner, as my helping included the triangular head, which had little or no meat. Frogs make a very interesting dish and are often ordered by foreigners once they have been introduced to yet another "very-delicious-and-good-for-you" Chinese cuisine!

Cows are scarce in China because what would be their pasture land is needed to grow fruits and vegetables for China's huge population. Perhaps the resultant lack of milk is why most moms breast feed their babies whenever and wherever they may be.

Beef is very scarce in the markets. Hamburger for McDonald's is shipped in, so we were told. In my thirteen years in China, I never saw steak, beef stew, or hamburger for sale. Now that Wal-Mart and Sam's are in the larger cities, these items may be available to urban residents.

In the countryside villages, where a few cows may be found, like the pig, all parts of the animal's body are used, the most unusual, of course, being the cow's udder. I was deprived of this delicacy but was told by the "more fortunate" that it was rubbery and tasteless. At first I took their word for it and made no effort to make a taste test myself. Later, I did indulge and found it chewy as had been described by others.

Buffaloes are more plentiful than cows. They are still used to plow through muddy rice paddies and can sometimes be seen pulling carts along the fields or roads. A piece of metal inserted through the buffalo's nose and attached to a rope guides the animal in the direction the driver chooses for it to go.

Some buffaloes are slaughtered for food. The stomach and

intestines are consumed as well as other body parts. Intestines are like hard rubber; the longer they are chewed, the bigger they seem to get. The stomach is like an unpaved bumpy road and is equally as tough as the intestines. They both provide good jaw exercise!

The chef will cut both of those exotic foods into small slices or pieces to make them easier to eat with chopsticks. The few times these were served in my presence, I learned after the first attempt to leave them in the containers and satisfy hunger with the other dishes. I cannot say either was very delicious, because I surreptitiously removed it when my friends were looking the other way. Extra tissues were part of my daily clothing for several reasons.

Snakes, turtles, and frogs were always available in the market. I never bought any but ate some of all three. Peasants brought bags of nonpoisonous snakes from the nearby wooded areas. The snakes would be writhing and crawling in bags as they came in on backs of peasants in small two- or three-wheeled carts.

Once a person bought the snake, the peasant would butcher it for the shopper. It all happened so quickly the poor snake didn't have time to know its head was off, skin stripped, and body pulled from the spine. The buyer would have fresh meat that day.

Snake meat looks like lean pork, much like pork tenderloin, but tastes and looks like the breast meat of chicken once it is cooked. It is a popular meat used in soups or fried a crispy brown. It was easier for me to eat, bones and all. "Very delicious." Yes, I would agree.

The bile of the snake is kept to use in making cold medication. Several vials were given to me, but my commode knew more about their effect than I did! Many "unusuals" are used in the production of medicines as well as of calories.

Grasshoppers and honey bees were like relatives to silk worms when they came from the deep fat in the wok, toasty brown and crispy. Like many other specialties, these were considered "good for you" and one should always "eat more!"

Scorpions looked like a cross between a crab and a lobster. These could be served fried, which made them easier to eat, or combined in a mix with assorted vegetables. They never became one of my favorites of the exotics, although they were classified as very delicious.

Most foods are cooked in China, including lettuce, cucumber, celery, and tomatoes, foods Americans eat freely uncooked in salads. Like most rules, there is one exception I encountered – live shrimp. These were swimming around in a large glass bowl as if watching the ten diners seated at their round table. How to eat a live shrimp? This was definitely a new experience, so I hesitated in order to let someone else take the first one. Oh, so that's how you do it. After capturing the poor thing, the diner should bite his head off. This way, he stops looking at you. Next, the shell and whiskers must be removed. The unwanted parts are deposited right beside your rice bowl. Now, on with the feast. You know that you are eating fresh shrimp! "Very delicious"? Debatable, as I preferred mine boiled or fried.

My heart was sad when I saw baby chicks still in their egg shell. The shell was cracked and the chicks were just ready to make their debut into the world. No, not yet! The poor little things were not allowed to complete their efforts. Rather, they were taken to the market for sale as another exotic and special treat. These babies were put into boiling water for a few minutes and then removed from their shell and eaten. "What about the feathers?" I asked. "Oh, you mean the fur. We just spit it out," was the response. "And the bones?" I asked. "Oh, they are soft, so we can eat them, too!" No, I cannot describe the taste because I let that specialty pass; however, they were labeled "very delicious!"

Small, tender bamboo shoots were very delicious and used in many mixed vegetable and meat dishes. Although bamboo was available in the market, I never bought any simply because I thought it should be left for the pandas. Sometimes the small shoots could be ground as pickles. They were tasty, but again, pandas need bamboo to survive. Let's leave it for them, even though it is "good for people" as well as for pandas.

Chinese are excellent chefs who make wonderful dishes. Even with the "unusuals" they can take simple, unheard-of ingredients and prepare a feast. Yes, I like Chinese cuisine and often visit Chinese restaurants in my area of North Carolina. Besides, it's very delicious, good for me, and yes, I will continue to eat more of it!

CHAPTER 17

Trips in and out of China

"...but he that is of a merry heart hath a continual feast."
  (Proverbs 15:15b KJV)

The local universities along with the local Educational Committee planned several exciting trips for foreign teachers. Occasionally, a university would take the dean, the head of the English Department, and foreign teachers on a more private trip. Needless to say, these were a perk for all in attendance and provided opportunities for us to see and explore sites of historical and legendary interest.

The Amity Foundation, the Chinese organization through which I worked, met for Winter Conference just prior to the Chinese Lunar New Year. This could be from late January to mid-February and lasted three to four weeks or more. Of three locations – Kunming, Guangzhou, and Xiamen – Amity officials chose one, Kunming, which borders Burma. Kunming, known as the flower capital of China, is a very exotic place to visit.

KUNMING

During Flower Festival in Kunming, streets are lined with big pots of beautiful flowers tastefully arranged by colors making exquisite displays of color throughout the city. Just strolling through the streets admiring the fresh, brightly colored flowers brought relaxation and a great pleasure within my soul.

A favorite part of visiting in Kunming was taking a short trip from the inner city to Stone Forest. From a distance, it appeared to be mountains; however, on arrival I learned those tall, high hills are solid gray stone. Adventurous tourists can choose to climb up to the top by carefully squeezing through openings between the granite walls. Near the top a gap exists which I declined to jump, leaving my roommate to go it alone. I made my way back to ground level and waited for her return. "Oh, the view is great from the top," she taunted. "I will take your word for it," was my reply.

GUANGZHOU

Guangzhou is a very modern city now, much like Hong Kong. When our conference first met there, we had hot water only from 6:00 a.m. to 8:00 a.m. and from 8:00 p.m. to 10:00 p.m. Bathing in warm water had to be done in early mornings or early nights. We managed!

I was introduced to country style chicken feet for breakfast at our first meeting in Guangzhou. I thought they were frog legs until a friend informed me otherwise. My son used to gig bullfrogs, and I had cooked the legs for him. I knew they had small bones, but chicken feet!! Truthfully, they were tasty and I ate them many times later.

XIAMEN

Xiamen is famous for its botanical garden and a large Buddhist Compound on top of the mountain just outside the city. The garden is beautifully arranged with flowering shrubs, flowers, and manicured walks, a perfect place for peace, rest, and meditation under the shade of a tree.

The Buddhist Compound had living quarters for monks and a large temple. Shops were filled with tourist items as well. Incense sticks burning in the temple produced a most unpleasant odor to me. My heart broke to see the young men in brown, baggy pants and with heads shaved, kneeling on pillows, bowing, and chanting to the most grotesque Buddha statues imaginable. The mournful drumbeat, to me, was like a funeral call. I wanted to tell them of a living Jesus who could give them a direct connection to our loving God.

All three locations were interesting in their own way, and I am grateful for opportunities to explore and enjoy, to some degree, what each had to offer. Jiangsu Educational Committee would take us to interesting places. A three-day trip to northern points within the Province, I remember so well.

YAN CHENG

It was March 29, 1989, and the day began at 5:30 a.m., when a bus came for Annette, Pat, Ricky – my colleagues, Wang Li – foreign affairs officer, and me. We were taken to a hotel where we met several foreign teachers for an eight-hour ride to Yan Cheng. Buses had to be serviced after we arrived at the hotel, but finally we pulled out for the long ride.

Along the way, we saw productive rice paddies and peasants with big hats working in paddies. Some were using a one-handle wooden plow pulled by a large buffalo, houseboats with fishermen on board floated in lakes and rivers, and some fishermen seemed to be pulling in nets. This was quite interesting to me. I felt as if these scenes were out of the past.

The day was long with only one rest stop. By 6:00 p.m. we were famished, so the foreign affairs officer on board decided to stop at a sizeable restaurant, where we were substantially fed. At this point, what I ate was not important if it filled my stomach.

Next we were taken to a large department store. Even if shopping had been on our agenda, it would have been basically impossible. Chinese shoppers surrounded us, gaping and staring as if we had escaped the zoo! Frankly, we were too tired for shopping and most wanted only a warm bath and bed, but this was not quite the plan. When we arrived at our hotel, we were told a banquet would be served at 7:30 p.m. Banquet? We had eaten less than two hours earlier! Wang Li, my foreign affairs officer, was disappointed that I did not attend, but my interest at that point was a bed, not more food. It had, indeed, been an interestingly different, long day!

Next morning we rode for two hours in pouring rain to see a crane sanctuary. In China, the crane is considered the symbol of longevity. The sanctuary is located well off any paved road. The bus plunged into the red clay mud, slipping and sliding, but finally reached the museum of stuffed cranes. No live crane with any amount of intelligence would have been trying to fly in the torrential rain. This was supposed to be their nesting ground but all we saw was a video and a few stuffed, dusty cranes with a few feathers missing. So much for the crane sanctuary!

After we boarded the bus again, it became stuck in the mud and slid into a side ditch as rain continued to fall. We got off the bus in flooded ruts of red clay and trampled back toward the paved road. A dear Chinese lady came out and put down a few flagstones for us to keep our already wet feet dry. We were muddy, our shoes were soggy, and our clothes were wringing wet, but we made the best of a wet situation by singing hymns and praising God for an entirely different experience.

The bus was finally pulled and pushed from the muddy ditch, so we boarded again, looking and feeling like mud turtles from a ditch!

LIUYANGANG

Our next adventure was to Liuyangang where yet another banquet was planned with the dignitaries of the city. My colleagues – Annette, Pat, and Ricky – and I were seated at the table with the mayor and other high officials. The number of glasses at each place setting clued me in on the beverages to be served. I had learned that simply to turn a goblet upside down was a polite way to refuse strong drinks. But our host enjoyed all the refills and was fully inebriated by the time the banquet ended – a disgusting sight to all.

Foreigners are royally received and feted but also expected to perform. This request always happened without prior notice, so we learned to be prepared. Usually I would sing "You Are My Sunshine," but on this occasion, we were in a group and accommodated our hosts with our rendition of "This Land Is Your Land." Later I used this song in class but changed the words to Chinese locations instead of American, such as "from Yuannan Province to Fuzhou City" instead of "from California to New York Island." It didn't matter that we were not talented vocalists; our singing was a delight to them and fun for us.

The following day we were taken to a 640-meter-high

mountain, and many people were walking to the summit. An enormous rock on a level plateau was the great attraction. One of the many Chinese legends claimed that the Monkey King hatched from this huge rock! A pagoda and Buddhist temple were an attraction for many people. The pagoda was a nice place for a picnic, but the fragrance from incense was so overpowering that I avoided the temple.

We rode the bus down the mountain to see the seaside. After we removed our shoes, we waded in the South China Sea. Nearby, Buddhist figures and various animals were sculpted on rocky mountain sides. What patience! What God-given skills! The animal figures were beautiful but the many Buddhas were hideous. My heart bleeds for those who can kneel and worship such ugly figures. They need to know the Spiritual Creator God who loves them as He loves us.

HUI AN

On the bus again, we left Lianyangang for Hui An, home of Zhou En Lai and the area where Mrs. Billy Graham's parents, Dr. and Mrs. L. Nelson Bell, served as Presbyterian missionaries many years ago. We were escorted through the compound of Zhou En Lai's family, and I actually touched the bed and desk he used as a child. He was schooled by a private tutor and in later life became a high official under Mao Tse-tung's regime. Zhou En Lai presented the two pandas to President Richard Nixon when he visited China in the late 70s. Hui An is a fairly small city but full of historical interest.

I was disappointed when our guides knew nothing of the Bell family, so we did not knowingly see where Ruth Bell Graham had lived as a child. In a Communist country, however, that omission should not come as a surprise.

It had been a good five-day vacation but now it was time to return to our universities and resume teaching duties. Surprises accompanied us along the way. As we crossed the river, a lady was sleeping while lying on a bridge railing as a small child played nearby. This neglect gave me chill bumps. Young girls and old ladies were tending geese and herding goats, and small boys and old men were sitting on buffaloes as they grazed or stood in a rice paddy canal. We were told that a buffalo's hide would crack if not wet from time to time. A few men were standing on a harrow pulled by a buffalo and smoothing the soil for planting another crop of rice or wheat. This was truly a historical adventure for me; however, it was good to get back to Nanjing, to Southeast University, to Room 402, and to my bed!

ANHUI PROVINCE

Yellow Mountain in Anhui Province is a must for every serious tourist. Xiao Yu and Shi Hong had just married, and I was invited to go on their honeymoon. Xiao Yu got the tickets and in mid-October we left on an old bus over a road under construction. We were in the very last seats, so we received full benefit of every bump along the way. Cracked, not crushed, rocks had been strewn in some areas and while we rode over them, our heads hit the top of the bus several times! Our driver seemed undisturbed and never slowed down. He was geared for one speed – FAST! After ten hours of bumping and jostling around, we arrived at the foot of the mountain. Xiao Yu rented two rooms, one for Shi Hong and me and one for himself. During the three nights we were there, the bride and I were roommates. Strange honeymoon! But they were intent on keeping the foreigner comfortable.

The discomfort of the travel was worth the gorgeous sunset we saw. From one of the tallest peaks, we watched as colors changed from silver to gold, pink, rose red, gray, and black. Only the Great Artist could paint such a perfect array of colors. I had viewed many beautiful sunsets, but this one excelled them all.

Many tall peaks with different shapes captured our attention. Various animals and faces were clearly identifiable. Some less physically able people were seated in a sedan chair carried by two young men. The steps were uneven and steep to reach the peaks, but every step was worth the effort.

The three of us were reluctant to leave such a display of

natural beauty, but our duties awaited us in Nanjing. On our last day at the top, as we were eating lunch, I dropped several morsels from the chopsticks. A waiter nearby said something in Chinese directed to me. I asked Xiao Yu for an interpretation. He really didn't want to tell me, but I insisted. Xaio Yu blushed and said, "He called you a Cuckoo Woman!" I laughed and continued to eat what I didn't drop. As we left, the waiter called out again, "big Cuckoo Woman!" Later, I became more proficient with chopsticks! The waiter most likely had learned that expression from some foreigner and perhaps didn't even know its meaning. It provided a good laugh for us.

"All good things must come to an end" is a cliché I had heard many times. The experiences on Yellow Mountain reinforced the meaning of that phrase in my mind. The weather had been ideal, the colors of trees in mid-October were beautiful, the scenery was breath-taking, but my legs were ready for no more climbing, at least for a while.

The ten-hour bus trip back to Nanjing was made in the rain. Several other firsts came to my attention as we passed villages along the way. One lady was catching rainwater in her wok. Many people with no umbrellas were sloshing through puddles. The bus passed an open-faced meat marker where toads, dogs, rats, cats, snakes, and numerous unidentifiable carcasses were lying on shelves for sale. I said a silent prayer for the consumers! Another cliché, "All's well that ends well," perfectly described my trip to Yellow Mountain as an escort for a couple on their honeymoon!

HAINAN ISLAND, KUNMING, DALI, and LI JIANG

Teachers and students enjoy a fairly long vacation between fall and spring semester. Timing, determined by the Chinese New Year and the Chinese lunar calendar, usually occurs from mid-January to late February, the usual time when foreigners travel in or out of China. Chinese look forward to celebrating the New Year with family and friends.

An interesting trip with Marie Melrose, my traveling

315

companion, to Hainan Island, Kunming, Dali, and Li Jiang was my next excursion. The first leg was made by overnight boat from Hong Kong to Hainan. Eight people, plus a young couple we did not know, shared a ten-bed compartment with us.

The overnight boat trip was fairly uneventful, but it lacked conveniences in some ways. The restrooms were on the level below us and had no western style commodes, only "squat, floor level" urinals. Since there was no toilet paper or lavatories, foreigners quickly learned to take along any tissue needed and "wet ones" if they could be found., We managed to sleep some in spite of the loud foghorn and snoring men in the compartment next to ours.

The boat docked at 10:30 a.m. the following morning, but we met with resistance by customs officials. At first, it seemed we would not be allowed to disembark, but after showing our passports, work cards, and resident cards, we moved on to customs. After being scrutinized and questioned again, we were finally allowed to get a van to the Chinese overseas Hotel in Haikou. This close inspection seemed unnecessary to us as Hainan Island is still in China and we were not coming in from another country.

Marie Melrose had lived for fourteen years on the island with her Presbyterian missionary parents and a brother. It was good to have her expertise in the Chinese language and her knowledge of places to see. She took us to the compound where her family had once lived, the hospital where her father had practiced medicine, the school she and her brother had attended, the house where they had lived, and the church where her father had been a pastor. I enjoyed her memorable stories as we walked the old grounds of her early childhood.

Our first night in Haikou was scary, exciting, and LOUD! It was the night before the Chinese New Year. We had retired early because both of us were a bit weary from the boat trip and the miles we had walked since arriving. We were sound asleep when suddenly the hotel lit up with red, orange, pink, and yellow shadows as what sounded like cannons shattered the solitude of the night. My first thoughts were Armageddon or WW III!! We were almost ejected from our beds as loud explosions continued for one full hour. The people, celebrating the arrival of New Year, were setting off firecrackers which literally jarred the hotel. The following morning the hotel grounds were a good six inches deep in bits of red paper, the remains of firecrackers exploded during the early hours of morning. Shouts of "Xing Liang Kuai Le" (Happy New Year) intermitted with the ear-splitting explosives. It was difficult to complete a night of sleep after that experience.

SANYA

The next morning Marie and I boarded a bus crowded with Chinese headed to Sanya, a six-hour ride from Haikou. Along the way, we saw rubber tree plantations, many cocoanut trees, and bananas growing by the roadside. The mountains were beautiful and valleys were filled with peasants plowing with water buffalo. I felt deep sympathy for one poor buffalo striving to free himself from belly-deep mud as the peasant in hip–deep mud thrashed him with the reins and a long stick. I said a silent prayer that they could be freed from this dilemma. At our only rest stop, the men disappeared in bushes on the right and the women, a little luckier, found a bamboo screen for privacy on the right. Marie and I nibbled on bread, oranges, and chocolates purchased in Hong Kong. It was a different bus ride in interesting ways.

We were seated behind the driver and could read some of his non-verbal behavior! The engine began to sputter and smoke until the bus finally stopped. Seemingly unperturbed, the driver took a large glass jar from under his seat, jumped from the bus, and filled the jar with dirty water from the roadside ditch. He poured three jars of water into the radiator and tried repeatedly to start the engine. Finally, after several attempts, the motor coughed, snapped, and sputtered. The driver hopped out, adjusted a few wires, and on the next attempt, the engine cranked and we were off again. This almost comical activity was repeated twice during our trip from Haikou to Sanya.

Arriving in Sanya, we met several other foreign teachers whom we knew – Jack and Judy Williamson, Wilma and William Wielink, and many others we had met during conferences in Hong Kong. A seaside restaurant became our favorite meeting place. Sitting outside, watching sunsets over the South China Sea as waves washed ashore, refreshing ourselves by light breezes blowing, holding friendly conversations – all those blended to produce my favorite time of day. On one occasion while dining, we watched the gorgeous full moon slowly rise even as we had observed earlier the beautiful sunset in the western sky. God's creation was made with no mistakes and with great beauty for those who take the time to enjoy His handiwork.

A very meaningful highlight of our stay in Sanya was a worship service on the beach. The blue water of the sea, the blue sky overhead, and the white sand of the beach made a perfect setting to sing hymns and praise songs, give testimonies, and hear an ordained minister in our group preach about "The Universal Father." I was spiritually fed at the conclusion of the service when the group sang "The Family of God."

Chinese salesmen were curious onlookers standing at a distance as we sang, prayed, and gave testimonies. They were waiting with hands and arms loaded with cheap jewelry, hoping to make sales to the worshipers. I wished all of them could have participated in the service and more importantly had a saving knowledge of the God whom the group was worshiping.

The six days in Sanya were truly a vacation. Sleeping, enjoying leisurely meals, walking the white, sandy beaches, picking up shells, sitting on the patio while reading, conversing with fellow teachers from other countries, and comparing traditions and customs all made for a restful, worthwhile holiday. Many Europeans, Canadians, Australians, Japanese, and Americans made up our group. We often talked late at night as we shared teaching ideas, philosophies, and, best of all, our faith experiences. Sanya had been a refreshing time for me.

On the last trip down the hill to the seaside restaurant, time slipped by too quickly, and Marie and I were scheduled to leave by bus for Nada. We usually walked down and back up to the hotel, but this morning to save time and not miss the bus, we joined several Chinese in a three-wheeler taxi. This is nothing more than a motorcycle with a small truck-like body fitted with narrow benches on each side. Because it was too heavily loaded, we got out when it reached the foot of the steep hill and pushed it part of the way up the hill. Marie, with her long legs, decided to walk rather than ride. The taxi slowly moved along and passed Marie shortly before it reached our hotel. She was loping up the hill as if to beat us to the top!

NADA

Our next destination was Nada, located in the center of the island. Marie and I boarded the bus already crowded with Chinese. Our seats being up front made observation and visibility easier for us. More rubber plantations claimed our attention as we moved along. A peasant on a bike had a basket tied on each side with an unhappy pig in each basket. The pigs were determined to escape, as the poor guy was desperately trying to keep the bicycle erect and the pigs contained. Pigs and peasant were still struggling as we went out of sight. The bus had to slow down several times for wandering goats, cows, and lumbering buffaloes to decide in which direction they wished to go.

More bus problems! The motor ran hot and again we pulled off the road. Side ditch water was poured into the radiator. Marie and I decided this was a common occurrence as each of the drivers had brought along glass jars to be used for dipping up the muddy water and pouring it into the radiator. Twice we stopped to "water the engine." Each time, to start the bus again, the driver had to adjust wires and hit some engine parts with a hammer he must have brought along just for re-starting the engine. Marie and I wondered whether the mud had solidified in water lines and only a hammer could loosen it. Needless to say, we had more than a few concerns about arriving in Nada!

God provided and after an uncertain bus ride, we rolled into Nada relieved that we had finally arrived. A three-wheeler taxi took us to the Protestant church which Marie and her parents had attended. The pastor, his sister, son-in-law, and caretaker warmly greeted us and then took us to a hostel where we were to stay. The price suited us well, only twenty-one renminbi (Chinese dollars), or $2.50 in U. S. currency. Accommodations were adequate, comfortable cots and a bathroom with a sink.

The pastor's sister invited us for dinner and since we were unsure of her location, she came for us and then walked us back after the evening meal. Our dinner of rice, chicken, and assorted veggies was well prepared and delicious. During the conversation, the hostess told of her twenty-one years of imprisonment because she was a Christian. With great emotion, she talked about how hard those years had been and how God had sustained her through many interrogations by the guards. We were deeply touched by her experiences and realized how fortunate we were to be Americans unafraid to practice our faith. Suddenly, her face lit up as she relayed her background experiences. "One of my greatest victories was leading my husband to the Lord," she smiled. What a wonderful evening with a tried and true Christian family!

The following morning, the pastor's granddaughter, her friend, and the friend's husband were escorting us to see a monument of Su Dong Pou, a poet exiled to the island during the Song Dynasty. The taxi was a small pickup truck with benches in the back for seats. Just a short distance away two tires went flat. Nails had punctured them, so we dismounted and waited for them to be repaired. Though streets were often littered with debris, drivers kept going unless mechanical failure or flat tires stopped them.

Tires repaired, we climbed aboard and began the hour drive to the monument. Su Dong Pou, though in exile, became a teacher and used his knowledge and skills to help educate young people in Nada. Alas, on arrival, the museum and surrounding fenced-in grounds were closed. A girl nearby climbed over the fence and pleaded with the official to let us in. He did and then followed us as we toured the museum and inspected a well which supposedly contained water that had tasted like wine until "a bad woman" had drunk from it and then it became bitter! Chinese have many such fascinating legends. This was a pleasant outing and the trip back to Nada was made without more flat tires; however, I stood most of the way because of bumpy road conditions and no hand rails to keep me from bouncing off the bench. I held to the overhead rod which supported the top of the truck body. Enjoying the informative and interesting trip, we decided it was well worth flat tires and the rough, bumpy ride.

Next we visited the home of the old bell ringer's daughter, who was a friend and classmate of Marie's when they were little girls. Family members were now caregivers for this dear lady who was now paralyzed and unable to take care of herself. When she saw Marie and realized who she was, a smile spread across her face and tears of joy filled her eyes. Grandchildren were called in to sing children's praise songs for us: "Jesus Loves me" and "Praise Him, Praise Him" among others. They blessed my heart as they sang about the same Jesus that my own grandchildren sing about and praise.

That night we went to midweek prayer services and sat on the same pew Marie had sat in as a child. After many songs and personal testimonies, the lady speaker began her sermon. Marie was happily surprised when she learned that the speaker was the daughter of her parent's cook so many years ago!

We were saddened to learn that the pianist and her husband had been incarcerated for twenty-two years because they would not denounce their Christianity. So many people were unjustly treated during those treacherous years. Now they were back serving God in their church and with seemingly no ill feelings for those who had mistreated them. They said, "God forgives and we must forgive, too!" Such faith and Christ-like love are essentials for a forgiving heart.

Time arrived to leave Nada. With many tight hugs and teary eyes, we said good-bye to our Christian sisters and brothers. The cook and her son escorted us to the bus station for the trip back to Haikou. People crowded on board with boxes containing live ducks and chickens, and one man had a butchered pig in a gunnysack with feet protruding out the side. All in all, the trip back was made without a thirsty engine and we were back in the overseas Chinese hotel for yet another night. Bathing, shampooing, and washing clothes were important duties of that night. Nada was a good place to visit, experiences there were inspirational and informative, and I was grateful for the opportunity to go there.

KUNMING in YUNNAN PROVINCE

The next leg of our journey was to Kunming in Yunnan Province, which joins Burma. After several trips to the CAAC (Chinese Airline) office, we finally bought tickets to Kunming. It was not always easy to get desired tickets, and negotiating seemed to be part of the plan. Today, getting tickets is easier as more flights are available.

Arriving in Kunming, we first needed to buy tickets back to Nanjing, where we were currently teaching. No flights to Nanjing but we could fly to Shanghai and take the train to Nanjing. Done! Now we could enjoy the remainder of our vacation, knowing we could get back to our schools on time.

As we checked into the Camille Hotel, we spotted Todd and Shiggy, two Amity teachers. They took us under their wings and hired a van to take ten foreign teachers to Stone Forest, where I had attended the Amity Winter Conferences on two previous occasions. Climbing those stone walls in Stone Forest once was enough for me!

Kunming is known as the Flower City of China and well it could be. A flower festival is held there each year usually around the Chinese New Year. Streets are lined with flowering pots of vibrant colors tastefully placed along the streets, and the sweet fragrance makes a walk along the streets most delightful. The climate is quite pleasant and I once requested being transferred there, but at that time Amity was not placing teachers in Yunnan Province, where Kunming is located.

Sunday came and we asked where the nearest church was

located. When we arrived at the spot, the building had been demolished. A young man from a nearby room came out and asked whether we were looking for the church. "Come with me," he said. "The church building was unsafe so it had to be taken down. We meet in another building," he continued. As we walked along with him, he spoke in broken English and explained how eager they were to rebuild and have enough space for all the people wishing to attend. He was a student at Jing Ling Seminary in Nanjing but since he was not in my English class, I did not know him.

The pastor was an older lady, who gave an hour-long sermon. Familiar hymns were sung for thirty minutes prior to the message, and the last hymn, "Down at the Cross," was sung with great feeling and gratitude. Two younger ministers served as assistants until their ordination took place. The lady pastor was a very good speaker and many people responded when the invitation was extended. We were blessed to be able to attend a true worship service with strangers, yet we sensed from all the members a warm feeling of sisterhood.

After worship as we were walking along the street heading back to our hotel, a lady slid to a stop on her bicycle and invited us to have lunch with her family. We accepted and her three grown sons, one grown daughter and her husband, and three grandchildren joined us for a lunch of fish soup, cabbage, shrimp, peanuts, raisins, and oranges. Hot tea was always the beverage in a Chinese home. We enjoyed a very good lunch and good fellowship with a gracious family of God's children – strangers, yet relatives, as all of us were Christians. A warm feeling of kinship existed between us, and we were grateful to the cyclist who had so graciously invited us into her home.

Lunch lasted two hours as eating was mixed with many questions and answers. Marie could communicate in Chinese and translate questions directed to me. The dear lady proudly showed us a Dispensation Chart she had been able to save which traced Chinese history back to Abraham and through all the dynasties up to 1949, when the Peoples Republic of China under

Mao Tse-tung was established. Her son-in-law showed us a box of Bibles in Chinese Braille that had been ordered from Hong Kong. These would be distributed to blind peasants in a nearby village. This was a committed family of Christians reaching out to share God's love with others.

Kunming is a city of two million people. Our hostess told us that over four hundred thousand of them are Christians. Sadly, there were only forty ordained pastors, so young seminarians were assigned weekend duties and older Christians assumed many leadership roles. There is still a great need for trained leaders.

The afternoon passed too quickly and when we had to leave, the entire family escorted us back to our hotel. They knew short cuts behind, beside, and in front of buildings. Soon back at our hotel, we felt the afternoon had been spent with part of our extended Christian family.

DALI

The following morning we were up at 4:45 to catch a bus for a nine-hour ride to Dali. The trip was quite picturesque as we moved along the winding mountainous border of Burma. Snow-capped mountains and lush green gardens below made the shaky, window-rattling trip worthwhile. I tried to squeeze a comb between the window and its frame but ended up with only a broken comb. Finally, I stuffed bits of tissue into my ears to shut out as much window and engine noise as possible. We were very happy on arrival to meet five other younger Amity teachers, who treated us as their mothers, and we felt secure in their care.

Hotel space being scarce, we were forced to settle for a room with twin beds but no bathroom. That communal facility was on second floor, we were on the first, and the only water available in our room was delivered in a liter size thermos, but things improved the next day. A room with a bath became available and we could have water after 7:00 p.m. We grabbed it!

We enjoyed our meals at the Coca Cola Restaurant, where my favorite breakfast consisted of banana pancakes. Many foreigners visit Dali and this restaurant had learned about sandwiches, pizza, and hamburgers, so our caloric needs were well met while we were in Dali.

Three pagodas were in a park-like area near our hotel, and festivals were held the three days we were there. Minorities dressed in colorful costumes were dancing, using decorated wands and feather-like fans. Quite skillful were even the older performers. Many tables and stalls were set up to sell warm drinks (no cold drinks), a variety of foods, and cheap souvenirs.

After a lunch of pizza and fruit salad in the Coca Cola Restaurant, I walked outside where I met a scam artist in a business suit. He boasted of his ministry among remote village churches and told of sermons he preached and the long distances he walked to conduct worship services. Of course, he needed money to buy Bibles and an accordion since the churches he supposedly served had no musical instrument. Convincing stories!

The following day was Sunday and as usual, Marie and I attended the church in Dali. When I saw the self-proclaimed minister present, I wondered why he was not out in one of those village churches. A Chinese lady came to us after the worship service and said, "Don't let David Li fool you. He has served time in prison for molesting female students. He was an abusive husband. He spends his time now befriending unsuspecting foreigners who accept his stories and make donations to his ministry which does not exist." From then on, Marie and I avoided him.

LI JIANG

The next morning at 5:45 a.m. we left by bus for Li Jiang, a small mountain town north of Dali. We followed the winding roads known during WW II as the Burma Road. The tall mountains, including Jade Dragon Mountain with its snowcap, were breathtakingly beautiful. At the breakfast stop, a dirty, unkempt mother and her young retarded son were very persistent as they held out their hands for a contribution. Marie and I gave them cookies, which the mother tucked into the bosom of her dress. We knew then that they were not hungry. As we continued on to Li Jiang, we were almost speechless while viewing God's beautiful creation of those magnificent hills.

Li Jiang had maintained its "Old Town." As we walked through the narrow, winding streets, we passed a group of men building a coffin and several old ladies whose feet had been bound when they were little girls. They were using sticks to help as they toddled along on their little, short, stumpy feet. A Chinese legend has it that an emperor had a daughter born with a clubfoot. He did not want her to feel she was different so he sent out the decree that all baby girls would have their feet bound. I cannot prove the truth of this legend, nor can I disprove it.

While in Li Jiang, we saw several different ethnic groups. Each group dresses differently in colors, headdresses, etc. In a field nearby, two boys and a buffalo were pulling a wooden plow guided by an old man. The three were wearing colorful caps representing their ethnic group.

Todd and Jamie, two Amity teachers, joined us at Peter's Café for a lunch of tenderloin and mashed potatoes. Afterwards, we toured the small town by foot. We visited the Dragon Pond, Phoenix Temple, and Museums of Art and Calligraphy. The latter I enjoyed but the temple was full of incense smoke and made me sad for the poor misinformed people worshiping Buddha as their God. Along the way, two soldiers were pushing another one in a wheelbarrow, but they chose not to tell us why!

Time to depart Li Jiang came, but it had been three good days enjoying the beautiful mountains and places of interest. So up at 4:30 a.m. to catch the bus, which I assumed would take us back to Dali. What a surprise – an old rickety bus with back window missing and seats on one side only, and we were facing a six-hour bus ride. Surprise again! The old bus stopped after fifteen minutes, and we boarded the second bus as people pushed children and bags through the windows. They were determined to get everything and everyone on that bus. It was packed but we, at least, had seats. We reluctantly left Li Jiang with gratitude for the three days there.

On our return journey the tall mountains, canyons, and lush green valleys seemed even more beautiful. We were told that these valleys produce much of the opium poppy trade, an illegal business that provides income for its producers. A bouquet of artificial flowers on the dashboard provided some entertainment as they swayed and bounced, and we kept expecting them to tumble off though they never did. As they swayed back and forth, a large bag of sunflower seeds above our heads began to drop, seed by seed. Entertainment back to Dali was cheap.

RETURN TO DALI
Back in Dali, we checked into a hotel and headed back to the Coca Cola Restaurant, where the semblance of western type food was tempting. We enjoyed a lunch of vegetable soup and French fries. Just as we completed our meal, we heard mournful music coming in our direction and went outside as a funeral procession was about to pass. Two young people marching in front of the entourage carried a large photo of the deceased man. Behind them was a young man carrying a black paper wreath. Two boys on each side of the wreath bearer were shooting strings of firecrackers as they moved along. They were followed by the band and then around sixteen other people scattering paper money for the deceased to use in the next world! Six men were carrying the coffin on poles and then came the family, weeping, moaning, and helping one another along. Behind them came mourners to enhance the sadness of the occasion. We watched as they marched up the mountainside to a cemetery and the burial site. Afterwards, I saw similar funeral processions on several occasions. Most Chinese are cremated after death, so seeing such a ceremony was considered unusual. We were glad to have been at the Coca Cola Restaurant in time to witness this event.

Vacation time coming to an end, it was time to return to our respective schools. We took a bus from Dali back to Kunming, traveling the same scenic route we had traveled earlier. Along the way, we saw several soldiers moving in small groups. A lady soldier was wearing high heeled shoes, a sight which seemed a little odd to us. The bus was stopped by police twice on the trip back, and certain passengers had their bags and pockets searched. We were not searched and were told that police were checking for drug smugglers. Yunnan Province joins Burma and is one section of the drug triangle in Southeast Asia with Thailand and Hong Kong making up the other two–thirds. After the ten-hour bus ride we arrived back in Kunming and checked into the Camilla Hotel for the night.

RETURN TO NANJING VIA KUNMING AND SHANGHAI

The following morning we were up again at the break of dawn for the flight from Kunming to Shanghai. No flights were made from Kunming to Nanjing at that time. Arriving in Shanghai, we took the CAAC bus to their downtown office. From there a taxi took us to the train station for $1.50 (USA. currency). We were fortunate to get tickets to Nanjing on a double-decker express train and were there in a mere four hours. The train station in Nanjing has many steps from arrival to exit gates, but it was a welcome sight to me. It had been a wonderful vacation but now it was time to go "home."

Prayers were on my lips from Shanghai to Nanjing. How to get the heavy luggage up those steps was a concern. Happily, two African students from my university were in the train station, assisted us with luggage, and hailed a taxi. One of them rode with us to Marie's campus first and then with me back to Southeast University. Back safely in my room, I bowed again with gratitude for an eventful vacation and a safe return. Christ was there all the time!

NANTONG

In March 1991, a trip to Nantong to attend the Kite festival was the spring outing. A delightful lady, Joyce Miller from Ohio, and I shared the bus seat and also a room. The first stop was for lunch in Taizhou, after which we toured the Mei Li Feng opera museum, a female impersonator's museum. That night we attended the Nantong Folk Arts Performance, a noisy, colorful troupe. It was a long day beginning at 6:00 a.m. and ending at

11:00 p.m., but an enjoyable one to say the least.

Next morning we were loaded onto a bus headed for the grounds of the Kite festival. Police with flashing lights escorted the five buses of foreign teachers and their foreign officers. People lined the roadways to gawk at this entourage as we made our way to the VIP section of the area. After we were seated, a colorful flag ceremony including the "Stars and Stripes" was presented. This was followed by the release of balloons, musical kites, huge dragons made of brightly colored paper, and hundreds of live birds, mostly pigeons. Choosing to fly over the spectators, the birds "anointed" Joyce and many others, backpackers, and even cameras! Since the wind was not very strong, only the small kites could be launched. This is an annual event so kite enthusiasts could have yet another opportunity if they so desired.

Next we toured an embroidery factory, where people were using brightly colored threads to sew designs into pillow tops, sheets, scarves, clothing, etc. Lighting was poor, no patterns were available, but skillful people embroidered from the image in their minds. From the factory we walked through a street lined so thickly with people that police had to make way for us. Residents reached out to shake our hands or just to touch us, and some mothers held their babies out for a gentle pat by a foreigner. This was a humbling experience for me, and inwardly I wished we could have shared the plan of salvation with all of them.

On to a banquet for the evening meal, with the food too plentiful and the speeches too long – before, during, and after the meal. But all that was not the end of the day's activities. Feeling tired and overly stuffed, we were taken to a fashion show of elegant lady models showing elegant fashions, which we never saw anyone wear afterwards. We assumed all of those clothes would be shipped or exported to classy shops elsewhere. The day's entertainment ended with a fireworks display lasting another hour. What a loud, boisterous, colorful, enjoyable way to end a long, long day!

The following day we toured a silk factory, where we witnessed the total process from silk worms to silk cloth. Worms were put into a vat of boiling water to soften the cocoons, each cocoon producing around three hundred meters of silk. After removing them from the hot water, a worker found one thread and fastened it to a wheel which unwound the entire cocoon. How fascinating to see this! Other workers took the thread to a loom where it was woven into cloth. Cloth was then dyed different colors and designs were made on the material that would be used on site or sent to a shop for sale or shipment. Some cloth was sent to a sewing department where silk dresses, suits, blouses, etc., were being made. These were available for sale and some foreigners bought several items. I found this to be the most interesting event of the trip – from silkworm to a silk jacket.

Again it was time to return to Nanjing with more surprises along the way. The middle bus of three buses traveling together gave out of gas and since we were the last, our bus driver stopped to offer assistance. When it was finally determined that there was no mechanical failure but rather some fuel was needed, our driver decided to siphon gas from our bus to relieve the situation. One big problem: it was raining quite heavily and water doesn't mix well with gas! How to get the gas and then pour it into the other bus offered much room for debate. A solution which finally worked was to roll up a magazine, put it into the tank, and suck on the rolled magazine until the gas flowed into the open bucket. One of the foreign affairs officers assisted by holding an umbrella over the entire operation and it worked! Our bus driver continued to drive behind to be sure the middle bus reached its destination. After a few pops and snaps, the bus took off with us bouncing along behind. When we arrived back in Nanjing, the bus leading us had unloaded and gone. Never mind, we were safely back and had more experiences to record in our memory banks.

BEIJING

My first trip to Beijing was Easter 1991, when a group of foreigners from all over eastern China assembled for a weekend of sightseeing and worshipping. A young teacher, Susan Harrelson, met me at the airport and took me to the Lido Holiday Inn, where she was living and serving as director of a kindergarten class. Beijing was interesting in many ways, and it was exciting to be in the capital of China.

After lunch, Susan and I met another friend, Thannis Phillips, at the Friendship Store nearby. From there Thannis took me to the Mining College where she and her husband, Charles, were teachers. I was spending the weekend with them. She, Charles, several other teacher friends, and I soon left for a tour of the Forbidden City, Tiananmen Square, Summer Palace, and Temple of Heaven. Lunch with Susan in the Holiday Inn was good, but dinner in The Pizza Hut near Tiananmen Square was a real treat!

An acrobatic show was our entertainment that night. Chinese are so skillful. The troupe included children from ages five to twelve in colorful costumes. The precision and accurate movements of those little tykes were at times breathtaking. Their performance made our day longer but it was well worth seeing, and no one expressed any discontent about the need for sleep

Sunday morning we were up again at 4:45 and caught a bus which took the group to the Great Wall for an Easter sunrise service. It was very cold as snow had fallen on Thursday and a cold north wind made for frigid conditions. We were wrapped in warm clothes, heavy coats, scarves, gloves, etc., and still the low temperature made our teeth chatter.

The scene was beautiful. Snow glistened on the mountain tops and the wall, and the sun coming over the tall mountain peaks turned the gray of dawn to a colorful reminder that this was a new day and a new sunrise to celebrate the resurrection of our living Savior! Dr. Ronald Winstead, our Baptist area leader, gave an inspirational message as he talked about the new life that awaits all born again believers. The service included appropriate hymns, "Were You There?" and "He Arose," and prayers of gratitude concluded the service, fairly short because of the intensity of the cold air. We left the Great Wall grateful to Dr. Winstead but most of all to our God, who through His Son, Jesus Christ, has provided the Way for us one day to experience resurrection as well. Hallelujah, what a Savior!

We boarded the bus quickly and were thankful for its warmth. A worship service followed a breakfast at the International Fellowship Club. A group of African students, some of whom I knew from Southeast University, Nanjing, led in several praise songs using their musical instruments brought from Africa. Many nationalities were present but the sweet, sweet Spirit prevailed, and a deep sense of unity and love permeated the entire service. There are no language differences while worshiping the same true and living God.

The time to leave Beijing and return to Nanjing came too quickly. My friend, Thannis, took me by taxi to the airport where I met a nice Japanese lady, who guarded my baggage while I stood in line for a boarding pass. A student from Nanjing took my bag and led me by the arm to the boarding gate. I did not know him but was deeply appreciative for his assistance. The flight was only an hour and a half, and it was good to be back in Nanjing again.

NANJING

Back home in Nanjing, I experienced yet another blessing, a nice surprise. The desk clerk in the guest house where I was living had arranged for one of the university cars to come for me. She was engaged to an engineering student and had asked him to meet me. God does, indeed, provide and on many occasions provisions were made that I could not have achieved myself. It had been a wonderful Easter weekend on the Great Wall of China with Christians from many nations, all celebrating the resurrection of our Lord.

XIAN

Two good friends, Glen and Rose Davis, had taught in Nanjing. When they transferred to Xian, a special young Chinese student of theirs adopted me as her surrogate mother. She was a very happy Christian who enjoyed Bible studies in the Protestant Church, and Sunday worship services were the highlight of her week. We often met for worship, after which we would have lunch usually in Jing Ling Hotel. There we could get hamburgers back in the early nineties. When the Davis couple invited us to spend a weekend with them in Xian, we were very excited as we could see not only our good friends but also places of great historical interest there.

The young student, Elizabeth, and I boarded a Russian made prop plane headed to Xian at 5:00 p.m. We were due in Xian at 7:00 p.m., but since there was no food on board and gas tanks needed refueling, a stop was made to satisfy both of these needs. As the plane was refueling, we were told to go to a restaurant for dinner only to discover no food had been prepared. Several passengers became very irate, so the manager raced out and came back with bags of cookies for our dinner. Each of us was given an orange bag with ten or twelve vanilla-like cookies. So much for a tasty dinner!

Back on the plane which shook and tottered all the way to Xian, we finally arrived two hours later than expected because of the slow speed of the flight. The Davises had gone to meet us at 7:00 but had given up and returned to their college. Elizabeth and I hired a taxi to take us to Xian Mining College, where our friends taught. They seemed relieved to see us and we were happy to see them. We had doubts if that old worn-out plane could ever airlift itself again.

Our friends had classes the following morning but had arranged for a car to take Elizabeth and me to see the terra cotta warriors, chariots, and horses buried for hundreds of years "to protect the emperor in the next world." Today, the excavation continues and the site is considered the eighth wonder of the world. Seeing this wide pit with statues facing north, east, south, and west to guard a deceased emperor was a wonder of wonders!

From the warriors' location, the car took us to the Hot Springs swimming pools. Lavish and extravagant was the pool for the emperor, his concubines, officials, and other important people. Those serving "his highness" and his selective personnel used pools, though impressive, that offered much less luxury. All of the pools are now obsolete and are used as a tourist attraction only.

Next we went to Banpo Village, which dates back some six thousand years. Deep excavations showed sites of simple tent-like constructions to more comfortable houses where people lived. We saw several graves of children buried right beside the houses. A large moat around the village protected villagers from would-be robbers.

The Silk Road Museum in the area provided more information of this ancient site. Bits of pottery, crude weapons, parts of straw shoes, faded fabric pieces, and other artifacts were of great historical interest. Many of the pottery pieces were quite similar to those I had seen in Mexico. The Silk Road stretched from western Xian all the way across China to the east coast. A worn, faded map on the wall showed the route taken by those making this trip. Standing there, I felt a reverse in time as images of people appeared moving along on this long, long, rough road toward the east coast of China.

Sunday morning came too quickly; however, we were on time for worship at the Protestant Church near the Goose pagoda. The choir robed in white marched in singing "Are Ye Able," after which the congregation joined them while singing "Holy, Holy, Holy" and "Down at the Cross." A blind soprano in the choir captured my heart as she sang. Her radiant face revealed what she was feeling in her heart. She blessed me as she sang. It was truly an inspiring worshipful experience, one I shall always treasure.

NANJING

The trip back to Nanjing was on a more comfortable plane, a jet to be exact. It was four hours late but returned us safely. Punctuality is not the most important aspect of Chinese culture as I viewed it. Arriving at 9:00 at night, I was concerned about someone meeting me. A student from Nanjing University said, "Don't worry. My school is near Southeast University. We can take a taxi together and then it can take Elizabeth on to her university, which was also nearby." What a relief! But when we deplaned there stood Ray Hill, the boy friend of the desk clerk in my guesthouse. She had sent him again to pick up "my American grandmother." Again God took care of all my needs.

XI HONG

Patrick lived in Xi Hong, a small town in northern Jiangsu Province. He and I left by bus on a Friday morning to spend the weekend with his family. Along the way we saw villages that had suffered extensive flood damage. Long brick buildings were under construction for homeless peasants who had lost all their possessions during the flood. "Each family will have one room," Patrick explained. One is better than none, I thought. Jiangsu is a fairly large province, but Xi Hong is small and yet large enough for a university and one hotel.

The five-hour bus ride was interesting and different from my past experiences while traveling. First, Patrick had bought a new suit which he carried in a large plastic bag like a small child with a new toy. When I suggested he put it on the overhead luggage rack, he exclaimed, "Oh, no, it would not be safe there!" So he caressed the bag and held it close to his body all the way. Later, I learned that this was his very first suit. Along the way many peasants were working in rice fields, some were using buffaloes to pull heavy plows, and some were on a packed dirt platform winnowing rice, while small children played nearby. The five hours passed rather quickly and we arrived safely in Xi Hong.

The bus station was not far from my would-be overnight headquarters. I was a bit surprised to learn that I would stay with Peng Tai and his wife rather than with Patrick's parents. The father was the head cadre (Communist leader) in Xi Hong. Patrick's brother was a governmental employee, and his wife a doctor and mother of a two-month-old baby girl. It was only a short walk to the brother's home, where I was warmly welcomed, fed, and escorted to my bedroom. It was furnished with a desk, a bed, and a washing machine, adequate for my needs.

Schools were still meeting on Saturdays, so Patrick suggested we visit his middle school. While we were in a class of fifteen-year-olds, Peng Tai appeared and asked for my passport and travel license. "Xi Hong is a closed city for tourists and a new rule has been recently passed," he said. Patrick was unaware of this. There was a small military unit in the area which accounted for this edict. We made visits to four classes where the "foreigner" sang "You Are My Sunshine" and answered a few questions asked in broken English. As we left the school Patrick announced, "You must go to the hospital." Shocked, I replied, "But I'm not sick!" We went by the principal's office to express our thanks and then made our exit.

Leaving the school, I was again informed that a foreigner could not spend nights in the home of a governmental employee. Relief came when Patrick took my weekend bag, crossed the street from Peng Tai's home, and checked me into the hotel, not the hospital. It was then that he informed me that I was not to leave the hotel. I was ready to return to Nanjing and must admit uneasiness disturbed my feeling of well-being. "Father, I'm in this situation. Please protect and help me, I silently prayed.

That afternoon turned out to be relaxing and pleasant. Patrick stretched out on the bed and called a friend who came to the hotel with fruit and other snacks. His friend spoke good English, so we discussed many issues of their concerns. They asked about life in the U.S.A., activities among young people, educational opportunities, etc. With no TV or radio in the room, they sang "Clementine," and "My Bonnie Lies over the Ocean," and then asked me to teach them "Do, Re, Me." They asked a few riddles and told many Chinese legends. Being exiled to a hotel was not so bad after all.

Peng Pao (Patrick), a Christian, had invited me to his church, which was meeting that night. Since I was confined to the hotel, it didn't seem feasible to venture out on the street. However, streets were poorly lit and I had a heavy jacket with a hood, so we surreptitiously stepped out as Patrick warned, "When we pass anyone, don't speak." He did not need to remind me, not even once! We walked on the dark side of the street as we made our way to the church. We had planned to attend worship the following morning, but the new policy stalled our intentions. When we arrived at a safe distance from the church, people were standing outside unable to get inside. "Our building will hold four hundred people, and it is always full," Patrick said. "One day we hope to build a large church so no one will have to stand outside," he added, his voice full of anticipation.

As we stood and listened, the congregation sang familiar hymns. Worshippers outside were singing along, and Patrick and I quietly hummed as they sang "What A Friend," "Blessed Assurance," and "The Old Rugged Cross" among others. This was a moving experience but we could not tarry. I was not supposed to be on the street. The musical sounds slowly died away as we headed back to the hotel, but in my heart God was still listening as these precious people praised Him in songs and in prayers.

Arriving back to the hotel room, we were just in time to prevent a flooded bathroom. Steam and piping hot water were just before going over the top of the bathtub. Having to wait for the water to cool enough to release it was my biggest problem. A big luxury was a western style commode and a shower over the tub. The night before, a pan of warm water and a "night pot" were my accommodations, so the hotel room was indeed a welcome sight.

Patrick was back early Sunday morning to return me to his brother's home for breakfast. Several others joined us for much more than the rice porridge usually eaten by Chinese – a big meal of different meats, vegetables, and fruits. Introductions were made and when the biggest man was introduced, he was Patrick's father, the top Communist official in town. He did not shake hands, as others did, but spread both arms, gave me a big bear hug, and asked whether I would come back and teach English during the summer holiday. Friendly, warm conversations took place the entire morning. My fears had no time or need to surface.

Patrick's two-month-old baby niece was a doll. Since I was not to be seen on the street, I asked Patrick to get one of the young ladies to go shopping for me. I wanted to buy an outfit for the baby. She graciously went and came back with a pink and white outfit. I could not have made a better choice.

The time to return to Nanjing came too early. Patrick was not going back for a couple of days but had a friend who took charge of my bag and me as she was taking the same bus. She and I shared the seat and had little conversation, since she spoke very little English. As we left for the bus station, everyone except the baby and her mom accompanied us. They stood and waved as our bus disappeared out of sight. This had been a wonderful, scary, different weekend but one I will always cherish.

Patrick returned a few days later and said, "My father is going to try to get you transferred to Xi Hong!" I knew then that I had been accepted even by a Communist leader. Of course, his request was never granted and truthfully, I didn't expect it would be. Some months later, Patrick rang to say he was so happy that his father was interested in God and the Bible and was attending church with him. His mother and girl friend were also interested, he added. My prayer was that the three would join Patrick in his Christian faith.

Patrick's greatest concern seemed to be marriage to the right girl for him. When asked to describe his ideal girl, he said, "She must have big eyes, be as tall as you (5'5"), and like to sing church songs." I hope that he found his "Miss Right" and is happily married and doing well as an electrical engineer, for which he was studying. He was an important part of my life during those years at Southeast University in Nanjing.

PU TIAN
Pu Tian is a fairly short bus trip from Fuzhou. Peng Zhao Deng and his fiancée, Qi Bi, were engaged but had not told Qi Bi's widowed mother. I was invited to go along to help break the news. They had been classmates in Jing Ling Seminary in Nanjing and were now assigned teaching positions in Fujian Theological Institute in Fuzhou. Peng had been in my English class in Nanjing and I had also met Qi Bi. Both were among my favorites in Nanjing. The bus trip was uneventful, and we arrived on schedule and checked into a hotel which belonged to Qi Bi's sister from Hong Kong.

My accommodations were adequate, though the bedroom and private bathroom were full of hungry mosquitoes! They really liked my type O positive blood. Dinner that night was a full banquet with too much food including various kinds of seafood, pork, beef, dog, vegetables, rice, and fruits. A pleasant evening with a feeling of love and acceptance!

After the meal, Peng and I left for the nearby church. He translated while I talked about life as a Christian in the U. S. A. Many people were present and asked several deep theological questions. They obviously had studied the Bible and were, indeed, committed Christians. We enjoyed meeting with them even though we arrived back at the hotel at 10:30 p.m. It is always a pleasure to meet with new members in the family of God.

Peng had been received and accepted as the groom-to-be. Smiles and words of encouragement to "Come back, come back" were issued warmly to Peng and to me. He thanked me over and over for making it easier for him to meet his future mother-in-law. All I did was just be there with Peng, but apparently he felt a little braver by my presence.

MEI ZHOU

While in Huanan Women's College, we made several day trips. It was a beautiful, sunny day when five foreigners and three staff members took a bus to a large lake near Mei Zhou Island. The purpose of this trip was to help celebrate the birthday of Mei Zhou, a goddess who reportedly lived a thousand years ago.

A large boat with many others heading to the island took us across the lake. Arriving there, we saw a large statue that was erected in memory of Mei Zhou. According to legend, she never cried as a baby until she was a month old. This made her quite special and different. The boat ride was pleasant, and our group enjoyed seats on the deck as we made the trip over.

Many steps led to the top of the hill where the statue stood looking somewhat like the Statue of Liberty in New York Harbor. Steps going up were lined with food that would be offered in the Buddhist temple, already belching smoke from so many incense sticks. A whole pig stood on one side of the entrance to the temple and a full-grown goat joined him on the other side. Both were ready for roasting. We wondered who would eat more, the Buddha statues in the temple or Mei Zhou! Coming down the steps, we saw numerous heads of pigs hanging from bicycle handlebars and heading for their part in the celebration.

To the left of the temple was a large incinerator, into which people were throwing paper money and other items made of paper to be burned and passed on to the other world for their deceased family members or friends to use. My heart bled for those dear souls who did not know of a living, loving, forgiving Christ.

Legend reported that Mei Zhou died at age twenty-eight on the peak of Mei Zhou Mountain. Each year many Chinese return to celebrate her birthday by shooting fire crackers, burning incense in the temple, and bowing before her statue.

The return trip proved interesting as we saw peasants harvesting shellfish from shallow water. Many were working in rice paddies and paid little or no attention to the group of curious foreigners. It had been a different day and yet another Chinese legend was placed in our memory banks.

On a bright Saturday the school van took eight foreign teachers to the East China Sea Coast. The wind was fierce and waves were high; however, the sunshine was warm in spite of high velocity winds. The foreign affairs officer, Xu Dao Feng, was with us and protected us as best she could. We began to walk along the beach picking up seashells, chatting as we strolled along. From a distance we saw a figure racing toward us waving her arms and yelling something we could not understand above the roar of the wind and the sound of waves bursting on shore. As she came nearer, we recognized Xu Dao Feng, panic and anxiety written on her face. Our outing on this beautiful day in this beautiful area was coming to an abrupt end!

At the end of the pier stood a sea wall wide enough at the top for a person to stand, if he so desired. Two men had decided to climb up and stand on top of the wall. We were told neither could swim. A strong, powerful gust of wind blew them into the raging water below and both drowned. What a pity! Rounding us up like wayward children, Xu Dao Feng soon had us on our way back to Huanan Women's College. She graciously served our picnic food in the van as we made the return trip. "I was afraid you all would drown and I am responsible for you," she explained. She was relieved only when we were safely back in our living quarters. Our disappointment turned to thanksgiving as later we discussed her anxious behavior. She was our acting mother taking care of her foreign children. She meant well.

Since the Agriculture University was located on the seashore, we decided to spend a weekend there. It was a nice, sunny, warm Friday when we checked into the guest house well before dark. Double rooms with twin beds and a private bathroom were our accommodations. This promised to be a relaxing and pleasant weekend.

Since my roommate was to arrive later, I went in to see whether all was well before she came. Whoa! The wooden door to the outside was fine but the screen door was full of holes. Suddenly, it sounded as though a full hive of bees had been released in the room. Mosquitoes swarmed from every direction. The bathroom window was placed too high for me to reach, and it was wide open! This would be a busy night swatting the varmints. Our twin cots were supposedly protected with mosquito netting, but mosquitoes can squeeze into unexpected spaces. They did, did, DID! My roommate took garlic tablets every day, I learned when she arrived. "Mosquitoes don't bother me," she boasted. Just then I would have eaten a peck of garlic buds had they been available!

Mosquitoes were not the only unwelcome "guests" that night. I woke up a number of times as the buzzing pests sang around and in my mosquito net. When my ankles covered by a sheet began to itch, I wondered what on earth could be biting me under the sheet. I hesitated to switch on the lamp but I was in agony, so after my apology to my now awakened roommate, she turned on the lamp. Big, healthy, well-fed bugs scattered in many directions. So much for any more sleep that night. Believe me, our next trip to that school was for one day only.

An interesting sight came into view as we were walking up

from the beach area where we had morning worship the next morning. We heard the sound of pat, pat, pat coming in our direction. Suddenly, two hundred or more ducks came into view followed by their herder carrying a long bamboo pole with a white cloth tied on the end. This was his tool for keeping them in order. It seemed they padded along almost in military formation heading to a grassy area for feeding. The herder needed only to flip the cloth and a wayward duck would step back in line. To see the precision steps made by the ducks led by only a white cloth the size of a man's handkerchief was almost worth the painful, annoying bites of bed bugs and pesky mosquitoes.

NAN PING

After the completion of a new church in Nan Ping, the pastor invited one of his former classmates from Jing Ling Seminary in Nanjing and me to the dedication. Both the pastor and Peng Zhao Deng had been in the English class I had taught at Jing Ling Seminary for three years. Peng Zhao Deng was assigned to Fujian Theological Seminary quite near Huanan Women's College, where I was then teaching. This connection proved very convenient for me on many occasions during the following years. The two-and-a-half-hour train trip to Nan Ping was fairly comfortable, as we were able to get tickets in the soft seat section of the train.

A couple from England were English teachers in Nan Ping University, so I spent the night with them. After settling in, we went to the church where the choir gave a wonderful rendition of "I Would Follow Jesus," "Now Thank We All Our God," "He Leadeth Me," and "Trust and Obey." The singing was followed by two reports, one given by Chen Zi Min entitled "The Spread of Christianity," and the other – a scholarly report on "Christian Literature" – given by Pastor Huang. Both did an excellent job.

The next morning being Sunday, back we went to the new church packed with worshipers on our arrival. We were escorted to the front and later I learned why! The English couple and

I were invited to sing a trio. It did not matter that we didn't consider ourselves vocalists. We sang "Blessed Assurance" and then we were asked to sing another hymn, so we did the favorite of most Chinese, "What A Friend."

A delightful lunch of frog soup, snails, much seafood, vegetable, fruits, and the ever-present rice was served in the basement of the building. The people were most cordial and seemed to appreciate our presence during this special occasion. I was quite honored to have been invited.

FUZHOU

The train ride back to Fuzhou was pleasant as we discussed the events of the past two days. It was obvious that the new Protestant Church in Nan Ping was on mission for our God.

Situated on the east coast just across from Taiwan, Fuzhou is a mountainous city. Its interesting rock formations along the riverbanks resemble pencils, shoes, boots, books, etc. Rivers and lakes are numerous in the area, and boat trips provide nice outings. We boarded a fairly large boat for the trip down Ming Jiang River one Saturday morning.

At 12:00 noon, the boat docked and suddenly McDonald's bags of hamburgers, fries, and warm drinks were being passed our way. Our school had engaged McDonald's to meet us with bag lunches. This was a nice gesture even though some of us did not care for fast foods. Of course, we did not complain, because our hostess had planned this nice surprise to show appreciation for our work.

The dean of the school was along and took care of me, holding tightly to my arm and helping me to get seated. The dear lady needed me more than I needed her, though she meant well and I appreciated her kind attention. I surely did not feel so helpless as she seemed to think, but she was doing her duty and doing it well.

I shall always treasure opportunities to travel in these different areas of China. Differences in ethnic groups and their traditions are quite fascinating and interesting. China, its cities, countryside, rivers, and sea are outstanding places in the world. Most important of all are the people who are endearing, deserving, talented, and appreciative of any kindness shown to them. May God bless all Chinese. He loves them and I do, too!.

CHAPTER 18

Literary Bits and Pieces

"Blessed is he that readeth...."
    (Revelation 1:3a KJV)

Students and friends liked to share their English skills. This chapter is made up of their bloopers, letters, legends, poems, stories, speeches, and a few sermons. Only in the last year that I was in China, 2000-2001, was an interpreter available to translate these sermons into English. They are included as the students wrote or submitted them.

Bloopers

1. Chinese clothes are redesigned to reshape body defects.

2. The line was too tired to hold the ropes.

3. Is it OK to love a girl taller then I am?

4. My boyfriend must have big eyes and be six meters tall (six feet!)

5. Most ladies wear sick stockings.

6. Is coffee mate coffee's wife?

7. What does John Cow mean? (John Bull)

8. In China, it is propitious to get near dead people

9. I hope to advance my tongue and speak English with another.

10. I'm an assistant engineer engaged in film finishing, that is to say, how to make a car become more beautiful in the face.

11. Air conditioning makes your bones soft.

12. Psychosis means a metal defect.

13. What happens when a chicken's head is chopped off? Eddy replied, "He wouldn't be able to see." Alex said, "He would have a mental problem."

14. I used hot steel (an iron) to press my pants.

15. Let's go to the mosquito (flea) market.

16. Keep your navel covered so gas can't escape.

17. It's bad luck to wash your socks with a married person.

18. Wind blowing on you causes rheumatism.

19. Why do Americans put cats in a bag? (Someone let the cat out of the bag.)

20. I was afraid to be late so I bought an alarmed clock.

21. My heart went down as soon as I heard my bride had an appendix.

22. I was as dumb as a wooden chicken.

23. Suddenly I had a bad limp and found that the heel of one of my shoes had run away.

24. The line (phone) stopped breathing.

25. The receiver is the instrument that hangs on someone's ear.

26. When swimming, tap the water with your legs and feet.

27. When the water is full of blisters, it is ready for tea.

28. The government says we must fire (cremate) dead people.

29. I felt comfortable when I rippled above the lake.

30. Her shoes are crying. (They were wet from walking in the rain.)

31. On the side of a bus was written, "Don't kiss me. It's very terrible."

32. I have an elastic stomach.

33. I slept on a high-heeled bed.

34. This broadened our eyeshots.

35. The trolley bus had two long braids.

36. I was frightened by a fish needle. (bone)

37. The boss can ask you to his office and give you a moving conversation until you are filled full and lose consciousness.

38. Eve slept with the dragon causing evil to enter the world.

39. I became a curly-haired monster when my cousin curled my hair.

40. On the back of a box of Ningman Teas was this information: "The tea is resignedly made of Thailand's high-quality lemon, mainly the fruit is tender, fresh, fragrant, sour, sweet, and delicious. It can give you a strong aftertaste, dispel your fatigue, whet the appetite, invigorate the function of the spleen, promote the secretion of the saliva glands, quench one's thirst, give you a lift, and make you relaxed. It is the healthy drink for anyone to take home, in hotels, in Kola OK (karaoke) Halls and in some other public places of entertainment. Ingredients: lemon, juochangus, licorice root, sugar, and table salt. Put this product with the paper bag into a glass and pour some boiling water on it for 3 to 5 minutes. If the glass does not break, the tea is then ready. Packaged in Guanzhou Shantou XiQing, Lianguochang."

41. It is pawing (pouring) cats and dogs.

42. Our company exports democratic (decorative) candles.

43. There are senses (scissors) for left hand and right handed people.

44. Pork (pop) music is good to here. (hear)

45. You class is horry intelligent.

46. Your class is holy intelligent.

47. Your class is holly intelligent.

48. Some people can never sing in tomb. (tune)

49. Some people can never sing in two moods. (tune)

50. There are ball people, short people, fat people, and thick people.

51. I am prepared to go home back.

52. I am very like to swoon. (swim)

53. I talk with my classmaids.

54. It made my arms ill and sour. (sore)

55. She enforced me to wilt, laugh, and cry.

56. When I see a policeman, I get a tension.

57. We talked, singed, and falled into love soon.

58. A neighbor took me off the file. (pile of wood)

59. We have different thinks.

60. The ship sat down. (sank)

61. I like to visit in your worming room.

62. Southeast is a good university because her graduates are originals.

63. I remember that afternoon when the sun fell down and the sky was red.

64. Ice sculpture shows absorb people even on the coldest days.

65. He fell into a swoon. (fainted)

66. Women wear beautiful colors in spring instead of their clumsy serious winter coats.

67. When I hear something good, I go into rapture.

68. Each won enjoyed the meal very up.

69. The duck was deftly. (gentle)

70. The sun broke through the dark cloud and jumped from the top of the mountain.

71. She is experiencing home illness. (sickness)

72. With education man can avail from foolish mistakes.

73. A man who has no education cannot be regarded as a man, only a creature.

74. Love makes our world vivid.

75. Many people diet (died) in WW 11.

76. Without health, everyday you must think of your bad boody. (body)

77. The progress of society makes us want more peas. (peace)

78. Love is mortar strength. (mortal)

79. Without love we live in a spiritual desert!

80. Truth is the basis to make friends, especially ordinary people – not politicians.

81. If everyone donates love, the word will be warmhearted.

82. That gave me a shark (shock) in my heart.

83. I'm writing to express my grievous heart to you.

84. You have an overcome problems faith.

85. Chopsticks make one more clever and develop the brain.

86. I wish the poor and sick were in varnish. (vanish)

87. When I smell flowers, it diminishes my tires. (fatigue)

88. Chairman Mao said, "Women lifted up have (half) the sky."

89. In typing class my fingers didn't listen to my eyes.

90. Michelle pronounces words with a coiled tongue, so her tongue often gets tired.

91. As a senior student, I feel I've developed enough in the school cocoon.

92. When I play the harmonica, I feel replenished.

93. Everyone has been faulted by this caustic woman.

94. He pulled so urgently that his heart almost broke out of his mouth.

95. He turned on his brains and passed the test.

96. I prefer an arresting (interesting) life.

97. I absorbed all the juice from the can of pineapple.

98. Nature's peace will flow to you as sunshine flows into trees.

99. The love of God will fill you to overflowing and as it spills out, it will bless those with whom you share it.

***

The first letter to my grandson, written by a student:

November 18, 1988

Mr. Matthew,

I'm a Chinese student of your mother. She costs one hour to have a practice for me everyday.

Now we are teacher-student and friends. We help each other. I accompany her to go out and buy foods for her sometimes. She came to have a dinner with our family when I was my birthday. Also, I was attended a congratulation for her. She gives me many stamps as she knows that I collect stamps.

Out country don't like your country which is a modern state, but our country has her special character. Mrs. Todd has been visited many cities and places. Welcome you to our state! Also, I wish to have a chance visiting your country.

Though Mrs. Todd is very business, her life is full of happy. She gave me an English name: Catherine. It's easy to call.

Your sincerely,

Gu Zhu Yun

(Catherine)

Shi Hong (Doris) was my "little girl Friday," running errands, shopping, etc., for me.

Whitney Sue is my granddaughter.

Dear younger sister Whitney:

You must be very confused. Maybe you will think where is this letter from? Who is she (he)? Why does it come to me? Well, I know. You must have many questions. Now don't be hurried, please. Let me tell you.

You can't forget which country your grandma is in now. Yes, I'm a Chinese girl. Your grandma Mrs. Todd's Chinese student. My Chinese name is Shi Hong. And now I have an English name: Doris, which your grandma gave me.

Mrs. Todd always mentions you and your brother Matthew while we talk. She also showed me your pictures. So I know you are a lovely girl and Matthew is a lovely sweet boy. I'm very glad to know both of you.

Now your grandma is learning Chinese and I'm glad to be

able to help her a bit. She is a very good teacher. Certainly she is also a nice grandma. I love her just as you. Mrs. Todd asked me to write letters to you and Matthew, using Chinese and English. And I'm very glad to have a chance to make friends with you. Are you willing?

I'm 21 years old now. I'm studying in the Graduate School of Southeast Univ. I should be older than you, is that right? My own grandma is in America. I miss her very much, and I think it is also with you. Maybe I will be able to study in USA. And then we can see each other. I do hope so!

Christmas is coming. Mail a card to you. Wishing you happy X-mas!

Doris Shi
1988.12.5

In writing class during mid-December, students were asked to write a letter to Santa Claus. The following was Tommy's letter.

Southeast Univ.
Nanjing, China
Dec. 21, 1988
Mr. Santa Claus
North Pole
Top of the World
Dear Santa Claus,

How are you? I miss you so much and I'm looking forward to your coming this year. It's sure you will bring all the things children need. The world will be happy when the youngsters are. Yet you can give us what the world need in a hurry. We want peace and no war. We want joy and no distress, happiness, no sadness. Come, and bring us those dear but necessary gifts. You can, at your presence, make the past enemy the friend forever. And you can, with your sleigh, give the poor the clothes for needy, the food for needy. It'll not be wonders that when you appear, something bad disappears. So come as soon as possible. I'd like to inform you that the situation between the two superpowers is getting well. We hope it's getting better and better. You may fly to the White House and Kremlin to tell Reagan and Gorbachev what they should go on doing. It's all depend on you. Good luck!

Yours truly,

Tommy

Dena shares the name of my daughter-in-law and felt a kinship with her because they had the same name.

Num. 0188

Southeast Univ.

Nanjing 210018

P. R. China

Jan. 10, 1989

Dear Dena:

How are you? Surely you must feel strange and wonder who I am. Who am I? I am Dena, too. Dena is my English name called by my English teacher Mrs. Todd. Then why does Mrs. Todd call me Dena? In my opinion I think this is because she always thinks of you, and secondly, perhaps you and I have something in common. Is it all right? (It's by my reasoning.)

I hear of you are very kind. You have two lovable children. I think you are very happy. Although we both are Dena, we are not in the same country and certainly have different fortune. Mrs. Todd like me to talk something about myself. In addition to this, I want to be understood by you – Dena, the real Dena. I regard you as my friend. I am glad to tell you my story, and I hope it'll not bore you.

I was born in a very happy harmonious family. I had a very good father who was not only kind but also strict. He loved me the most because I am the youngest child in our family. But something happened. My father was beaten down by the wrong people in the wrong period – the Great Cultural Revolution. This was a catastrophe from heavens. The reason was that he had written something he thought was the truth but different from the rule of the day. Not long after that, he died of tiredness in 1974 when I was only 11 years old. We were sad. It was the hardest strike on my heart. But surely will go dark and come dawn. Now all my sisters and brothers in my family have been to universitys. I am studying in the University for the Master degree. (Perhaps I'll go to America to study more some day.)

I am very happy now. But I feel sad as soon as I think of my father. I often pray for his returning and staying with me. I can tell every scene when was beside me. But I couldn't get any answer to all of this. Perhaps I shouldn't be so disappointed because I have a long way to go and our country is getting better and better. Do you think so?

I'll feel very happy if you are willing to be my friend. Could you tell me something about you and your family? (Certainly when it is appropriate to you.) Thank you very much.

Yours sincerely,
Zhou Guo Yen
(Dena)

Abdi from Morocco, Africa, wrote this short note and sent it to me by a friend. He confused March for May. Word was being spread that foreigners would be required to leave China because of the Tiananmen Square demonstrations taking place at that time.

Dear Mrs. Todd,

After I knew your departure time to USA, I felt sorrowful to leave Nanking (Nanjing) as I will be alone that time and will miss you. Because our friendship is very important and much intrest [sic].

Will you come back again?

Thank you.

Abdi

March 22, 1989
Another letter from Dena, writer after the Tiananmen Square massacre:

Dormitory No. 520
Post Box 0188
Southeast Univ.

Nanjing, China
7-21-89 Dear Mrs. Todd,

How are you? It's a pity that I couldn't see you off. I don't know whether I can meet you in the future or not. I hope I can.

It seems true that I had a lot to tell you just before I started to write this letter. But now, I can't express myself very well somehow. I miss you and all the other members of your family. I miss all of your friends who are kind to us young students. I love my country but I can't understand many things which happened in our country, such as anti-Right Deviation Movement in 1958, the Great Cultural Revolution, etc. I don't know why these things have happened in my country!

Your departure makes me feel as if I lost something. I recognize you as my best friend. I think you understand me.

I feel despair. I am crying in the heart. "Why do you cry? You may ask. I don't know why. I can't gain harmony in the heart. I am not a weak woman although I usually don't talk much. I felt I was a woman full of self esteem. I doubt now! I doubt myself! I doubt everything! Please, Mrs. Todd, help me out of the sad situation. I need spiritual support. What I need the most at this moment is the Bible.

It's time for me to say goodbye to you.

Please give my love to everyone in your family and please send my respects to Mr. Wilson whom I met in Southeast Univ. Thank you.

Yours sincerely,
Zhou Guo Yen
(Dena) Chen

A letter from Dena to my daughter-in-law:
Dormitory No. 520
Post Box 0188
Southeast Univ.
Nanjing, China
9-9-91
Dear Dena,

355

Please forgive me for not being able to write to you earlier. I think you did know what had happened in my country sometime before. To tell you the truth, I don't want to speak a word of it. Perhaps it is because I have the idea of myself. I feel despair about myself.

I appreciate your harmony family. I think you have your own idea and experience which makes you live in harmony much well with everyone of your family. I regard it a difficult thing to deal with the relation among several generations, especially in the field of educating your children. Could you tell me something about your idea and your children? I am sure you love your children very much.

Knowing that Mrs. Todd like Chinese history and Chinese food, I feel very happy I am majoring in architecture, special in Chinese architectural history. If possible I'll go to America to study architectural theory or designing. So in my opinion, perhaps, we have common interests in some field. I think I can make delicious Chinese food. I'll make for you if I ever have the opportunity to come to U.S. Do you like Chinese food?

I am preparing for TOEFL (Test of English as Foreign Language). I know there is little hope for me to go to U.S. now. But I'll try. God will give me strength.

Best wishes to all of you!

Sincerely yours,

Zhou Guo Yen

(Dena)

Students requested English names. This young man asked to be called Matthew, after my grandson.

January 2, 1992

Matthew:

I'm glad to write this letter to you. I'm one of your grandmother's students and she maybe qualify as my grandmother too. I'm Matthew, the same name as you. I want to know you, though you are 7 years old and I'm 22.

From your photography, I'm sure you'll be and just be now a

gentleman. Isn't it? I think so. You live in a peace harmony and happy family. So do I. We have much in common, haven't we?

I hope we'll stick to communicate and our friendship will last forever, for we both are Matthew and anyone of us has and will have high spirits. We'll have different experiences and so we can help each other. I wish your success in immediate future.

Jan. 2 is your birthday. I'll you but I'm sorry to write this letter and air-mail this picture so late to you. You just like the sun risen early in the morning. I wish you would shine your lights to the world with the addition of your age. I hope we can keep up the bridge between us and improve us with our experiences, thoughts, and knowledge.

Wish you a very happy new year!

My best wishes to you and your family!

Your sincerely,

Matthew

Late one night in Xiamen, I met David, whom I named Toby after my pet name for my son, Carl Glenn. My friend and I needed direction on which ferry to take to return to our hotel. Toby walked up with books in hand and asked in English whether he could help us. He had attended a night class, and another American teacher and I had visited a former student, who was a desk clerk in a recently opened western-style hotel.

Each day Toby traveled the ferry we needed since he lived on the island where our hotel was located. He escorted us to our rooms and chatted for around thirty minutes before bidding us good night.

Our friendship continued and grew through the years. He made a profession of faith and shares his beliefs with colleagues, family, and friends. He often visited and in 1996 spent Chinese New Year with me.

The last time I saw him, he introduced me to his lovely wife and promised to visit me when he came to the U.S.A. He had become a successful businessman with dreams of establishing a company selling cooking oil in America. I hope this will become a reality for him.

It was not easy saying goodbye to this endearing young couple. In his exact words, this was his letter to me soon after we met:

Zhou Shimin
Jishan Ra. No. 16
Gulangyu, Xiamen
PRC 361002
Apr. 7, 1993
Dear Mrs. Sue,

Very sorry to return your letter so late that I almost have nothing to say in reply. You treat me so kindly, but face to God I will pray. Almost every time I cherish the memory of you.

During these days I feel very busy. First, it took me lots of time to do my graduate work. Another, I took a job in ad company as an amateur designer. Each day there are many work need I to do. I must accumulate experiences and earn money. Usually more than 15 hours per day.

I will appreciate you for let me know what is Christianity. These days I went to church more. I couldn't without it in my life, when I was tied, when I was sad. I can feel there was nothing around me, encourage me. It make me know the meaning of life.

I have a request. Please give me a name, a new name. I don't like "David." It was named casually by myself and was too popular. I like the name you give me. Because you are my guider, my teacher. I will keep this name forever. Please.

Maybe I will have a trip to Fuzhou. If so, I am sure to visit you. I am so yearn to meet you. I have many things to talk with you. Please write again soon. So am I. I want to know which name you give me. Thank you. God bless you.

Sincerely yours,
Zhou Shimin

Jian Zheng was a student of mine in Jing Ling Seminary, Nanjing, from 1990-1992.

Teacher Sue Todd:

I very excitedly receive helping you given. God bless you for your selflessness offering. I tell you, whenever you did this for one of the least important of these brothers of mine you did it for me! (Matthew 25:40) We are all one body in Lord or brother and sister.

We do not recognize that race, color, language, or national boundaries will separate and divide us. I think that you come China for loving Chinese people and your loving heart was sacrificed us.

I hope you had lived in China forever. Everyday is full of laughing.

May God bless you.

Thank you!

Your student,

Jian Zheng

1993.4.23

Bruce was one of the engineering students at Southeast University, Nanjing. He was an interesting young man who grew spiritually as he read his Bible, attended church, and shared his faith with classmates. After graduation, he began work with an electrical company and, so far as I know, is still working in the same company.

I am so grateful that our paths crossed because he blessed my life with his excitement as a disciple of Christ.

Dec. 1, 1993

Dear Sue Todd,

I'm glad to make friends with you. Whenever I go, your warm smiles and balmy kindness linger on my mind. I can't imagine if I hadn't met you and got your help.

God gives me a good chance, which makes it possible for me to have such a benign friend. Those moments when you told me how we open our heart to God Lord will never fade away from my mind.

Thanks for what you have done for me and may our friendship will last to eternity.

Yours love,
Bruce

Candi was a student in Huanan Women's College, a three-year institution for girls. Upon graduation in 1995 she was employed as a secretary. She had aspirations for a higher education which materialized when she passed the required examination for a four-year university in Fuzhou. She continued to work and attended classes at night.

After a couple of years' work, Candi surprised me one day when she appeared with application forms to a university in Sidney, Australia. Her next step up was for a Master's degree from a foreign university.

She was indeed accepted, went to Australia, and graduated with a Master's in English. Shortly after graduation, she was hired by a large business firm where she works today.

She never gave up on her dreams and with her strong faith and hard work, she is now a citizen of Sidney, Australia. She hopes to bring her parents from Fuzhou to live in her newly purchased home in Sidney. May this dream also become a reality for this wonderful Christian whose plans and future are in God's hand.

Candi was an inspiration to me as a student for three years and as a friend since her graduation. I'm grateful that e-mail makes it possible to keep in touch with this very special Chinese Christian lady!

May 17, 1995
Dear Sue,
I was so glad to get your letter. From your letter, can see you always optimist. This influence me and also cheer me up.

On the first Sunday night of May, I joined a service in the church to get together with a choir which came from Taiwan. This is a special choir made of criminal and drug addicts. Sure, now they believed God and began to serve God. They sang lots hymns for us. It was very nice. I thought they must sing with their heart. They looked pious and tears while singing. (They were moved first by their hymns.) This made the audience moved and tears blurreded [sic] their eyes. Hope sometimes I can sing as good as them and really put my feeling completely into the hymns.

Thanks God, He let me meet a good boss. He didn't treat me as a secretary. I meant not like a clerk. Besides copy, fax, booking, he also want me to learn the technical things. Now I start to learn from engineering side. Not so deep, just some general knowledge, so as I can help him a little in the business side. That make my job more interesting.

I just get Kitty's letter. She told me she would go to LA (Los Angeles) next month. She is a lucky bird. God really took good care of her. I was very happy with her. But I didn't understand why she said her working conditions not so good and felt her work hard to be carried out. She said she didn't want to quit the job just for the good payment. But I think she should feel lucky that she has opportunities to travel around the world. OK. See you on next letter.

Grace and peace to you from God our father and the Lord Jesus Christ. Philippines 1:2.

Candi

* * *

The following is a miraculous testimony as shared with me by a Chinese:

Christian friend,

Here I give you a testimony. There is a sister in Christian family in Xian City, Shangzi province. Her son is a pilot in the army. One day, when he was flying, the weather was very bad. When the plane came to a mountain, he missed the way and couldn't find the route. Just at this very moment, he thought of his mother's God. He prayed: "My mother's God save me please! Jesus save me please!" Just after he prayed appeared a bright cloud from the dark cloud in front of his plane. This piece of cloud is different from the others. It's pure, white, and beautiful. He had never seen such a bright cloud. He then decided to follow the cloud. The cloud wasn't too large, not too small, not too far and not too close, and always kept the same distance from the plane. Because he liked the cloud so much, he took a photo of this cloud when his plane was coming to the destination. After he had developed the photo, he couldn't believe that it was a picture of a man's head. He soon wrote a letter to his mother and enclosed the photo. He asked his mother to write to him as quickly as possible if this is the picture of Jesus. His mother received the letter and wrote to him and told him it was the picture of Jesus. He soon developed 50 copies and sent to Xian big church as a testimony. This witness was spread to Luo Yang and many other places. It confirmed the Christian's faith that only through God, we can be saved.

The Chinese Lunar Calendar features twelve animals. Written by one of my students, the following is one description of how they were chosen. The order according to this legend is rat, ox, tiger, rabbit, dragon, snake, horse, sheep, monkey, rooster, dog, and pig. Each year is appropriately celebrated with its particular animal. Stuffed "lunars" fill the shop shelves.

Long, long ago, Heaven emperor called all animals together and chose twelve animals to commemorate year, put them in order according to their ability.

Cat and rat were good friends. They would take part in meeting together tomorrow. On next morning, rat wanted to win first position in a name list. He didn't call cat and went (wanted) to be elected himself.

Rat met ox on the way. They arrived the meeting place in the same time. Rat used his head and said to ox, "We had a race to see who would win first position and ox agreed to it. So they went on the street. Rat was very clever and jumped up on the ox's back. The people felt very surprised and cried, "Big rat!" So rat won first position. Ox was in second position.

Dragon followed tiger to the meeting place. Suddenly rabbit jumped up from a brush and forced his way in front of the dragon. So tiger won third position. Rabbit was fourth position. Dragon wanted to occupy fifth position. Snake arrived at the meeting place and wanted to compete with the dragon. But dragon said,

"You have no horns on your head and no foot under your body. You must fail."

Dragon won fifth position. Snake was in sixth position. At that moment, horse came to the meeting place and occupied the seventh position.

Sheep and monkey now came here. So the heavenly emperor arranged the sheep in eighth position, monkey is in ninth position.

Rooster and dog came to the meeting place at the same time. Rooster said to the dog, "I tell time in the morning. You defend at night. I am before you. You are behind. So Rooster is in tenth position. Dog stood in the eleventh position.

At last the pig came to the meeting place. All the animals said, "You are lazy and came late." So pig stood in the twelfth position. It was time for the heavenly emperor to announce the results.

Rat first, ox second, tiger third, rabbit fourth, dragon fifth, snake sixth, horse seventh, sheep eighth, monkey ninth, rooster tenth, dog eleventh, pig twelfth.

The race was over. When rat came back home, he told the cat how he won first position. After the cat heard the rat's report, he was very angry and rushed at the rat and killed him. From that time on, the cat became rat's enemy forever.

There are different versions of several reports made about Chinese customs and special festivals. Included are two such reports.

Chinese Customs
by
Yang Fan

China is an age-old country. In the five thousand years historial long river, it took shape of its own special culture and custom. China also is a multinational country. There are fifty-six nationalities altogether. So, we have much abundant custom and culture. Today, I would like to talk about some of them.

Among these fifty-six nationalities, Han is the biggest one.

Most of us are Han. So, I want to introduce Han at first.

Do you know what is the biggest and the most special custom of Han Nationality? Yeah, that is animal years. Each one of us has an animal year. There are 12 animal years altogether. They are: mouse (rat), ox, tiger, rabbit, dragon, snake, horse, goat (sheep), monkey, rooster, dog, and pig. Do you know your animal years? I'm sure you do!

We can say, to know about festival can help us to know about our custom much better. So, I now want to introduce several big festivals.

Everyone in China knows Spring Festival. Yes, this is the most important festival for the Han ethnic group. In the Spring Festival, children like to let off fireworks and firecrackers. These beautiful fireworks bring an animated and jubilant atmosphere. Not excepting playing fireworks, people live in the north of China like to eat jiaozi. At the lunar New Year's Eve, the whole family sits around the table together and makes jiaozi. They make many, many jiaozi and put them into gunnysacks then put into the yard. Because of the low temperature, the yard becomes a natural refrigerator, so jiaozi will be frozen soon. When people want to eat it, they catch some and cook them.

Different from them, people live in the south don't eat jiaozi but make much delicious food. In some places, it is a tradition that there (they) must have a plate of fish on the table but can't eat it. It should be left to the next day. This means we can have enough luck and money in the coming new year. Recent years, we have a new custom at the Lunar New Year's eve – all the families sit in front of TV set to watch the Spring Festival Get-together. In China, most areas have a tradition that gives money to children; this is called "Ya Sui Money." On the New Year's Day, people go out and visit others or pay a New Year call. Some places in north, people also brandish dragon or lion in order to celebrate.

New Year will continue fifteen days. The last day is the Lantern Day. This festival is also called "Shang Yuan Day." It stems from Han Dynasty, the date is the 15th day of the first month in Lunar. At that night, people eat "Yuanxiao," a kind of food made of glutinous rice. "Yuanxiao" means reunion, happiness, and harmony, so people like to eat it. When night comes, children first fire the festival lanterns, which are made of paper and bamboo. There are many kinds of lanterns, such a rabbit, fish, folding lantern, palace lantern, and so on. At the night, all the lanterns are fired, how magnificent the scene is! In the north of China, people also go to appreciate Ice Lantern. Ice Lantern is an old traditional art. These years, there is a great ice lantern meeting every year in Heilongjiang province. At the Lantern Day, there are other customs such as guessing lantern riddles, putting flash willow on the door or playing tug-of-war.

After the Lantern Day, it enters the Spring. Then, the Pure Brightness is coming. The Pure Brightness is 4th April. Because it is the beginning of the Spring, weather becomes warm and grasses turn green, flowers come out, people go for an outing, so we call it "jaqing" also. "Jaqing" means to go for an outing. On that day, people just can eat uncooked food and can't have a fire. The traditional food is "oing ming guo." At Pure Brightness, people go to sweep graves, plant trees, and play with kites.

Dragon Boat Day is another important festival in China. It came from the War Period before B.C. 2000. It is in order to commemorate Qiu Yuen – an honest official of Cu in the War Period. Once Dragon Boat Day comes, people make zhongzi and paddle dragon boat. That is said that in the ancient age, people paddled dragon boat and threw zhongzi into the river in order to dispel fish and let them eat zhongzi but not eat Qiu Yuen's body. People also hung calamus on the door to escape unlucky things. In some places, people put atractyclodes chinensis, sweet grass, and other sweet plants into a little bag, then hung it on the waist. Old men say it can bless you to escape bad luck.

I 'm sure everyone knows that the 15th of the 8th month in Lunar is the Mid-autumn Festival. Your grandma would tell you: "In the whole year, today's moon is the brightest. Do you see those black points in the middle of the moon? That is Moon Palace. Chaner Lady lives in there with her cute hare. At night, families sit around a table, eat moon cakes and fruit, appreciate the bright and beautiful moon. As our tradition, at the Moon Day, everyone in the family must come back home. If someone can't come back or died, others leave a seat for him/her. We see the moon and think about those members who are not here.

All the above are five important festivals of Han nationality. Of course, we have many other customs, such as Diet culture, marriage and burial custom, and so on.

Now let us talk about them.

I've met many foreigners. When I asked them, "What do you think about China?" most of them answer this first: "Oh, Chinese food is very delicious." That is true. There are many different kinds of food in our country. Among them, there are eight kinds more famous than others. They are: Chuan Cai, Ming Cai, Yue Cai, Jing Cai, Lu Cai, Shu Cai, Hui Cai, Zhe Cai. All of them are delicious. But today I don't want to talk about the food, I want to ask you a question: "Do you know any custom in eating?" I would like to talk about this. Because we live in Fuzhou, I want to introduce Fuzhou's eating customs specially. In Fuzhou, when you go to visit a friend who lives in the country, the hostel will serve you a big bowl of xianmian – a kind of noodle – with two eggs. We call the egg Security Egg. It means if you eat the egg, you will get lucky and have peace. When the hostess serves you such a bowl of xianmian, you must eat all the noodle and an egg. Please remember, you just can eat one egg and leave the other in the bowl. Then, if they ask you to have dinner with them, and you sit down at the table, the host and hostess will pick up food to you with chopsticks continuously till your bowl looks like a hill. But if you eat some food in your bowl, they will add food in your bowl. So if you don't want anymore, you don't say, "Thank you, that's enough." You just cover your bowl with your hand. They will know your meaning.

Once I went to one of my father's friend's house with my father to attend feast. I was very surprised to find from beginning to end, there were thirty-six courses altogether. Later my Dad told me that this was Fuzhou's custom. Among these thirty-six courses, the first course must be cold dishes, the last one must be sweet food. Of course, these years, because of Reform & Opening, there are lots of new customs appearing, such as people like drinking tea before eating, or when waiter/waitress pours you wine, you would bend your forefinger and middle finger together and knock them on the table. It is to say, "thank You," or people like MTV, KTV after dinner and so on. From the above, it is not difficult to see our society is developing. People's living level is increasing.

Tea, it is a favorite drink for most Chinese. Chinese people have known how to plant tea trees for at least 1,000 years. China is the home of tea. Tea can be divided into four big kinds: red tea, green tea, Oolong tea and perfumed tea. Each of them also can be divided into many small kinds. Fujian is a big tea province. Fujian has many famous kinds of tea, such as Wuyi Rock Tea, Oolong Tea, Anni Tie Guanyin and jasmine tea. Fujian people like drinking tea, especially in Minnan south of Fujian. When you visit Minnan, those enthusiastic hosts will invite you to sample tea. Please pay attention. I say "sample tea" but not "drink tea," because they only invite you to drink three small cups of tea. But these three small cups can make you drunk. The knowledge of cooking tea is very tastefully. Sampling tea has 3 steps. The first step is to heat up water; it is best to use spring water or well water. The water needn't to be boiling completely. When the surface of water is full of blisters, the water gets the best degree to make tea. Then, we will enter the 2nd step – make tea. You should put tea in the teapot and add a little boiled water and wait for the tea's leaves to spread. After about 3 or 5 minutes, put more water into the teapot till it is full. The last step is, make cups one by one into a line or a circle, then pour tea into cups continuous, not to stop. Now you can sample it. It is very important that the container used to cook water and the cups are made of earthware. These are some customs about drinking tea.

Old men often say that when you are living in the world, there are three important things which everyone must undergo – birth, marriage, and death. So there are many customs about marriage and funerals among the people. In some places, especially in countries, young people's marriage usually is arranged by parents or matchmakers. Man's side must give woman's father or eldest brother a certain number of betrothal money. If woman's side isn't satisfied with it, the marriage becomes unable. Many young people can't marry their own lover; many love tragedies take place in those areas.

In the cities, before the wedding, men should send betrothal gifts to ladies' house. About 10 years ago, people paid attention to "36 legs" – 9 pieces of big furniture. Recently, they began to emphasize "6 machines" – TV set, tape recorder, washing machine, refrigerator, sewing machine, and video recorder. Formerly, people held wedding banquet that must have at least 20 tables' food. Now, many young couples like to have travel wedding. Some of them also take video for the wedding.

Death is the sure result for everyone. There are many kinds of funerals. In Fuzhou, if one dies, the body must stay at home for at least 7 days, formerly it should be left for 49 days, then it can be buried. Some families also invite monks to read for the dead person. And if there are young people who are suitable to marry in the family, he/she must marry within 3 months, otherwise they will wait 3 years. In other places, there are many ways to deal with the body. But now government calls us to put into practice with firing bury, so some old customs are cancelled little by little.

Up to here, I've introduced some customs about Han nationality. But we know there are 55 other nationalities living with us in China's ground. They also have many customs. Now, I'll talk about them.

Do you know the Mangu Great Grasslands? Do you know that people live there? Do you know the name of their house?

This nationality is Mengu Nationality. It is distributed mainly over Nui Men Gu, Xing Jiang, Lias Ning, Ji Ling, Hei Long Jiang, Gan Su and Qing Hai provinces. Mengu people have bold and unconstrained character, they are very warm. If you go there, whether or not they know you, they would invite you to go to their home. They live in Mengu Bas, when you enter it, please remember you should sit at the left side. After you sit down, you can draw snuff and change your snuff bottle with others. Then, the hostess would pour your milk, tea or wine. And they also would serve you beef or mutton. Mengu people don't get rid of bone when they eat meat. In their opinion, the meat on the bone is the best part of the whole ox or sheep. If they offer beef, they usually serve the backbone and half a rib; if they offer mutton, they usually serve the backbone and four ribs. These mean they respect you and they would like to share their happiness with you.

Every year, between July and August, Mengu people receive their traditional festival – Na Da Mu Great Meeting. This is very important in Mengu people's living. Na Da Mu is Mengu language; it means "Entertainment" and "Game." It is not only a simple entertainment meeting but also a fire. People have many matches in the meeting, such as wrestling, archery, horse race, volleyball match, basketball match, and so on. People also like "Has Lai Bas" – a kind of speaking & singing art. It has firmly tune, words are usually made at time by the singer, he sings with horsehead qin – a kind of musical instrument. "Has Lai Bas" also can be sung by two persons. Night comes, the voice of horsehead qin spreads over the grasslands, young men and young ladies dance and sing around bonfire. How happy they are!

You go towards west side from Mengu, you will come to Xinjiang Province. Here, you could see Weiwuer Nationality. As soon as you meet Weiwuer people, you must pay attention to their little flower cap at first. This cap is called "Duopa" in Weiwuer language. It not only is a kind of art and craft but it also has religious meaning. According to Islam's rule, people can't let head face the sky without anything on it outside the house. "Duopa has two kinds, one is "Qiuman Duopa," one's "Badannu Duopa." "Qiuman Duopa" is very bright-colored; it has many varieties. Young people usually wear it. "Badannu Duopa"uses Badan apricot as its main variety, at the same time adds up white point or line. Mid-age men like it.

Corban is Islam's big festival. It is at the 10th day of the 12th month in the Islam calendar. On that day, every family must clean rooms, make cakes. In the early morning, they go to mosque. They should kill a goat or an ox or a camel, bone and blood must be buried underground, and the meat can't be sold. Some of them visit others, some go to sweep grave, some pray. But wherever you live, when Corban comes, Weiwuer people always hold great Singing and Dancing Meeting on the square. Going to Weiwuer people's home, please be careful that you must knock at the door at first, and don't interrupt others' conversation, don't sneeze, and say something clearly. They call uncle "Ah Kang," aunt "Ah Qia," grandpa "Dada" and grandma "Ah Na." Do you remember?

Next to Xing Jiang is Xi Zhang Province. Zhang nationality lives there. Among their living, tea is an important drink. But the way they drink tea is different from the Han nationality. They put butter and salt into a special water tube, then add the water to it and mix until the butter and teawater become well-distributed. This is the special drink of Zhang. It's name is Butter Tea. When you drink Butter Tea, you should take care of some customs. Host pours you the tea and gives the bowl to you with two hands. You must receive it with two hands and drink it slowly, little bit by little bit. Host will add tea into your bowl continuously. You can't drink it all at once. This means you don't want more. But Zhang people's home, you couldn't leave after just drinking one bowl of tea because this shows you don't respect host and it's an impolite action.

The Zhang calendar New Year's is the most ceremonious festival for the Zhang nationality. This is similar with our Spring Festival. In order to welcome the festival people will prepare ahead of time. They put highland barley seeds and wheat seeds into water so that it can grow up into green seedlings. When the day comes, they put seedlings on the niche for a statue of Buddha, which in the coming year can harvest more. At the Zhang calendar New Year's Day, people draw on the door to pray for happiness and forever. According to custom, everyone should eat nine bowls of rice on that night, but don't eat all of every bowl – put the rest into a container. After the dinner, they go to every room with the container and a torch. This is done to get rid of ghosts. Is it funny?

Do you know the peacock? Do you know that the peacock is the symbol of Dai nationality? Dai live in Yuanan Province, among the original forest. As soon as we say Dai, the first thing we think of is the Water-Sprinkling Festival. Ladies put bunches of flowers in pails, mothers make cakes and delicious food, children cut down bamboo and make water guns. The Water-Sprinkling Festival includes 3 days. The first day, called "Sangkan Day" in the Dai language, means let all old things go. On the 1st day, people paddle a dragon boat. The grandest action on the 2nd day is to sprinkle water. On that day, people sprinkle each other very happy, if you are sprinkled much more water, it is to say you are respected by more persons and you get many good wishes. Young men run into ladies' room to sprinkle water in order to tell girls their love. The last day, people get together to play games. Young men and young ladies play "Throw Bag" game. This is a game for them to find their lover with each other. To play the game, young men stand on one side, ladies stand on the opposite side of men, and they throw bags from each side. If you like a girl or a boy, throw your bag to her/him, then I think you will have a romantic love story.

Another game is "Fly Gao Sheng." "Gao Sheng" is one kind of fireworks that is made by Dai people themselves. On the top of a long thin bamboo, put a bamboo tube that is full of gunpowder. When you fire it, it flies to the sky with a sharp whistle and spurts beautiful fireworks in the sky and makes the night more beautiful. "Fly Gao Sheng" has three meanings: the 1st is to welcome the new year; the 2nd is to escape the fire in the hot season; and the 3rd is to let "Gao Sheng" chase sickness, sadness, and catastrophe away. There are some other games in the Water-Sprinkling Festival.

Dai also has a strange custom; that is after the wedding, the bridegroom must stay at brides home for 7 days, then the new couple can go back to the bridegroom's home.

There are many other nationalities in China that have their

own customs. For example, Yi nationality's marriage is very interesting. When a boy falls in love with a girl, he will play erhu (a kind of instrument) behind the girl's house. At first the girl's parents would defend carefully, but if the boy plays erhu one night after another, they will feel boring. Then the boy rushes into the girl's room to rob her.

Another example is about Miao Nationality. Miao has a traditional festival, that is "Lusheng Jie." Lusheng is a reed pipe wind instrument. The Festival is on the 27th day of the 9th month in Lunar. It lasts 2 or 3 days. During the festival, Miao people come from everywhere with Lusheng, Dize, Suona, Dong gu (all of these are instruments) to get together. People dance "Lusheng Wu." When they dance, dancers make a circle, several dancers play Lusheng and dance first, other dance hand in hand. Sometimes men play Lusheng and women dance, sometimes just one dancer dances in the middle, others sit around the dancer and look.

I will tell you something about Hui nationality. Hui people like cleanliness. Each time before they go to mosque, or they come back from distant place, or they attend a wedding or meet at a festival, they will take a bath. They consider that used water can't be used again, so when they wash their face, they use their hands from forehead to mouth, and can't do the opposite. They never use a washbasin. They don't allow to wash things in the well or container. Otherwise, you would be punished sternly.

There are many other nationalities, but I'm sorry I can't introduce them at this time. I think we can continue it next time. And I wish you can know about some customs about China through this essay. If you do that, I'll be very happy.

Chinese Special Festivals
by
Peng Cao Yang
China is a numerous population's country. So they have many celebration days among them. Traditional celebration days are the most important. They are the Spring Festival, the Lantern

Festival, the Dragon Boat Festival, the Mid-Autumn Festival, and the Qing Ming Festival.

Spring Festival is the biggest, the most important, and the most influential one for us. A long time ago, the Spring Festival prayed for a rich harvest.

Several days before the lunar new year, in large shops preparations for the Spring Festival are made five or six weeks before the exact day. Shop owners like Spring Festival because it is a time that people exchange presents. This means more goods have a ready sale than any other time of the year. In large cities, decorations are put up in the main streets two or three weeks before Spring Festival. Preparations are made at home, too. The children are going to decorate the home; Mother is going to prepare a lot of good food. They are going to have a family dinner. Father will be home soon. We clean our house and decorate it. The old folk says that everything must be new and clean for the Spring Festival for the people so that the new year will bring happiness and good luck. The celebration begins on the eve of the lunar new year, when the family gathers for dinner. No matter how far away from home a person is, he will always try to get home in time for this big dinner, which lasts a couple of hours.

On the first day of the Spring Festival, we usually stay at home. We get up fairly early. The first thing we should do is exchange New Year greetings. On the second and the third days, we go visiting relatives and friends. We sit around chatting and eating candy and all kinds of delicacies. Every family prepares something special. My elder brother and I go outside and explode fire crackers. My parents stand by the window and look at us.

The celebration sometimes lasts 15 days. The 15th night of the first lunar month is called the Lantern Festival. This is the day when young people go out to enjoy themselves and sometimes we have folk dances far into the night.

The Lantern Festival is on the 15th day of the first month according to the Lunar calendar. We eat a kind of food at supper. It is sweet dumplings made of glutinous rice flour. Since Tang

Dynasty, all the family goes outside and watches lanterns at night. During the Lantern Festival, everyone is filled with joy and it's a carnival. They enjoy themselves with poems or some beautiful sentences. I'll let you solve a riddle. Some people dress in clothes from Tang Dynasty and sing a song in the street. Some people have fairy tales about all kinds of people.

The other minority peoples in China have Spring Festival, too. For example, Tong, Cheoxian, and Zhueng. Other countries also have Spring Festival – Korea, Vietnam, and Japan.

The Dragon Boat Festival is a commemoration of a poet of ancient times – Qiu Yuen. He died on May 5th in legend based on the Chinese lunar calendar. Qiu Yuen was a prime minister of Chu Country. He was not only a good poet but also a good statesman. He persuaded his emperor to take precautions against Qin country. But the emperor didn't believe him. He was removed from his office. Not before long, he knew Chu army attacked and occupied Chu Capital. He committed suicide in the Milu River. When people knew this thing, they rowed a dragon boat and found his corpse. In order to prevent his body from being eaten by fish, people spread glutinous rice in the river. Today, people don't spread glutinous rice in the river, but we eat zhongzi and make competition of dragon boat.

In Mid-Autumn Festival, family people often sit down in the year and eat moon cakes, drink wine, and enjoy the moon and light. When I was a little girl, my mother told me a mystical story about the moon. "Once upon a time, there were ten suns in the sky. Hanyu shot nine suns with nine arrows and saved people's lives. So the emperor of the sky gave him a miracle ball. If he ate it, he wouldn't die for ever. But he loved his wife very much. He didn't eat it. One day, he went outside and told his wife to keep the ball. His wife ate it, and she flew toward the moon and lived on it. She stole the ball, so the emperor punished her. She lonely lived on the moon about one thousand years. There is a picture of his wife on each moon cake today.

During the Qing Ming Festival, we will visit graves and pray for our forefathers. This custom commemorates our ancestors and our forefathers' ancestors.

The arrival of spring is celebrated through rural China in a variety of colorful and unusual festivals. The Yao people, one of the country's 56 minority nationalities, have their own special way of welcoming the new season and "ensuring" the harvest.

On the first day of the lunar new year, the village of Xuankeu, Qingxi, and Gudiao in Jian Yeng country, Hunan province, select two stout young men to lead the festivities. Both are dressed as oxen – their heads covered by elaborate structures of bamboo and paper, and their bodies by hides of coarse black cloth and black leg wrappings. Accompanied by the roar of drums, gongs, and firecrackers, the "oxen" make their way from village to village. A drum band and a skilled plowing team follow the oxen through the crowds of excited onlookers. "Black oxen have black ears. They plow and harrow. They climb hills and wade through gullies. Their hard work will give us a good harvest," chant the villagers as they try to touch the foreheads of the oxen for good luck. The young men, however, are very selective, and nimble sidestep these advances unless they are made by a beautiful girl!

The plowing team, meanwhile, has more serious things in mind. Working barefoot, whatever the weather, they plow and sow the fields. They too sing as they work:

> We sing a spring song
> As we harness the oxen.
> We plow deep
> And carefully sow the rice seeds.
> In October we will make wine
> From the fragrant rice.
> And lovers will invite each other
> To drink.

The workers also sing impromptu verses they have made up about the activities of the different seasons. Here is one year's song:

> In the first month of the year
> Flowers are blooming.

Don't play around in this busy season.
The pond leaks and needs repair.
The plows are rusty and need sharpening.
In the third month of the year
Flowers are blooming.
Go to the field to weed.
First the rice and then the hemp.
Mushrooms need covering with cattle dung.
Insects threaten the tender vegetables.

In the sixth month of the year
Flowers are blooming.
Early rice is ripening and
Late rice awaits planting.
During the harvest we have white rice.
After the harvest we cut grass.

When the songs are over, a man carrying a basket on his back enters the fields. He mimics the action of sowing, tossing rice husks to the ground and over the villagers' heads. To round off the day's festivities, a village woman (played by a man) and a child bring baskets of food to the hungry workers. Their appetites satisfied, the "harbingers of spring" are escorted back to the village – secure in the hope that their efforts will bring a plentiful harvest in the new year.

There are 56 minority nationalities in China. We cannot list all of their special celebration days, but five of the most famous are as follows:

The Water-Sprinkling Festival is held by the Dai people living in southern Yunnan Province. It begins on New Year's Day in the Dai calendar, which falls on the seventh day after the Qing Ming Festival and lasts three or four days. The celebration starts with Buddhist sutra chanting and prayers for a good harvest, after which everyone carries two pails of water and sprinkles the water on the figure of Buddha to clean it. After that, the Dai people go out into the streets and sprinkle water on each other to wish them good luck. Dragon boat races and "Peacock Dance" performances also take place during the festival. Young men and women throw embroidered purses to look for wives and husbands. Whoever picks up your purse can end up as your life partner.

The Torch Festival is traditional with the Zi, Bai, Wa, Buleng, Naxi and Lahu nationalities in Yunnan and Sichuan Provinces. It starts on the 24th or 25th day of the sixth month in the Chinese lunar calendar (July in the Gregorian calendar) and lasts three days. Because of differences in language and customs, the various nationalities celebrate and amuse themselves differently during the Torch Festival. For the Naxi nationality in Yunnan Province, the climax of the festival comes on the third day; people carry large torches high above their heads, hoping to illuminate the crops and thus drive out the insects and gain a good harvest. On that day, everyone sings and dances happily all night long.

Flowery Mountain Festival is a celebration for the Miao people, who live in western and central Guizhou Province and in southern Yunnan and Sichuan Provinces. Dates of this festival differ because of their different localities. Given by the Gregorian calendar, some take place in February, some in June, some in July, and some in September. During this particular festival, people sing and dance to their hearts' content, accompanied by their traditional instrument lusheng (a reed pipe). It is also a good day for young men and women to get engaged. If you go there in the Huahan Festival (Flowery Mountain Festival), you will see lovers pair off under colorful umbrellas.

Nadam Fair is a Mongol Festival that takes place in July or August on the grasslands of Inner Mongolia. In the Mongolian language, nadam means "amusement" or "gathering." At this fair there is wrestling, archery and horse racing. In addition, there is entertainment in the form of arts and music, sports events and booths for selling local goods. Tourists can also travel over the vast and beautiful grasslands, live in the Mongolian yurts (tents) and taste special Mongolian foods.

Xudon Festival is important to Tibetans. It starts on the first day of the seventh month in the Tibetan calendar (August of the Gregorian calendar) and lasts four or five days. Tibetans like to sit comfortably on the ground, drink buttered tea and enjoy watching Tibetan opera at this time. In the afternoons, they drop in at each other's homes. The hosts welcome guests with a toast and sing songs urging them to drink wine. You have to be ready to drink if you visit Tibet during the Xudon Festival.

There are 56 minority nationalities in China. They have themselves special celebration days and special celebration activities. So I only introduce the most famous celebration days for Han minority nationalities and other minority nationalities. Welcome to China!

**

English classes included writing poems. Chinese tend to be very poetic.

My Tree
by
Xu Ling Yan
When people lead me away,
You comfort me to wait in patience –
It's always you who accompanies me during those endless cold days,
So tolerable you are.
When people close me up,
You remind me to keep a sober mind –
You know I hide a calmless heart,
So impulsive I am.
The tree encourages me,
Step out of my shadow –
Sing the song the river sang,
With the rock characteristics,
Build another haven for the people
– for the people of the world.

My River
by
Yuan Guang Jie
With my boat of live wandering,

I happened to flow into the river
I had longed for in the past,
With my helm losing control,
I let the river lead me,
I kept going, kept going,
Suddenly I was led into the sea.
I turned my head,
Asking for help, and found out
The river's heart had my answers.

My Rock
by
Chen Xue Jin
Is there a rock to
Wipe my tears when I cry,
Hug me when I am lonely,
Encourage me when I'm despaired,
For me?
Is there?
You are a rock
Solid, strong, unbreakable.
But I wonder
Whether you ever cried
When nobody is looking.
Does a rock need a rock?

Happy Nineteen Eighty-Nine Year
By
Henry
Nice Spring with hundreds fragrant flowers
Beautiful summer night follow long day time.
Harvest autumn with delicious grains and fruits.
Wonderful winter receive splendid cards for Christmas.
We sing hymns to praise merciful God.
Hopefully God give us a happy New Year.

The following was translated from a Chinese newspaper. No

author was given.

Life is a challenge, deal with it.
Life is charity, accept it.
Life is adventure, experience it.
Life is sadness, conquer it.
Life is duty, perform it.
Life is recreation, enjoy it.
Life is mystery, discover it.
Life is opportunity, grasp it.
Life is a good thing, praise it.
Life is struggle, participate in it.
Life is goal, attain it.
Life is journey, complete it.
Life is a purpose, fulfill it.
Life is a well, drink from it.
Life is a ship, navigate it.
Life is a book, read it.
Life is a river, voyage in it.
Life is a monster, kill it.
Life is a dream, don't break it.
Life is a gift, receive it.
Life is a mistake, begin again.
Life is a piece of white paper, color it.
Life is a song, sing it.
Life is a stage, perform on it.
Life is a blessing, repeat it.
Life is time, take hold of it.
Life is a poem, write it.
Life is a glass of bitter wine, drink it.
Life is a candle, light it.
Life is love, sacrifice it.
Life is a lock, open it.
Life is an olive, taste it.
Life is a rock, carve it.
Life is nothing, forget it.
Life is regret, give it your best.

Life is a train, catch it.
Life is a treasure, search it.
Life is an art, appreciate it.
Life is a mine, dig it.
Life is a flower, smell it.
Life is a spouse, marry it.
Life is a memory, cherish it.
Life is a tune, compose it.
Life is philosophy, study it.
Life is giving, please it.
Life is a Virgin, treasure it.
Life is everything, hug it quickly.
Life is pleasure, enjoy it.

Betts Rivet was graduation speaker at Huanan Women's College, Fuzhou, PR China, in 1995. She closed her address with this poem.

Life
by
Betts Rivet
Not once, not twice but hundreds of times
Life gives us twists and turns of many kinds.
There will be dilemmas and difficulties to unravel,
Questions, puzzles, and predicaments that baffle.
But as you follow this unwritten rule,
Your troubles will be minor, I guarantee you!
The rule is: Never look back with regret;
Instead recall the positive episodes you have met.
Take each day that is given to you,
Make the best of it and don't be blue!
Doors will open and doors will close.
If you accept it all, you'll have no woes.
Life doesn't always follow your will.
But as you go over and around each hill
Something more exciting will come into view.
And with your mind focused ahead, life stays new.

Remember, at your very best you must always be,
The happiness in your face, people will see.
So get in the habit of looking at life
As being full of more joy than there is strife.
You'll be making this world a better place to live.
For your family and friends, what more can you give?
So as you graduate, I wish you the best!!!
Your whole life is ahead. It is always a test!
So think about this advice, you can't go wrong.
Life can be as good as a beautiful song.
Melodious and clear, harmonious and pure,
But your attitude is the key, you can be sure.
Now off you go to meet whatever is ahead!
I hope you'll remember some of the things I have said.
Wherever I am, I will NEVER forget you.
Good luck to you as you begin life anew!

"Graduation Speech" was made by a student from one of the twelve classes I was teaching in the spring semester of 1989.

A Little Speech for the Graduate Ceremony of the 18th Oral English Class.by

Jim

Now it is my turn to give a speech. Truly, I have many butterflies in my stomach. But before the end of the class, I would like to say something to you.

First, as one of the organizers and sponsors, we thank the dean of Studies. Professor Jianyan Qin, the director of Foreign Affairs Office, Mr. Xu Huiyan, the director of Teacher's Department, Mrs. Wang Yun, and other teachers and guests who attend our oral English graduate ceremony.

Second, as student of the 18th oral English class, we are feeling very grateful to our University for sponsoring this class. With its support, we can get together to improve and practice our oral English. Here, greatly, sincerely, we like to express our deep thanks to our American English teacher, our grandmother, Martha Sue Todd! For us, Mrs. Todd is not only a good teacher but also a good educator. She not only teaches us how to study English but also educates us how to be a good person. From her class, we learned many stories, new words, proverbs, and tongue twisters. From her class, we know that in our lives, we must equally treat any person with our tender love and care. From her class, we understood that beauty is as beauty does. Also, from her class we remembered that we can if we think we can! Although the class has ended, we will continue to learn and speak English. Because we believe that a winner never quits and a quitter never wins, and we also believe that practice makes perfect!

Third, as a monitor of our class, I must thank all of my classmates. It is your help and support that I can take my responsibility and complete my duty. Personally, I am very happy that I can have a chance to study English with you. I am delighted that, with the class, we have got along well with one another. And with the time passing by, we have planted a tree of friendship. Now, we have to separate and return to our units again after the ceremony, but the tree of friendship is still thriving, and it will thrive and blossom forever!

Last, I hope all of my teachers and classmates have a rich, wonderful, prosperous and successful future. I hope all of your dreams can come into reality in your lives.

****

Ho Ruo Ying was like a Chinese sister to me until her death in 1995. She served as the director of the Home for the Blind until the Cultural Revolution (1966-76) closed the school. Later she taught piano at her alma mater, Huanan Women's College, Fuzhou, China. This is a report she shared with me.

A Friend Whom I Respect (1990)

by

Ho Ruo Ying

Miss Yu Ching Zhu helped the girls' blind school for her whole adult life. She came to the blind school when she was 17 years old. She came from Rou-Yann, a district a hundred miles away from Fuzhou. She had very little education, but she was very clever, diligent, and trusted. She was as good as any good and knowledgeable person with the most noble heart.

When she first came to the blind school she was an assistant helper to take care of the sick and blind girls, to measure the temperature of the sickness. She also helped the young blind students to know how to use the loom, how to roll the thread, and also take care of the older blind girls who wove in the school's weaving factory when they had troubles in the weaving. Yu was so capable that not very long afterward she was matron Ni-Suek Kuang's great friend and great helper.

Matron Ni-Suek Kuang was a crippled old lady, with two sticks to help her walk around the school. She found all students were good and in order, because the sound of her footsteps helped her discipline the noises. I wondered if she knew that her two sticks had some magic for her job.

Matron had a granddaughter, Chen Rong, 3-4 years old. Yu also helped her to take care of this small girl, because Ni's daughter had died. Her son-in-law had gone to Taiwan, with no news of him since his wife died. Yu was very busy; besides her school work she did a lot of work for her friend, Ni.

Yu had reached middle age when the Japanese occupied Fuzhou. She was one of the important staff of the school. She took charge of the school weaving factory, also helped Ni to take responsibility for the school. For example, when Fuzhou was occupied by Japanese, all official offices moved away to a far village district. The church missionary office also moved away. The missionary schools all moved away except for the blind school, which was impossible to move away. The school stayed in Fuzhou. The school had a very difficult time because of its lack of money, lack of food. At last Yu and Ms. Chen, a knitting teacher, tried to go to Ming Ching to meet the church office people, to get some money back to school. They did bring back a big sum of money for the school. They separated all the money into several parcels and tied them inside their clothes. They had to go through some village roads to reach Fuzhou. They may have met the Japanese. Very fortunately they arrived at the school safely. Really, it was a very dangerous journey.

The summer of 1945 was an excited season for our Chinese. The eight-year anti-Japanese War was ended in victory, but for Yu it was not so happy; her only brother had migrated to the North part of Fujian in 1942, when the Japanese had come. Her brother's whole family was killed by the plague except for one nephew, Yu Ming Xing, who was 6 years old. So now, there are two children for Yu to take care of. Yu now had two adopted children to take care of with her low salary. But she never said any unkind word or showed her unhappiness. She still worked hard for the school and her two adopted children.

Many years passed by; both of her adopted children had graduated from senior high school. Both of them had good scores in the school, both of them were good enough to go to the university, but Yu could only afford for one of them to go to the university, and the other one had to go to the senior technical school. According to Chinese habit, her nephew had the privilege to go to the university. If so, her friend's granddaughter had no chance to go to the university so which one would go to the university? Yu had a very hard time to make clear her thought. Yu made her decision at last. Yu let her friend's granddaughter study in the university and her nephew study at the senior technical school. When I heard of her decision, I was very surprised and deeply moved by her unselfishness and noble behavior. All the staff at the blind school knew that Ni left nothing for her granddaughter, no money, no property. We all were moved by Yu's truly loyal friendship. Another person who also moved me deeply was her nephew, Yu Ming Xing. He gave his opportunity to his adopted sister with no complaint. He was really his aunt's good nephew.

Three years, four years passed, both of her adopted children graduated from the senior technical school and the university. Both of them took care of Yu. Yu had her happy time in her old age. She stayed with her adopted daughter's family, sometimes she stayed with her nephew. She is worthy to have her reward.

****

The first Monday in March is Women's Day in China. Gifts

are given, speeches made, and a big luncheon served to those in attendance. Women are given the day off from work, and foreigners are expected to perform, a custom which usually meant singing a song. My favorite to use was "You Are My Sunshine."

Commemorating the International Working Women's Day
by
Wu An'an

This year is the 81st anniversary of the March 8th International Working Women's Day.

On this day in 1909, the working women in Chicago of the United States went to the streets on strike and held a demonstration demanding for the increase of salaries, the enforcement of the eight-hour working system, and their legal right to vote. Their actions and demands received great response and supports from the people not only in their own country, but also worldwide. In order to remember this brilliant day, to unite the working women all over the world and to fight continuously for their liberation, many countries have been celebrating March 8th as International Working Women's Day.

The first time the Chinese women commemorated this day was in 1924, when a mass rally in Guangzhou brought the public awareness to the discrimination and oppression of women in the society and addressed the importance of women's liberation. As soon as the founding of the new China in 1949, the Chinese government set up March 8th – the International Working Women's Day – as an official holiday for the working women in the country. The Chinese women have enjoyed this holiday ever since because it is not only a holiday to them, but also a time to remind them of their own commitment and tasks of fighting persistently for their equal rights in the society.

In the feudal China, the Chinese women were deprived of property rights, excluded from working outside the home, and reduced to the level of household slaves and virtually an appendage of men. The Chinese women's liberation movements started during the Republican period (1911-1949), when many women intellectuals, by new Western ideas, moved out of the homes into society and fought alongside the men for women's equal legal rights and their liberation. According to the Marxist theory, the degree of women's liberation is a natural yard stick to measure the degree of liberation of all people. Therefore, the Chinese Communist Party advocated the liberation of women from its inception in 1921. During its revolutionary cause before 1949, the Party often subordinated the women liberation to other revolutionary goals, campaigns to end wife-beating and ban arranged marriages were carried out in rural revolutionary base areas. Increasingly, the Party emphasized bringing women into the paid labor force, as it firmly believed that to help the women to be economically independent was an important precondition of women's liberation.

Thereupon, after the New China was founded in 1949, the Chinese government made continued efforts to expand employment opportunities for women. Women's equality and right to work and vote were guaranteed in the Constitution in 1950, and the Marriage Law of the same year gave women the right to choose their own marriage partners and demand a divorce. Measures to guarantee women's participation in employment and state affairs were taken and the principle of equal pay for equal work for men and women alike was adopted, which greatly stimulated the enthusiasm of women for social labor. Nowadays in the city, people can easily see men and women working side by side everywhere, in the factories, the hospitals, the schools, the companies, and other institutions. Statistics show that 43 percent of all women are now working outside the home, a proportion much higher than in most Western countries, as well as other developing Asian countries. The final analysis shows that economic independence has greatly elevated the Chinese women's status both at home and in the society.

Great changes have taken place in the women's lives today. For instance, the Chinese women keep their own family names instead of following their husbands' names after they get married. In the people's daily life, especially in the cities, there are a lot of contrast between old and new pictures. In the streets, one can easily see some men carry the baby or child instead of women. Men also carry baskets to buy food in the market. At homes it is not difficult to find men sharing housework with their wives, such as cooking, house cleaning, and doing laundry, which are usually considered women's work. "Hen-pecking" is a common word used to tease a hard working husband at home. The women in China also enjoy the social and health care services. For example, they have paid maternity leave and have health insurance covered by their work units. They receive physical check-ups during their pregnancy period about five times. After giving birth of a baby, they also have home visits by their local medical workers two-three times. In many workplaces and factories, nurseries and day-care centers are run for female workers with small children, and mothers of babies are given time breaks so that they can nurse their kids.

In the countryside, people's attitudes towards women have changed greatly, too, for women are playing a great role not only in farming but also in sideline production. Since the introduction of the responsibility system centered on the household contract system in the countryside, the percentage of women engaged in diversified endeavors, such as animal husbandry, fishery, handicraft industry and service, was up to 40-60. They have become a vital new force in the economic development of their areas.

However, in spite of all these achievements gained in women liberation, it is still too early to say that women are equal in China because deep down in everyone's mentality, tradition and culture still unconsciously play an important part in perpetuating inequality between the sexes. One disturbing fact is that the number of women participating in political life is far less that of men in this country. According to the statistical information, less than a quarter of the Communist Party members were women in Shanghai, a significant handicap in a nation where the Party makes policy and controls political life. Women as a percentage of the total membership of legislatures in China are very limited:

about one third in the lower levels; (diminishing towards the higher levels) less than five percent women in the Central Committee; and only two women ministers in the Standing Committee. Even more disturbing, female access to education in this country remained limited because of popular belief that girls were less capable than boys. As a result, women were barely represented in the ranks of those studying for advanced degrees. Taking Shanghai for example, there were only 50 women out of 410 Ph. D. students; and 156 women out of 7753 master's degree students in 1986.

Many old problems concerning women discrimination resurfaced after the reform and open door policy in the 1980s. As industrial enterprises are given self-decision power to hire and fire workers and staff, and are made responsible for their own profits and losses, they promptly decided that they would prefer to hire men rather than women, who were considered incapable of devoting themselves to jobs as fully as men because of their responsibilities for child-care and housework at home. What's more, according to the press, when many institutions of higher learning in Shanghai recruited new students in 1989, they set much higher standards for prospective girl students because the institutions had found the difficulties in finding jobs for the female graduates.

The old ways of thinking that men are more important than women because sons can carry family names still has strong influence in the countryside. That not only hinders the implementation of one-child policy, but also sometimes leads to the illegal abandonment of female infants. There are still cases as wives are abused and beaten because of their giving birth to a female child. There is sometimes an implicit assumption in Chinese policy that expects women to fulfill two major roles: that is of a good mother and a hard worker. Therefore double duty women do working both inside and outside the home haven't changed very much.

Another aspect of women liberation seems to be the critical awareness of women of their own dignity and worth. Many women in today's society are still hesitant in accepting their own status and equality. An opinion poll at Beijing University found that more than one-fifth of the women students surveyed wanted their prospective husbands with more education, ability, and income than themselves. The old idea that women are to be dependent on men dies hard. What's more, there are still women today who totally forget their own respect and dignity. In order to make money they would do anything to please men including selling their own souls and bodies. Some women, in order to go abroad, are even willing to be married to any man as long as he has a foreign passport.

In brief, sex-based discrimination lingers on in the new period, but finds its root back in the feudal time. So, women's liberation is a long-term historical process. In order to solve them, not only the government efforts, but also the awareness of the whole society to these gender inequalities are needed. On the other hand, the task to educate women to raise their competence in the spirit of self-respect, self-confidence and self-improvement is crucial, too. Being a Chinese woman myself and a feminist worker in the Amity Foundation, I feel it my responsibility and also one of the Amity's tasks to work for women and the role they play in each of our projects so as to help them to stand up in solidarity and confidence. Only when women themselves are united with each other and also with men who are committed to ending exploitation and oppression in the world, can women's liberation and equality be really fulfilled.

CHAPTER 19

Testimonials

"How sweet are thy words unto my taste! Yea, sweeter than honey to my mouth!"
(Psalm 119:103 KJV)

These sermons appear as written by my students. Only in the last year when I was in China, 2000-2001, was an interpreter available to translate these sermons into English.

Taiping Road is one of the main shopping streets in Nanjing. Among the many stores, restaurants, and night clubs with their glittering neon lights, the grey church building at No. 369 looks somewhat out of place. St. Paul's Church, built by missionaries in the 1920s, is today one of the main churches in the city. It is also the church where students from Nanjing Union Theological Seminary do field work. The Communist Government began to allow churches to reopen in the late 1970s. The following is a report regarding the church I attended while teaching in Nanjing (1988-1992). ANS editor Claudia Wahrisch-Oblau, a minister from Germany, has known St. Paul's since its reopening in 1985.

St. Paul's in Nanjing – Portrait of a Chinese City Church
by
Claudia W. Oblau

Sunday mornings are busy times at St. Paul's church. By 7:00 a.m., the sanctuary has begun to fill with worshippers for the early morning service, which will begin at 7:30 a.m. Old ladies in faded blue trousers and jackets, bent over by age, mingle with smartly dressed young entrepreneurs. Even at this early hour, the church is packed, and latecomers are directed towards the little church hall next door to which the service is broadcast. By 8:30, space in the small courtyard is at a premium, with hundreds of bicycles parked in orderly rows, people crowding around a table where Bibles, hymnals, catechisms, devotionals, and calendars are sold, and early morning worshippers leaving the church while others arrive for the 9 a.m. service.

Amid the melee is another table, staffed by young teachers and senior students of Nanjing Seminary. A large sign announces "Counselling." Rev. Ji Tai, one of the young teachers involved in this service, tells me that problems discussed here span a wide range: "About one third of the people coming to us are just curious. They come in from the street to see what is going on here, and then, when they see our sign, they come up to ask all kinds of questions about Christianity. A second group of people who come to us are seekers, those who have been attending church for a while already. They may have questions about a Bible passage, or about the sermon they have just heard. The third group are Christians from this church. They come when they have problems in their faith, their work, or in their families."

Before the service begins, there is hymn singing, with a young student leading the congregation. By 9 a.m., the church is packed even more tightly than for the early service, with chairs and small benches in every aisle, hardly leaving room for people to pass. Recently, a closed circuit video system was installed at St. Paul's; now people directed to sit in the hall next to the church actually get a better view of the preacher than those at the back of the big sanctuary.

The service itself is simple, with hymns, Bible readings, some liturgical singing (a St. Paul's specialty), and a sermon that at 20-30 minutes is short by Chinese standards. Meanwhile, about 30 noisy children are crammed into the church office for Sunday school, taught by some seminary students. This is a new program, started only recently. Peng Yaqian, the young seminary teacher in charge, says that most of the children come from Christian families and have been brought up in the faith. "When we tell them Bible stories, they often know the ending before we get to it," she laughs.

After the service, many people stay behind to pray privately. Small prayer groups are scattered all over the sanctuary. Twice yearly, in early spring and in late fall, catechism classes are held after church. Anybody who wants to be baptized must participate in these classes and pass an exam first. Says Ji Tai: "We not only ask them whether they have understood the basic teachings of the gospel, but also about their faith, what Jesus means to them personally." Before Christmas and on Easter, St. Paul's celebrates huge baptismal services. Rev. Chen Zemin, Vice Principal of Nanjing Seminary and St. Paul's pastor-in-charge: "When the church was re-opened in 1985, we had about 300 members. Since then we have baptized about 2,000 people in this church alone, an average of 250 per year. That means that in every baptism service, more than one hundred people are baptized.

Even with this kind of growth, St. Paul's is not exceptional. Many rural churches are growing at an even faster rate. What is it that attracts people to Christian churches? Li Fuyang, a theological student involved in church work, explains: "Many young people feel a great emptiness. They think their life has no meaning. There is nothing you can rely on; what used to be important 20 years ago has now been completely discredited. So many young people think that there is no meaning whatsoever. Some of them look for love, but even human relations aren't very good today. So people cannot find what they are searching for. Such people easily become Christians, because they realize that Jesus is one who will not forsake them."

Wan Xixian, a woman minister with the Nanjing Christian Council, adds that the changed lives of many Christians are a great witness. She cites the examples of families who always quarreled until one or two members became Christians. "Now that they have accepted Christ, they are full of love, they live differently." Wang adds: "I also know some private entrepreneurs who prefer to hire Christians because they are honest and reliable. Some of these entrepreneurs have become Christians themselves." Recently, Rev. Wang was told by a senior policeman that there were no Christians among the many people in the Nanjing area who had been arrested for robbery in recent months.

For Chinese Christians, it is important that faith become manifest in a life that is obviously changed. Sermons therefore often center on how Christians should lead their lives, how they should deal with money, how they should order family life. Zhao Qiusheng, the young seminary teacher in charge of youth work at St. Paul's, underscores this: "Our aim is not just to win new converts – we also want to train them. We don't want people to become Christians only in name. We need to help them understand the new life in Jesus that they have received must become evident; the new person they become must be visible to others."

Young people have been coming to St. Paul's church in greater numbers since the church started its own youth work. Every Saturday evening, about one hundred young people, most of them between 18 and 25 years of age, gather for a lively youth meeting. There is hymn singing, an evangelistic sermon, and then group discussion. It is those discussions that draw the many high school and university students who regularly attend the youth meeting. In school or university, they are often just spoon-fed knowledge, without many possibilities for questioning what the teachers say. Here, in church, they can finally ask all the questions they will not find answers for anywhere else.

Still, more than half of the members of St. Paul's are elderly, most of the women with very little education. Chen Zemin says that it is not easy to meet their needs, especially as many Sunday preachers come from the seminary. He feels that St. Paul's strength lies in reaching out to intellectuals, and that the church should do this consciously. But as the large majority of worshippers are either still seekers or recently baptized, sermons need to concentrate on the basics of the gospel no matter what, even though the questions of intellectuals and illiterates may not be the same.

There are other problems, too. Recently, sectarian groups have been active in and around Nanjing, telling new believers that their baptisms are not valid because they were not conducted in a river. Especially for older, less-educated Christians, this has caused some confusion. It is obvious why the education of Christians is so high on everyone's agenda at St. Paul's.

Regardless of all this, St. Paul's is a thriving church. Sunday services are pervaded by a very strong sense of worship. Church music is flourishing, with the church and the seminary choir taking turns in making services festive. Wan Xixian looks back at the time of the Cultural Revolution, when St. Paul's church was turned into a factory workshop and she herself was imprisoned in a "cow shed." "Then we thought that all was over, that the church had come to its end. But nothing happened to us that God did not allow. Then we were scattered and buried, like seeds in the soil. And now is the time of growth, of resurrection. God has opened the door for the gospel."

****

Many people doubt that the Gospel can be preached in China. The following sermons are proof of messages I heard in 2000! They were translated by a Chinese English teacher who converted from Buddhism to Christianity.

Invitation and Following
September 24, 2000 – Song of Solomon 1:4; Psalms 63:8
by
Ren Wu Rong
It is commonly known in Christian theology that God has used his love to attract people to follow him even before the human being knew how to seek his truth. In Genesis, after Adam and Eve committed sin, afraid to face God and hiding themselves among the trees of the garden, God called to Adam, "Where are you?" the very first question God asked of man. Starting from that moment, God has prepared salvation for man and applied his love to overcoming man's fear after committing sins, ready to take man back to his love.

A person's darkness, fear, and sins should be got rid of before he is able to develop a thirst for God, seeking and praying to God. Today we have the knowledge that we can know God better through reading the Bible, prayer, sermons, and communion.

This is because God has instilled the truth of seeking him in our hearts.

There are three kinds of attractions in the Bible for God. The first is revealed in John 6:44: "No one can come to me unless the Father who sent me draws him (NIV)." Drawn by God's glory, man is willing to come to the Father, a similar remark made by King David in Psalm 9:1-6. The second is revealed in John 12:32: "But I, when I am lifted up from the earth, will draw all men to myself." Jesus' death on the cross has manifested and completed his love for the mankind. Third, God says in Jeremiah 31:3 that "I have loved you with an everlasting love; I have drawn you with lovingkindness." We can learn that God always loves his people, protecting them and eliminating their unfaithfulness, not withstanding that his children go against him and worship idols from time to time. We can tell this from Israel's history, especially from the fact that God commanded Hosea, the prophet, to marry Gomer, a wanton woman, in order to draw his people from wandering, with the rein of love. In a word, God represents three attractions: godly glory, grace of salvation, and fatherly, everlasting love. The reason that we are able to run after God and spread the Gospel is because we are attracted by (to) him.

The immediate effect of this attraction is that we will follow God closely. In Psalm 42:1-2, King David made a metaphor that "As the deer pants for streams of water, so my soul pants for you, O God. My soul thirsts for God, for the living God. When can I go and meet with God?" We can also learn Moses' pursuit, ambition and faith in God. Moses asked God in Exodus 33:13, "If you are pleased with me, teach me your ways so I may know you and continue to find favor with you." Our problem is: have we prayed hard to be closer to God? Often we have the preliminary faith and no further knowledge or crave for God. This narrowness is due to lack of more yearning for God. Man cannot feel the genuine peace unless he has a strong crave for God and follows him closely. I quote from *The Lord of the Last Age* as an encouragement for both you and me: Devote yourself to the Lord with your gentleness and love. Simply think about Him, not merely his goodness. Furthermore, you should discard yourself. Accept God, then there is nothing more you will think of. You should be simple-hearted with the only God and no trace of your own conception. (Translator's note: it is original English and here is the back translation.) If only we can say to the Lord, "My Savior, my love, may your love attract me and I can follow you fast and steadily."

I also need to point out that attraction comes before the following. God is active. It is not us seeking after God but God is seeking for us from the very beginning. It is not we who love God but God loves us first. Since God attracts us with his steadfast love, we have no boast before God. "Salvation comes from faith." God is in control when we are attracted by his love, and are willing to follow him. King David said: "My heart follows you and your might supports me steadily." There is no contradiction between God's invitation and man's following as God is one and he is almighty and deals with everything. Amen.

How to Develop Good Soil to Absorb God's Word
Sunday, October 8, 2000 – Luke 8:4-15
by
Jiang Guiying
Our Jesus Christ used sowing seeds as a parable in listening to and receiving the word of God: the one who sows the seed is God himself, the seed is God's word, and the field is just like the human being's heart. How the heart can be pleasing to God and receive God's word well depends on the following three factors:

1. Seek after God's word. A field that can yield a crop of a hundred times calls for soil loosening, stone removing, weeding, and watering. In this way, the seed can grow freely without the hinder from stones or the wild weed. In this parable, soil loosening, stone removing and weeding all refer to the cleansing of sins. In order to cleanse sins, a person will seek after and value God's word. "Therefore, rid yourselves of all malice and all deceit, hypocrisy, envy, and slander of every kind. Like newborn babies, crave pure spiritual milk, so that by it you may grow up in your salvation, now that you have tasted that the Lord is good" (1 Peter 2:1-2, NIV). Only a person who seeks for God's word can find and keep God's word. In the church, some people hold that it makes little difference in reading the Bible or listening to God's word. However, a person who has been saved will value God's word, as the growing of the spiritual life needs God's word.

2. Be pure, kind and honest in heart. Before God, we should be of integrity, like Nathaniel., who was "a person in whom there is nothing false," always saying what was in his heart (John 1:45-49). This kind of person is pleasing to God and will receive God. Jesus said: "Simply let your 'Yes' be 'yes' and your 'No,' 'No,' anything beyond this comes from the evil one (Matthew 5:37). The pure heart also means that a person has a pure motive in seeking God. Those who go to church to seek girlfriends or boyfriends, to just obey their parents, or to save face, or kill time, are not pure before God. A pure motive before God is to seek God only, plus faith, sincerity, awe and carrying out his word.

With different motives, people receive different messages from God. For instance, in Sunday's church, some people meet with God, some feel the pushing and rushing of people, some get rid of worries and anxieties with replacement of delightfulness and joy, while some keep in grief. Only those who seek God with simplicity, constancy and holiness will find God and receive the blessing from God and will his heart to become good soil that absorbs God's word.

3. Be patient. Fruits are borne with the nutrition of patience. Keep God's word and never forfeit it even before trial, or temptation or adverse surroundings. Instead, let's face an unfavorable situation with patience and then bear fruit. James 5:7 reads: "Be patient, then, brothers, until the Lord's coming. See how the farmer waits for the land to yield its valuable crop and how patient he is for the autumn and spring rains." It is evident that there is a time for sowing as well as a time for harvesting. Without patience, there is no yielding. Nevertheless, we should be aware that patience is not inborn but the fruit of the Holy Spirit. The Bible teaches us how to bear the fruit of patience. Romans 15:4-5 says that "For everything that was written in the past was written to teach us, so that through endurance and the encouragement of the Scripture we might have hope. May the God who gives endurance and encouragement give you a spirit of unity among yourselves as you follow Christ Jesus...." Romans 5:3 instructs again that "Not only so, but we also rejoice in our sufferings, because we know that suffering produces perseverance." The above scriptures help us know that patience is yielded after experiencing hardship and trial. Those figures like Noah, Enoch, Abraham, and Moses, were all with patience and bore good fruit. With the heart of patience, we are able to develop good soil and the seed (God's word) will grow, blossom, and bear fruit of 30 times, 60 times, and even 100 times of that has been sown.

In conclusion, good soil is not born with but developed by God's word through Christ Jesus. If we are willing to follow God's guidance, good soil will result, sinfulness will become righteous, and wilderness will turn fertile. Brothers and sisters, let's love God's word and bear fruit with pure heart and persevering. Be glory to the name of God. Amen.

****

Offer Yourselves to God
March 18, 2001 – Romans 12:1-2
by
Pastor Cai

These two verses are the key to Romans, which is the link between the preceding Chapter 1:11 ("For the wages of sin is death. God's salvation comes to human beings as a gift so that we are saved by faith.") and the following chapters, which are about the life and service of Christians. Paul advised us to present our bodies as a living sacrifice, which was a severe blow to the then philosophy. At that time, the philosophy of "school of wisdom" was in fashion, which maintained that the spirit inside human beings was holy, but the body where the spirit was located was evil, i.e. "spirit is holy while material is evil." The body belonged to material, so it was evil too. Thus brought about asceticism and self-indulgence. Asceticism advocates that evil bodies should be ill treated by not providing food and drinks. Galatians 5 mentioned the various kinds of manifestations of self-indulgence, which maintained that soul was inside us and bodies were evil, so we were justified to be irresponsible, self-indulgent, immoral, and to lead a dissolute life.

Our bodies are very important to God, which lies in the following aspects:

1. Bodies are instruments glorifying God. Sacrifice offered to God in Old Testament is a dead one; in New Testament, Jesus Christ has offered himself to God for us. He is the Lamb of God and fulfilled the redemption of human beings on the Cross. Once offered, it works forever. As Christians of New Testament, we needn't offer sacrifice in the holy temple any more, what we should offer is the living sacrifice and to put our rights in God's hands. When we present ourselves to God, we will glorify God with our bodies because our bodies, which were redeemed by Jesus Christ, are the temples of the Holy Spirit. We live in this world to testimony and glorify God.

We sacrifice ourselves to God every time every moment as if we are on a sacrificial altar. It is not just pastors or reverends who should offer themselves to God, but also the Christians who have been saved because of God's grace, and who are justified by faith. In the Old Testament, we find wherever Abraham went, he did two important things: pitching a tent for daily necessities and building a sacrificial altar. The sacrificial altar embodied the relationship between God and Abraham. He came near to God and offered himself to God through the altar, which had great impact on his life. Whenever he built sacrificial altar offering himself to God, his spiritual life and faith grew amazingly.

Bible records two failures of Abraham, which did not involve the altar. First is because of famine, he lacked in faith and ran away from Canaan to Egypt and lied about his wife to be his sister. As a result, Pharaoh nearly took her as his wife. Abraham didn't offer sacrifice during this period. Another time is recorded in Genesis from the end of Chapter 16 to Chapter 17, that the thirteen years' life of Abraham from the age of 86 to 99 was not recorded in the Bible, because these thirteen years were a failure to him. As he lacked faith in God's promise, he listened to his wife Sarai and went in to her slave girl Hagar, who bore him Ishmael. Then he had to suffer from the distress of the conflicts between his wife and concubine. This family conflict let to the national hostility between the Jews and the Arabians, which derives from his not offering himself to God and living in his own way instead of obeying God's will.

Thus we see that Christians should live to testimony and glorify God, not depending on our own but on our relationship with God. We should offer ourselves to God any time and put our life and rights into God's hands completely. When we do so, God's glory will show on us, and that's why God created human beings and the universe. Today, God puts us in this world to glorify Him and we will use our life to testimony and glorify Him.

2. Bodies are instruments bearing God's grace. "To present our bodies as a living sacrifice," bodies involve life and external things. Living in this world we need God giving us grace of material and money, just that we Christians hold different perspectives towards money. Money and material are grace from God and we beg God to help us manage money well. Bible says, "Some day wings will come out from money and money will fly away. " Job says, "The Lord gave, and the Lord has taken away; blessed be the name of the Lord." Therefore, when God's kingdom is in need, we should offer the money.

Bodies are the instruments bearing God's grace. With "bodies" we can take the grace of material things and money that God gives us, and serve God more to glorify Him.

3. Bodies are instruments participating in God's plan. God's plan is God's ways of work, is His grace. For example, in Exodus, God chose Moses and guided Moses to lead the Israelis to leave Egypt. Why didn't God take the Israelis to Canaan directly? Instead, He made them trudge over a long distance. He wanted them to participate in His plan and to temper and redeem them. In the times of the New Testament, Jesus entrusted the Church with the task of spreading the Gospel for the involvement of human beings in God's plan.

We should commit ourselves to God completely, and be used by God where we are most needed. Chinese said, "Money is not with you when you were born or when you pass away." One passes away empty-handed. But we Christians will not meet our God empty-handed. Revelation 14 says, "Blessed are the dead who from now on die in the Lord." "Yes," says the Spirit, "they will rest from their labors, for their deeds follow them." The deeds and the values of serving the Lord will be there forever.

Bodies and health are very precious in God's kingdom. Bodies are for serving the Lord. The deeds are done when our bodies are healthy. Therefore, we should protect and cherish our bodies and health in order to serve God better.

Brothers and sisters, today, we all have a body, but have we committed it? May we all commit our rights to God and our body, heart, and spirit be used by our Lord. Thanks be to God. Amen.

****

Sacrifices That Please God
Hebrews 13:10-16
by
Minister Huang Chaozhang
Hebrews 13 focuses on how to please God with our love and faith. Love is one of the most beautiful sacrifices that we offer God. What are the sacrifices that please God?

First, tolerate humiliation. What does the "altar" in

Hebrews 10 refer to? It refers to Jesus Christ. Hebrews 13:12-13 tells us clearly that Jesus suffered and died outside the city, where his blood washed our sins away. Jesus not only became our altar, but he also offered himself as a sacrifice to God for us. Therefore, our Lord Jesus is both an altar and a sacrifice. Thus we should come to the cross to accept salvation and sacrifice ourselves to God. We should be willing to sacrifice our human desires such as position, power, wealth, vanity, etc., to endure the humiliation that Jesus has experienced. Only when we suffer with our Lord can we enjoy glory with him. Matthew 16:24-27 points out the principle of life for every Christian. Christians may be discriminated against, humiliated, and persecuted. This is common. We have to experience a lot of hardship to enter the world of God. In ancient churches, many saints, for Jesus' sake, remained faithful and unyielding until death. They were praised by the Lord. The Lord said, "You are well-blessed if you are insulted, persecuted, and slandered because of me." Dear brothers and sisters, if you are humiliated for our Lord, the Lord is pleased because you love Him wholeheartedly.

Next, offer the sacrifice of praise. Praise is the sacrifice of giving thanks, which is pleasing to God. Hebrews 13:15 says that we praise God and that all glories be to God. This is the sacrifice of appreciation, worship, and praise. Philippians 4:13 says, "I can do everything God asks me to win the help of Christ who gives me the strength and power." We will gain victory and joy only when we rely on our Lord in all ways. We give thanks for everything and praise our Lord for both success and failure. It is easy to praise God when we are happy, but difficult to do so when we are in trouble. We should offer up sacrifice for everything to be with God. Meanwhile, we should tell others the glory of His name. Only when our heart is touched by the gift from God can we offer our sacrifice of praise to God. Moreover, we should prevent ourselves from saying anything deceptive and from speaking evil. God will be very pleased by our sacrifice of praise to Him by telling others of the glory of His name.

Last, offer the sacrifice of doing good. Hebrews 13:16

says that God is not only pleased by our suffering for Him and praising Him, but also by our doing good and sharing what we have with those in need. God is more pleased if we do good and share what we have with those in need even when we are suffering for Him. But we shouldn't take what we do for others as an achievement or favor. We should take what we do to others as our dedication and love for God, which is pleasing to God. For our life should be a life of glorifying God and for benefiting people, a life of loving God and His people. I hope that we all sacrifice ourselves for Jesus and we offer our sacrifice of love for all people because God is love.

****

The following sermon disputes those who claim the Second Coming of Christ cannot be preached in the opened Church, the Government State approved church.

The Relationship between the Ascension of Jesus and Us
May 17, 2001 – Acts 1:6-11
by
Rev. Jiang Guiying

The ascension of Jesus refers to our Lord's returning to heaven, which is after 40 days of His Resurrection. Let's commemorate the ascension of the Lord today.

Psalms 68:18 and 110:1 of the Old Testament predict the ascension of Jesus. In John 7:33, the Lord predicts his own ascension to heaven. What a glorious thing it is that our Lord ascends to heaven! It is not the holy place built by human beings but the kingdom of heaven that He enters. Being nailed on the cross for humankind, the Lord Jesus fulfills God's plan of salvation. On the day of His ascension, thousands of angels are singing loudly the song of victory. Then, what's the relationship between the ascension of Jesus and us? Let's share the following three aspects.

First, give us Holy Spirit. Before his ascension to heaven, the Lord Jesus promised to give us Holy Spirit. In modern era of the Holy Spirit, the called children know that the work of the

Holy Spirit among us is endless.

What is the work of the Holy Spirit? First, the Holy Spirit makes us know our sin. "And when He comes, He will prove the world wrong about the sin and righteousness and judgment." (John 16:8) The Lord came to the world to love people, to give value to people and to make people righteous through faith. "About sin, because they do not believe in me," i.e., those who do not believe that Jesus is the Son of God will be declared guilty and be blamed. "About righteousness" means he goes to the father gloriously and we will not see Him. The death, resurrection, ascension to heaven and being lifted up high by Father God of Jesus prove that He is "about righteousness." When Jesus breathed his last, the centurion saw what had taken place and cried, "Certainly this man was innocent." The Lord died on the cross so that we are righteous through faith and saved through faith. "About judgment" means that the ruler of this world will be judged (John 12:21-32). The king of the world is Satan. The Bible tells us that the world is in the hands of the evil and people's hearts are controlled by vileness. If it were not the work of the Holy Spirit, human beings would not have realized or admitted that they were sinners. "All have sinned and fall short of the glory of God." Many people think that they are law-abiding and not guilty. Thank God that those who know God fall to the ground in the light of the Lord, admitting their need for the salvation of Jesus Christ. There was once a priest named Hogaman who had preached Gospel in a city for ten years, but nobody was converted to the Lord. He thought that the people in the city would not repent. When he was preaching one evening, the Holy Spirit descended on the get-together. Miraculously, many who had not been touched before then cried loudly and repented and were converted to the Lord. Among them was a person who had committed crimes two times and had not been willing to admit his guilt even under cruel torture; but touched by the Holy Spirit, he admitted guilt in public.

Second, the Holy Spirit directs our work. The Holy Spirit can lead us to every truth and to the depth of truth to understand

God's will. When we are slow to God's love and God's things, or even confused, the Holy Spirit will make us understand and know God's will. "…because God's love has been poured into our hearts through the Holy Spirit that has been given to us" so that we are asked to walk on the right road which God has prepared for us without divergence (ref. 1 Corinthians 5:5). The guidance of the Holy Spirit is just like the pillars of cloud and fire that guided the Israelites in the wilderness. Having been forbidden by the Holy Spirit to speak the word in Asia, Paul and his fellow Christians were led by the Holy Spirit to Troas and had a vision of hearing the cries from Macedonia. He experienced the lead of the Holy Spirit and obeyed the lead of the Holy Spirit. At a pastoral meeting, Pastor Kou Shiyuan obeyed the touch from the Holy Spirit, gave up the message he had prepared and repeated the message of "love" that he had shared several days ago. As a result, at the end of the get-together an officer went to the front desk and took out a gun and two bullets. It turned out that he had prepared the gun to kill his battle companion and himself as well. In God's love, he laid down his hatred and wrote a letter to his battle companion telling him the whole story and saying clearly that it was because of his converting to the Lord that he changed his original intention. Shortly afterwards, his battle companion was converted to the Lord, too.

Third, the Holy Spirit gives us the ability to work. In Chapters 2 and 4 of the Acts, we see the ability of the disciples after they get the Holy Spirit. The ability from the Holy Spirit involves courage, guts and faith, etc. Having obtained the ability from the Holy Spirit, Peter's preaching was like the arrow cutting to the heart and leading three thousand or even five thousand people to repent and be converted to the Lord. Human beings were born to be hopeless to resist the evil and unable to defeat the control of evil. There is a brother who used to be a big gambler and who also loved his wife very much. His wife exerted all her efforts, even bumped her head against the wall, to change her husband's bad habit but she was unable to. She tried to handle by means of human being but failed. The husband, though feeling a prick of conscience, was unable to free himself from evildoing. But when he accepted God's words one day, he naturally gave up his craving for gambling. Now he is an enthusiastic brother serving the Lord in the church. Thanks be to the Lord!

Lastly, the Lord is with us in the form of the Holy Spirit. John 14:16-18 tells us that though the Lord has ascended to heaven, He gives us the Holy Spirit and makes us enjoy the sweetness of being with God. Yes, this is our hope as well as our satisfaction.

Besides, there are other abilities of the Holy Spirit such as comforting people, giving testimony, worrying for us, praying for us, touching us, inspiring us, and giving us all kinds of grace, etc.

Jesus returned to heaven to be the high priest for us in front of God. Hebrews 8:1 tells us that the Lord Jesus becomes our high priest after he ascends to heaven. The day of a priest is to offer fragrant incense and to set up the lamps (ref. Exodus 30 and Numbers 8). The Church is for the called to get together. Revelations 1:20 tells us that churches are lamp stands. Christians are lamps. To illuminate, light should be put on the lamp stands rather than under them. How important the light is! Christians are light to glow for the Lord in the world. The lamp needs oil to illuminate, which cannot be done by us. Only the Lord Jesus adds the oil, sets up the lamps and is our help when we are weak. Revelations 5:8 says that "incense" is the prayers. Romans 8:34 and Hebrews 7:25 mention that the Lord Jesus prays and intercedes for us in front of God because the Lord knows our weaknesses and shows solicitude for our weaknesses. He is the only mediator between God and us. He prays for us in front of God, offers incense for us and blesses for us. Exodus records that the priest shoulders the names of twelve tribes, which shows that the Lord remembers and cares about every child of God until eternity.

Prepare a place for us. John 14:1-4 records the Lord Jesus' promise of "preparing a place for you." Modern people are fastidious about their houses, but whether the houses are good or bad will be gone. What the Christians hope is the eternal heavenly home. The heavenly home predicted and revealed in Revelation is extremely beautiful. It is not material but solid, imperishable, never out of date and forever new, where there are no tears, wars or pains, and where God is with us and lives with us. This is our hope. The heavenly home is the forever homeland prepared for the redeemed people. Having ascended to heaven, the Lord Jesus not only prepares a place for us but also comes again and takes us to the place where He is going. The Lord's coming again enjoys popular confidence and it is also an important part in Christian belief. Therefore, we should be prudent in the rest of our life, prepare ourselves and be cautious all the time to welcome the coming again of the Lord.

****

I received the following testimony by e-mail. Lin Feng, Xiao Wu, and their son, Bobby, now live in Burnaby, British Columbia.

A Personal Testimony

Wednesday, October 13, 2004

by

Lin Feng

I interviewed Bobby when I received your e-mail request about how we became Christians. "He gives us food, shelter and earth and air," Bobby told me when I asked him why he believed in God. "He helps us and gives us confidence to overcome fears," Bobby continued, "such as raising my hands, working harder, participating more in sports." Bobby also commented about the teachers at Sunday School of our church. "Teachers in the Sunday School teach us how to be a good kid. Stories in the Bible are interesting to read and if you start reading it you want to continue forever," he said.

Believe it or not, God is working on us all the time. After checking with Bobby about his reasons in believing in Jesus, my heart was touched again by what God has been showing us.

One of the main reasons that we decided to believe in God is because of Bobby. After arriving in Canada, we realized that we had to find a shelter to help Bobby from being "polluted" by different allusions in this "New World." We thought that sending Bobby to church might be a good idea to keep him from the devil spirits. It proved to be quite effective and the church has helped us build a solid moral foundation for Bobby. Every time, whenever we finish the service in our church, we can immediately feel the impact that God has created on Bobby, who appeared to be a totally new born adorable kid. As Bobby described, God gives him more confidence in working harder, participating more in sports and giving him the Good Books to read. Bobby said to me, "Stories in the Bible are interesting to read and if you start reading it, you don't want to stop."

As to myself and Xiao Wu, our hearts were touched by God after we came back from my mother's funeral. In the funeral, one thing puzzled me so much was seeing how Chinese treated the diseased and how scared they were towards the who-knows-what spirit. (Imagine – someone runs away from his/her mother's body before the cremation!) I was shocked seeing this happened to my siblings and confused as to why they were so afraid of my mother!!!

Two weeks after we came back from the funeral, we were invited to attend a movie party (that's how they called it in Chinese) at our church. We had no idea that it was actually a preaching testimony until we arrived at the church. The speaker was a lady from Hong Kong, the film that evening was about her husband, a movie star who finally believed in God. My heart was touched when she mentioned about how her family had been changed through God and how God had helped her husband overcome the fear and how her husband finally passed away in peace. My heart was really touched when she mentioned about her husband's passing away and being summoned by God. I was also deeply moved by her preaching about how Christians love each other through their love to Jesus. "Married couples come closer through Jesus," she told me. I agreed and was totally convinced. It was at the moment when the lady asked if anyone would like to believe in God, I stood up, took Xiao Wu's and Bobby's hands and walked to the front.

Xiao Wu told me that my eyes were shining all the time

during the month that we decided to follow Jesus and I treated her just like we were newly married.

****

He Hui Bing not only graduated from Candler School of Theology at Emory University, Atlanta, Georgia, but also received her Doctor of Ministry from Columbia Seminary in Decatur, Georgia. Later, she completed special training in Clinical Pastoral Education at Episcopal Health Services Institute in New York City, New York. Today, she is the pastor of First United Methodist Church at Port Jefferson, New York.

Becoming a Christian and Receiving God's Call to the Ministry
January 27, 1996
He Hui Bing

To begin, I would say that the response to God's calling is my life long commitment. Even as a child, when I did not know God, I looked out at the sky and the world about me and asked, "Who controls this world and Who manages this nature so full of beauty?"

When I was ten years old, the beauty and peace I had known all my life was shattered with the so-called "Cultural Revolution" in China. Bishop K. H. Ting says correctly that it was neither "Cultural" nor was it a "Revolution." It was madness. I saw many things I could not understand and accept. I saw hate, persecution, fighting, struggle, and bloodshed among my people. I lived through the destruction of order as I had known it, and the destruction of life as it is to be lived. I felt confused. Nature is so full of beauty, but this world and the human mind had lost harmony, peace, and to Chinese, "balance."

As a child, I loved to draw everything I saw. Because during this time, my father, owner of a pharmaceutical factory and a capitalist, was sent away to labor farm for fifteen years. Because of his record, and our family file, I could not enter college, but quietly and secretly was encouraged by teachers who had the courage to risk that support. I did not give up drawing, painting, reading and writing. My teachers considered me the best student in all of my grades, but when I graduated from high school, I was not admitted in Art College as I had hoped. My family file hung over me as a shadow of doom once again.

I was assigned to work in a coal company, and for few years I did very hard physical labor in a coal factory. During this time I got to know how people lived in hardship, poverty, and need. I shared their physical and mental suffering. They looked for the meaning of life, but it was difficult because everything was filled with "struggle," meetings, rallies, parades.

When the church in Guangzhou re-opened in 1980, my brother and I were having lunch when we heard a bell ringing. "What's that?" we cried, and ran to see. We saw the people smiling with tears, and they were singing. The music was beautiful. After the service, I immediately asked if I could join that singing group. The pastor said, "Yes, you are welcome." Even though I attended church, it was hard for me to believe that anything was really true because I had grown up in an atheistic society and experienced the Cultural Revolution; I was very skeptical to religion and yet my soul yearned for something. I questioned and studied to prove whether it was true and worthy. Through the preaching and church fellowship and Bible study, I finally came to believe that the message of the Bible is for me. I heard the message of hope, love, and forgiveness as if it were the voice of Jesus, the Son of God, talking to me. How thirsty I had been for this good news! Words cannot express the joy I found in my faith. I found a new dimension to discover the meaning of life, besides art. I joined a group of young artists in Guangzhou. We met together, not only for studying art, but also for seeking value and meaning for life. I found my faith and accepted Jesus in my life that year. It was 1981, a year of new beginning.

After baptism, I read, studied, and sang in the church choir. In 1982, I felt that God's message through Jesus Christ was the only hope for the world. I knew I had to do something, and then I felt that I must enter the seminary to study. I became more active and enthusiastic in my local church. My pastor worried that I might not continue my art, for the ministry in China is very demanding and there is little time for much else except the pastoral visiting, preaching, and work with the needy. Yet, at that time I strongly felt God's call and when they asked me, "Are you willing to give up your art?" I looked about me at the many young people who needed help in seeking the truth, love, and meaning for life. They were so thirsty for faith. I knew them and I knew their language. I wanted to be trained for the ministry. I said, "Yes, I am prepared to give up all for the sake of the Gospel our people need so much." I met all the requirements, and soon was in the seminary.

When I arrived at the Nanjing Theological Seminary, much to my surprise and joy, I was encouraged to continue my study in art, as well as artistic creations: painting with oils, watercolors, sketching in ink and the Chinese art of drawing and painting. I also began a serious study of Chinese Paper-Cut, which I later taught. Besides teaching I was commissioned to design covers for the various theological, educational textbooks being printed by the Seminary, and pointed out that art form is needed and helpful in the ministry on many levels.

These activities prompted much discussion about Christian art among teachers and students. We shared our personal feelings of God's image. We were challenged to think about the encounter between Christianity and Chinese culture, and how the Chinese people experience God's Presence among them. We meditated on how the Incarnate Christ is with us as we receive Him as our Savior and Lord. I thought Chinese art could be a powerful language to speak out our feeling, thoughts and experience of our faith, and a way to share this faith with others where there is no knowledge of a Loving God, no Christian memory, and no background to receive faith. So once again I heard the calling: "Pick up the brush and tell people about the Truth of God," from whom I have found the source of beauty and hope, love and salvation, in my painting – to tell God's message with color and line, fire and desire in my art.

Reviewing the path of my growth in faith has helped me remember that God's love and grace have never failed me since the day I first felt His hand touch my life and deliver me from the darkness of not knowing Him. He sent Jesus, the Light of the World, to lead me through dark valleys. Each step has brought me to deeper dimensions of faith and to richer experiences of Him. Each life experience has been a mileage mark in my faith journey.

Today as I hear Him calling me to experience Him in further study, marriage and family and in sharing His Good News in singing, choir leadership, preaching, and serving Him, I look back to recall those encounters which taught me His ways and led me to a commitment and a vision for the future.

In 1989, I was awarded a full scholarship to study in England. While I was applying for my passport, the student's Democracy movement occurred in Tiananmen Square in Beijing. A smaller movement occurred as well in many cities, and very strongly in Nanjing. I led the Seminary students to carry water to those involved in the protest. I was considered a participant. Then I was denied the right to receive my passport. I was not allowed to travel, and the opportunity to study abroad with a full scholarship was lost. At the time, it was a disappointment, and painful to lose the chance to study in England, but I believed that everything was in God's hands. Now, I see that Romans 8:28 is as true as words can describe the powerful love and care of God.

As I said in the opening sentence, "The response to God's call is my life long commitment." Ever since I have sensed this call, and made the commitment, I have been serving God in any and every condition – in my home church in Guangzhou, in Nanjing Seminary, in St. Paul's Church in Nanjing, through counseling fellow students, and with art creativity.

In 1991 I married an American citizen and applied for the exit permit. One year later I got my passport to come to USA. Due to my vocation for the ministry and for the Christian mission between two countries, I needed to further my study in this field. It is my intention to return to China and teach in the Seminary in Nanjing. I did not have a denominational background. The Church in China now is post-denominational. I joined St. James United Methodist Church and became a member after I entered

Candler School of Theology at Emory University.

To help in paying my tuition and living expenses during these terms, I have been leading two church choirs: one in the United Methodist Church in Cumming, Georgia, and the other at the First Chinese Christian Church of Atlanta. I also preach there on a regular basis, so that I could better prepare myself for the ministry at large and acclimate with the culture and life in this country.

My original intention to study abroad was to extend my research in theology and art. During my teaching in China, I realized that it is very necessary to go further in my study in these fields. Not only because I myself am a Christian artist, I feel that art has a function of transcendence which applies to the context of history and culture to theology and faith. Art itself is an interpreter and reflection of theology and God's work through culture and history. In Nanjing Seminary we established the art course to apply visual art to the church worship, and Christian Art History to study the image of God. We are still in the process of experiment that seeks to apply art to our ministry and dialogue between Christianity and society. My hope for the future is that I may continue to study and then teach in art history and research and apply the art creatively in theological concepts to increase the effectiveness of my ministry and pastoral care, as well as spiritual therapy and outreach.

I am from a Post-denominational background, and inter-denominational spirit, that has influenced my theological views of the church and life. I hope to study in the D. Min. program, that I will be able to serve the Church in China and continue to teach the History of Christian Art. I have been asked by Dean Chen Zemin to teach and apply them in the ministry. This is my calling, and now my life's goal, and I believe it is God's purpose for my life.

****

"And we know all things work together for good to them that love God, to them who are called according to His purpose." *(Romans 8:28 KJV)*

CHAPTER 20

Going Back

"...Let us go again and visit our brethren...."
(Acts 15:36a KJV)

Three years passed since I had left China, leaving behind dear friends and loved ones. Not surprisingly I was overjoyed when I was able to return to my second home country, China! A great feeling of excitement and expectation filled my thoughts after bidding farewell to members of my family – Glenn, Dee, Matthew, Whitney, Steve, Doris, and Max. The time to board the plane for Japan and China had arrived on June 5, 2004. A prelude to the overseas flight included a stopover in Orange, California, to connect with my traveling companion, Betts Rivet, and her Japanese born adopted granddaughter. We were taking Bethany, Betts' granddaughter, to Nagoya, Japan, to meet the American missionary, Betty Loudermilk, who had assisted in Bethany's adoption fifteen years ago.

Since the following day was Sunday, we attended worship at Aldersgate United Methodist Church in Orange. A moving sermon was given by a lady pastor on the topic of "I Choose to Hope." Scripture was taken from 1 Peter 3: 13-22. After worship, a nice surprise awaited us when Jim, a Chinese doctor from Fuzhou, his wife, Connie, and eight-year old son, Matthew, appeared. Jim was a surgeon in Fuzhou and is presently preparing for exams related to obtaining his American medical license. Jim insisted that he treat us to dinner that night.

Off we went to meet Jim, Connie, and Matthew at the Green Tree, a Chinese restaurant not far from Betts' home. During the dinner, I learned that Connie, a biologist, was preparing for graduate school, and that Matthew is a budding architect, as he can already design and build originals using the logos blocks. For his sixth birthday, Matthew asked for a dictionary! His future? Only our Father knows.

We spent one more day in Orange as we awaited Bethany's arrival from Roanoke, Virginia. This wait provided time for a visit from Kay Grimmesey, a teacher from nearby Upland and also from Huanan Women's College, where we would stay during our upcoming visit in China. She gave us an update of the past year's events, which whetted our appetites even more to experience our plans. It was good to see Kay again and enjoy lunch and fellowship with her and Betts. I had known both of them from our working together in China.

The day arrived sunny and warm as we made our way to Los Angeles International Airport. We would fly the Japanese Airline (JAL) to Nagoya, Japan, by way of Tokyo; Betts and Bethany were seated on the opposite side of the plane from me. I sat between a sweet Japanese girl, who had just graduated from the University of Nevada, and Ben, a graduate student from Brown University in Rhode Island. From Hiroshima, the young Japanese lady showed great interest in Christianity. She knew of a church near her home and promised to attend it. She had graduated as an accountant. Ben, an instructor at Brown University in the field of philosophy, is at the same time working on his Ph. D. In Tokyo he was to meet a friend with whom to backpack through much of Japan. Sharing the seat with these two made the twelve-hour flight quite interesting and pleasant.

Another short one-hour flight was necessary from Tokyo to Nagoya. It seemed that we could almost walk that distance!

On arrival in Nagoya, we expected to see Betty, our hostess. She was returning from Atlanta, Georgia, with a three-month-old Japanese baby boy and his adoptive mother. She had taken the baby to Atlanta for the prospective parents to see him. The young, adoptive mother and baby returned with Betty, since a visa was required for the baby to reside in the United States. This requirement entailed a trip to the United States Embassy in Tokyo to obtain a parent's signature on behalf of the baby.

So we waited and no sign of Betty. As we were about to go to a hotel, out of the milling crowd, a young man walked up and said, "Mama asked me to meet you, and I am late because of the traffic. So sorry." From him we learned that Betty's plane had come in four hours ahead of ours. Since she had a church friend to meet her, she was not there to greet us. No matter. We were relieved and happy to see one of Betty's sixteen children, all of whom she had reared from infancy.

Betty had been a Baptist missionary in Japan for forty-nine years. Besides Bible studies and teaching, early on she began to rescue unwanted babies and to help place them with adoptive parents. The walls in her large, six-bedroom home are lined with many group and individual photos of the sixteen children she reared. Bethany was posed as a baby with ten others in one of the photos. Betty's sixteen children are grown now, married with families, and all are still in Japan except one girl who is in Atlanta. The long, long dining table, which seats eight on each side, and the multiple bunk beds were evidence of a lively household. Betty never married. "I was too busy having children," she laughed.

One night in Nagoya, Betty and I walked down the steep hill to a food store. As we started back to her home, she suggested we walk around the hill and circle back, a longer walk, but less strenuous. As we were making our way back, I spied a cross on top of a building. When I questioned Betty about it, she told me it was a combination kindergarten and church. My interest aroused, I was glad I had chosen to accompany her to the food store.

The following morning, Saturday, Bethany and I walked to the kindergarten-church. Of course, no children were there but the director, a handsome, six-foot Swedish man, greeted us and invited us to see the facility. It was well furnished and spotlessly clean, but there were no chairs for the children. They sit on the floor to hear instructions, to play, and to eat. Live rabbits, gerbils, turtles, two baby ducks, parakeets, and one snake were housed in appropriate cages and looked well fed. Their surroundings were very well kept.

The director, who was born of Swedish missionaries, proudly explained their goal and objective as we walked upstairs to a large playroom. He stated, "Our purpose is to reach parents and grandparents for Christ through their children." Only five percent of Japanese are Christians, according to him and Betty. We wished him God's blessings as he works to realize this goal.

The playroom was arranged with adult-sized chairs and a podium in front. "We have worship every Sunday for adults," the director explained. "Our attendance runs about fifty each Sunday, and we have baptized several into church membership." Buddhism and Shinto religions are the most predominant in this area," he reported.

A lot was being cleared behind the school for a parking lot. "More people are driving in, so we need space for them to park. We hope our attendance will grow once we complete the parking space," the director said.

Bethany and I bade the director farewell and thanked him for the tour of the facility. We wished him Godspeed in his work as a Christian witness in this unchristian country.

We were in Nagoya for three nights. Our hearts overflowed with gratitude as Betty took us to the airport for our flight on to Beijing, China. In spite of jet lag and five extra people, Betty had been a good hostess for us. She is certainly one of God's saints in Nagoya, where she will most likely live out her life.

On the first leg of the trip from Nagoya to Tokyo, I shared a seat with a Japanese lady married to a Greek man and living in Switzerland. She had a very sad story. Her father has never accepted nor seen her husband of fifteen years, nor his two grandchildren, ages nine and twelve. "My father is dying of cancer. He is a Buddhist. We are Christians. Please pray for him and my mother," she asked. She and her husband are accountants in Berne, Switzerland. Prayers are needed for her and for her parents.

Arriving in Beijing, we were met at the airport by Australian friends, Bruce and Faye Michaels, English teachers, and Beth Roberts from Ohio, also an English teacher in China for several years. They had been faithful participants in Thursday night

Bible study held in my living quarters. Our friendship goes back many years, so it was great to see their smiling faces and waving hands on our arrival at Beijing International Airport.

It was about eight o'clock at night and an hour's drive from the airport to the Michaels' apartment. Beth Roberts would spend the night, as she was teaching in a university many miles away. By the time we got to the Michaels' seventh floor apartment, it was time to begin thinking of sleeping arrangements. First, we decided to have a short Bible study with Bruce leading. For his scripture, he used the fourteenth chapter of John's gospel, one of my favorites. This study brought back memories of other times when the same group, along with a few others, had enjoyed similar occasions together.

Early the next morning, Bruce went with me by taxi to the airport. Now I was bound to Fuzhou, where my last nine years in China had been spent. Bruce was quite helpful getting the construction tax of fifty yuan ($6.20 U.S.A) paid and asking the check-in clerk to give me an up-front boarding pass. I was given seat No. 5! After saying goodbye to Bruce, I made my way to the departure gate for Fuzhou.

It was a short one-and one-half hour, uneventful flight, but things changed on my arrival. May Zheng, one of my former students, was alarming everyone around her jumping, clapping, yelling, "Sue, Sue, you are here! You are here!" The security guard restrained her from rushing out to the carousel to greet me! May has been working for nine years in an export company that specializes in sportswear shipped to many European countries, Japan, and the United States. Her job is quality control officer. "Last year our company made one million dollars in profit," she said.

May is a Christian as is her boss, the owner of the company. May's boss is affectionately known as Sister Lin. Sister Lin had told May to use the company's new van to meet me. There are two other vehicles owned by her company. As we made our way to the city, May used her cell phone to ring Sister Lin. We were urgently invited to come by and have lunch with Sister Lin. Surprise! Not only Sister Lin but her sister, brother-in-law, two nieces, and a nephew joined us for a typical Chinese feast. May was jubilant all the way into town and chattered about their successful business. Indeed, I am happy for May and grateful to Sister Lin for the use of her van and the delicious luncheon.

It was early afternoon when lunch was finished. Sister Lin and her sister wanted to climb Gu Shan, a mountain nearby. I declined their invitation to join them, so the van driver and May drove me to Huanan Women's College, where I would spend the next three weeks.

Arriving at Huanan was a welcome sight! May called the foreign affairs officer, who literally ran up the mountain to unlock room #205, my assigned post. She eagerly handed me a 4 x 6 photo of her newly constructed church. What a nice surprise! Her former church building had been demolished for a new, wider street. The new church is quite modern and a beautiful structure. At last, I was in Fuzhou, in a bedroom with a bath. All I needed now was about a two-hour nap!

Xu Dao Feng, the Foreign Affairs Officer, soon left and I suggested to May that she visit Amy, a former student of mine, who had become mother to a baby girl, now six months old. Soon after May left, I was fast asleep! Two hours later, loud knocks and louder voices claimed my attention.

Hugs, laughter, and tears mixed as Eli and Ann burst through the door just as I awoke from my deep sleep. Eli had been my "little boy Friday" for eight years. His wife, Ann, had been my student back in 1992. Both are English teachers at the Fujian Medical School in Fuzhou. "You must have dinner with us," they insisted. I felt right at home with them, as we had spent many hours together through those wonderful years.

We enjoyed dinner down the mountain in a modern restaurant that was once a "hole-in-the-wall noodle shop." We could hardly eat for chatting. After all, it had been three years since I had seen them. Eli seemed very proud and insisted on paying for our dinner.

Because it was Sunday night, May, Eli, and I decided to go to the night service in the church we had attended together. Since Anne's parents lived near the restaurant, she went to visit them.

We took a bus but the routes had been changed, so I hardly knew where we were. A new bridge, a wider street, and more vehicles added to my confusion. But with Eli and May as my guides, we arrived at Flower Lane Church in good time.

Another big surprise occurred as we entered the gate – there sat Professor Li, a retired pharmaceutical professor who had audited my English classes when I taught for two years (1995 – 1997) at Fujian Medical University. We often visited in each other's homes and frequently dined together. Both he and his wife are retired and doing well.

After greeting him and several older ladies whom I knew from previous years of worship together, we moved on to the sanctuary where we were escorted to the second row up front. Prof. Li accompanied us. A large group of Malaysians were seated just behind us.

The guest speaker, a young pastor from Malaysia, did a wonderful job using I Corinthians 13 as his text. His sermon on Faith, Hope, and Love was delivered in a professional manner. The choir of forty young people blessed the congregation with their enthusiastic and harmonious voices. It was a good way to end a Sunday night.

After a 7:30 a.m. breakfast, I met other foreign teachers who were assigned to Huanan: two Nigerians, three Americans, and three Japanese, all of whom were finishing the semester's work and preparing to go to their homes.

A small Chinese lady and her husband live in one room adjoining the kitchen. Each morning a warm breakfast of oatmeal, boiled egg, toast and fruit – usually an orange, an apple, a peach, or a banana – was served to each diner. The cooks took great pride in their work and fed us well.

Bus routes and bus numbers had changed since my years there, and I needed to cash traveler's checks at the Bank of China. Rose, one of the Foreign Affairs Officers, rode the bus with me to May's office. Her office faces the bank I had always used while working in Fuzhou. Rose returned to Huanan Women's College while May and I went to the bank.

Going to the Bank of China was one of my least favorite things to do. In the bank, there are many stations and many employees. A visit to the bank is a very time consuming and tiresome chore. This day we were able to gain a window with a clerk who was evidently in training as another employee double-checked all that was done. I made the mistake of taking $50.00 checks, an error which meant a wait twice as long had I wisely carried $100.00 checks. Each check was stretched, scrutinized front and back, and held up high and then down low. Between each examination, I was stared at as if I were a suspected counterfeiter. Forty-five minutes later, I was handed the money and my passport. "Let's get out of here before the clerk decides to take it back and have me incarcerated!" I jokingly said to May.

The following day, May and I went to the school for blind children. Five children who had been supported since 1996 by some special friends and family were in the conference room awaiting our arrival. One young man is twenty-one, two are nineteen, one boy is eighteen, and the girl is eighteen. What a happy reunion to see them again!

The twenty-one-year-old has completed junior high and is employed as a masseur in a Chinese medical clinic. Through the interpreter he said, "I am so happy to be working. Now I can help support my very poor mother." When I asked whether he would like to attend senior high, he replied, "No, I must help my mother and grandparents."

One of the nineteen-year-olds is working part-time and is equally pleased to earn some money. He expects to work full-time come next July. The other three will complete junior high next June and likewise will work as masseurs in traditional Chinese medical clinics. All of them seemed eager to go to work rather than to attend senior high. May will stay in touch with these children and keep me informed of their plans. We made an appointment to meet at church on the next Sunday.

Medical students whom I had taught English planned a lunch the following day. Dr. Chen, head of hematology at the Medical University, introduced them using the English names I had given them in class four years earlier. All are now medical doctors working in hospitals in Fuzhou. As we hugged and shook hands, they would say I am Matthew or whatever their English names happened to be. My cup overflowed as I visited with these very special former students now working as doctors.

Lunch consisted of sheep belly soup and chewy cow udders, among other things. The fellowship made up for the unusual dishes. After two hours of dining, they needed to get back to their hospitals. It was such a treat to see them looking so well and seemingly being so happy in their work.

When Eli came for me, we went to his apartment so I could rest. He and Ann were still grading exam papers in their office on campus. I was alone and in an air-conditioned bedroom. Eli wanted to put a mosquito netting around the bed so cool air would not blow on me as I rested – slept! The temperature outside was 93 degrees and the humidity was 90%, so cool air was more than welcome. Eli was hardly down the stairs before I fell asleep, awaking only as Eli and Ann came in around 5:30 p.m.

A very good cook, Eli prepared dinner. His parents had a restaurant in the past. Our menu for that evening consisted of fruit salad, tofu, oysters, and melon. I could recognize all of the ingredients. What a treat to visit with two special former students, a husband-wife team and university English teachers.

The dean of Fujian Theological Institute, Charles Huang, called that night. He had audited my English classes held on Friday afternoons from 2:00 – 5:00 p.m. He extended an invitation to me for the following day. He had recently moved his family to a new housing development known as Garden City. "I can come for you," he said.

The next morning around 11:00 a.m., up roared Charles on a motorcycle. "Can you ride this?" he asked. "It's only ten minutes to my home," he explained.

Astride the motorcycle, I arrived in Garden City, where another surprise awaited me. Tall, high-rise apartments dotted the landscape. The guard at the gate eyed us closely but allowed me to enter. Charles, his wife, and two daughters had lived previously in three very shabby rooms over in the area of Fujian Theological Institute.

Charles proudly punched in the code numbers to open the door to the stairs. Up six flights we climbed to his apartment. Squeals of laughter ensued amid tears and hugs as his wife and daughters greeted us. It had been three years since we last saw each other.

Besides working as dean of the Theological Institute, Charles pastors a church near Fuzhou. He had invited four of the church leaders to join us for lunch. None of them spoke any English; however, a feeling of oneness in spirit prevailed during the luncheon of twelve courses! Charles was obviously better off financially than he had been three years ago.

The three-bedroom apartment was well furnished and boasted of air conditioning. A large screen TV, comfortable sofa with two matching chairs, coffee table, end tables, lamps, and walls tastefully decorated spoke of his hard work and higher income. Each daughter's bedroom was equipped with a bed, desk, and computer. A modern bathroom with a tub and shower was a step-up from the communal toilet they had shared with many others prior to their move to this new, modern home. A stainless steel kitchen, including a dishwasher, was another big surprise for me. I was truly happy for them because I had seen them many times in far less desirable circumstances.

After lunch, the oldest daughter played hymns for about an hour as we sang in Chinese and English many favorite hymns of those present. Included were "What a Friend We Have In Jesus," "Amazing Grace," "Oh Happy Day" (my choice), "When We All Get to Heaven," "The Old Rugged Cross," "How Great Thou Art," "Redeemed," and many more. There was a sweet, sweet spirit in that place as we rejoiced and sang of a Christ who gave Himself for all peoples. We would probably still be singing, but Charles had to return to his office! My cup was filled to overflowing as we said good-bye until we meet again.

Next day, May Zheng invited Akiko and Mami, two Japanese teachers, for lunch in her home. May's mother, a younger daughter, her husband, a four-year-old granddaughter, and May live in a five-room, well-furnished apartment. The son-in-law is the son of a Protestant minister; however, his wife and May's mother are not Christians yet. May became a Believer several years ago and is greatly concerned for her mother and sister.

Another delicious meal was served, after which May insisted that I take a nap in her air-conditioned bedroom. I needed little persuasion to accept her invitation! With a full stomach, firm bed (no mattress), and cool temps, I slept for almost two hours. I appreciated May's thoughtfulness and her hard bed!

May's four-year-old niece is a budding artist. Some of her drawings have been on exhibit in art galleries at an international art showing of children's work. Her certificate of recognition is prominently displayed in their living room. Her winning drawing was of three giraffes. Most of her work consists of an animal family – father, mother, and child. She drew three monkeys for my gift from her since I was born in the lunar year of the monkey. It measures 12 inches by 18 inches, and I treasure it quite highly.

Charlie Lin, a cancer victim back in the late '90s, and a former engineer, phoned to ask whether he could visit. Dear Charlie! The last time I saw him in 2001, he had no hair and was the epitome of a cancer patient. How great to hear from him, and still greater to see him. He had a clear complexion, a head full of neatly combed hair, and a big smile on his face. "God has given me another chance," he smiled. He has been a Christian for several years.

Since his recovery, he works now with a satellite company as their representative to foreign countries. He had many photos to share of his travels to Vietnam, Los Angeles, and Las Vegas. "My next trip is to Mexico," he said. He is a walking miracle and gives God all of the credit for his new job and new lease on life. What a joy to see him, to talk with him, and to hear his testimony of faith. He is an inspiration to me!

Sunday morning meant having breakfast at 7:30 a.m. and getting to Flower Lane Church by 9:30 a.m. The bus route had changed, but I soon mastered those changes and rode the bus to the correct stop. Friends planned to meet me in the courtyard of the church. As I approached the street where the church is located, crowds of people who had attended the 7:30 a.m. service flowed out into the street. Among them was Rachel, a former student of mine at the Fujian Medical University. She proudly introduced her husband and asked for my phone number. "We have to see you," she said. They left, pushing bikes through the mass of people, and I continued on to the gate in the wall that surrounds the church.

Entering the gate, I saw several older ladies I had known in years gone by. Amid hugs and tears, they welcomed me back. Among the group was Rachel's mother, who had been my seamstress for the last eight years I was in China. Another woman, seventy-five-years old, toothless, and very thin, handed me a scroll on which she had written Galatians 5:22 in Chinese calligraphy. It hangs in my living room today!

Dr. Hannah Lin, a retired pediatrician, and Charlie's aunt met me inside as did several other friends and former students. After worship, Hannah, Leslie, Charlie, Eli, May, and I trekked over to Kentucky Fried Chicken for lunch. The restaurant was full of people; however, the manager put up a folding table and found enough stools to seat the seven of us. Chicken never tasted better as I enjoyed it with these very special friends. Eli graciously treated all of us with an ice cream cone for dessert. Leslie, a converted Buddhist, invited us to her home as fifteen of her students from the Agricultural University were planning a sing-a-long there that night. Charlie and I were the only two free to go and off we went to Leslie's home where her two sisters, daughter, and husband were preparing for the guests. Leslie had won her parents and sisters to Christ, and she is still rejoicing in their newfound faith.

Students began to arrive along with three of the blind boys and their music teacher from the Blind School I had visited many times. One plays the piano like a professional, one the flute, and another the "erho," a two-string instrument played with a bow.

They favored us with many selections. Their teacher played the guitar and sang a song he had composed, entitled "When Humanity Ends, God Shall Reign."

Charlie is a novice pianist and entertained the group with old tunes, "Moon River," "I'll Be Seeing You," and "Yankee Doodle." After he played "Good-night Ladies," I told him it was nearing my bedtime. We had foot tapped and sung until almost 10:00 p.m. What a deep pleasure to be with such a group for a wonderful evening of fellowship and fun in songs!

Leslie, our hostess, is teaching a Bible Class to her students. She has used *My Utmost for His Highest* by Oswald Chambers and is presently using *The Purpose Driven Life* by Rick Warren. In my humble opinion, she is being a missionary in her classroom, church, and city.

Chester, Xia Rong Qiang, director of blind services for Fujian Province and also a good friend of Betts Rivet's and mine, invited us to his office and later for dinner in his home. It was good to see his new office equipped with a computer that could read his e-mails and a telephone into which he could type responses. Hadley School for the Blind in Chicago provided these for him.

Chester showed us around the five-room facility with the greatest of ease. It was amazing to observe his movements almost as if he could see. At the time of my return visit, he was hoping to get a vehicle soon to expedite travel demands, and now his prayers have been answered. He has to meet many people in different areas of his work.

Chester's daughter came to his office to escort us to their home where his wife had prepared a big dinner. Conversation centered on his work and his retirement plans. He is fifty-nine and men generally retire at sixty. Whatever he decides to do, I feel it will still include services for visually handicapped. Our best wishes and prayers are with him, his wife, and daughter.

A few days before leaving Fuzhou, Betts, Bethany, and I made a trip to Metro near Huanan. Rose, one of the Foreign Affairs Officers, was expecting a baby in November, and Betts thought a baby stroller would be a nice gift for her. We purchased it and gave it to a very surprised mother-to-be.The English department insisted on treating us to a very nice luncheon. A taxi was called and the head of the Foreign Affairs Office went with us. We enjoyed a bountiful meal as a fierce thunderstorm raged outside. It had blown itself dry by the time we were ready to return to Huanan.

Betts, Bethany, Xu Dao Feng, and I went to the Blind School since Betts has known the students from years ago. The eldest one was working, so only four students were available. Since there were four of them and four of us, each of us was given an absolutely wonderful back massage. The masseurs seemed to enjoy this as much as their patients did.

It was hard to bid them farewell but with a job on the horizon for them, it was helpful knowing they would be self-supporting in another year. Their gratitude and smiling faces have been rewards enough through the years.

Hosted by Huanan Women's College in a nice restaurant down the mountain today, we were provided another feast. About two hundred faculty and staff filled the entire area. Betts, Bethany, and I were guests of honor, and we were seated with the top administrators. It was good for the faculty and staff since they are often overlooked on such occasions. We surely didn't expect such an extravaganza but were grateful for their kind intentions.

After the luncheon, the parents of Sandy took us by car to their penthouse apartment. Sandy hopes to study in the United States and needs a guardian since she is still a high school student. Her father, who appears quite wealthy, has done well in business ventures.

Their three-story apartment overlooks that part of Fuzhou city. A gate with a guard provides the only entrance to the compound. Elegant furniture and an aquarium, which covered one wall at least twelve feet high, represented financial success. Large fish, some as long as seven to eight inches, along with huge goldfish, seemed to feel it their duty to entertain us! They almost smiled as they scooted back and forth, up and down to our amazement and pleasure.

There were three spacious, elaborately furnished bedrooms, and on the top floor was the father's tearoom that has a table made from a tree root about five feet wide. The seats around it are made from shorter, smaller tree stumps. An assortment of tea was stored in an ornate cabinet behind the table.

A balcony outside the tearoom had comfortable chairs and a bench for guests wishing to enjoy their tea outside. This set-up indicates, in some ways, just how much the "open door policy" of Deng Zhao Peng has opened the door of prosperity to many Chinese.

Eli and Ann came for dinner at Huanan that night. Both continue to work on their required theses for a Master's Degree in English. Resources and reference materials are hard for them to find. They do have a computer, and I hope it will be useful in locating needed information.

Yet another lunch, sponsored this time by the Foreign Affairs Officers, Pizza Hut was our destination, and, frankly, Betts and I were glad. A good fresh garden salad would be greatly appreciated. They had ordered too many pizzas and the urgency to eat more, typical when dining with Chinese friends in the past, was the order of that meal. Our hosts thoroughly enjoyed the variety of pizzas and followed the advice to eat more! Their intentions, as they were at the other special meals, were for friendship and appreciation for our teaching services in Huanan. We were touched by their efforts to offer us the "best food available."

To reciprocate the hospitality of May, a former student, and her family, I took them to the Pizza Hut. The four-year-old niece was very excited and had a hard time trying to manage a slice of pizza. She is quite proficient with chopsticks but not with any finger food. The adults managed well and enjoyed the change in diet, I think.

My last Sunday in Fuzhou arrived too quickly. I was impressed with the choir's special music and the well-presented sermon on "God's Grace." Eli, May, Hannah, and Leslie were with me. My heart was blessed as we sang together and I heard them saying "Amen" during prayers, a common practice in the Chinese church.

We were among the last to leave and as we approached the gate, a lady came in and presented me with two white shirts trimmed in blue. On the back of each is printed, "Jesus Christ loves you." A red cross on the front with Flower Lane Protestant Church, Fuzhou, PR China all in Chinese makes them very special to me. I shall wear them with pride.

The next day, Connie, one of my 1995 graduates, came to take me out for dinner. She is a happy Christian and has a good job in a very successful business company.

After dinner, we walked several blocks and behold! We came to the shop of my favorite hairdresser in all Fuzhou. We recognized each other about the same time. He rushed from his shop, leaving his customers looking a little more than surprised. He jabbered away in Chinese and gestured for us to come in, but I told Connie to make an appointment for me later. This she did, and I went back the morning of my departure for the United States to get a shampoo, massage, and a blow dry. I would like a repeat at least once every week.

Lorna, a 1995 graduate working in the large Foreign Trade Center as a business lady, called and invited me to dinner. Her father, mother, older sister, and Lorna drove up in a new air-conditioned Toyota. Off we went to a restaurant near May's office. As I was getting out of the car, I heard a distressful call, "Sue, Sue, what are you doing here?" When she saw Lorna, she calmed down but could not accept the invitation to join us. She had other plans that night. Lorna is not a Christian yet but is giving thought to becoming one. Her sister is encouraging her to accept Christ as she herself did some years ago. Lorna and her parents are in my prayers.

Shirley, an English teacher and also one of my former students, came to pour out her disappointment when she was denied a visa to study in the United States. We talked for about two hours, after which she accepted Christ. Every time I saw her after that all-important decision, she was smiling.

One of the Foreign Affairs Officers had been wearing a white floral blouse that I admired. The next day she brought it to me freshly washed and neatly folded. I should have told her it looked nice on her rather than saying I like your blouse. Chinese will literally take the shirt off their backs if they think you like it.

Dr. Chen rounded up six more of my former students for our last dinner together. Among them were three lady doctors still using the English names I gave them: Whitney, Dee, and Doris (the names of my granddaughter, son's wife, and sister). The young men were still using their English names, too: Tommy, David, Joe (the names of my brothers). Good food, fun, and fellowship all too soon ended as most of the group had night duty at the hospital.

Eli and Ann invited us to "Champ Elissey," the Chinese spelling of a French restaurant in downtown Fuzhou. May also joined us and brought along a large tea set, several small Chinese lanterns, and six small chipao bottle holders. Chinese are generous and believe in presenting going away gifts. Eli and Ann seemed proud to be able to entertain Betts, Bethany, May, and me.

Rachel, now a teacher at the Fujian Medical University, and her mother came to say goodbye, since I was leaving the next day. They rode bikes in 90 degree weather and had to push the bikes up the mountain to Huanan. What an effort!

Rachel had recently represented her university at a conference in Xian. An uncle she had not seen for many years lives there. Her eyes glistened with tears as she told of witnessing to him about Jesus Christ. To the joy of both, he accepted Christ as his Savior. "I don't know which one was happier," she said. She then quoted I Chronicles 4:9-10 known as the prayer of Jabez. "Oh, that you would wonderfully bless me and help me in my work; please be with me in all that I do, and keep me from all evil and disaster."(*Living Bible*). My heart rejoiced with her. She, her husband, and mother are strong Christians and are devoted supporters of the Flower Lane Church in Fuzhou, PR China.

Another visitor, Xue Han Hui, a retired architect and designer of the International Airports in Beijing and Fuzhou, had dinner with Betts, Bethany, and me at Huanan. Han Hui lost her husband to cancer two years ago, and now her aged and deaf mother lives with her. With a live-in caregiver helping to take care of her mother, Han Hui is free to attend "The Old People's University," where several courses are taught of interest to older people. She decided to study painting and enjoys making beautiful landscapes of trees, lakes, typical Chinese houses, mountains, and streams. She paints these using thin rice paper, and the results look professional to Betts and me. "Choose one," she insisted. So I chose one of a small stream with a boat floating under lofty green trees and with a cluster of Chinese homes teetering on a mountainside. To me it is a work of art by a master artist.

On the day of our departure, our friends came to say good-bye. Eli and Ann with teary eyes, tight hugs, and pats said, "Hurry back!" Clarence, an Afro-American former English teacher whom we had not seen during the three-week visit, came to bid us farewell. He chose to stay in China, learned the Chinese language, and is now a businessman there. Sandy's wealthy father came to help with the baggage, and several staff and faculty members came to see us off. The courtyard was abuzz with activity when Guo Ping, the van driver for Huanan, pulled up at the gate. Emotions ran high as final good-byes were said.

The van was crowded with our luggage and the seven passengers aboard. Sandy's father used his cell phone to notify the airport of our arrival. Uniformed airport employees helped with our baggage as we were rushed over to First Class check-in, although we were flying in economy class. The Foreign Affairs Officer stood in the Security Line to reserve a place for the three of us, Betts, Bethany, and me. Guo Ping, the driver, refused a tip, as this was his gift to foreign friends. Neither royalty nor political big wigs would have received more attention and assistance!

As we cleared security, we waved a final farewell and made our way to the departure gate. Mixed emotions and deep gratitude for the privilege of visiting China again filled my total being as the plane lifted off for Shanghai, where we would spend the night before flying back to the United States.

Arriving in Shanghai, we were met by a business acquaintance of Sandy's father. She and her van driver took us to Jin Lin Inn near Pu Dong International Airport, an elaborate facility that looks like wonderland at night with hanging neon fluorescent lights on driveways and streets leading into the airport. The building itself was like a giant white palace as it glowed from all its fluorescent lights. I wondered about its monthly electrical bill! The business lady was quite courteous even though she had never seen either of us before. Connections and friendship are assets when traveling that distance!

Although we had ordered a triple room at Jin Lin Inn, we were given a double. When we made an inquiry, the desk clerk simply said, "No more rooms." In the closet we found two quilts for Bethany to use, so she slept on the floor.

A double room furnished for two, although we had asked for a triple, provided linens for only two guests. Back to the desk I went to ask for more towels. The young man on duty said, "No more towels until day after tomorrow!"

By then we were ready for dinner. An adequate menu was available so we had a nice, relaxing Chinese meal. As we headed back to our room, we noticed a young lady at the desk. Betts asked her for more linens, and without hesitation, she took a bunch of keys and said, "Come with me." She unlocked a room filled with wooden cloth racks full of wash cloths and hand and bath towels. From the quantity of linens, apparently the hotel had a washing machine, but no dryer. At least, we can each have a bath and a towel! The beds were comfortable, and Bethany, the youngest, was okay on the floor. The three of us slept well and were ready when the wake-up call came at 6:00 a.m. We had survived another night in less than a five-star hotel.

A fifteen-minute ride took us back to Pu Dong Airport. There we boarded a Japanese plane to Tokyo and from there to Los Angeles, California. The three of us shared a seat on the overseas flight. We chatted and read, Bethany watched movies, and we slept. It had been an absolutely fantastic trip from the start. We arrived in Los Angeles on time – tired, happy, and ready to start all over again!

The Pacific Northwest

After two days of rest in the home of Betts' daughter, Lynette, we were off again to visit more former Chinese students working in California, Washington State, Burnaby and Vancouver, Canada. Lynette's husband, Les, loaded the bags and ice chest, which provided "calories" for lunch each day. Betts' 1994 Buick had been checked and fueled for the last two weeks of our journey.

Up the coast of California we went from Orange to our first stop in Fresno, where we spent the night with Janice, another one of Betts' daughters, and her hospitable family. The golden mountainsides along our route probably account for California's nickname "The Golden State." It was quite relaxing as we took turns driving and enjoying the beautiful scenery along the way.

After a restful night we began the next leg of our trip – destination, Campbell, near San Francisco. Gu Nian, a computer and English-Chinese major, awaited us in her home. When we arrived a little before noon, sounds of piano music filled our ears. We knew Gu Nian is an accomplished pianist, having been taught by her grandmother back in Fuzhou, China. We hesitated to interrupt such melodious sounds! We were excited as the music stopped and she with seven-month-old Aaron opened the door. What a handsome baby and beautiful mother!

By now it was a little past noon, and Gu Nian insisted on treating us to lunch in a nice restaurant she and her husband enjoyed from time to time. During the meal she shared her deepest thoughts about family connections and relationships in marriage and American society. A very devout Christian, she is the daughter of Christian parents and the granddaughter of the Protestant Bishop in Fujian Province for many years prior to his death. Much of her concern stems from the differences in Chinese and American culture.

Our visit was fairly short because another couple in Berkeley was expecting us for dinner. Wei Wen Bin (see "From Rice Straw to PhD" chapter), and Zou Lin, his wife, along with his parents had planned another feast for us. Betts had consulted Map Quest for directions to our destinations. As we neared his address, now Professor Wei was on the walk to welcome us. I had not seen him in several years, so our meeting was one of great enthusiasm and happiness. Before we went inside, he pointed to the Golden Gate Bridge some distance away. "When I was a child, I never dreamed I would see this," he said.

Inside the apartment we saw the two-month-old daughter. She is absolutely beautiful, and I threatened to kidnap her! "She looks as if she should grow up in North Carolina," I told him and Zou Lin. They have every right to be proud of Yi Yen, which means "beautiful cloud."

Wei Wen Bin, or Wade, (English name), chauffeured us to the campus at Berkley University. This is where he and Zou Lin had received their Ph.D.s. He received his Ph.D. in civil engineering, and Zou Lin received her Ph.D. in comparative literature. With great pleasure we walked on the campus as they pointed out various buildings and the location of their offices. I felt such a feeling of humility as he held my hand while we strolled along because I knew about his humble beginning and now more about his accomplishments. Both are more than qualified as university professors in their specialized fields.

Back to their home and to baby Yi Yen, who was cared for by Wade's parents. They came to America shortly before the baby's birth to help with babysitting when Zou Lin returned to her job on campus. His parents had prepared a delicious meal but retired to their bedroom while we dined. Since they speak no English, they probably were not comfortable listening to a conversation they could not understand.

Many photos were taken after dinner with the new parents, grandparents, (whom I had visited in China), Betts, and me. The baby was handed from first one and then another so each of us could have an opportunity to hold her. She was probably glad when the time came for Betts and me to leave! What a pleasure to see two more special students and friends in their present setting. Wade stood on the walk and waved us out of sight.

Crossing Oregon to reach Burnaby was our next intention. This meant spending one night in Motel 6 in Redding, California. Both of us were ready for an "ice chest" dinner of mostly fruit, followed by a bath and bed. Next morning we were up early and headed to Vancouver, Washington. Here were our dear friends, Joan and Don Whitehead, who had also taught in Nanjing with me. Gracious host and hostess they were. Reminiscing of those earlier times and sharing faith stories added much to our time with them.

Off to Burnaby we went the next day and again enjoyed a beautiful drive. Green mountains lush with trees and well-kept four-lane highways brought us to the Canadian border. Before 9/11, crossing the border was simple and quick. This day we were in a crowded line of cars for one hour, which seemed much longer in the hot sunshine. More questions and closer scrutiny caused delays.

The weatherman had been smiling on us every day, but when we arrived in Burnaby, heavy rain blocked street signs and the wind blew nearby shrubs. With visibility too poor for us to see the names of streets, we stopped at a service station whose operator gave us misinformation. Back we went to the station just as a taxi driver was running through the pouring rain to his car. Betts hastily opened her umbrella and stopped him as he was just before leaving. He had to check his city map before he could lead us to the high-rise apartment of our good friends, Xiao Wu; her husband, Lin Feng; and son, Bobby. The rain had stopped before we arrived there and the sun came out to welcome us to Burnaby.

This is a gated condominium that, of course, requires codes to enter. We rushed in behind a car and found a visitor's parking space. We waited a few minutes until a friendly Korean lady drove in, parked her car, and allowed us into the hallway and to the elevators. Our friends were more than surprised when we appeared at their door. They fully expected to escort us into the underground parking lot and up to their eighth floor, two-bedroom apartment. We laughingly told them, "What two old ladies can do should never be underestimated."

The three nights and two days we spent in Burnaby were great. The first day we went on a bus trip to the beautiful harbor and onto Stanley Park. There we took a one-hour carriage trip around the park, where we saw cormorant, long-beaked birds, fishing for food; old, old redwood trees; and many fir trees which lincd the pathway. Because Lin Feng needed the family car, we took the "Sky Bus" above the ground subway to and from the harbor area. Xiao Wu wanted to be sure we were having a good time!

The Fengs are Christians, including the eleven-year-old son, so we attended their Chinese church the next morning. As in China, so it was in Burnaby, packed with people! The first service was conducted in Chinese, and the one we attended was in English. A young Chinese used Psalm 37:4 as his text for a moving sermon entitled "Touching the Mist – the Glory of God. Delight yourself in the Lord and He will give you the desires of your heart." He expounded this with a four-point outline, which included journey in prayer, journey in worship, journey in the Word, and journey through doors through obedience to God.

He was most impressive in his presentation and seemed to hold the rapt attention of all the worshippers. I was fortunate to be one of them.

Ten of our students met us at a Chinese restaurant that night. Precious thirty-one- year-old Danny was among them. He apologized for crying the last time I had seen him in Fuzhou six years ago.

Danny had come to my room for advice. As we talked, of course I introduced him to Jesus Christ. He left Fuzhou and spent two years in Singapore as an electrical engineer. There he earned money to build a nice home for his fisherman father and peasant mother. "I gave them all the money I had except ten thousand dollars," he said. "I wanted to immigrate to Canada, and I needed that much to pass immigration," he went on.

In Canada, Danny faced problems finding a job in his electrical background. He took a job as a dishwasher while studying at a community college to become a pharmaceutical assistant. After completing the course, he found a suitable job, but now he would like to be a radiologist in a hospital or a licensed practical nurse. "I like to help people," he explained. If he pursues either, he will do well, in my opinion.

Another major concern of Danny's is finding a Christian Chinese girlfriend. Because his work requires Sunday duties, he cannot attend either of the Chinese churches. We hope this will soon change, and he will be able to find Miss Right and then can start his family. He deserves the best, and I sincerely hope he gets it.

Lucy had a successful story to share. She first settled in Montreal and worked as a clerk in a food store. She enrolled in accountant classes and today works as an accountant with a thriving business. She was well groomed, stylishly dressed, and looked like a native born Canadian.

Albert was a mechanical engineer in Fuzhou. When he came to Burnaby, he took menial jobs while he went to classes to study computers. Today he, his wife, and small son are living quite well as he is now a computer specialist in a large firm in Vancouver. He still retains the English name of Albert I gave to him when he was in my classes back in Nanjing (1990-1992).

Another young man had gone to a university in Calgary and graduated with a degree in accounting. The Vancouver Central Government had just employed him. So the stories continued as these deserving young people were finding freedom and success, all the while giving God credit for all of their accomplishments. My cup overflowed again and again as I rejoiced with them.

Dinner finally ended and our former students, now business people, had to go their separate ways. The next day was a workday for them, and Betts and I were heading back to Orange, California.

That night, Xiao Wu shared her interest in attending law school. She has worked five years in a progressive law firm for three attorneys. I hope her dream of being a lawyer will become a reality. Lin Feng heads a travel agency and is doing well. Self-educated, he hopes to earn a college degree in business as he continues his job. With their work ethic and desire for improvement, they will most likely fulfill these goals.

Our departure came too soon but our schedules necessitated that we head back to Issaquah, near Seattle, Washington. Alan, Doris, their three children, and his parents were expecting us. They were among my first students at Southeast University in Nanjing in 1988 – 1989.

Alan, a computer consultant, was out front looking for us as we arrived. Dressed in white shirt and dark pants in typical Chinese business fashion, he waved jubilantly as we pulled into the double garage driveway. His parents rushed from the house to greet us. I had visited in their home several times in Nanjing, so they knew me. Doris was at work and came in later.

Alan said that taking off work to meet us was no problem, since, after all, he is one of the top executives in his company. Previously he had worked with Carrier Heating and Air Conditioning as a mechanical engineer. Doris had worked with Motorola but now works with Honeywell. Their nice two-story home and well-kept lawns spoke of their prosperity.

The next morning Alan, nine-year-old Junior, Betts, and I toured Seattle. First stop was the Space Needle to overlook the city with Mt. Hood visible many miles away. We were taken to a massive water fountain in a park where many children were racing in and out of the spray. Squeals of delight expressed their feelings and thoughts.

"You must see the Flying Fish Market," Alan told us. We took a bus over to a huge market place. The main attraction was the fish market where the employee who sold the fish tossed the twelve-to-fifteen inch fish to a second employee, who cleaned it. Salmon are big and among the favorites, we were told. This was certainly interesting in a different way.

At lunch time Alan took us to the restaurant "Where I take my best clients," he said. The smoked salmon was quite tasty but very costly, I felt. The atmosphere was expensive as well as the food, but he was determined that we should have the best.

Doris was entertaining us that afternoon. She met us at

Alan's office so we changed from his expensive van to her Saab automobile. Alan had important appointments to keep. "I want you to see the waterfall that comes from melted glaciers," she told us. Off we went through gorgeous mountains to see the waterfall with her and Junior. We did not have the heart to tell her that Betts grew up in Niagara Falls, New York, and I had seen it twice in years past.

Returning to their home, we found the grandparents, five-year-old Sophia, and active, three-year-old Ethan enjoying the spacious, fenced-in backyard. A gazebo with ample chairs, a small pool for the children, granddad's vegetable garden, and many flowering shrubs made an ideal place to relax and enjoy chilled watermelon the grandmother served. How delightful just to sit and chat with Doris and watch the children ride wheel toys and play in the water. I could have stayed on and on and enjoyed every minute of it.

Horror filled my soul that night. Alan and Doris insisted we have another dinner at a fancy restaurant. As we were eating, Betts, a psychologist by training, was making statements about proper child rearing. Alan and Doris' three-year-old is a typical hyper, inquisitive youngster with muscles and strength to carry out most of his explorations. Suddenly Doris told us, "I almost aborted him!" She went through all required preliminaries, and she and Alan had gone back for the procedure. "We sat in the car for one hour discussing whether we should follow through, he admitted. Finally, we said, "No!" and returned home. Both of them believe in God!!

"I would have walked from North Carolina to Seattle had I known you even thought of that. Please don't ever let Ethan know you gave that a thought," I warned. I felt sick just thinking such was ever even considered.

The next morning, Betts and I left for Vancouver, Washington, where we planned to spend the night with the Whiteheads. This was just what we needed in body and in soul. We were there in time for a good walk around the area and enjoyed meeting some of their friends. This was the only night I slept in air conditioning.

Since the afternoon sun shines into the room I was to use, a window unit cooled it so that I slept very well and very comfortably.

Breakfast the next morning consisted of hotcakes with blueberries and sausage. Both Joan and Don are excellent chefs and seemed to enjoy kitchen duty. We are blessed to have them as friends.

Back across Oregon we came, still admiring the scenery as we drove along. We made it into Redding, California, again for the night. As we passed massive Mt. Shasta, I marveled at its snow-covered peaks as we were using air conditioning down below. We made a rest stop across from the spectacular mountain, and the cool air outside the car was apparently being blown from Mt. Shasta's direction.

A visit in Fresno the following day with one of Betts' longtime friends was quite pleasant. Her backyard was full of loaded olive trees and a black and white grape vine with long bunches of grapes just waiting to be picked. She was very generous and told us to help ourselves. They were the sweetest grapes I ever tasted.

From Fresno we drove to Orange the next day. There had not been a glitch in the entire trip. Our formula in the beginning included three P's – pray, plan, pack lightly. Those three made it a wonderfully satisfying experience for me.

The next day I said farewell to Betts, Lynette, Les, and Aaron, their fifteen-year-old son, and boarded an American Airliner back to Raleigh-Durham, North Carolina. My dream of returning to China and seeing dear Chinese friends had become a living reality. For this, I will be eternally grateful.

EPILOGUE

My childhood dream of serving God in China had finally become a completed reality. One regret – it was not longer; however, I shall always treasure those thirteen years (1988-2001) and the opportunities to share the message of God's love with students who had never heard of "The Old Rugged Cross" and "Amazing Grace."

With my eighty-first birthday on the horizon, time had come to bid farewell to the gentle breezes off South China Sea, walks around the track with Eli Huang, my little boy Friday, on moonlit nights. He referred to these as our moon walks. One last visit with the precious baby orphans with outstretched arms and attention-getting eyes pulled at my innermost heartstrings. Weeping blind students and elderly church friends saying, "Don't go, please, don't leave us," made my departure very difficult. Our last goodbye was quite emotional and not an easy task.

I still miss the bicycle bells, loud voices on the streets, vigorous singing in the churches, noisy children during break time at schools, horns blowing as buses roared through crowded streets dodging pedestrians and cyclists, and early morning loud and mournful music when a Buddhist neighbor had passed away. Most of all, I miss the visits of inquiring students who want and need to know that God does exist, that He loves Chinese people, and that His Son gave His life for them, not just for foreigners. My prayer is that this knowledge will continue to deepen as Christianity spreads in China.

The day arrived for my departure to Buies Creek, N.C., and Campbell University, my first institution of higher learning. Dr. Norman A. Wiggins, then president of Campbell University, made arrangements for me to live in campus housing, where I am available for mission discussion and also ESL (English as a Second Language) classes. To him I owe a great debt of gratitude.

It was a genuine pleasure, after three years in Buies Creek, to return to China for a three-week visit and to attend church with close friends and former students. How happy they are, worshiping and sharing the gospel with family and friends. Through them, many other souls are finding the peace that passes understanding.

True! I shall always miss them and their motherland, but God opened the door for me now to serve him in my motherland. How pleased I am to serve Him again in my native country. May God bless China! May God bless America!

APPENDIX

Without the following supplementary material, my memoirs would be incomplete. It is my hope that these pages will further reveal not only the difficulty of learning any language second to one's own native language but also the humor and enjoyment in such a challenge.

My Chinese students' version of the "Twelve Days of Christmas":

1.A partridge in a pear tree ---------------long life noodles
2.Two turtle doves ------------------------chopsticks
3.Three French hens ----------------------red banners
4.Four calling (colly or collie) birds ----dragon boats
5.Five golden rings -----------------------bicycles
6.Six geese a'laying ----------------------fluttering kites
7.Seven swans a'swimming ---------------- beautiful Chinese jackets
8.Eight maids a'milking ------------------silk scarves
9.Nine ladies dancing -------------------- babies laughing
10.Ten lords a'leaping-------------------- juicy jiaozi
11.Eleven pipers piping ------------------smooth pearls
12.Twelve drummers drumming---------bowls of rice

****

The following four letters were written to Santa Claus by my Chinese students:

Southeast University
P.O. Box 0888
Nanjing, 210018,PRC
December 19, 1988
Santa Claus
North Pole

Top of the World

Dear Santa Claus,

I'll have my first Christmas Day six days later though I have lived in this world for 22 years, for in our country there is no customs to recognize a happy Christmas. Thanks to Mrs. Todd, she taught me lots of useful and good things which are fresh to me.

I've a lump in my throat, I have so many things which I want to tell you. I wish you can give all your love and happiness to the world and share with those who have little opportunity to enjoy themselves. I wish you bring peace and every good things to the people. I want to devote my loyalty to you and become your representative and serve all the people.

I was born in a poor country family. My parents sacrificed too much to bring up us four children. I wish they will be rich rewarded. I'm away from my dad and mum for so long a time. I wish you can bring me a happy dream on Christmas night and let me have a good time with my family.

I wish you a merry Christmas, Santa Claus.

Yours Sincerely,

Matthew

****

Post Box 712

South-East University

Nanjing, P.R. China Dec. 20, 1988

Mr. Santa Claus

North Pole

Top of the World

I'm Lizzy, a Chinese girl. As Christmas is coming, I'm sure you're coming from North-pole on your sleigh to distribute presents to the world.

As a young girl, I've heard of you. Here I've a little will and I desire you to fulfill it. I hope you to bring friendliness to the world. I hope from now on there's no war, no malice. Everybody will love each other and do his or her best to the society.

I believe that most people in the world also have this request. We all wish you to bring it to the world.

Truly yours,
Huang Xiao-tao
(Lizzy)

****

Southeast University
Nanjing Jiang Su
The P. R. China
December 21, 1988
Mr. Santa Claus
North Pole
Top of the World
Dear Santa Claus:

I know you are very kind and of generosity. You know what people want and always help poor people or children. I wish you long life long long life.

Now, I don't want everything but a flower. I want to put this flower on the altar for my father. He left me 15 years ago because of the bad treatment of the bad people. Every year especially on Christmas I think of him. I remember every scene while I was living with him. He was very kind also like you. So as soon as I think of you I think of my father. I love you as I love my father. Please give me a flower which I'll give it to my father to express my feeling of love for him and at the same time I'll wish my father always with me. Thank you!

Yours sincerely,
Zhou Guo Yen

****

Southeast University
Nanjing 210018
China
Dec. 22, 1988
Mr. Santa Claus
North Pole
Top of the World
Dear Santa Claus.

I am a student of Southeast University in Nanjing, China.

446

Christmas Day is coming. I send my best wish to you from far away. In the meanwhile, I want to express my best hope in this year.

I hope our mankind will realize the pollution made by ourselves more profoundly. Air we breathe, water we drink is especially important to our health. To develop industry is to raise the life level, but in a long run a good circumstance to live in is more important.

I hope this new Christmas Day will bring peace in the world. Human beings should spend less money in military and much to develop people's live standard.

Yours truly,
Mr. White

****

These were the wedding vows I used in the western style wedding at Shangdong Institute of Education in the summer of 1996 in Jinan, PR China:

Wedding Ceremony

Shandong Institute of Education Jinan, P.R. China July 31, 1996

"Dearly beloved, we are gathered here in the presence of the Lord and this congregation to join together this man, Tom, and this woman, Janice, in the holy bonds of matrimony. If anyone knows why this man and this woman should not be joined together in matrimony, let him speak now or forever hold his peace."

"Who gives this woman to be married to this man?"

The bride's father: _____, "her mother and I."

"In the beginning God created man and gave him responsibilities. Then the Lord said, 'It is not good for man to be alone. I will make a woman who is right for him. Then he brought the woman to the man. For this cause a man will leave his father and mother and be united with his wife, and the two will become one body.' You must promise to obey each other because you respect Christ. The husband must love his wife as he loves himself, and a wife must respect her husband. There should be a commitment as expressed by Ruth in the O. T. when she said, 'Where you go I will go, where you live, I will live. Your

447

people shall be my people and your God shall be my God.'"

"Tom and Janice, we are happy with you today. I'm sure for months you have looked forward to this day. And now here we are! You will remember this day for the rest of your lives. We are so glad that we can be part of your special day."

"Marriage is a wonderful and joyous relationship. It is full of many privileges, but also responsibilities. It is a privilege always to have someone to share your life with – to share your happiness as well as your sadness – to have someone who will always be there for you."

"With marriage come responsibilities. Tom, you are to take care of Janice, to be sensitive to her needs, and always to be kind to her. Janice, you are responsible to take care of Tom, to be sensitive to his needs, and always to be kind to him. Both of you must try to put each other first, to consider your own needs and wishes second."

"In just a few moments you will make vows to one another and to God. You will promise to be faithful to one another for the rest of your lives. That is a big promise – and with God's help, we believe you can keep that promise."

"Maybe in the beginning you will feel that you have a wonderful marriage. Everything will seem so exciting and romantic. After some time maybe those romantic feelings will not always be there. Then you must remember that real love is not just a feeling. Real love is expressed in actions and in commitment. The Bible says much about love."

"Love is patient, love is kind. It does not envy, it does not boast, it is not proud. It is not rude, it is not self-seeking. It is not easily angered, it keeps no record of wrongs.' With this kind of love, I believe that your marriage will be successful. May God lead and guide you in your new life together. Now will you, please, turn and face each other as you make these very important vows."

"Do you, Tom, take Janice to be your lawfully wedded wife to have and to hold, to love and to cherish, for richer, for poorer, in sickness and in health till death do you part?"

Tom: "I do."

(The vow is then given to Janice)

Janice: "I do"

"Please give me the ring."

"The ring symbolizes the encircling love of God. It is a circle that signifies continuing, never-ending love. It is made of precious metal as is the relationship of marriage. As you exchange them, may they be symbolic of your never-ending love for each other until death do you part."

(Give ring to Tom.)

"Repeat after me, 'With this ring, I thee wed and pledge to you my never-ending love as long as we both shall live.'"

"Ladies and gentlemen, you have heard these vows, and now may I be the first to introduce to you, Mr. and Mrs. Tom Liang."

(Libby sings "The Lord's Prayer.")

****

Daily devotions, Bible reading, prayers, and meditation began my days. Keeping a prayer diary brought an assurance and inspiration as answers came, many in ways far different from my requests, but I trusted God to grant the best answers. The following scriptures, some of which are paraphrased, have blessed me mightily.

Isaiah 12:2-6: Praise the Lord. He comforts me. I will trust and not be afraid. He is my salvation. Oh, the joy of drinking from His fountain of salvation. Thank the Lord. Praise His name. Tell the world (China) about His wondrous love. How mighty He is. Sing to the Lord for He has done wonderful things. Make known His praise around the world. Let all the people shout His praise and glory!

Philippians 4:13: I can do all things through Christ who gives me strength and power.

Philippians 4:19: It is He who will supply all your needs from His riches in glory.

11 Corinthians 12:9: My grace is sufficient for you. My strength is made perfect in weakness.

Philippians 1:21: For to me to live is opportunities to serve Christ.

James 4:10: When we humble ourselves and realize our need for God, He will come to us and encourage us.

James 4:11: Don't criticize (Chinese) and speak evil about one another.

Jude 1:21-22: Stay always within the boundaries where God's love can reach and bless you. Be merciful to those who doubt.

Acts 26:16: Now get up and stand on your feet. I have appeared to you to appoint you as a servant and as a witness of what you have seen and what I will show you.

Psalm 164:33-34: I will sing to the Lord as long as I live. I will praise God to my last breath. May He be pleased by all these thoughts about Him, for He is the source of all my joy.

Revelation 14:6: Strengthen disciples, encourage them to proclaim the eternal gospel to every nation, tribe, language, and people.

Hebrews 5:12: The Word of God is alive and active in China.

1 Chronicles 16:8-9: Sing unto Him. Talk of all His wondrous works. Glory in His holy name. Let the heart of them rejoice that seek the Lord. Seek the Lord and His strength. Seek His face continually. Remember the marvelous things He has done.

Psalm 139:1-7: You engineered me and wired me. You searched me and know me. You know when I sit, when I stand up, what my thoughts are when I go out, when I lie down; even before I speak you know the words on my tongue. Your knowledge of me is too wonderful for me, too lofty for me to attain. Humility overflows me and gratitude explodes with me. Where can I go from your Spirit, or where can I flee from your presence?

2 Timothy 1:7: For God did not give us the spirit of timidity, but a spirit of power, of love, and of self-discipline.

Philippians 2:20: My deep desire and hope is that I shall never fail in my duty, but at all times and especially now, I shall be full of courage, so that with my whole being I shall bring honor to Christ whether I live or die.

****

Evidences of the Holy Spirit's work in China and in the hearts of students there:

Nancy: "My life and mind are empty. Tell me why you are so high spirited and kind."

Franny: "Tell me how to be a Christian, please."

Sandra: "Please tell me what the Trinity means."

Miller: "My name is in the same Book as yours."

Erica: "I have nine roommates. I have to be their salt and light. Please pray for me."

Debbie: "I close my door every day and pray."

Selena: "My parents are Buddhist. No one ever told them about Jesus. Now when I read my Bible, I feel so calm and peaceful. I will tell my parents about Jesus Christ."

Ho Ru Ying, an older student: "I survived the Cultural Revolution by singing 'I Know That My Redeemer Lives.'"

Xiu Ping , a grandfather: "I would not have survived the twenty years labor of the Cultural Revolution if God had not been with me."

Dr. Li: "I wasted 45 years away from God. Now I must work hard and try to make up that time."

Patrick: "My father, who is a Communist official (a cadre), now attends church with me."

Qi Wei, an engineer: "In a vision, Jesus told me to follow Him. Things are better now that He is my guide."

Eli: "Now I believe Jesus." Eli, a Bahai believer, converted to Christianity and was baptized Easter Sunday 2001. It took five years to lead him to Christ.

Madam Su: "The greatest need in the world is to love God and to love others."

Guo Zin Yin (Kathy's) Birthday Menu

Translated by ZhiCheng Lin

Cold Dishes (冷盘)
Salt Duck (壠水鸭)
Fried Shimp (油爆虾)
Thousand-year old eggs (皮蛋)
Chicken (白切鸡)

Hot Dishes (热盘）
Eels with Wild Rice Stem （交瓜炒鳝鱼）
Sweet and Sour Fish （糖醋叉扁鱼）
Shirmp with Green Pepper （青椒炒虾仁）
Fried Chinese Cabbage （开洋菜心）
Fried Vegetable （炒素）
Fried Pork with Green Soya Been （毛豆炒肉丁）

Refreshments （点心）
Noddles （生白面）
Eight-Treasure Rice （八宝饭）
Steamed Dumplings （虾仁蒸饺）
Cakes （蛋糕）

Fruits （水果）
Water Melon （西瓜）
Bananas （香蕉）
Apples （苹果）
Pears （梨）

Drinks （饮料）
Beer-Non-alcoholic (啤酒）
Organge Juice （柳橙汁）
Coca-Cola （可口可乐）

Rats invading her bedroom, fireworks exploding at funerals, and delectable baby mice soup served to the author were not her expectations when she signed the necessary forms to go to China as an English teacher through the Amity Foundation. Nor did she foresee riding a motorcycle behind a most polite Chinese man or eating a mystery meat later identified as canine raised solely for food.

Even from a devout teenager, Martha Sue Todd was convinced that the Lord was calling her to become a missionary to China, and she never gave up on that pursuit. In her early years of teaching, however, a handsome young man proposed to her, they married, and they became the parents of one son. After the death of her husband of forty-one years, she again felt a strong pull to serve in China. Accordingly, she learned about Amity Foundation, which allows foreign organizations to send English teachers into China.

The author met the requirements and left the United States in 1988 at the age of 67 to serve for 13 years a people she came to love with an undying devotion.

Few western amenities awaited her, but she never failed to adjust. Walking four flights of stairs, living in one room, and having access to a usually non-functional toilet failed to diminish her enthusiasm, and soon many of her students visited her in her various lodgings.

She learned to appreciate Chinese customs, such as red wedding dresses, fireworks at funerals, and strange food that would make most Americans wince.

When the author returned to the United States in 2002, she dreamed of revisiting her second home country and was able to return to China in the summer of 2004, when she visited many of her former students and other Chinese friends

ISBN 1425109365-5

9 781425 109363